Sources of the River

TRACKING DAVID THOMPSON
ACROSS WESTERN NORTH AMERICA

Jack Nisbet

MAPS AND ILLUSTRATIONS BY
JACK McMASTER

SASQUATCH BOOKS
SEATTLE

To J. D. and to Claire

Copyright © 1994 by Jack Nisbet.
Maps and illustrations copyright © 1994 by Jack McMaster.

04 03 02 01 00   5 6 7 8 9

Printed in the United States of America.

Published by Sasquatch Books.
Distributed in Canada by Raincoast Books Ltd.

Cover design, interior design, and composition: Cameron Mason
Cover art: David Thompson's map "The Northwest Territories of the Province of Canada," 1814 (detail). Actual dimensions: 10 x 6½ feet. AO 1541; Archives of Ontario. Page from Thompson's April 1808 journal; vol. 8, book 19, page 306. David Thompson Papers; F 443; Archives of Ontario.
Cover illustration and calligraphy: Jack McMaster
Endpaper are (hardcover): page from Thompson's June 1810 journal; vol. 10, book 22, page 51. David Thompson Papers; F 443; Archives of Ontario.

Cataloging in Publication Data
Nisbet, Jack, 1949–
     Sources of the river : tracking David Thompson across western North America / Jack Nisbet.
          p. cm.
     Includes bibliographical references and index.
     ISBN 1-57061-020-7 : Hrdbck.
     ISBN 1-57061-006-1 : Pprbck.
     1. Columbia River Region—Discovery and exploration. 2. Northwest, Pacific—Discovery and exploration. 3. Explorers—Biography.
5. Cartographers—Northwest, Pacific—Biography.
I. Thompson, David, 1770–1857. II. Title
F1060.7.T48N57 1994
971.03'092—dc20   94-6478
                                                            CIP

Sasquatch Books
615 Second Avenue
Seattle, Washington 98104
(206) 467-4300
books@SasquatchBooks.com
www.SasquatchBooks.com

CONTENTS

LIST OF MAPS

AUTHOR'S NOTE

When David Thompson died in 1857, he left behind a wealth of written material in the form of journals, letters, reports, and four drafts of reminiscences about his life in the fur trade. In retracing Thompson's travels through the West, I have chosen to rely on his original field notes for the backbone of the story, both for chronological integrity and for the sense of immediacy they bring to his journeys. In many cases, I draw passages from his other writings to clarify or embellish events, and on such occasions I credit the source in order to make clear the perspective. If no source is named, the reader can assume that Thompson's words come directly from his field journals. Since, as far as we know, he did not begin keeping a journal until 1789, all selections previous to that time necessarily come from his memoirs.

When quoting from the original daybooks, I have retained Thompson's idiosyncrasies of spelling and punctuation as much as possible. Over the years he developed his own personal shorthand, using, for example, ⊙ for sun, d° for ditto, &c for etc., SRC for strong rapid current, and similar abbreviations for latitude and longitude. These few symbols I have written out for ease of understanding. Thompson was, for the most part, an excellent speller, and I saw no reason to modernize the few words that have changed since 1800. As for the names of places and peoples he visited, I have tried to follow current tribal usage and to render geographical locations as they appear on the most recent maps. Sometimes this means that a tribe name is spelled one way by Thompson and another way by me, or that a river changes its spelling when it crosses the border between Canada and the United States.

I have had a great deal of help on this book from the kind staff members of numerous libraries, especially the Archives of Ontario, the Fisher and Robarts Libraries at the University of Toronto, the Toronto Public Library, the Hudson's Bay Company Archives in Winnipeg, the Royal Ontario Museum, the Glenbow Museum in Calgary, the Spokane Public Library, the University of Montana Library, the Suzzallo Library at the University of Washington, the Rosenbach Library in Philadelphia, and the Habersham County Library in Clarkesville, Georgia. I also received encouragement, information, comments, places to stay, and extended tours from many individuals, and single out only a few of them here: Tom and Susie Bristol, Cary Cleaver, Ivan Doig, Charles Ferree, Harriet Huber, Nancy Hunn, Connie Poten, Ann Rittenberg, Terry Webster, Steve Zender, and Joan Gregory and all the people at Sasquatch Books. I want to thank them all very much. Special appreciation is due to John Stern for his insights, to Sean Peake, Hugh Dempsey, and Gene Hunn for generously sharing their files, and to Emily for being such a good sport.

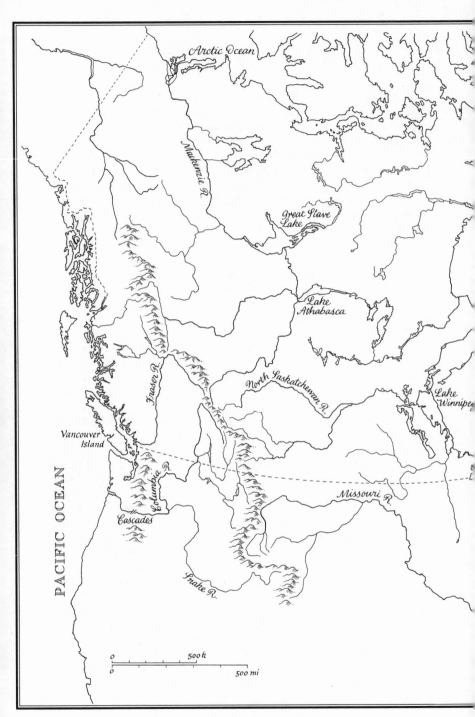

Arctic Ocean

Mackenzie R.

Great Slave Lake

Lake Athabasca

North Saskatchewan R.

Lake Winnipeg

Fraser R.

Vancouver Island

PACIFIC OCEAN

Columbia R.

Cascades

Missouri R.

Snake R.

0   500 k
0   500 mi

DAVID THOMPSON'S TERRITORY

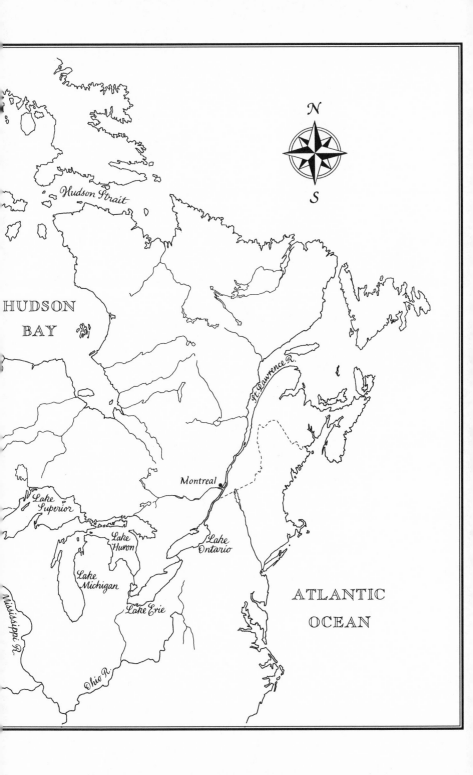

PROLOGUE

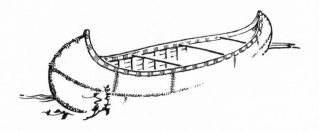

U P ON THE hill, the March morning was seared with a
frigid light that preceded the sun, locking the mud-
frosty ground up tight. As I wound down the slope past the
old town dump, a horde of ravens and magpies broke out of
the black pines, and we sank together into the ocean of white
ground fog that hugged the valley floor. My eyes followed
the course of the local creek, bare cottonwood arms that led
to the Colville River. Not a whole lot wider than a creek
itself, the Colville meanders north for thirty more miles
before dribbling into the Columbia River, and that was the
way I was headed.

This was a route I had followed many times during the
years I lived in northeast Washington, and I remembered
again how much I liked this part of the country, with its
open, piney hillsides and comfortable valleys. As I drove
north the fog thinned, and I looked out over easy swales of
farmland where lumps of stubble and umber muck shadowed
the snow's receding face. The peat bottoms seemed impossibly rich for a place that receives less than twenty inches of

rain a year. This rich dirt had been one of the first things the Canadian explorer and fur trader David Thompson noticed when he passed through this valley almost two centuries ago: "The ground of the day seems very fit for cultivation, black deep mould & the higher Ground a kind of black gray greasy earth." Thompson had been right. A couple of months from now, grain and alfalfa would be sprouting in that black earth all across the valley floor. The tamaracks in the hills would be budding out, matching the barley's yellow-green, adding depth to the mix of pine and Douglas fir. But even in high spring, the most visible feature of the landscape would be rocks. From the worn quartzite cliffs that ring the valley to the rubble piles left by small-time miners, you could always see the bones of this place.

It was still early when I reached the Kettle Falls bridge over the Columbia, and I rolled down my window to let in a blast of cold air as I crept along beneath the old steel trusses. Clouds of mist clung to the surface of the water, and a delicious turpentine smell seeped down from the wood-burning power plant up on the east bank. Over on the west side of the river, I could see the familiar slope of Bisbee Mountain, spotted with scrub maple and sumac. Along its ragged face, outcrops of dark quartzite have weathered into shades of fawn and chocolate, ferrous red and sulfur yellow, so that the hillside throws off an aura of heat and pressure and time.

At the foot of this hill sits Barney's Cafe, a rambling structure veneered from footings to chimney top with the forged colors of the local stone. I stopped in for a short stack of Barney's buckwheat cakes, sliding into an empty booth to gaze through one of the big windows at the river. Outside, in air that hovered right at freezing, a waitress in a thin blue sweater squeegeed away at the plate glass. When she was done, I could see every faint burble on the Columbia's surface.

Barney's Cafe and the Kettle Falls bridge lie just below the Canadian border, about midway along the length of the great river: five hundred and fifty circuitous miles from its source lake up in British Columbia, another seven hundred down to the treacherous bar where its fresh water meets the Pacific. Many stories revolve around the site of Kettle Falls, which once divided the river so neatly. But the cascades for which this place was named have been silent for half a century, and the water framed by Barney's windows is now officially known as Lake Franklin Delano Roosevelt, the backup from Grand Coulee Dam a hundred miles downstream.

On this particular morning, the Columbia's surface seemed gray and ordinary, its current sluggish. Much more alive was the scene in Barney's parking lot, a huge asphalt rendezvous for vehicles from both sides of the border. While cars and work trucks came and went, I sat inside amid the breakfast clamor and thought about all the other traffic this stretch of river had seen. Fingers of great ice sheets had descended on this crossing several times, leaving behind scratches on the bedrock and spewings of unsorted gravel. The hooves of great camel herds had tromped past, preyed upon by big cats and bears and scavenged by nodding condors. Around ten thousand years ago, humans began filtering in, and through the millennia successive cultures appeared, shaped tools from the local quartzite, and faded away. In historic times the falls marked a summer fishing place; when David Thompson arrived here in the early 1800s, he found a large village of Colville Indians drying salmon in long cedar sheds. Succeeding traders beat down a portage trail for their canoes and fur packs, and built a small fort on a bluff above the river. White missionaries soon followed with Bibles and primers, and prospectors rushed in to grub for ore around every little cliff and outwash. Turn-of-the-century homesteaders plowed and planted, froze and flooded, dried out and blew out and burned out, and some still hung on.

I thought of my old neighbor Lynn Walker in the Colville Valley, one of the homesteaders still hanging on, and about a piano I had once helped him move. His wife had just inherited the big black upright from her mother, whose mother in turn had ordered it from New York City in 1892, then watched it come ashore many months later at the bustling port just below the falls.

"You bet," Lynn had puffed as we tried to steer the out-of-tune hulk through a narrow doorway. "This baby's been around the Horn and up the river. Clipper ship to Astoria, then mules around all the rapids, then a big sternwheeler up to Kettle Falls. They used to race all up and down that Columbia before the dams. Yes sir. They had this country opened up like a can of sardines."

David Thompson was the man who began to open up this country. Thompson was the first person to chart the entire length of the Columbia River; he also explored its source lake and the nest of tributaries that wind through the area we now call the Inland Northwest—southeastern British Columbia, western Montana, northern Idaho, and eastern Washington. As he traveled he carried a compass, a sextant, and a business proposition for the native tribes he met. For Thompson was not just a geographer out to map a river, he was also a fur trader with the North West Company of Montreal, out to expand its domain and convert the natives to its commercial purposes. He was an agent of revolutionary change in the region: its history turns on the moment of his arrival.

I first became acquainted with Thompson in the 1970s, when I was writing a series of articles about the natural history of eastern Washington. In the Northwest Room of the Spokane Public Library, I found a book he had written, called *A Narrative of Travels in Western North America, 1784–1812*. It was a story that sprawled across the continent, full of hair-raising adventures and sharp descriptions of wild country. He touched on subjects that ranged from the mechanics of the fur business to details of natural history. He had a special eye for the mosaic of native cultures he encountered, noting their various characters and social customs even as he proceeded to indelibly alter their future. During a long career that took him from Hudson Bay to the Pacific, he never seemed to lose his enthusiasm for new country.

There was something contagious about the man's particular brand of curiosity, and I found myself making detours to walk a trail he had walked or to canoe a river he had paddled. Thompson wrote his *Narrative* after he retired, and several footnotes in the text referred to his original field journals. These I wanted to see, because from the time he crossed the Continental Divide in 1807 until he reached the junction of the Columbia with the Snake River four years later, he was moving through territory that had never been described on paper. Anything that he had to say about what he saw, no matter how casual, carries the weight of that first contact.

Scattered portions of his field notebooks had been transcribed and published in regional history journals, and I stitched these together, then fretted about what Thompson might have been up to during the periods that had not been transcribed. I ordered microfilm copies of some of his notebooks and began learning to read eighteenth-century script. At first his rough field notes bewildered me. Many entries contained more numbers than words—paragraphs filled with notations of distance and direction, pages dominated by column after column of astronomical observations. Sometimes he would get partway through one journal only to turn it upside down and begin at the other end, and sometimes he would write two versions of the same trip in different books. He capitalized most of his nouns and often seemed to be in too much of a hurry for punctuation, so that one thought piled into another. A few passages looked like he might have written them while standing up in a canoe. After a while, though, I got the hang of his style and started looking forward to the next page. As I read on, I became absorbed in the flow of his daily life, and began to get a sense of wonderful randomness bursting from the mind of an orderly man— one day he wouldn't enter anything more than the weather and what he had to eat, the next he might fill a whole page with the submarine habits of a water ouzel or note that bears make a humming noise when they lick their feet.

PANCAKES FINISHED, I wandered out of Barney's and over to the river, picking my way along the rocky bank toward a stunted yellow pine that stuck up from a ledge of fractured rock. I knew this tree well, as a favorite perch for raptors, and once had almost put my pickup in the river trying to focus on a rough-legged hawk that had landed in its broken top. It was a fat, ancient tree, its bark broken into rough jigsaw plates. The rays of morning sun drew a deep orange cast from the trunk.

Straight across the river rose the hill where fur traders who followed Thompson had built their first small trading post, and where Catholic missionaries later established St. Paul's Mission. The hill juts out into the river, terminating in staggered bluffs, and its height commands the bay that broadens out upstream. A big black-and-white enlargement of this part of the river used to hang in Barney's cocktail lounge, taken with a box camera in some year before 1940, when the gates of Grand Coulee Dam first closed. In the photograph the bay was no longer a bay, but an extensive mud flat that spread out beneath the bluffs. From the base of Bisbee Mountain, a series of tall blocks of quartzite stepped across the river toward Mission Hill, and their path created the falls. For eons the waters of the Columbia's upper half had plunged over these ledges, hammering scores of pocks and craters into the rock below. Churning pools at the bottom of the twenty-foot drop inspired French voyageurs to name these falls La Chaudière (The Boiler). Rocks and boulders swept over the edge were tossed about with tremendous circular force, polishing certain potholes as smooth as the inside of a cooking kettle.

I leaned against the yellow pine and looked across the river, trying to imagine the scene that greeted David

Thompson when he first arrived on the opposite shore: the spectacle of many families gathering for the season's fishing, the shouts of spearmen below the pounding falls, the smell of split salmon hung up to dry. It had been late June, and the explorer had sampled some of the first of the summer chinooks, then boated across the river with the Colville chief and climbed Bisbee Mountain in search of cedar wood for a canoe.

From behind my head I slowly became aware of a faint noise that seemed to be coming from inside the tree. It was a series of anxious creaks, like the joints of a chair coming unglued. The sound was vaguely familiar, and as I tried to place it, a chorus of sneezy whines circled overhead and a phalanx of nuthatches landed in the top of the pine. The birds went directly to work, spiraling around the trunk from top to bottom as they probed crevices in the bark for insects and pupae. Insects. Bark beetles, that's what the noise was: the pincer jaws of soft-bodied larvae boring their galleries between the bark and sapwood of the pine. And now these masked bandits were coming after the beetles and all their kin; each quick yank meant another morsel of food. It was the kind of small event that David Thompson might have noticed as he tramped toward his next destination, sextant in hand. There was something appealing in the notion that a man who had traveled tens of thousands of miles would stop to watch a flock of little birds, would still bend down to finger the soil in the Colville Valley.

A lumber truck rumbled across the Columbia River bridge, then downshifted to toil up Mission Hill. Above my head the nuthatches skittered around the trunk and bare limbs of the yellow pine. Just beyond their reach I could hear the creak of bark beetles chewing away inside the old tree, gnawing at the edges of time.

CHAPTER ONE

IN THE COUNTRY OF SAUKAMAPPEE

1700–1787

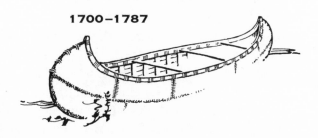

D AVID THOMPSON WAS born in London of Welsh parents in 1770. His father died when David was two, and at age seven he was sent to the Grey Coat School near Westminster Abbey, a charity school that aimed to "educate poor children in the principles of piety and virtue and thereby lay a foundation for a sober and Christian life." He spent seven years there, and though several of the textbooks he studied from had been published almost a century before, he apparently received a solid grounding in the basic skills of his day, including geography, algebra, navigation, and the workings of the tides. In his free time he read such popular adventure stories as *The Arabian Nights*, *Robinson Crusoe*, and *Gulliver's Travels*, and on outings he walked to London Bridge and St. James's Park. Thompson would later write that he had been given a "mathematical education" in preparation for service in the Royal Navy, but as his graduation neared, England was signing the peace treaty that ended the American Revolution, and the Navy no longer needed large numbers of new sailors. He probably would have wound up in the merchant marine had not his headmaster received a letter from the secretary of the Hudson's Bay Company, which sometimes recruited young clerks from orphanages and charity schools and was looking for four students to serve apprenticeships in the North American fur trade. Only two upcoming Grey Coat graduates were considered eligible; one of these ran away, the other was David Thompson.

In May 1784 Thompson sailed from London aboard the Bay Company's *Prince Rupert.* They crossed the North Atlantic, then spent a month weaving through the summer icebergs in Hudson Strait; by the time the ship traversed Hudson Bay and docked at Churchill Factory on the western shore, it was early September. Supplies for the trading post were unloaded and furs from the warehouse taken on as quickly as possible. Two weeks after arriving, the *Prince Rupert* set sail again, trying to beat winter ice-up in the strait. She left behind a fourteen-year-old boy who, as far as is known, had never before been out of London; he would receive no word from home until the arrival of the next supply ship a year later. Thompson recorded memories of his early years with the Bay Company in his *Narrative of Travels in Western North America, 1784–1812.* In one draft of these memoirs, he described watching the *Prince Rupert* sail away: "While the ship remained at anchor, from my parent and friends it appeared only a few weeks' distance, but when the ship sailed and from the top of the rocks I lost sight of her, the distance became immeasurable, and I bid a long and sad farewell to my noble, my sacred country, an exile for ever."

David Thompson had been set down in a vast wilderness territory inextricably bound to the fur business. Ever since the beginning of the sixteenth century, natives along the North American coast had been swapping their beaver robes and other furs for the extra iron kettles and similar useful articles of European cod fishermen who put ashore in sheltered coves and river mouths. Pelts that had previously served as everyday clothes and coverings suddenly took on new value.

When Jacques Cartier sailed up the St. Lawrence River in 1535 in search of the Northwest Passage, he met canoeloads of men, probably Micmacs, waving furs on sticks. During the trading session that followed, "they bartered all they had to such an extent that they all went back naked without anything on them; and they made signs to us that they would return on the morrow with more furs."

By the end of the century, the French had established a colony on the St. Lawrence, and European gentlemen and military officers had developed a taste for expensive beaver hats fashioned from the skins of these New World rodents. In the ensuing rush for pelts, French entrepreneurs set up shop in New France, importing wool cloth, iron utensils, firearms, and trinkets for exchange with the nearby tribes. Vigorous hunting quickly depleted the beaver grounds along the St. Lawrence, and intertribal warfare over who would control the trade disrupted the supply of furs coming in from the hinterlands. In response, some of the more adventurous Frenchmen took to the interior in pursuit of pelts, paddling with the natives in their birchbark canoes along aboriginal trade routes through Quebec's network of rivers and lakes. They moved north toward Hudson Bay and south across the Great Lakes into the Ohio Valley, where they began bumping into trappers from the British colonies.

The French soon found themselves squeezed by English interests to the north as well when the British Crown granted a charter to the Hudson's Bay Company of London in 1670, ceding it rights to all the lands drained by all the rivers that feed that huge bay. French traders, however, had already discovered the value of the thick pelts coming in from the cold northern regions, and chose to ignore the claims of Great Britain. The two countries and the tribes with whom they each were allied skirmished in the north and in the south until their spats grew into the long series of French and Indian Wars. When the British finally prevailed and the French surrendered all claim to New France in 1763, the

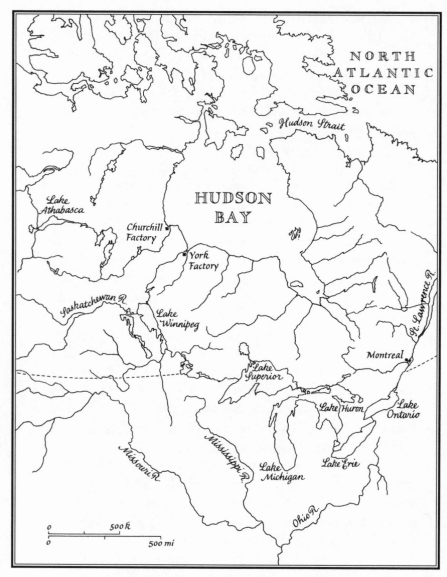

EMPIRE OF THE EARLY FUR TRADE

Hudson's Bay Company expected to have the bulk of the northern fur trade to itself.

But it wasn't long before a new generation of "pedlars from Quebec" took over the business. Experienced French traders teamed up with Scots moving in from the depressed Highlands, Yankee opportunists from the American colonies, and Englishmen who saw potential on the Canadian frontier. By the time David Thompson arrived on Hudson Bay, several of these independent operators had pooled their resources to form the North West Fur Company, headquartered in Montreal, and their upstart coalition was gaining strength.Up until this point, the Hudson's Bay Company had taken a conservative approach to its fiefdom, building forts at the mouths of the major rivers that feed the bay and relying on Cree and Assiniboine emissaries to ferry goods to the interior tribes and bring pelts back to the bay. Geography gave the Bay Company a major advantage, for ships docking at its posts on the bay's western shore were already halfway across the continent, right on the doorstep of rich fur country. In 1774 the company built a pair of inland posts, but the effort was expensive, and a series of difficulties delayed further expansion. The North West Company, despite the long distances from its port in Montreal, was far more aggressive. Organized into efficient brigades, the "Nor'Westers" forged across Lake Winnipeg into the prairies and penetrated northwest as far as Lake Athabasca, where they tapped into an enormous lode of prime pelts. They built a succession of new trade houses at strategic intervals and intercepted the native middlemen on their way east to Hudson Bay, treating them to rum and bartering for their choicest furs. They strangled the flow of pelts that had previously poured into the posts on the bay, and the Bay Company's profits were suffering when David Thompson landed at Churchill Factory in 1784.

Churchill was, by many accounts, a miserable posting. Thompson spent the winter "growling at the cold" and the summer "quarrelling with mosquitoes and sand flies." He learned to walk in snowshoes and shoot a gun, and borrowed books on history and "animated nature," but chafed at what he saw as the meager opportunities at the post. The London governors of the Hudson's Bay Company had sent along a glowing letter with the boy, recommending "that he may be kept from the common men and employed in the writings, accounts & Warehouse Duty . . . so that he may by degrees be made capable of business & become useful in our Service." Thompson was not feeling very useful, and his complaint that his penmanship was going to ruin for lack of practice won him the attention of the post's chief officer, Samuel Hearne. Hearne was working on a book about a journey he had made to the Arctic Ocean a few years earlier, and he allowed the new apprentice to copy out part of the manuscript that became *A Journey to the Northern Ocean*, a classic tale of resourceful travel under the most rugged conditions.

When the annual supply ship arrived in the early fall of 1785, it carried orders from London reassigning David Thompson to the supply depot at York Factory, 150 miles to the south. The boy made the journey to York on foot with two native couriers, called "packet Indians," whom the Bay Company employed to carry messages between posts. Their course lay down the muddy beach of Hudson Bay, with the drift ice and driven boulders of the sea on their left and a treeless bog on their right. Each man carried a blanket for cover and a gun for hunting; for food they roasted any ducks and geese they could shoot. Along the way they often passed clusters of polar bears lying on their bellies, heads together and bodies radiating out like the spokes of a wheel. The two couriers taught the boy to walk past the bears with a steady, direct step, eyes focused straight ahead. One afternoon they prepared to cross a fair-sized creek, and saw that

> on the opposite side of the ford was a large polar bear
> feasting on a beluga; we boldly took the ford thinking
> the bear would go away, but when halfway across, he

lifted his head, placed his forepaws on the beluga, and uttering a loud growl, showed to us such a set of teeth as made us turn up the stream, and for fifty yards wade up to our middle before we could cross, during this time the bear eyed us, growling like a mastiff dog.

Narrative

The couriers delivered their charge safely to York Factory, where he helped hunt geese and ducks in the surrounding marshes and learned to build snares for rabbits. In 1786 the Bay Company resolved to make a renewed push inland, and that summer young Thompson was one of forty-four men sent on an expedition to the interior to compete with the Nor'Westers. From York Factory, the group pushed west up the Nelson River, fighting its current all the way. There were tedious portages, where the canoes and cargo had to be carried around rapids. The current was often so strong that the three-man crews could not make any progress by paddling, and they would try to keep going by poling with iron-tipped rods. When that didn't work, they would stop, attach long ropes to the bow, and put two men ashore to haul the boat upstream while the third stayed aboard to steer. This was known as line-hauling, or tracking, and since Thompson was too inexperienced to steer a boat, he labored for days at the end of a tracking line, trudging through blistering heat and clouds of mosquitoes. "To alleviate this latter," he wrote, "the men make for themselves wide, loose caps of coarse cotton with a piece of green bunting in the front, but the sweat from toil and heat makes it unbearable in the day time, but serves well at night."

On the go fourteen hours a day, the brigade made its way to Lake Winnipeg and around its windy north shore to the mouth of the Saskatchewan River. After a brief stop at Cumberland House, erected twelve years earlier as a hub for inland canoe traffic, the Bay men continued up the Saskatchewan. This great river flows east from the base of the

Rocky Mountains all the way across the prairies, making it a natural highway for the fur trade. As the canoes traveled upstream, they gradually left behind the dense forests of eastern Canada and entered the more open landscape that borders the Great Plains. David Thompson liked the change: "Every hour appeared to bring us to a better country, instead of dark pine forests the woods were of well grown Poplar, Aspen and white Birch and for the first time saplings of Ash. The whistling and calls of the Red Deer [elk] echoed through the woods, and we often heard the butting of the Staghorns."

The flotilla split up at the north and south forks of the Saskatchewan, with Thompson's party of five canoes ascending the south branch. About a hundred miles upriver, they spotted two adjacent trading posts, one belonging to the fledgling North West Company and the other to an independent from Montreal who had not yet joined the coalition. Here the Bay men stopped and selected a spot for their own house just upstream. It was a common practice throughout the history of the fur trade for rival companies to establish such close quarters, and they got along with varying degrees of amiability. In this case the newcomers were greeted warmly by the gentlemen in charge of both posts. One of them was French—"Every sentence he spoke or answer he made was attended by a smile and a slight bow, our men grave and stiff as pokers"—the other a Scot, who was happy to "have the pleasure of speaking english." (The Hudson's Bay Company imported almost all of its workers from England and Scotland's Orkney Islands, whereas most of the men from Montreal spoke French.)

The post that Thompson helped build that fall was named South Branch House. It was a large log building divided into three sections—the "Master's Room" on one end; a "Guard Room" in the middle, where the actual trade transpired; and three men's "Cabbins" on the other end. Here the apprentice's handwriting got plenty of practice, for the house master was illiterate. As clerk, or "writer," one of Thompson's jobs was keeping the post journal, and in a careful, copybook script he followed the standard Bay Company format, listing the day's weather, the jobs the men were doing, who came in to trade, food brought by the hunters, and any other arrivals, departures, or "unusual occurrences." On Sundays he recorded only the weather.

Around the little trading post, Thompson began his education in the ways of Canada's vast prairies. Native hunters supplied bison and elk meat, a welcome change from the constant diet of fish and fowl on Hudson Bay. The post had a few horses, and it seems likely that the young clerk learned to ride here, for he mentions traveling up to fifty miles away from the trade house to find the hunters' tents. His duties brought him into close contact with the Cree and Stoney Assiniboine Indians who traded there, and he learned how to hand out gifts of brandy and tobacco during the rituals of greeting, and how to smoke the introductory pipe that always preceded the actual exchange of goods for pelts. Although beaver remained the backbone of the trade, the furs of other animals were accepted as well. At South Branch House that winter, the skins included fox and wolf, lynx and wolverine, coyote and badger.

As soon as the snow began melting in the spring, the natives left their winter camps to move out onto the plains for their spring buffalo hunt. The Bay men sorted the furs they had collected over the winter and built a wooden press to squeeze the pelts into compact bales. An average beaver pelt weighed a little better than a pound, and one pressed pack, designed to be carried around a portage, usually topped ninety pounds. Warm or wet weather would draw out the smell of any unscraped fat, and the fur bundles often made rancid traveling companions.

When the ice broke up on the river, the packs were loaded into canoes, and Thompson floated downstream with them as far as Cumberland House. There he passed the summer mending nets and fishing for sturgeon while the boats made their round-trip journey to York Factory. When

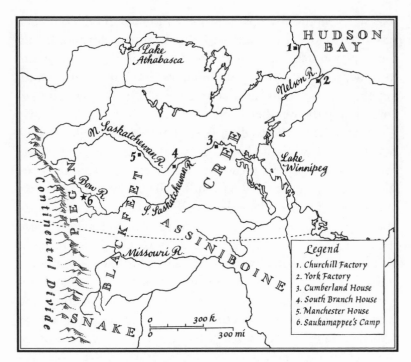

THOMPSON'S EARLY TRAVELS

they returned with fresh trade goods, he joined a brigade heading to the new Manchester House, midway up the north fork of the Saskatchewan. Their trip west across the prairies coincided with the migration of several buffalo herds crossing the river in search of fresh pasture, and for days the Bay men maneuvered their boats through swarms of bison dog-paddling across the current, only their big heads visible above the water. Undeviating in their course toward the opposite shore, the beasts "often came against our file of canoes and to prevent them coming on the canoes we had to shove them off with the paddle."

When the boats arrived at Manchester House, Thompson learned that his travels were not finished. The year before, a Bay trader had made an excursion west to trade with a group of Blackfeet Indians, and his trip had been so successful that the company was sending him back with five men; the young clerk was assigned to go along and learn the Blackfeet language. When they set off in early October, Thompson's kit consisted of "the clothes I had on, which was a cotton shirt, a blue cloth jacket and leather trowsers . . . another shirt, a leather coat, a blanket and Bison robe, forty rounds of ammunition, two long knives, six flints, a few awls, needles etc. with a few pounds of tobacco, and a horse to carry myself and baggage, which obliged me to walk the greatest part of the journey."

After about a month's march across the prairies, the men saw a line of brilliant white clouds coming into view on the horizon. Their guide said that these were the Rocky Mountains, but Thompson and the others found this hard to believe—at this time only a handful of white men had ever seen these mountains, and nothing in Thompson's experience had prepared him for the apparition of the east front of the Rockies rising from the plains. "As we proceeded they rose in height, their immense masses of snow appeared above the clouds and formed an impassable barrier, even to the Eagle." The furmen continued west, and near the foothills of the mountains crossed the Bow River, where they met a dozen "Peeagan" Indians on horseback. Thompson's "Peeagans" (now spelled Piegan in the United States and Peigan in Canada) belonged to the great Blackfeet Nation, along with two other tribes, the Bloods and the Blackfeet proper. The loosely associated bands of these three tribes lived a nomadic life, shadowing the seasonal movements of buffalo and the ripening of berries around the western plains. Their hunting territory extended from the Saskatchewan River south to the Missouri, with the Piegan bands tending to stay farthest west, along the foothills of the Rockies.

The Piegan scouts that Thompson's group had chanced upon gave the Bay men a hearty welcome and led them to a nearby camp. The elders who gathered to greet them said they were thankful the traders had come; according to

Thompson, they were especially grateful for fresh tobacco, which was "the great luxury, and like money commanded all things." The elders also were anxious to know how many animals the Bay men had seen on their way west, and were happy to hear that the buffalo had not already migrated north. After the exchange of news, three of the most prominent men invited the visitors to lodge in their tipis.

> The Peeagan in whose tent I passed the winter was an old man of at least 75 to 80 years of age; his height six feet, two or three inches, broad shouldered, strong limbed, his hair gray and plentiful, forehead high and nose prominent, his face slightly marked with the small pox, and alltogether his countenance mild, and even, sometimes playful . . . his name was Saukamappee (Young Man).
>
> *Narrative*

Saukamappee was by birth a Cree, a large tribe ranging all the way from Hudson Bay through the eastern woodlands and west along the Saskatchewan. Thompson had learned enough of the Cree language the previous winter at South Branch House to be able to converse with the old man and to understand the stories that he spun out during the long winter evenings. In his *Narrative*, Thompson recounted many of Saukamappee's stories, tales that outlined the history of the northern plains through a native's eyes. Saukamappee said that he had grown up in a Cree band that lived along the eastern fringe of the prairies. During his youth, his people were allies of the western Blackfeet Nation against their mutual enemies the Snakes, or Shoshones, who lived farther to the south and west. He was still a young man (from what Saukamappee told him, Thompson estimated that this was sometime around 1730) when Piegan Blackfeet messengers came to his band with reports of a skirmish in which several Snakes had appeared atop strange, four-legged animals, "swift as a deer." The Crees could not imagine what this meant, for dogs were the only domesticated animals they knew. Saukamappee had recently married, and hoping to bring back an enemy scalp for his father-in-law's medicine bag, he set off with two other young men to help the Blackfeet fight the Snakes. By this time many of the Crees had acquired guns, and there were enough firearms in Saukamappee's camp for him and each of his friends to carry one.

At the war camp they met bands of Blackfeet and Piegans armed with stone-pointed lances and bows and arrows, plus seven Assiniboine men with seven more guns. The war chief positioned the ten guns on the front line; this would be their first test in battle, for until then they had been used only for hunting. Saukamappee remembered that it was with great nervousness that he lay behind a big buffalo-hide shield, clutching his single-shot musket, two extra balls in his mouth and a load of powder in his left hand. As he watched the ritual display of weapons that always preceded a pitched battle, he saw no way to win, for the Snakes filing into position opposite him far outnumbered the Blackfeet, and many of them carried *pukamoggans*, the short stone clubs that were so dangerous in close combat. But when he and his companions opened fire with their muskets a few minutes later, there was "consternation and dismay" among the Snakes, followed by a confused retreat. The delighted Blackfeet and Piegans begged the Cree gunners to stay and live with them, promising handsome young wives as incentives. There were no takers, but Saukamappee and his friends did stay on for a few days of hunting before returning east.

None of the Snakes' mysterious four-legged beasts had been present at this battle, and when the hunting party chanced upon a dead stallion, they gathered around it in awe. "We all admired him," Saukamappee told Thompson, "he put us in mind of a Stag that had lost his horns, and we did not know what name to give him. But as he was a slave to Man, like the dog, which carried our things; he was named the Big Dog."

Soon afterward the Crees started their long walk home, each carrying a Snake scalp carefully stretched on a round willow hoop. As they approached one of their tribe's camps, the travelers stopped to paint their faces in anticipation of the night of singing, dancing, and feasting that would greet their return. Saukamappee imagined the grand appearance he would make before his wife and in-laws, but they were not at the camp. The three warriors had been gone for several months by now, and Saukamappee soon learned that his bride had run away with another man. The next morning he gave his prized scalp to a friend and left his people. He retraced his steps to one of the Piegan Blackfeet camps, where the chief made good his promise and gave his eldest daughter to Saukamappee as his new wife.

Saukamappee came to live among the Piegan Blackfeet as two dramatic waves of change converged on the northwestern plains. From the south came Spanish horses, their natural dispersal accelerated by trading and thievery. The animals thrived in the open grasslands, and the pedestrians of the plains took enthusiastically to horsemanship. Aside from their obvious utilitarian uses for hunting and transport, "Big Dogs" became new symbols of prestige and favored war prizes. From the east, emanating from Montreal and Hudson Bay, came the manufactured goods imported by the fur companies. These items, which had been embraced so wholeheartedly by the eastern tribes, met with a more mixed reaction out on the prairies. When an early envoy from the Hudson's Bay Company visited some of the plains tribes in the mid-1700s and encouraged them to bring their furs to York Factory to trade, the chiefs listened with interest. But when they learned that they would have to ride in canoes and eat fish along the way, they declined the invitation. Still, guns and iron arrowheads were greatly desired. Although white traders made only occasional forays onto the plains at this time, the Blackfeet were able to get some firearms from Cree and Assiniboine middlemen, but at a considerable markup. The Crees charged the Blackfeet fifty beaver or wolf pelts for one musket; back on Hudson Bay the going rate was fourteen pelts per gun.

The Blackfeet tribes were the first in their part of the country to own both horses and guns, and with their new-found mobility and firepower, they soon forced their rivals off the choicest buffalo grounds and made them their own. The Piegans chased the Snakes, who had horses but no guns, away from the rich Bow River country and south into the mountains, and for many years afterward the Blackfeet bands maintained their freewheeling dominance of the northern plains. Then one day Piegan scouts brought word of a peculiar Snake encampment within their territory, and Saukamappee related how he and the other warriors in his band determined to raid it. "Next morning at dawn of day, we attacked the Tents, and with our sharp flat daggers and knives, cut through the tents and entered for the fight; but our war whoop instantly stopt, our eyes were appalled with terror; there was no one to fight but the dead and the dying, each a mass of corruption." Saukamappee was describing the devastating smallpox epidemic that swept across the continent in the early 1780s. Because the Piegans had no concept of contagious disease, they did not hesitate to loot the infected camp, carrying home blankets and tents with their plunder. "The second day after this dreadful disease broke out in our camp, and spread from one tent to another as if the Bad Spirit carried it. We had no belief that one Man could give it to another, any more than a wounded Man could give his wound to another." Saukamappee said that many people drowned when they rushed into the river to relieve the unbearable itching. One-third of his own band was wiped out, while in other camps everyone died, he said. "When at length it left us, and we moved about to find our people, it was no longer with the song and the dance; but with tears, shrieks, and howlings of despair . . . Our hearts were low and dejected, and we shall never be again the same people."

It was about seven years after the smallpox plague when

Thompson met the Piegans, and scars were still visible on many of their faces. Those who had survived carried on the lifestyle and customs of their ancestors, and the winter that Thompson spent among them gave him an inside look at a traditional plains culture relatively untouched by contact with white men. Despite the introduction of guns and horses into their territory, many of the warriors still had only bows and arrows, and Saukamappee still walked wherever he went, carrying his pipestems and medicine bag over his shoulder. Whenever the Piegans struck camp, one of the old men would scoop burning embers from a campfire into a rough wooden bowl filled with dirt, then carefully tend the hot coals all the way to the next camp, where a new fire was stoked from the bowl.

The Piegans hospitably accepted the young white visitor into their daily lives. When scouts reported buffalo nearby, he sometimes rode out with the hunters to shoot a few days' provisions. As cold weather came on and the bison moved toward the foothills for food and shelter from the wind, the people herded small groups of them into rough impoundments and butchered them. The women sliced and smoked strips of jerky, then pounded some of the dried meat into a coarse meal called beat meat. This they mixed with dried berries and buffalo grease to make pemmican. Shaped into croquettes and packed into skin bags, these dense cakes provided a staple food that kept for months without spoiling. In Thompson's opinion, the women at his camp were too heavy-handed with the bitter chokecherries, and the result "required the powers of an Ostrich to digest."

Whatever he thought of their pemmican recipe, he did have the sensibility to see that the endless chores of the Piegan women—gathering firewood, cooking, curing and drying meat, preparing animal skins and sewing clothes, setting up the tipi and breaking it down—amounted to a crushing burden, and that for them the value of European trade goods went beyond bright beads and baubles: "See the wife of an Indian sewing their leather clothing with a pointed brittle bone or a sharp thorn and the time and trouble it takes. Show them an awl or strong needle and they will gladly give the finest Beaver or Wolf skin they have to purchase it."

Thompson took a great interest in the routines and everyday doings of the camp. He watched young bachelors painstakingly paint their faces in the little mirrors the traders had brought, then plant themselves in a conspicuous spot to be admired. He listened to the camp's civil chief deliver his evening bulletins of news from other bands and daily instructions for hunting. He turned a curious eye on the gambling games that dominated the leisure time of the men, and decided that the need for extra help around the tent might justify polygamy. His musings about Blackfeet theology and morals, though filtered through his devout Christian eyes, still show a real fascination for a different world view. Thompson was at the time only seventeen years old, and his winter among the Piegans instilled in him a romantic admiration.

> Their walk is erect, light and easy, and may be said to be graceful. When on the plains in company with white men, the erect walk of the Indian is shown to great advantage. The Indian with his arms folded in his robe seems to glide over the ground; and the white people seldom in an erect posture, their bodies swayed from right to left, and some with their arms, as if to saw a passage through the air. I have often been vexed at the comparison.
>
> *Narrative*

During his stay Thompson also learned something of the differences that horses had made in the lives of the Piegans. One afternoon in early January, a group of young men arrived in camp singing victory songs. More than two moons earlier, Saukamappee explained, a large war party of about 250 warriors under the leadership of the war chief Kootanae Appee had departed on horseback on a mission of revenge against the Snakes, who had murdered a small group of Piegans hunting bighorn sheep in the mountains the previous fall. When days of travel failed to turn up any sign of their foes, Kootanae Appee had pressed on, riding farther and farther south until he and his men came upon a silver caravan led by Spaniards in what must have been southern Colorado. After routing the pack train, the Piegans had discarded saddlebags full of the "white stone" as nuisances, then ridden back north with a herd of horses and mules, some of them still wearing saddles of "thick well tanned leather of a chocolate color with figures of flowers as if done by a hot iron."

A few days after the arrival of the warriors, Kootanae Appee himself paid a visit to the camp, leading a dark brown Spanish mule as a gift for Saukamappee so that the old man would no longer have to walk from camp to camp. Thompson, who was in the tent with his mentor, had heard many stories about the great war chief, but this was their first meeting. "He was apparently forty years of age and his height between six feet two to four inches, more formed for activity than strength yet well formed for either; his face a full oval, high forehead and nose somewhat aquiline; his large black eyes, and countenance, were open, frank but somewhat stern; he was a noble specimen of the Indian warrior of the great plains." When Kootanae Appee turned to greet Thompson, the awed teenager unwittingly committed a Piegan faux pas. "On entering the tent he gave me his left hand, and I gave him my right hand, upon which he looked at me and smiled as much as to say a contest would not be equal; at his going away the same took place." Saukamappee later cautioned his young guest that to the Blackfeet, the left hand was the hand of greeting, whereas offering the right—the hand that threw spears and pulled triggers—was an insult, and a challenge to fight: "If one of our people offers you his left hand, give him your left hand, for the right hand is no mark of friendship."

I HAD BEEN driving through Saukamappee's old territory all day, across the prairies of western Alberta, and I was tired. Evening seems to linger forever here in the summer, making it hard to know when to stop. As I drove numbly along, the grassland and wheat fields began to undulate like ocean swells; the only turnoffs were wide tractor entrances to the grain fields, and I passed by each one slower and slower, wondering if I should drag out my sleeping bag and nestle in between the furrows. I finally did pull off, to stumble through a forest of stiff barley, but there were too many clods for comfort. To the west a line of thick, dark clouds strung out along the horizon. That would be the Rockies, and there would be trees growing out of the hills at their feet. A canopy to sleep under, and a carpet of soft, dry needles. I wondered how long it might take to reach that haven, and how hard it might be raining when I got there.

I supposed that Saukamappee would have made this trip from flatlands to foothills many times, after berries or late buffalo, or to escape the summer's heat, or to catch the same whiff of trees that I was after now. He would have made his trips on foot, though, season after season, from the time he came to live with the Piegans until the day Kootanae Appee brought home that dark brown Spanish mule. Their ancestors would have made the same trek, and every one of them, from the time they wandered in behind the melting ice, would have walked to get there.

I wheeled into a farm-town grocery store and bought three sticks of venison jerky, then almost lost my snack to a couple of mutts in the parking lot. They were a mismatched pair, one yellow, one a piebald blue, sharing a lean, sinewy build and wary reserve. They sniffed around my heels on the way to the car, but the moment I turned to offer a pet they cowered back toward a dumpster. When I pulled out of the parking lot a few minutes later, they were laying for me beside the road, and I left town in a flurry of tire-biting yips and snarls. They soon lost interest and dropped back, and in my rearview mirror I watched them tussle over a potato chip bag beside the road.

I finished my last bite of jerky, and the miles began to unroll again. A few last rays of sun shot out beneath the low clouds, and the grasslands came alive. An upland sandpiper landed on a fence post just ahead of the car to arch its wings in a relaxing stretch. Sky, birds, and landscape all assumed the colors of ripening wheat. A huge splotch of yellow-black thunderhead hung over the road far, far ahead. I wondered how close Saukamappee had let the thunderheads move in before he stopped to camp, and how often his tipi smelled of wet dog fur. Because dogs would have been along, too, walking at the heels of his people: generation after generation of companions and load-bearers and mischief makers. Before the Big Dogs arrived, little dogs were the beasts of burden. They were the ones strapped into harness winter and summer, pulling travois and sleds.

I thought of all the little dogs whose pace had ever matched mine. I never knew any to follow a straight line for very long, and I tried to imagine how I would keep them on course from here to the mountains. Probably I wouldn't. David Thompson once watched a group of plains women on the way from one camp to another on a hot summer day. (The men always had urgent hunting to do on moving day, he said.) The dogs were all carrying saddlebags or pulling loaded travois, and the women were mushing them down the trail when a fair-sized pond appeared in the distance. In an instant the dogs made straight for the lake; once there they lay down and wallowed in the cool water, baggage and all. While the old men cheered, the women threw off their own packs and ran into the pond, swinging big sticks to chase the mongrels back onto the trail. Some of the dogs swam for deep water to avoid a beating and surely would have drowned if the women hadn't hauled them out.

I could picture that bolt toward the pond, bright tongues lapping at muddy water. My own tongue flapped out with a deep yawn, and I wheeled the radio dial in search of entertainment. Beyond country music and the CBC, I chanced on a live boxing card being broadcast from the Agricultural Pavilion in Edmonton. The first match was just under way, and no one had even thrown a punch when my path intersected with the blooming thunderheads. Raindrops came large and hard, and I crept along in the deluge, listening to static punctuated by an occasional lucid word. I thought I heard a knockdown, but everything else was lost in the sheets of water that swept across the road and down into the fields. By the time I drove out the other side of the storm, it was night.

A great horned owl leaped up from the path of my headlights, took five stiff beats, and glided into the trees. Trees. The highway curved for the first time in hours. A dirt road, messy with the tracks of logging trailers, angled off into the forest. I followed it over one gentle hill and down, then up onto another. It was a narrow track, with no place to pull off. I crept along, waiting for that flat spot. The pugilists up in Edmonton were still at it, and as I searched for a camping place, the radio bell rang on a late round of the last match on the card. Two boxers named David Fiddler and Danny Stonewalker seemed to be going at it pretty good, and the crowd was whooping it up.

I came to a crossroads at the end of the round and left the radio on while I circled the car to test the ground, clasping and unclasping my cramped fists. The earth felt spongy and extremely inviting. Then, just as Fiddler walked into a solid right hand, the mosquitoes arrived. I slapped at my ankles and neck for a couple of minutes, trying to gauge their density, while Stonewalker dispatched his opponent. I stepped around to the back of my car and dug into the trunk for tarp and sleeping bag.

The sky above the hilltop was impossibly deep. Moonlight revealed the landscape around me as a shadowy ruin of skidder tracks and small, splintered trees. I thought I could smell moose. I cleared a couple of springy limbs out of the way and curled up in my bag, already asleep. The bugs weren't bad at all, and the small dogs of Saukamappee scampered through my dreams.

CHAPTER TWO

A WELL-REGULATED WATCH

1788–1799

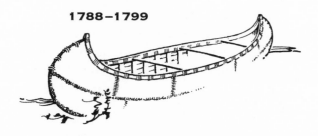

W ITH THE COMING of spring of 1788, Thompson and his companions left Saukamappee's camp and led a small contingent of Piegans loaded with beaver, fox, and wolf pelts back to Manchester House. House Master William Tomison was shocked at his apprentice's appearance: "He viewed me all round and muttered 'ragged, very ragged, can't be mended, must have a new jacket.'" The resident tailor made Thompson presentable again, and the routines of life at the trading post occupied the rest of the year. One of the things requiring attention was the state of the trade tobacco that the Bay Company had sent inland that fall. Tomison compared its taste to rotten turnips and had his men rub it down with sugar in hopes of improving its flavor; he was afraid the natives would refuse to trade with him when they learned that the Nor'Westers were offering an excellent crop next door. Tomison had no fondness for these neighbors, whom he called "those rogues from Canada," and argued with them throughout the winter. He didn't approve of the profligacy with which they dispensed rum among the natives, and it galled him that they had more than twice as many workers as he did.

Two days before Christmas, Tomison lost one of his valuable hands when David Thompson tumbled down a steep riverbank while hauling home a sledload of meat and broke the large bone in his right leg. The apprentice was across the river from the trade house and over a mile away when the accident happened, and his leg was extremely swollen by the time his co-workers got him home. William Tomison wrote that he set the leg and "put splinters around it with bandages in the best manner I could but such accidents would require a more skilful person than I am." Tomison's journal entries for the next few months indicate that the boy had a rough time of it.

> December 24: William Folster making a cradle Bed for David Thompson.
>
> December 31: David Thompson has been but indifferent for these three days past.
>
> January 12, 1789: David Thompson so far recovered as not to want any attendance at night.
>
> January 17: Took the bandages off David Thompson's leg and looked at it then bound it up again, he has but little pain in it, but still very weak.
>
> March 29: David Thompson was out of bed today for the first time but had not set long before his foot and ancle swelled a good deal so that he was obliged to lie down again. God only knows how it may turn out.
>
> April 13: As to David Thompson he mends but very slowly.
>
> May 1: David Thompson's leg I am afraid will turn out to be a mortification as the joint of his ancle has never lowered of the swelling.

Thompson later wrote that "Mr. Tomison behaved with the tenderness of a father to me, and alleviated my sufferings all he could."

When the spring canoes left with the furs for York Factory, Tomison floated the invalid downstream as far as Cumberland House. There it was decided that young Thompson could not continue on to York Factory, because he was in so much pain that he could not bear to be moved. He was left with Cumberland House Master Malcolm Ross, who wrote that he was concerned about a wound that had opened up over the fracture, "which I am afraid will prove bad." Ross set up a bed for Thompson in the warehouse, where the boy lay "helpless" for two months. He finally sat up in a chair on August 10, but it wasn't until the end of that month that he began to hobble around on crutches. He made slow progress for the rest of the fall and, possibly as a way to keep himself occupied, began keeping a daily journal. He ruled off neat columns for temperature, wind direction, wind speed, and general remarks on the weather, then filled them in three or four times a day.

The slow healing of his leg kept Thompson pinned to Cumberland House and meant that he was on hand for the October arrival of Philip Turnor, the Hudson's Bay Company "surveyor and astronomer." Most of the interior of North America at this time remained uncharted ground, and the company governors had hired Turnor to scientifically survey and map several of the river routes in their territory. Thompson had learned the rudiments of navigation at the Grey Coat School, and under Turnor's professional tutelage he renewed his study of practical astronomy, as the trade was then known.

In 1790 this was not a straightforward skill to master. To begin with, a student needed a full knowledge of the solar system, because the relative movements of stars and planets formed the basis for all calculations. Latitude could be reckoned fairly easily by measuring the altitude of the sun or a nighttime star with a sextant, then referring to set tables and formulas. Longitude, on the other hand, was determined by comparing the exact time at one's location with the exact time

on the prime meridian, which required an accurate clock set
to Greenwich Mean Time. The timepieces of Thompson's
day could stand up to the rolling motions of a ship, but not
the hard jarring of land travel, and an astronomer had to constantly adjust his watch to the Greenwich standard. He could
do this by timing the appearance and immersion of one of
Jupiter's moons, if he had a good telescope, or by watching a
lunar eclipse, if one happened to be on the schedule. More
commonly he would use the Earth's moon as one hand of a
giant celestial clock, then perform three or four hours of
trigonometry to interpolate the angle between its location
and that of certain stars. For this purpose all navigators and
surveyors were issued the annual *Nautical Almanac* in advance
of each year. The *Almanac* and its companion, *Tables Requisite*,
laid out the positions of specific stars and planets at set times
for every day of the year. Thus an astronomer in the field
needed a steady hand and eye, a firm grasp of mathematics,
and the stamina to stay up through the night, waiting for a favorable turn in the weather or the right configuration of
heavenly bodies. Because so many parts of the process were
subject to error, a surveyor would take two or more observations at the same location whenever possible, then average his
results to obtain the mean longitude or latitude.

David Thompson showed a knack for the meticulous
points of celestial observation. Throughout the winter and
spring of 1790, using a small sextant that Turnor loaned him,
the apprentice tested his progress by taking readings on
Cumberland House over and over again, doggedly reshooting
the points and refactoring the tedious equations. After compiling two and a half pages of minutely numbered shots,
neatly stacked up in his notebook, Thompson was satisfied
that he had the trading depot firmly located on the globe:

> The mean of the foregoing observations places
> Cumberland House in Latitude 53° 56' 44" N
> Longitude 102° 13' West of Greenwich and the

Variation by the Transits of the Sun and a well regulated Watch is 11° 30' East.

(sgn) David Thompson

Thompson's work so impressed Philip Turnor that the astronomer sent his student's coordinates for Cumberland House back to the Bay Company in London, along with a note:

I have inserted some Observations which were made and worked by Your Honors' unfortunate apprentice, David Thompson. I am fully convinced they are genuine, and should he ever recover his strength far enough to be capable of undertaking expeditions I think Your Honors may rely on his reports of the situation of any place he may visit.

Turnor and Malcolm Ross were planning a surveying expedition north into the Athabasca region the next fall, and Turnor needed an assistant. Thompson wanted the position, but his leg was still very weak and, in addition, "by much attention to my calculations in the night, with no other light than a small candle my right eye became so much inflamed that I lost its sight, and in the early part of May when the rivers and lakes became navigable, my health and strength were thought too weak to accompany Mr. Turnor as his assistant." There was a bright young clerk named Peter Fidler on hand, and when Thompson's health proved too unstable, Turnor quickly trained Fidler for the trip to Athabasca instead.

Thompson might have been disappointed, but he had found his focus, and relying on his one good eye, he soon began taking observations again. From then on, no matter how bizarre or troubled the conditions, he doggedly practiced his craft, which remained an arcane, incomprehensible occupation to most of his companions.

Both Canadians and Indians often inquired of me why I observed the Sun, and sometimes the Moon, in the day time, and passed whole nights with my instruments looking at the Moon and Stars. I told them it was to determine the distance and direction from the place I observed to other places; neither the Canadians nor the Indians believed me for both argued that if what I said was truth, I ought to look to the ground, and over it; and not to the Stars.

Narrative

Thompson *did* look to the ground a good deal, in fact, for it was necessary for an astronomer to supplement his celestial observations with detailed land surveys. In the summer of 1790, the budding geographer put his surveying skills to work by charting the 750-mile route from Cumberland House to York Factory. With a notebook in his lap and a compass in hand, he jotted down each twist and turn in the river's course: "S40E ¼ M[ile] S20E ½ M strong rapid on the right S8W 1 M S55E ¹⁄₁₀ M" and on and on and on. Later he sent these lists of distances and directions, along with any coordinates of latitude and longitude that he had been able to obtain, to the Bay Company headquarters in London, where they were passed on to professional cartographers and plotted onto the official maps of the region.

Thompson was twenty years old upon his arrival at York Factory, with his apprenticeship due to expire the next May. The customary reward for a young clerk who completed the program was a new suit of clothes. But in a letter to London, Thompson asked the governors to apply the price of his suit toward a set of surveying instruments, with any outstanding balance to be charged against his future wages. The company governors obviously decided his talents were worth encouraging, for in the summer of 1791, the supply ship brought him not only new clothes but also the gift of a ten-inch brass sextant made by Dollond—the standard navigational instrument of that era. They also sent a standard contract for three years' service at fifteen pounds per year.

The next summer Thompson received a brass compass, a Fahrenheit thermometer, and a case of instruments, along with a letter from the governors stating that these were "a reward for your assiduity." In a supply order to London that same year, he requested astronomical almanacs to go along with his instruments, plus two dozen coat buttons, a quire of tracing paper, and ten books, including a spelling dictionary, a pocket-sized New Testament, four volumes of Dr. Johnson's *Rambler,* and Milton's *Paradise Lost.* On the same supply list, Malcolm Ross and Peter Fidler both asked for an array of surveying implements, but not all of their co-workers displayed such a serious bent: one man ordered a magic lantern, an umbrella, and fiddle strings, as well as "12 skyrockets and other curious fireworks."

Two years later, when it was time to renew his contract, Thompson was bold enough to ask for a raise. The governors awarded him the substantial sum of sixty pounds per year— quadruple his previous salary and more than his superior, twenty-year company veteran Malcolm Ross, was making at the time. They also sent him another gift crucial to his surveying work: a fine watch made by London clockmaker Joseph Jolly, worth more than twelve pounds in itself. During these years between 1791 and 1796, Thompson worked all over the Bay Company's territory, spending another winter with William Tomison at a new post on the Saskatchewan and helping build several trade houses in what the furmen called the Muskrat Country north of Lake Winnipeg. All the while he made observations with his new instruments and surveyed every route he traveled. He also became well acquainted with the Cree and Chipewyan peoples who lived in the area.

> I had always admired the tact of the Indian in being able
> to guide himself through the darkest pine forests to
> exactly the place he intended to go, his keen, constant

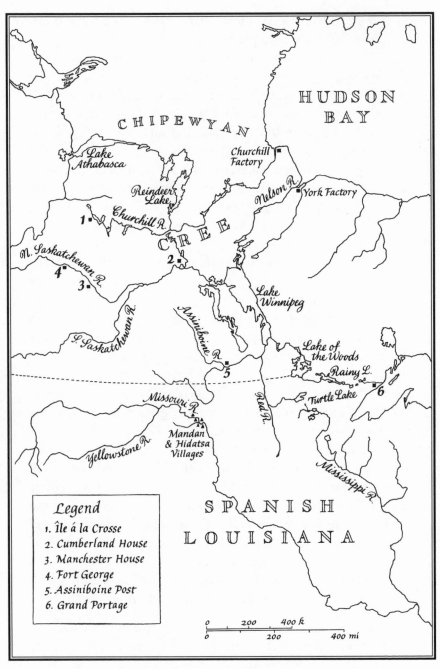

HUDSON BAY

CHIPEWYAN

Lake Athabasca

Reindeer Lake

Churchill Factory

Nelson R.

York Factory

Churchill R.

CREE

1. ▪

N. Saskatchewan R.

2. ▪

4. ▪

3. ▪

Lake Winnipeg

S. Saskatchewan R.

Assiniboine R.

Lake of the Woods

Rainy L.

5. ▪

Red R.

Turtle Lake

6. ▪

Missouri R.

Mandan & Hidatsa Villages

Yellowstone R.

Mississippi R.

SPANISH LOUISIANA

Legend
1. Île á la Crosse
2. Cumberland House
3. Manchester House
4. Fort George
5. Assiniboine Post
6. Grand Portage

0   200   400 k
0   200   400 mi

THOMPSON'S FIRST SURVEYS

attention on every thing; the removal of the smallest stone, the bent or broken twig; a slight mark on the ground, all spoke plain language to him. I was anxious to acquire this knowledge, and often being in company with them, sometimes for several months, I paid attention to what they pointed out to me, and became almost equal to some of them; which became of great use to me.

Narrative

However instructive Thompson's relations with the local tribes, these five years were not without their frustrations. For much of this time, he and Malcolm Ross were supposed to be looking for a more direct way from York Factory to Lake Athabasca, but they were repeatedly thwarted by manpower shortages and contradictory orders from the governors in London, the head of York Factory, and William Tomison, who was in charge of the inland trade. In the summer of 1796, after many delays, Thompson set off to scout a new route with two Chipewyans. It was a rugged venture, and in a canoe accident he lost everything he had with him, including his shoes. He located his precious cork-lined box of instruments some distance downstream, repaired the canoe, and made it back to his appointed meeting place with Ross. Certain that he had been on the right track, Thompson convinced his boss to try again with three canoes that September. By then, however, the water level of the river he wanted to follow had dropped too low for their boats, and the men were forced to retreat and build an impromptu shack for the winter on Reindeer Lake, far removed from any of the other Bay Company houses. They spent the next six months cramped, cold, and hungry.

Thompson's contract was up for renewal in the spring of 1797, and he had already been informed that he was slated to succeed Malcolm Ross, who was retiring that summer, as the person in charge of extending the trade northward to Lake Athabasca. But on May 21, Ross entered a surprising piece of news in his journal: "2 Geese from the Indians. This morning Mr. David Thompson acquainted Me with his time being out with your Honours and thought himself a freeborn subject and at liberty to choose any service he thought to be most to his advantage and is to quit your service and enter the Canadian company's Employ." Although this decision to cross over to the rival North West Company was a dramatic move, Thompson's own notes shed no further light on the subject. "May 22 Monday. A Cold Day put my baggage in Order, etc. etc." Ignoring the Hudson's Bay Company's policy that a year's notice of intent be given so that the London governors would have time to appoint a replacement, Thompson left Reindeer Lake on snowshoes early the next morning in a heavy snowstorm. "May 23 Tuesday. At 3½ A.M. set off... This day left the Service of the Hudsons Bay Co and entered that of the Company of Merchants from Canada." He then added the words "May God Almighty prosper me," and closed his journal.

In his *Narrative*, Thompson cites as his motivation for quitting a letter from York Factory that ordered him to stop exploring. But the chief of York Factory, upon hearing of Thompson's departure, noted that he had received information indicating that the surveyor had been "in treaty" with the Nor'Westers for some time. This would explain why Thompson had not sent any of his survey notes back to London for the previous two years, and it might also explain why Alexander Fraser, a partner of the North West Company, had visited Thompson and Ross in early April. One thing that is clear from both Ross's and Thompson's brief accounts is that Thompson felt certain of a job with the competition.

At any rate, it was to Fraser's trade house, eighty miles south, that Thompson went upon leaving Reindeer Lake. He helped around the post for a few days and wrote two letters to his former employers at York Factory—one berating the chief factor there and the other asking a favor of the governing council, in a rather testy tone:

Gentlemen—

As I am now in the employ of the NW Co. of Merchants from Canada you may perhaps not think it consistent with your Duty to send my Books, Mathematical Instruments etc. etc. to Cumberland House, should this be the Case you will please to reship them for England; tho' I must confess I am utterly at a loss to know how the reading of Books or observing the motions of the heavenly Bodies can be detrimental to the interest of the Honble. Hudsons Bay Company.

Your Humble Servant
David Thompson

The books and instruments he was so anxious to receive included *Nautical Almanac*s and an expensive new telescope that he had ordered from London the previous year. As it turned out, his parcel had already been sent inland before word of his resignation arrived at York. His former boss, William Tomison, upon learning of the incident, railed that any man who had forwarded a package for "so base a man as Thompson ought to have both his ears cut off which I should not have scrupled at had he been my brother."

Thompson, meanwhile, had made his way south to Grand Portage, the North West Company's field headquarters on Lake Superior. This was the site of the company's gala summer rendezvous, where traders from all over the territory convened to turn in their year's furs and pick up new trade goods and supplies that had been ferried in from Montreal. This was also the occasion for an annual meeting between the two arms of the company: the "agents," who handled the business in Montreal, and the "proprietors," or wintering partners, who oversaw the trade at the interior posts. Unlike the highly centralized bureaucracy of the Hudson's Bay Company, the Nor'Westers were more democratic, with major decisions being approved at these annual meetings at Grand Portage. They also paid better than the Bay Company.

Thompson did not record his salary that first year, but by 1799 he was listed as one of the better-paid clerks of the company, pulling down one hundred pounds a year plus twenty pounds' worth of such "equipment and necessaries" as clothing, tea, sugar, and chocolate. There was additional economic incentive as well, for it was possible for a diligent clerk to work his way up to the rank of field partner and share in the annual profits.

In the big dining hall at Grand Portage, Thompson drank fresh milk from cows the company pastured nearby and dined with the partners and other clerks. He also met head agents William McGillivray and Alexander Mackenzie, up from Montreal for the rendezvous. Both men had begun their careers as clerks in the field, and Mackenzie had become Canada's most celebrated explorer by leading expeditions to the Arctic and Pacific Oceans several years earlier. Now these men had an important expedition planned for their new employee. At the end of the American Revolution, diplomats had established the border between the United States and British Canada as a line that ran through the centers of Lake Superior, Rainy Lake, and Lake of the Woods, then west along the 49th parallel to an undetermined point north of the headwaters of the Mississippi River. There was now a movement down in the States to restrict trade south of this line, but no one was sure exactly where the boundary lay, and the partners wanted Thompson to find out. He was also to pay a goodwill visit to some Mandan villages on the Missouri River and, while he was at it, collect any large fossils he came across—new discoveries of the bones of mammoths and other big Ice Age mammals had excited great interest among collectors, including someone in the North West Company.

In early August, a little more than two weeks after he had arrived at Grand Portage, Thompson hitched a ride with a canoe brigade heading to Rainy Lake and started his survey. This was his first trip in the company of the French Canadian voyageurs that the North West Company hired from the large French population of Quebec. These men signed contracts with the company according to their paddling position in the canoe: the *gouvernail* in the stern and the *avant* in the bow were the key men, and the best paid. Thompson found the voyageurs "a fine, hardy, good humoured set of Men, fond of full feeding . . . eating full eight pounds of fresh meat per day." They were also noted for their short, stocky frames, their repertoire of paddle songs, and their fondness for a smoke—distances on rivers and lakes were measured in "pipes," for the amount of water the men could cover before putting down their paddles to fill a bowl. The patois of the voyageurs was the everyday language of the Nor'Westers, and if Thompson didn't speak French already, he started learning it now.

By late November the surveyor had made a big loop north through Lake Winnipeg and back south to a North West Company house on the Assiniboine River in what is now southern Manitoba. Even though winter had already set in, he decided to travel overland to the Mandan villages on the Missouri. He found an interpreter who knew the Mandan language and organized a trading party of French Canadians outfitted with dog teams purchased from local Assiniboine Indians. The first night out, November 30, 1797, his thermometer read twenty below zero. The next day it plummeted to thirty-seven below, and steady high winds kept smoke from their fire swirling inside the tent; the men spent most of the day out wandering in the woods for relief. "We could not proceed, but had the good fortune to kill a good bison cow, which kept us in good humor."

The Assiniboine dogs were not accustomed to hauling sleds, and the French Canadians flogged them enthusiastically to keep them in line. "When on the march the noise was intolerable, and made me keep 2 or 3 miles ahead." Over the next four weeks, they trudged through the gamut of winter weather. When a blizzard bore down across the plains, Thompson amazed his companions by using his compass to direct them to a protective grove of trees that he had spotted before the blowing snow engulfed them. A few days later, a howling chinook raised the temperature fifty-six degrees in twelve hours. As they entered the hilly country near the Missouri River, the rough terrain slowed their progress, as did retrieving dogs who kept breaking away to chase herds of buffalo. On December 30, after thirty-three days and over two hundred miles, they reached the frozen Missouri and walked on the ice to a cluster of Mandan and Hidatsa villages.

Here Thompson encountered an agricultural society very different from anything he had seen before. He took a census of the five stockaded villages and described large, earth-domed lodges furnished with wooden sofas covered in bison robes. He ate the corn porridge seasoned with ashes that the villagers offered him, and purchased a quantity of dried corn and beans. He learned that they also raised pumpkins and melons in the rich river bottoms, which they cultivated with hoes fashioned from the shoulder blades of bison and deer. In one of the villages, Thompson met a Frenchman who had been living among the Mandans for fifteen years and had risen to a position of prominence. While presenting him with gifts of tobacco, soap, a bottle of peppermint, a lump of sugar, and a dog, Thompson heard that two visitors had recently arrived from the headwaters of the Missouri, near the Rocky Mountains. The surveyor immediately arranged to meet the pair and spent a day questioning them about the course of the upper Missouri.

The Missouri River at that time was still part of the Spanish-owned Louisiana Territory, but Canadian fur traders frequently visited the Mandan villages, and the North West Company was very interested in trade possibilities farther up-river. The two men from the mountains described their homeland, measuring distances between landmarks in days of good walking, and Thompson drew out rough maps for them to examine and correct. They told him about large tributaries called the Yellow Stone and the Shell, about a high fall at the source of the Missouri, and three high ridges of mountains. This last bit of information ran contrary to the generally accepted notion that the Rockies consisted of a single low ridge or "Height of Land" that could be crossed by a short portage, but Thompson had good reason to believe that the natives knew something the European geographers did not. "They appeared to be very intelligent, as almost all the Natives of the Mountains are – They fully comprehended with a little explanation the drift of all my Questions, and answered direct to them. When done I gave them a little Tobacco – for which they were thankful."

Thompson was staying in the lodge of one of the chiefs, and during a few days of bad weather, he conversed with the people about their traditions while making himself a pair of snowshoes. He spent one clear night observing for latitude and longitude, and on other evenings watched "their Amusements of Dancing Singing etc. which were always conducted with the highest order and Decorum after their Idea of thinking; but to me, a stranger, I could not help thinking them the most uxorious Race I have seen and one of the old Priests of Venus would quickly have got them to build a Temple." In his *Narrative*, Thompson recalled a group of handsome young women dressed in thin white deerskins, who danced to the accompaniment of drum, tambour, rattle, and flute. "When the music struck up, part of the men sang, and the women keeping a straight line and respective distance, danced with a light step and slow, graceful motion."

THE DOUBLE DOORS of the tavern swung open, and I turned to watch as a dozen men and women, singing in what sounded like raucous Norwegian, burst through and swept past me like a breaking wave. The leader of the mob balanced an anvil-sized box on the tips of his raised fingers. He swooped his arms low to reveal a miniature black coffin, its lid sparkling with lit candles and a painted inscription: THE END OF YOUTH. The wave re-formed and rolled away on a direct line toward a crowded back corner, where the casket was laid down in front of one youthful, aging man. Amid a flurry of cheers, he blew out the candles and pulled mementos from the box—a baby doll, an inkwell, and an Indian headdress decorated with brightly dyed chicken feathers.

"Hey Carl, throw me down a pack a them Camels."

The bartender, with the slightest of nods, tossed a fresh pack down the row of stools to a lean, hatchet-faced guy who had wandered in behind the parade. He made a nice catch, hung a cigarette between his lips, and patted his pockets for matches as he settled onto the stool next to mine. Flakes of sawdust drifted away from his flannel shirt.

"Got a light, friend?" he asked, with a grizzled smile. He spoke with a Dakotan's deliberate, wide-voweled accent, and although I shook my head no, his smile didn't fade a bit. He wheeled around so he could scan the crowd and hailed a passing logger for a match. He took a long drag on his Camel, then rolled his stool back to front position and turned his ear toward a conversation that was going on to our right.

It had begun when the woman sitting next to me mentioned that she had recently unearthed the remains of a steam-powered tractor from a gully on her grandmother's ranch. The stack was as thick as a tree trunk, she said, and at first she had thought it was a train locomotive. The bartender had taken an interest and started prodding the lady for more details; her description of waffle cleats on great cast-iron wheels and a rivet-dimpled boiler tank touched off a discussion about the age of the thing. Estimates ranged from the first Homestead Act to the Battle of Midway. The Dakotan listened for a minute, then tossed his head toward me with a snort.

"Aaaaah," he said. "You think that steamer's old? Don't talk to me about no *old*. I've been there. I've seen the Mandan villages."

I started to ask him which villages, but he was gazing intently at the bottles behind the bar. "I've been lucky," he growled. "I've got to go places nobody else's ever been."

The Norwegian drinking chorus was now back on its feet, snaking around in front of the bar as a human chain. My neighbor lit up another cigarette and ignored the ruckus.

"I've got to touch things that hasn't been touched," he said. "I'll tell ya what—you're looking at somebody that had free run of the whole Standing Rock Indian Reservation. Prince Maximilian? You read his diary and it's just the same now as it was then. You look off to where he saw that butte, and there it is." He looked out over the crowded bar, beyond the curl of the line dance.

"Those Mandans. The stuff they left behind—shoot, you're tripping over 'em all the time. We used to take a bucket for the arrowheads, and have to pack the rest. I got spearpoints as long as your forearm."

The Dakotan wiped at the bartop with his sleeve. "I was out there one day, on a long mud flat, and I found this pipe, made out of soapstone. Not much bigger than this." He held out his curled left hand and stared at it, whistling in admiration.

"That sucker was beautiful, but it was only half there— split right down the middle. Some compadre must have carried off that other half, and meant to join it back together one day.

"That was right about the time they closed up the gates on the big dam. I got out there in my canoe and paddled all around. For a long time the water level didn't change that much, and I went from one island to the next. I just had a feeling like I was going to find it. That water kept coming up, and I kept on mucking around, but I never did find the other half of that pipe."

He brought his right hand slowly across to clasp his left. The glow in his eyes damped down, then rekindled.

"There was another day, across the river. There had come

a big rain, and I was trucking down this wash, slipping and sliding in the gumbo. I'd been that way one thousand times, always picking up things, and I come around a corner I knew like the back of my hand and whoooa, here's a whole crew of people. The Smithsonian boys. They're out there picking away with their little scrapers and tweezers. And they've dug up a whole, complete skeleton, TRI-CER-O-TOPS! Head bigger'n a wheelbarrow! Oh, I'll tell ya about it. Don't talk to me about no *old*. I cut my teeth in the Mandan country."

ON JANUARY 10, 1798, Thompson and his party left the Mandan villages with wolf pelts and buffalo robes, but no large fossil bones. By the end of the month, they had made their way back to the North West post on the Assiniboine River, where they had started. Here Thompson spent three weeks calculating the positions he had shot on the trip and drafting a rough map. In late February he hit the trail again, and by early spring he had used a light canoe to trace the headwaters of the Mississippi to Turtle Lake, which he decided must be the source of the river. Although later surveyors selected another pothole nearby as the Mississippi's official point of origin, Thompson did perform the first accurate survey of its upper drainages, near latitude 48° N.

Struggling downstream from Turtle Lake through the emerging shoots of wild rice, he crossed to Lake Superior and followed the lake's south shore to the site of modern Sault Ste. Marie. There he met North West agent Alexander Mackenzie, on his way to Grand Portage for the summer rendezvous. Describing their encounter in his *Narrative*, Thompson wrote, "Upon my report to him of the surveys I had made, and the number of astronomical observations for latitude, longitude, and variation of the compass, he was pleased to say I had performed more in ten months than he expected could be done in two years." Thompson continued his work along the east and north shores of Lake Superior, and his arrival back at Grand Portage in June 1798 completed a circuit of four thousand miles. He had discovered that several North West trading houses, as well as Grand Portage itself, lay south of the proposed U.S. boundary, and in the process he had filled in a large blank space on the map of North America. When Alexander Mackenzie published an account of his own explorations three years later, he included, with a small credit, Thompson's map work of points from Lake Winnipeg down into the headwaters of the Mississippi.

The North West partners next sent Thompson off to the opposite corner of their domain, the Athabasca region, where he built a new trade house and explored along the Athabasca River. In the spring, returning south with a load of furs, he stopped at Île à la Crosse on the Churchill River, and there, on June 10, 1799, he married Charlotte Small. Charlotte was the daughter of Patrick Small, one of the original North West Company partners. After living and trading at Île à la Crosse for several years, Small had retired to England with his fur profits, leaving his native wife and half-breed children behind. Charlotte's mother was a Cree, a tribe that Thompson knew well. In one draft of his *Narrative*, he wrote: "My lovely wife is of the blood of these people, speaking their language, and well educated in the English language, which gives me a great advantage." According to an entry in the Thompson family Bible, Charlotte was born on September 1, 1785, which would have made her not quite fourteen years old in the spring of 1799; Thompson had just turned twenty-nine. It was accepted practice for a winterer to take a young teenage wife of native or mixed blood, "after the fashion of the country," as official company documents phrased it. This was also in keeping with the nuptial customs of the Crees, as recorded by Thompson: "Their marriages are without noise or ceremony; nothing is requisite but the consent of the parties and the parents . . . when contrariety of disposition prevails, so that they cannot live peaceably together, they separate with as little ceremony as they came together, and both parties are free to attach themselves to whom they will, without any stain on their characters."

The newlyweds spent the winter at Fort George on the upper Saskatchewan, where Thompson laid out big sheets of drawing paper that had been sent from Montreal and began transforming the columns of figures from his notebooks into points on a map. He also took his first tentative stab at writing up his adventures in narrative form. During the winter, he was visited by John McDonald of Garth. (There were so many McDonalds in the North West Company that this one identified himself by the name of his ancestral estate in Scotland.) McDonald of Garth was Thompson's new brother-in-law, having married another of Patrick Small's daughters, and he also worked in the western Saskatchewan district, known as "Fort des Prairies."

For several years, McDonald of Garth and other traders along the Saskatchewan had been hearing about a tribe that lived on the west side of the Rocky Mountains. The name of these people is variously spelled in the early records as the "Cotta na haos," "Cuttenchas," "Cottonahaws," and "Coutonees"; Thompson called them the Kootanaes. (Today they are known as the Kutenais or Kootenays in Canada and the Kootenais in the United States.) Their country was reputed to abound in fur-bearing animals of all types, which they were anxious to trade; but the east-side posts were far away. This untapped source of furs was of great interest to everyone in the Fort des Prairies Department, for as that district filled with trade houses, the number of pelts taken in steadily dwindled. In order to give the Kootenais a convenient place to trade, McDonald of Garth had spent of the fall of 1799 building a new post far up the Saskatchewan at the base of the mountains. In the spring of 1800, Thompson rode up on horseback for a quick reconnaissance, and that fall he and Charlotte took up residence at the company's westernmost establishment, the new Rocky Mountain House.

CHAPTER THREE

SMOKING
WITH EAGLES

1800–1806

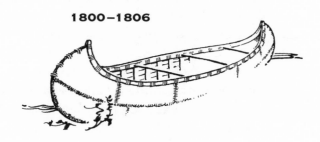

ALL THE WHILE I read Thompson, I had pictured Rocky Mountain House as being in the foothills, but as I approached the provincial park that preserves its site, the flatness of the surrounding countryside was what impressed me most. A pasture of tall grasses could have been a rug unrolled; its only relief was a small group of buffalo, their round backs bunched up black and shiny within a stout wire fence. Beyond the animals the white cone of a tipi stuck up from the grassland, and a line of stubby spruce trees stretched along the Saskatchewan River. I knew that a wall of mountains rose up fifty miles or so behind me, but today the whole horizon had sunk into a yellow haze.

I walked toward the river and the tipi, which stands near the site of the first rough fort that McDonald of Garth built for the North West Company in the fall of 1799. The Hudson's Bay Company built its Acton House that same fall less than a mile away, and during the next eight decades edifices were raised, added on to, burned, rebuilt in different spots, and neglected for seasons at a time. A sign notes that one carefully preserved rotted timber might have belonged to that first trading post, but it's hard to tell for sure. Later incarnations are better documented, with foundation outlines and a reconstructed bastion. Down by the landing beach is a replica of one of the flat-bottomed bateaux that sometimes hauled cargo on the river, and when I punched a button on the kiosk nearby I heard the slap of fat oars against the water, followed by the grunts and hissing *Sacré bleu*s of paddlers as they worked themselves silly for the Englishmen.

Remnants from the various sites are displayed inside an interpretive center on the grounds, and as I stepped inside, a silver-haired man was questioning a young guide. "I'll tell you what I want to know," the man said. "What I want to know is, if this place is called Rocky Mountain House, then where the hell are the mountains?"

I noticed that several people around the lobby leaned in to catch the answer. The guide explained that usually you could see the Rockies off to the west, but that smoke from a big forest fire up in the Northwest Territories was obscuring the view today. The man still looked vaguely dissatisfied, as if the ranger were somehow responsible for the lack of visibility. I was about to step up and tell him that there had often been prairie fires even back in David Thompson's time, when a woman with a troubled expression entered the foyer and walked directly up to the guide. "Excuse me," she said, "but I thought there were supposed to be mountains around here..."

I moved on into the adjacent exhibit hall, which was momentarily empty of visitors. The first display I came upon was a collection of antique surveying instruments. Here was a ten-inch brass Dollond sextant, exactly like the one Thompson had carried, and a smaller box full of drawing equipment: pens and nibs, protractors, compasses, dividers, and rules. There was even a copy of a *Nautical Almanac*, and a Jolly watch that looked as if it would still keep pretty good time.

Across the corridor I stopped at an array of trade items, several of which I had wondered about when I came across them in Thompson's journals. A "dag" turned out to be a wide, heavy knife, shipped without a handle to save space and weight in the canoes. "Hawks bells" were the same little jingle bells that falconers hang from the jesses of captive hawks; farther along I saw them used as decorations on buckskin jackets and bags. A small copper pot, plain metal rings, glass beads of different colors, a sewing awl, a thick twist of tobacco—every one of these items had gone through an epic of packing and repacking, wetting and drying, loading and unloading, inventorying and pricing, on its journey to this spot.

In the next hallway I almost bumped my head on the vessel that had ferried all this stuff across the continent: a genuine birchbark canoe. It looked to be about fourteen feet long, which would have made it a "light" canoe, used for running messages and carrying small loads. I reached one hand up and touched the birch rind. It was paper, yet wood, calked solid at each seam, sewn neatly to the wooden gunwales. The tribes of the eastern woodlands had developed these craft, and the early French traders had been quick to see their value. Light enough for two men to carry, yet strong enough to hold many times their own weight, they could be built in different sizes depending on where and how they were to be used. Twenty-five feet was the standard length for the *canots du nord* (Northern canoes) that Thompson used for hauling cargo; he estimated that one of these boats, fully loaded, could carry twenty-nine hundred pounds of supplies. During his years with the woodland tribes, he became skilled in their construction and repair. The first requirement for a good canoe was quality bark, or rind, and it took an experienced eye to spot the right tree. Cree canoe builders taught Thompson to pay special attention to the dark horizontal nicks, or "cores," that mark every birch trunk. They told him that these nicks were scars left from floggings by Weesaukajauk, the Flatterer, an impish deity whom the birch species once disobeyed. Some trees had been whipped so severely that the nicks penetrated all the way through the rind, and this made for a leaky boat. After the bark was carefully peeled from the trees, thin tendrils of coniferous roots, called *watap*, were stripped out of the ground and used to sew the canoe together. Then the seams were calked with the rendered sap of fir, spruce, or pine. A bundle of watap and a bucket of gum rode along as necessities on every voyage to repair rips in the bark or leaks around the nicks of Weesaukajauk.

Other exhibits along the hallways showed off native costumes and accoutrements, and weapons of hunting and war. One small case held miscellaneous relics that had been found in the immediate vicinity of the old trade houses, and it was this random collection of everyday objects that evoked most strongly the meeting of disparate cultures that had taken place around those rotting timbers out in the yard. There were stone arrowheads, buttons, a small bottle, a child's whizzer toy, and a delicate whistle sectioned from a bird's hollow wing bone.

Back outside, there was plenty of light left in the day, and I thought I would climb across a fence and take a shortcut over to a nature trail marked on the map. The park is nestled in a pocket between prairie and muskeg, where the effects of the last glacial ice sheet linger like a slow-drying sponge, and when I hopped down I landed in ankle-deep ooze. After five squishy steps I retreated to a gravel road that led through the grassland and ended at a walking-beam oil pump. The blue steel grasshopper bobbed slowly up and down, surrounded by a knobby, unnavigable bog of spruce. A heavy petroleum smell hung in the air, and as I drove away from the park I passed the twin flames of a small natural gas plant. The odor hung with me until I reached the bridge over the Saskatchewan River and climbed a hill toward town.

The settlement of Rocky Mountain House sits in open country set back from the river. The main street is laid out wide enough for a cattle drive, and the evening traffic suggested that the trading-post culture of the last century had moved only a few miles up to the crossroads. At the bottom of the main drag, I spotted the David Thompson Hotel, a two-story concrete-block affair, blue with a bright red false front. A Conestoga wagon rides across its roof, above a cowboy mural touting "Rocky's Largest Country Party Bar." When I tried to jaywalk across to the saloon, I found myself dodging a series of big-tired pickups that rumbled along the rolling streets. Back at my car a note on the windshield informed me that although I had parked a little crooked, the city fathers were going to let me off this time, and they hoped that I enjoyed my visit.

Later that evening I wandered back down to the Saskatchewan. Fresh out of the mountains, the river ran fast and milky under the bridge. I followed a trail that led upstream to a point opposite the cluster of old trade houses and sat down beside a clump of wolf willows to watch it get dark. Along the flat, big cottonwoods rose above the dark green of alder and serviceberry bushes. Pearly wolf willow berries, beads for Blackfeet children, mirrored the ice-green color of the Saskatchewan. A muted laugh rang across the water, followed by the dips and drips of smooth paddle strokes. By the light reflected off the river, I could make out bright orange flags and life jackets suspended over a loose formation of canoes. As they came closer, the laughter increased. Then three dark fiberglass hulls coasted quietly into the big eddy, and the paddlers drew them in, one by one, to scuff up on to the gravel bar for their final stop of the day.

AS DAVID THOMPSON approached that same landing spot in the fall of 1800, he was paddling through territory frequented by several tribes. His old Piegan friends, along with their Blood and Blackfeet kin, still ranged freely between the Saskatchewan and Missouri Rivers. Several Cree and Stoney Assiniboine bands had moved into the vicinity, and some of

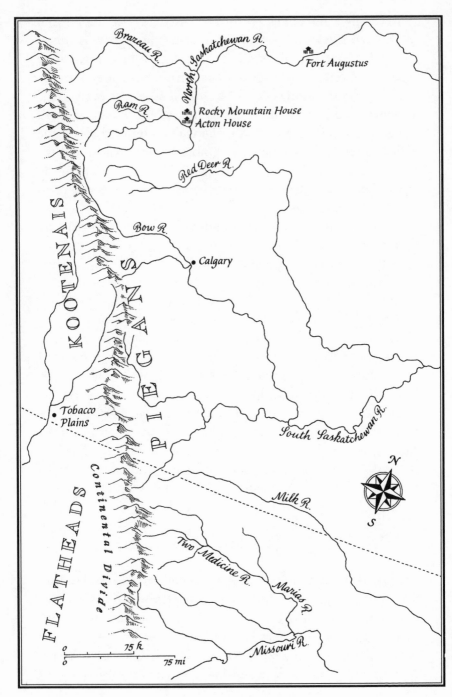

RIVERS OF THE EAST SLOPE

them worked as hunters for the fur companies. Then there were the Kootenais across the Divide, whom the traders were counting on to bring in the next great bounty of beaver.

Thompson had not been at Rocky Mountain House very long when he heard that a group of Kootenais was heading over the mountains with a load of pelts. He quickly hired two guides—a Cree named He Dog and a Piegan named Old Bear—and gathered five men and eleven horses to go and meet the new customers and guide them to the trade house. The Nor'Westers set out on October 5 and were a few hours down the trail before someone realized that they had forgotten to bring a cooking pot. The voyageur La Gasse hurried back to the post and caught up with the party that evening, two kettles in hand. On the second day out, they stopped for a brief smoke with five tents of Piegans, then continued south until they struck the Red Deer River, which they followed upstream to an open plain. "Here we had a grand view of the Rocky Mountains, forming a concave Segment of a Circle ... all its snowy cliffs to the Southward ever bright in the Beams of the Sun, while the most northern were darkened by a Tempest & by the Storm, which spent its Force only on the summits." As they climbed higher into the foothills, Thompson studied the huge piles of driftwood far up on the riverbanks, untouched by high-water marks for several years. Had so much of the mountain been eroded away that it no longer attracted storm clouds, he wondered, or had there been a change in local weather patterns?

Late on the third afternoon, Old Bear brought them to his own small camp, and here they put up for a few days. Thompson hunted and took observations for latitude and longitude while he waited for another guide who had promised to come and lead them farther into the mountains. When the new guide did show up, he immediately made clear that his primary interest was tobacco. As for the other Piegans in camp, "They are so jealous of the Kootanaes coming in to Trade that they do all they can to persuade me to return, assuring me that it is impossible for me to find them and that in endeavoring to search them out, our Horses will fall by Fatigue and Hunger, and perhaps also ourselves."

The Piegans seemed to have an on-again, off-again relationship with the Kootenais. Both tribes had long traditions of travel back and forth across the Divide for hunting and trade; sometimes they were in a state of war, at other times they would declare a truce and meet amiably. In 1792 Hudson's Bay Company surveyor Peter Fidler had traveled with a group of Piegans up into the foothills to meet a Kootenai band that had come across the mountains to trade. He was the first white man to meet the Kootenais, and he watched as they chopped firewood with hatchets crafted from sharpened elk antlers, then swapped their good horses and furs for the old kettles and broken iron tools that the Piegans had brought along. Fidler figured that any trade house would have given the Kootenais as much for one pelt as the Piegans gave them for ten, but the Kootenais walked home happy with their trifles, and wanted more. What they wanted most was guns. In the years that followed, however, the Piegans would trade them only a few, jealously preserving their own arms superiority as well as the healthy profit margin they gained as middlemen. The Kootenais repeatedly tried to elude the Piegans and other Blackfeet tribes and go directly to the trade houses, but they were rarely successful.

Now traders had come in search of the Kootenais, and the Piegans were trying to scare them off by feigning concern for their safety. The new guide told the Nor'Westers to ignore these dissuasions, and led them upriver. The first afternoon out, Thompson shot a bighorn sheep whose horns measured thirty-five inches along the curl. The next day he had a chance to climb a high knoll, where he had a good view of range after range of wooded hills rippling toward a distinctive peak. He killed a fisher, another example of the plentiful variety of game they were finding—so far they had seen wolverine, elk, moose, mule deer, and "Grisled Bears but too many." They stopped to camp that night with two tents of Piegans who had spent the day eagle hunting, a sport Thompson had observed closely during his first winter on the plains:

> The natives made shallow pits which they covered with slender willows and grass under which they lay, with a large piece of fresh meat opposite their breasts; thus arranged they patiently await the flight of the eagle, which is first seen very high, scaling in rude circles, but gradually lowering, till at length he seems determined to pounce upon the meat, his descent is then very swift with his claws extended, the moment he touches the meat the Indians grasp his two legs in his hands, and dashes him, through the slender willows to the bottom of the pit and strikes his head till he is dead . . . Lying in this position, and frequently somewhat benumbed, it requires an active man to pull down an Eagle with his wings expanded, and dash him to the ground . . . As the Eagle never loses his courage, the whole must be quickly done, or the Eagle will dart his beak in the mans face, and thus get away.
>
> *Narrative*

Eight birds had been captured on this hunt, and that evening the Piegans cleared a spot in the back of their tent and laid the eagles on a patch of clean grass with their heads pointing toward the fire. During the next three hours, the Piegans sang and shook a rattle while a medicine pipe was passed; each man in turn smoked the pipe and then presented it to each of the eagles. These birds' feathers would adorn war bonnets and shields, and the claws, beaks, and other parts would be preserved for ceremonial uses. After the consecration, Thompson went out for some stellar observations, and noted the latitude of the camp (51° 41' 41" N) in his journal the next morning.

They all stayed put for a day of bad weather and fruitless

hunting. That evening two young Piegans showed up with a pair of mares and reported that the Kootenais, from whom they had stolen the horses, "would be on the Heights of the Mountain the Morrow." The morrow was October 14, a Tuesday, and their guide led the Nor'Westers high up the headwaters of the Red Deer River in what is now Banff National Park. In midafternoon, at the base of some high cliffs, they met a Kootenai chief with twenty-six men and seven women. The chief presented Thompson with a bow and a quiver of arrows, a red foxskin cap, and a fine yellow horse loaded with fifty beaver pelts. Thompson told him to hold on to the horse and furs until they could trade properly at Rocky Mountain House and pulled out a fathom of his good tobacco for an introductory smoke. The Kootenais were poorly clothed for the cold weather and had only eleven horses among them—they said they had started out with more, but several had been stolen by Piegans who met them on the way over. Despite such discouragements, the travelers assured the surveyor that they were ready to make for the trading post, and together they camped for the night.

They headed down the mountain on Wednesday, and by the time they made camp, the sun had already set. It was not too dark, however, for one of the men from a nearby Piegan camp to notice a handsome black horse and boldly snatch it on the spot. The Kootenais grabbed their weapons, the thief let go his prize, and the commotion brought out a Piegan chief who lectured his men on their rude behavior, "that it was an Act neither brave nor manly to rob a few Strangers, their allies, of their poor starved horses." The Kootenais decided they had seen enough and prepared to head home that night. Thompson enlisted the help of a voyageur named Michel Boulard, who was good with native languages; together the two men reasoned with the travelers until midnight and finally convinced them to continue.

The next morning they discovered that the incorrigible Piegans had stolen five more horses during the night, including the yellow one given to Thompson. The Kootenais again determined to turn around, and it was only after "much ado" and the loan of a horse to carry some of their baggage that Thompson was able to get them to come with him. The thought of the guns they would be able to get at the trade house helped move them in that direction. "They complained much & bitterly to me of what had been stolen & plundered from them . . . several of the principal of them went so far as to kneel down and swear by the Sun, the Skies, and Earth, that they would revenge themselves."

For the next five days, Thompson refereed a running game of cat-and-mouse as several young Piegans followed along to pester the Kootenais. On Thursday an altercation seemed certain to end in bloodshed until Thompson and Boulard rushed up and chased away three young rowdies who were trying to stop the caravan. They camped Friday night near a friendly Piegan chief who invited them all to come and feast with him. Some of the young men at this camp challenged the Kootenais to a gambling match, then lost every game until the party broke up at midnight. On Saturday morning the Kootenais awoke to find they had only two horses left. Thompson quickly rode back to Rocky Mountain House to fetch fresh mounts so that he could keep things moving. Still hassling with young Piegans, the party arrived safely at the trading post on Monday afternoon. "Thank God," wrote Thompson, and passed out rum all around.

The next day he purchased ten bear, two wolverine, five fisher, and over a hundred beaver pelts from the Kootenais. One old man was savvy enough to take his five bear hides next door to Acton House to see if he could strike a better deal with the Hudson's Bay trader there. Throughout their ordeal, Thompson had been impressed by the Kootenais' spirit and fortitude, and by the steady demeanor of the four old men who led them. After the trading was finished, the surveyor questioned these elders about the geography of their homeland and about the mountains between. He learned that the Kootenais were a small tribe with a broad knowledge of both sides of the Divide. Two or three times a year, several of their bands would get together and cross over to hunt buffalo on the east side. Sometimes they were harassed by Blackfeet, but often they were able to dry their meat and stretch their hides in peace. They had once had many routes across the mountains, they said, but smallpox had decimated their numbers, and all but a few trails had fallen into disuse.

This was the sort of information Thompson needed, and he asked the Kootenais to come back the next spring and guide him to their country. He loaned the chief a horse to carry his baggage and fitted out two voyageurs, La Gasse and Le Blanc, to go home with them and spend the winter. In hopes of avoiding any more Piegan woes, the Kootenais decided to return home by a northerly route, through wooded country where the Blackfeet rarely ventured. On October 22 they set off along the north bank of the Saskatchewan. When it was time to depart, La Gasse and Le Blanc couldn't find their horses, but by the next morning they were ready. Thompson rode along with them until they caught up with the Kootenai party just past noon, then he bid his pioneers adieu and returned to Rocky Mountain House.

Upon his return he found that Duncan McGillivray had just arrived. The younger brother of Chief Superintendent William McGillivray, Duncan had worked in the Fort des Prairies Department for seven years and had helped build many of the posts that had leapfrogged up the Saskatchewan. Now that the trade had pushed all the way to the foot of the Rocky Mountains, Duncan was one of several prominent partners who saw no reason to stop there. As their network had stretched farther and farther north and west, the long commutes across the continent had grown increasingly inefficient. Precious time and manpower were being spent getting from the outposts back and forth to Grand Portage, and from Lake Superior back and forth to Montreal; by the time a canoe brigade reached Lake Athabasca or Rocky Mountain

House, it was actually much closer to the Pacific Ocean than to Montreal. The explorations of Captain James Cook and other mariners had failed to uncover any Northwest Passage by sea, but for years furmen had been talking about the "Great River of the West," rumored to run all the way from the Rockies to the Pacific. If such a river could be found, it would not only provide them with a transcontinental passage and a western port, but also open a lucrative trade route to China and Russia.

In the 1780s Alexander Mackenzie, working around Lake Athabasca, had become convinced that just such a river lay close at hand. In 1789 he had led a small party from Lake Athabasca to Great Slave Lake, then west along the river he assumed would quickly take him to the Pacific. But that river, later named for him, soon turned north and led him straight to the Arctic Ocean—a remarkable piece of pioneering, but the wrong ocean on which to found an economic empire. Four years later Mackenzie tried another route. This time he made his way up a tributary of the Peace River and carried his canoe 817 paces across the Continental Divide. On the other side he traced a river that he called the Tacoutche Tesse to the beginnings of a wild canyon in what is now west-central British Columbia. As the river turned south, Mackenzie broke away from its tortuous course and followed native trails through dense rain forest to Bella Coola, a village on the Pacific Coast near latitude 52° N. Again his trip provided landmark information about the geography of the Northwest, but did little to further commerce.

When Mackenzie returned from his disappointing trip to Bella Coola in 1793, he learned that the previous May an American sea captain named Robert Gray had discovered the mouth of a big river on the west coast just north of the 46th parallel. Gray had claimed the river for the United States and named it after his ship, the *Columbia*. George Vancouver's British expedition had arrived at the same wide mouth five months later, and his lieutenant William Broughton had

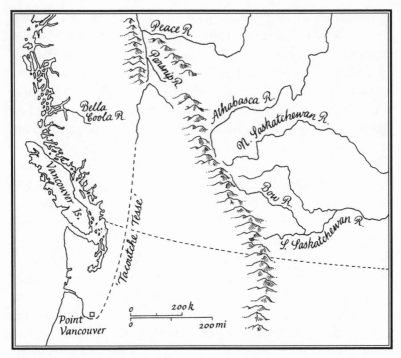

ALEXANDER MACKENZIE'S CONJECTURE

crossed the bar and rowed a dory a hundred miles upstream before reaching impassable cascades. Broughton decided that the Americans had never made it into the river proper; he drew a chart of his discoveries, named the prominent landmarks he passed, and with Vancouver claimed the Columbia for Great Britain. Such a large river, lying to the south of his own route, rekindled Mackenzie's hope for a trade artery to the Pacific. He was convinced that the Tacoutche Tesse and the Columbia were the same river, and dotted in its projected course on a map that appeared in his book about his two great adventures.

For the next several years, Mackenzie lobbied for an expedition to follow this dotted line and find out how much of it was navigable, both to extend the fur trade across the continent and to secure for Great Britain that wedge of uncharted country between the Rocky Mountains and the dark green coast. Disgruntled with his partners, Mackenzie resigned from the North West Company in 1799, but William and Duncan McGillivray remained enthusiastic supporters of his vision of transcontinental trade. Now Duncan had come to Rocky Mountain House to lead an expedition across the mountains to the Pacific Ocean the next spring, and David Thompson was to go along as his astronomer.

In mid-November, Thompson took McGillivray on a scouting expedition southward to look for an eligible pass over the Continental Divide. Along the way they stopped to visit a Piegan band on the Bow River, in the same area as Saukamappee's old winter camp. In the twelve years since Thompson had wintered there, the Piegans and other Blackfeet tribes had continued to fight with the Snakes and to live out their seasonal chase for the buffalo. Though the bison herds remained the most important commodity in their lives, it was inevitable that the proximity of the Saskatchewan trade houses would undermine the tribes' self-sufficiency. The Blackfeet now had large numbers of muskets, but they always needed more powder and lead balls. They had stopped growing their own varieties of tobacco because they preferred the smooth Brazilian and Virginia strains offered by the traders. Some of them had developed an unfortunate taste for the whiskey that both companies used to gain a competitive edge. None of the Blackfeet tribes, however, had entered the beaver-trapping culture with much enthusiasm, preferring to offer wolf pelts and buffalo meat for trade.

McGillivray and Thompson had not been in the Piegan camp long when Sac o tow wow, the principal chief, paid them a visit. Sac o tow wow had guns on his mind, complaining that the Nor'Westers had traded arms to the Kootenais and that the Flatheads would soon have guns, too, and would use them to attack his people. The Flatheads, a populous tribe who lived south of the Kootenais, were steadfast enemies of the Blackfeet. Thompson reminded Sac o tow wow that it was the Blackfeet themselves who had introduced firearms to the west-side tribes, by trading the Kootenais guns for horses.

The furmen had another agenda for their visit. Many of the beaver grounds in eastern Canada were now completely trapped out, and some of the Iroquois who lived there wanted to move west. Since the Blackfeet had not shown much interest in hunting beaver, the North West Company thought it might be a good idea to resettle some experienced Iroquois trappers nearby: "Those Indians would behave quietly, would reside in the woody Hills at the foot of the Mountain and serve as a Barrier between them and their Enemies – upon these Terms they gave us Permission to bring them up as soon as we pleased. Cut a Pipe of Tobacco to each Man & gave them a few pints of Mixed Rum to drink." ("Mixed rum" was rum mixed with water; the traders varied the strength of the mixture according to the occasion and the tribe.)

As McGillivray and Thompson pushed on up the Bow River, they amused themselves by dogging buffalo that grazed in the foothills. They came upon a second Piegan camp, of about forty tents, and made another pitch for relocating Iroquois. These Piegans responded quite favorably to the idea, but when they learned that the white men were planning to go up into the mountains, they warned them to beware of the Flatheads, who were "constantly hovering about there to steal horses or to dispatch any small weak party they might chance to fall in with." The two explorers kept a sharp watch but encountered only buffalo, moose, bighorn sheep, and expansive views of the snowcapped Rockies: "Never before did I behold so just, so perfect a resemblance to the waves of the ocean in the wintry storm," wrote Thompson. Here he and McGillivray could see the daunting breadth of these mountains: this was no single ridge, and it would take more than Mackenzie's 817-step portage to make it across the "Height of Land" in these latitudes. They would need a guide who knew the country, and horses to pack the goods.

The two explorers were back at Rocky Mountain House by early December, and Thompson remained there while Duncan McGillivray rode north to examine a possible crossing up the Brazeau River. McGillivray returned after two weeks, having found the river's course too rugged for horses, and apparently having pushed himself beyond his physical limits. According to Thompson, McGillivray "took no precautions against the effect of exposure to the weather, wet feet, etc. The consequence was that early in February he began to feel attacks of acute rheumatism, which became so violent as to oblige him to keep his bed." Though still a young man, McGillivray had suffered for at least five years from what he called "rheumatism or some other vile disorder of that nature."

McGillivray had spent the previous year in Montreal and had apparently brought west with him extracts from George Vancouver's recently published *Voyage of Discovery to the North Pacific Ocean.* Over the winter Thompson copied the parts pertaining to the Columbia River and the Northwest coast into a separate notebook, presumably so that he and McGillivray would be able to use the information when they arrived at the Pacific. What these men were planning was a historic transcontinental crossing, only the second north of Mexico. By the time they returned, they hoped to be the first to have pioneered a practical trade route to the sea.

Of what lay between Rocky Mountain House and the Pacific Ocean, they knew nothing except for what the Kootenais had told Thompson the previous fall. Before they left, the Kootenai chiefs had promised to send someone to guide the Nor'Westers as far west as their country in the spring. At the end of May, La Gasse and Le Blanc, the two voyageurs who had gone to winter with the Kootenais, did return to Rocky Mountain House. They brought with them a load of beaver pelts and valuable information about the country across the mountains, but not the native guide that McGillivray and Thompson were waiting for—a young

Kootenai had accompanied the two voyageurs east, as agreed, but he had been killed by a group of Stoney Assiniboines along the way. Despite this setback, McGillivray remained determined to launch his expedition. For some reason, neither La Gasse nor Le Blanc was mentioned as a possible guide, and McGillivray hired a Cree named the Rook who said he knew a good horse trail up a tributary of the Saskatchewan and across the Divide. Thompson thought the Rook "a Man so timourous by Nature, of so wavering a Disposition, & withal so addicted to flattering & lying, as to make every Thing he said or did, equivocal and doubtful." McGillivray, who also had reservations about the man's character, promised him a large reward if he performed well. As an extra precaution, he made the Rook swear an oath to the Great Spirit over his medicine pipe.

When it was time to leave, McGillivray's poor health prevented him from making the journey, and in his place he appointed James Hughes, the proprietor in charge of Rocky Mountain House, to head the party. Thompson's journals for this part of 1801 have never been found, and the only description of this trip comes from a report he wrote for Duncan and William McGillivray. The account begins on June 6, 1801, with Thompson and Hughes starting west "in order to penetrate to the Pacific Ocean." They had with them the Rook, his wife, and an old Kootenai woman who had been captured by the Blackfeet years before and wanted to return to her people. Nine voyageurs led thirteen horses loaded with trade goods, necessities, and enough birch rind to build a canoe once they reached the west side of the mountains. They made slow but steady headway through the woods on the north shore of the Saskatchewan until the second afternoon, when a deep ravine blocked their path. They were traveling along a bench high above the river, and as they prepared to descend the steep bank, one of the horses stumbled and began rolling toward the lip of the sheer cliff. A pine tree stopped the animal just short of the edge, but partway down the bank another horse lost its footing and plunged into the river. The voyageur who volunteered to rescue it from the opposite shore was swamped by a wave in the middle of the river and bucked off *his* horse, leaving a man, two horses, and 120 pounds of valuables on the wrong side of the river.

Mishaps of this sort happened several times during the next few days, as the explorers continually found themselves pinned between steep slopes and fast water. The horses "rolled down so often, & received such violent Shocks from the Trees against which they brought up, as to deprive them for a Time of Motion." When they did reach a flat bench, the ground was so boggy that the animals sometimes sank up to their bellies in the mud. Part of their troubles could be put down to inexperience, because none of these men had ever tried to cross mountains with packhorses before. Learning on the job, the Nor'Westers slogged on through steady rain into the front range of mountains, and this time Thompson did not rhapsodize about the rugged landscape as he had back on the Red Deer: "The Scene around us has nothing of the agreeable in it, All Nature seems to frown, the Mountains are dreary, rude & wild, beyond the power of the Pencil."

The Rook led them along animal trails over the first ridge of the Rockies and then turned up the north branch of the Ram River. Fresh buffalo for dinner and the sight of greening hills to the west improved Thompson's spirits. But now the Rook was visibly discouraged, and when a violent thunderstorm forced them to make camp early, Hughes thought some rum might perk him up. While thunder and lightning crashed across the hills, the guide proceeded to get drunk with his wife. The next morning, feeling rough, he asked for "a little Medicine." Hughes obliged, but whatever he administered did not help. Sitting around the campfire with the rest of the men, the Rook called his wife to him. He took a sharp flint and sliced open a vein in her forearm, "she assisting him with great good Will." In front of the astonished furmen, he drew a cup of her blood into a wooden bowl and drank it down.

"While I was considering from whence so savage an Action could arise, one of our Men with Indignation exclaimed to our Guide, I have eaten & smoked with thee, but henceforward thou & me shall never eat & smoke together."

The Rook assured the white men that his wife's healthy blood was an invigorating tonic, that this was an established custom among his people, and that he would certainly offer his own arm to refresh his wife if her stomach were out of order. He smoked his morning pipe "with great tranquility," and soon the party was on its way again. Their route for the day led along a steep sidehill with patches of ice that tumbled two more horses into the river and wet their supply of salt and sugar. The next day they climbed up a narrow streambed high into the mountains, where the willows had not even started to bud and there was no fresh grass for the horses. Late that evening the Rook came to Thompson and Hughes "with a woful countenance"; he had dreamed about "bad Indians" and asked permission to go home lest he die without seeing his children again. When Hughes kidded him that there was nothing to fear besides mountain goats, and that he himself would personally defend him from these, the Rook whined, "That is the way of all you white Men, you joke at every Thing 'till you are fairly Killed."

The next day, floundering through two to three feet of snow, they reached the headwaters of the Ram—a narrow lake hemmed in by a sheer mountain on one side and steep talus all the way down to the waterline on the other. When the leaders asked their guide how he had gotten his horses around this obstacle on his previous trip, the Rook replied that he had forgotten about this part of the mountain. Furious, Hughes and Thompson set out to see if they could find a way out of the cul-de-sac. After crawling on all fours across the talus to the opposite end of the lake, they calculated that their route up the Ram had paralleled the Saskatchewan, which they guessed to be only ten or twelve miles away. They decided to salvage their expedition by sending the Rook home with the horses and most of their baggage. Then they would quickly make a skin boat, float their men and a minimum of gear across the lake, descend the precipitous slope into the next valley, and bushwhack a few miles cross-country to the Saskatchewan. Once there, they would build a canoe and explore the headwaters of the larger river for a pass. But when the rest of the men heard this plan, they balked; they were used to portages that lasted for hours, not weeks, and protested that their contracts did not include undertakings such as this. Hughes and Thompson even offered to carry their shares of the load, but the voyageurs could not be persuaded. Thompson noted that the men had been reluctant to come on this trip in the first place, "however we must do them the Justice to say, that it was improbable that they could have got down the Mountain with the Baggage, without at least one half of them being crippled." The leaders had no choice but to turn around and retrace their steps.

Three days later they had followed the Ram back to its junction with the Saskatchewan. It took more than a week to find wood and split out enough boards to construct a frame for their birchbark shell, and all that time the river was rising with spring runoff and torrential rain. Hughes needed to get back to Rocky Mountain House, so he took the Rook and the horses home, leaving Thompson to launch the boat. For three days the surveyor and eight voyageurs fought their way upriver, using every trick they knew. On the afternoon of the fourth day, as they pulled themselves along by trees protruding from the riverbank, they were brought up short by a set of whirlpool rapids running through a tight canyon. There was no shore for tracking, and no way to stem the volume of water pouring down at them. Thompson climbed up the bank and walked upstream far enough to conclude that during lower water the river should be quite passable, and he resolved to start his next trip before spring runoff reached its peak. After measuring the current at twelve to fifteen knots within the canyon, he and his men turned around and shot the seventy-four miles down to Rocky Mountain House in five hours and fifty minutes.

Back at the trade house on June 30, Thompson learned that while he was gone Charlotte had given birth to their first child, a daughter they named Fanny. He stayed close to home for the rest of the summer, trading for furs and watching swarms of locusts engulf the local vegetation. In his report to the McGillivrays analyzing the pitfalls of the trip, he briefly referred to what was probably the chief cause for its failure: "How unfortunate has this Journey been from the beginning, when we had got all ready & waited a long Time! At length a Kootanae came to guide us, & he when within a few miles of the fort was murdered." But Thompson did not explain why the two voyageurs La Gasse and Le Blanc, who had just returned from the Kootenai country, had not gone along to show him and Hughes the way west.

THE CITY OF Calgary rolled up like a great ship from the trough of a wave. It was just past dawn, difficult to discern any exact features among the lights, but easy to feel the daily surge of human energy already kicking off. The Quebecois hitchhiker I had picked up in the mountains stirred around in his woolly blanket as we sailed in on the Trans-Canada Highway. He had been quiet, almost sullen, since I had picked him up an hour before. My French was as bad as his English, but he had made me understand that he was headed east and was looking for a bus. As we passed the specter of an Olympic ski ramp beside the road, he began to communicate in the language of food.

"So big mountains," he said, eyeing the grocery bag in my back seat. I signaled with a wave of my hand that he could help himself, and he gobbled down a sizable wedge of hoop cheese and half a loaf of sourdough bread from my bag. Then he fished a tin of chocolate pudding out of his rucksack and slathered it across the last portion of bread. With a river otter's smile, he raised his creation in a toast, and when I pointed at an exit sign for the Blackfoot Trail, he nodded heartily. I turned off and let the flow of morning traffic funnel us toward the angular skyline that has been laid down upon the curves of the Bow River bottoms.

We ground to a halt among the morning commuters, right beside the stately facade of a Bay Company retail store. There in the window, above the company's ironclad guarantee, hung a striped blanket very much like the one wrapped around my hitchhiker. Beneath the building's polished granite windowsills, a handful of natives napped on the promenade. The Quebecois pointed down a side street at the bus station, and I dropped him under the Greyhound sign, hard by the Bow River and the old winter camps of the Piegan Blackfeet.

Ten minutes later I arrived at the library of the Glenbow Museum. The records kept here cover all aspects of Alberta history, and as I flipped through the card catalogue, the familiar names of La Gasse and Le Blanc appeared at the top of one of the cards, in the title of a paper written by an anthropologist named Claude Schaeffer. Schaeffer studied the Blackfeet and Kootenai people for over thirty years beginning in the 1930s, and recorded many of their oral traditions. He had several contacts among the Tobacco Plains band of Kootenais, which was most likely the same band that Thompson sent La Gasse and Le Blanc home with in October 1800. In a 1965 interview, two Tobacco Plains elders began telling Schaeffer about the first white men in the memory of their tribe. As the chief and another elder recounted their story, Schaeffer saw enough parallels with what he knew of La Gasse and Le Blanc to make a connection.

There was a pair of French Canadians, the elders said, who came one year to winter with the band at Tobacco Plains. The Kootenais called the one who liked a big, roaring blaze K!isuk-ing!uku (Good Fire) and the one who let his embers burn small and quiet Sahaning!uku (Poor Fire). The Frenchmen trapped some animals that winter and spent part of their time teaching the Kootenais more efficient ways to kill beaver and how to prepare skins without damaging the pelage. In the spring they took the furs they had accumulated over the mountains to a trade house.

The two white men returned to the Tobacco Plains either in the summer or the fall, and one of them married the daughter of Kulsmayuk, the Tobacco Plains chief. After their second winter with the tribe, the trappers made another delivery east. Sometime during the next year, Kulsmayuk's daughter had a baby, and the following spring the mother and child went along with the white men to the trading post. Schaeffer's storytellers at first thought that the men had taken their furs east for three years, then upped it to five. They did agree that Chief Kulsmayuk had often warned Good Fire and Poor Fire not to take a certain route over the mountains that was frequented by the Stoney Assiniboine. In either the third spring or the fifth spring, Kulsmayuk suggested that they take a southerly trail, and sent his son along to guide them. On the east side the three men ran into a party of Stoney Assiniboine. Using sign language, the Stoneys asked where they were from and who the guide was. The Frenchmen replied that the chief's son was from an eastern tribe and continued on their way, hoping their deception worked. But the Stoneys suspected the truth and followed the voyageurs' tracks back down to the camp of the Tobacco Plains band. The Kootenai men were out hunting, and the Stoneys attacked, killing a number of women and children.

When Kulsmayuk and his hunters returned home and discovered the massacre, they believed that their white guests had knowingly betrayed them by revealing the location of the camp. When Good Fire and Poor Fire returned that fall, the chief killed them both. He was about to kill his own grandchild, the infant child of the Frenchman, but his daughter prevented him. Eventually, Kulsmayuk's son convinced his father that the two white men had been blameless, and the story of the ill-fated fire-builders passed into the pool of Kootenai tribal lore.

IN HIS ACCOUNT to the McGillivrays describing the failed trip to the Pacific in the summer of 1801, Thompson made no mention of La Gasse and Le Blanc, their fire-building abilities, or whether they had gone back to winter with the Kootenais again. He did note that in the future he would be certain to find a guide who knew where he was going, and he included other insights that would ensure the success of a second expedition. But by the spring of 1802, North West Company plans for expansion had been replaced by worries about the company's survival. After his resignation from the North West Company in 1799, Alexander Mackenzie had joined forces with another group of traders from Quebec known as the XY Fur Company. Over the next several years the XY rivalry commanded the full attention of the North West partners. They shut down Rocky Mountain House in 1802 and assigned Thompson to a post in the Peace River country near Lake Athabasca, where the XY Company was trying to establish itself.

Thompson spent two winters in the Peace River region, trading and surveying during the good weather months, inking in maps when shut in by cold. He wrote up reports and corresponded with a variety of fur agents, including Peter Fidler, his surveying counterpart with the Bay Company. He read a popular French novel that was making the rounds of the trade houses and lent his XY competitors some food when they were in a pinch. In the summer of 1804, he traveled to the North West Company's annual rendezvous, but this year it was not held at Grand Portage—in order to be clear of the American border, the company had moved its depot farther north on Lake Superior. At the expansive new compound that was soon to be named Fort William, David Thompson was elected a field partner and given two shares in the company, valued at more than four thousand pounds sterling.

Later that fall Alexander Mackenzie capitulated in his at-tempt to build a third major fur-trading concern. Although the destructive rivalry ended, it took accountants in Montreal another year to work out a merger between the XY and North West Companies. During this period, David Thompson worked around the Muskrat Country west of Hudson Bay, the same region where he had once surveyed for the Hudson's Bay Company.

Meanwhile, down in the United States, Thomas Jefferson had made the fortuitous purchase of the vast Louisiana Territory, stretching from the Mississippi River to the Rocky Mountains, and had obtained full funding from the U.S. Congress for a military expedition to assess his new acquisition. When Meriwether Lewis and William Clark started up the Missouri River in 1804, they carried a copy of the chart that David Thompson had made on his trip to the Mandans seven years earlier. They also carried the most up-to-date map of North America available at that time. Drawn by the London cartographer Aaron Arrowsmith, it contained a great deal of information gathered by Thompson, Alexander Mackenzie, and Peter Fidler. The area west of the Rocky Mountains was almost completely blank, except for Mackenzie's travels and a conjectural river called the "Great Lake River," which flowed from the Rockies straight toward the dotted line of Mackenzie's Tacoutche Tesse and the mouth of the Columbia. A legend noted that "the Indians say they sleep 8 Nights in descending this River to the Sea." Lewis and Clark hoped to descend just such a river, for they did not intend to stop at the edge of the Louisiana Territory, but to proceed on to the Pacific. With transcontinental expansion clearly in mind, Thomas Jefferson had given his men instructions to find the "most direct and practicable water communication across this continent for the purposes of commerce."

William and Duncan McGillivray and some of the other North West partners understood the implications of Lewis and Clark's trip, and with the XY situation in hand, they again turned their attention west. In the summer of 1805 they sent Simon Fraser to Lake Athabasca, where he was to cross the

Continental Divide by Mackenzie's northern route and build a post in the area they called New Caledonia. From there he was to follow the Tacoutche Tesse south to its supposed junction with the Columbia and find out if it was navigable to the sea. The partners also resolved to make a new attempt to reach the still untapped source of furs in the Kootenai country. John McDonald of Garth was now in charge of the Fort des Prairies Department, and in the summer of 1806 he recruited David Thompson to return to Rocky Mountain House and put his previous experience to use.

IN EARLY JULY of that same year, on the way home from their long swing to the Pacific, Lewis and Clark decided to split their expedition and further explore the northern tributaries of the Missouri River. Within three weeks Meriwether Lewis and three men on horseback had worked their way up into the headwaters of the Two Medicine River, in present-day Montana, but poor weather and the formidable east front of the Rockies turned them around. As the men rode down the grassy breaks of the Two Medicine, they surprised a party of eight Piegans with thirty horses. Lewis was not certain of the identity of the horsemen, but he had heard unpleasant stories about the tribes of the northern plains and had hoped to avoid them. He considered his situation—it was late afternoon, and his interpreter was hunting separately downriver—and decided to approach in a friendly manner. He was relieved to see that only two of the Piegans carried muskets; the rest were armed with bows and arrows. During the drawn-out rituals of greeting, Lewis dutifully presented a flag, a handkerchief, and a medal to all three Piegans who identified themselves as chiefs. Then the two parties pitched camp together on a wide flat beside the river.

Lewis found the Piegans "extreemly fond of smoking and plyed them with the pipe untill late at night." The explorer told the band about his long trip and about his hopes for friendly trade among all tribes at a post he planned to build on the Missouri. The Piegans in turn described a British house on the Saskatchewan River, about six days' easy march north, to which they traveled to trade wolf and beaver skins for "arms amunition speritous liquor blankets &c."

Other tribes had told the explorers that the Piegans had a penchant for thievery, and Lewis stood the first watch himself that night. Around midnight he warned his replacement to keep a sharp eye out, then retired inside a buffalo-skin shelter set up by the Piegans. There he fell into a "profound sleep," from which he did not stir until after dawn, when he was awakened by his tentmate shouting, "Damn you let go my gun." The Piegans had gotten up early and stoked the fire, then taken advantage of a lapse in the watchman's attention to grab guns and powder pouches. By the time the groggy Americans chased down the thieves and recovered their firearms, one Piegan had been stabbed through the heart, and Lewis had shot another in the stomach.

Back at the deserted campsite, Lewis took a moment to burn two bows and quivers of arrows that the Piegans had left behind. He retrieved the flag he had presented the previous afternoon, but left an inscribed peace medal around the neck of the stabbed man, "that they might be informed who we were." Quickly choosing the best of the remaining horses, the four white men struck a cross-country course for the Missouri River, riding hard all day and deep into the night. When they finally stretched out on the plains at two the next morning, Lewis wrote that "my Indian horse carried me very well in short much better than my own would have done and leaves me with but little reason to complain of the robery."

The Piegans felt otherwise. They still remember the name of Side Hill Calf, the man stabbed to death that morning in 1806. Thereafter, all the Blackfeet tribes made a sharp distinction between the Canadian traders, dubbed "Northern White Men," and the American white men, whom they called "Big Knives."

CHAPTER FOUR

NEUTRAL GROUND

FALL 1806–WINTER 1807

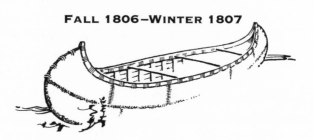

WHILE MERIWETHER LEWIS was scuffling with the Piegan Blackfeet on the Two Medicine River, David Thompson was attending the North West Company's summer rendezvous at Fort William, where it was decided that he would lead the expedition across the Rocky Mountains to the Kootenai country. Up the Saskatchewan River he went, stopping to visit his friend James Hughes at Fort Augustus, the headquarters for the Fort des Prairies Department. He continued on upriver another 120 miles and arrived at Rocky Mountain House in late October. John McDonald of Garth had recently come up from Fort Augustus to check on the post, and the two men spent a couple of days inventorying the warehouse and presumably discussing logistics for Thompson's upcoming trip. Earlier that summer McDonald had set plans in motion by sending four men to cut a pack trail along an old Kootenai route through the mountains near the headwaters of the Saskatchewan. The leader of this team was Jacques Raphael Finlay, the son of an early Nor'Wester and a Chipewyan woman. Jaco, as he was known, had already worked for several years on the Saskatchewan as a clerk and interpreter and seemed a good choice for a scout. Thompson had been at Rocky Mountain House only a couple of days when two of Jaco's crew arrived back at the post. They had left Jaco building canoes across the mountains and reported that the Kootenais they had met, delighted at the news of the furmen's coming, had set off to work beaver. After a general holiday for All Saints' Day, McDonald of Garth returned to Fort Augustus and Thompson took charge of Rocky Mountain House. From then on through the turn of the year, he was taking care of post business and keeping an eye on the Hudson's Bay Company "blockheads" next door at Acton House, who, he complained, were passing out too much rum.

November 19 began as a typical day. Thompson sent two of his men out to get meat from the native hunters and traded with some Piegans. He sent off another man with presents for a band of Blood Indians, who had been fighting with the Crees, to encourage them to make peace. At some point during the activities of the day, he must have left his pen unattended, for this page of his journal is covered with the enthusiastic scribbles of a small child. In the afternoon Jaco Finlay arrived back at the post, having finished his work across the Divide. Thompson would certainly have been anxious to hear details about the unknown country, and it may have been during this visit that Jaco drew a map that later turned up among Peter Fidler's papers with the note "drawn by Jean Findley 1806." The rough sketch outlined a trail up the north branch of the Saskatchewan, across two rows of bumps labeled Stony Mountains, and down to a river running through "a fine valley between more mountains."

As the year 1806 drew to a close, Thompson made snowshoes and a sled and shared Christmas dinner with his rivals at Acton House. On New Year's Day of 1807, he received word that Kootanae Appee and eighteen of his relatives were on their way to the post. Thompson sent tobacco ahead to welcome the storied war chief he had met in Saukamappee's tent as a teenager, and delayed his own New Year's celebrations until the Piegans had finished trading and drinking the rum he gave them. When the Nor'Westers did get around to calling the holiday on January 3, the Bay men came over to help, and Thompson calculated that the party cost him five gallons of French rum.

At the end of January, Thompson turned his attention to his spring expedition. He had not forgotten the obstacles that had turned him and James Hughes around in 1801. Aside from following the Rook up the wrong trail, one of their biggest problems had been the horses, which had proved so unwieldy in the mountainous terrain. There was no way to get across the pass without pack animals, but this time Thompson intended to supplement them with canoes as far as possible. Remembering what he had seen of the Saskatchewan's narrow channel on his previous trip, he planned to get moving before spring runoff swelled the river and flooded the shorelines they needed for tracking. With an early start in mind, he sent dogsleds up the frozen Saskatchewan as far as the first ridge of mountains. There the men cached over a thousand pounds of nonperishable supplies, so both canoes and horses would have lighter loads on the first leg of the trip.

In April, after another visit from Kootanae Appee, Thompson began working on a birchbark cargo canoe and making pemmican. In mid-month a dozen Kootenais came over the mountains to trade and reported that the snow on the Divide was still "equal in height to the top of a tall Pine." Thompson sent them home with gifts for their chiefs and word that he was on his way. On April 26 he heard the first frogs of spring croaking. On the 27th he saw cranes, then a small plover on the 29th. On May 4 the ice broke up on the river, and the explorer started packing.

"May 10th Sunday A very fine Day. At 9½ A.M. sent off Mr. Finan McDonald & 5 Men in a Canoe with Goods &

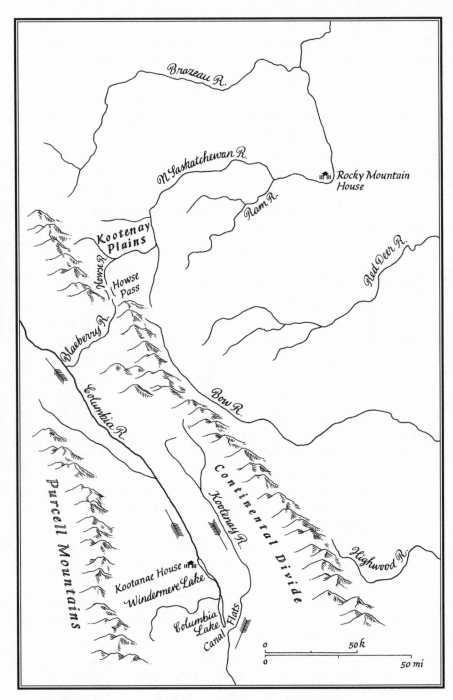

CROSSING THE ROCKY MOUNTAINS

Necessaries to the expedition across the Mountains." Finan McDonald, a tall, red-headed young Scot, was Thompson's clerk and deputy. He and five voyageurs—Boisverd, Lussier, Le Camble, Beaulieu, and Buché—began paddling and line-hauling their way up the Saskatchewan. Since the snow hadn't yet started to melt in the Rockies, the level of the river remained low, but its current still ran so fast that it frequently snapped the two new tracking lines Thompson had brought from Fort William. At intervals, steep canyons closed in, and the voyageurs had to track right up the riverbed. In a report to the partners, Thompson detailed the men's troubles: "The greatest Hardship of the People lay in being continually wet up to the Waist, exposed to cold high winds, & the water, coming direct from the Snows on the Mountains, was always so excessively cold as to deprive them of all feeling in their Limbs."

While Finan McDonald and the voyageurs towed the canoe upriver, Thompson paralleled their course overland with a string of horses, several dogs, and the women and children who were going along. These included Charlotte and three Thompson children, plus Lussier's family and one other woman. He also had with him three men: Clement, Bercier, and Boulard (Thompson seemed to prefer voyageurs whose names began with the letter B). Both Boulard and Bercier had been across the Divide with Jaco Finlay the previous summer; this time the explorer was sure he had guides who knew where they were going. For the next two weeks, they followed a route through thick woods that was short on grass and hard on the horses. Thompson took advantage of the slow pace, climbing hills for views of the countryside and studying the layout of the mountains and the course of the river. His men had good luck hunting along the way, bringing in buffalo, bighorn sheep, elk, and several porcupines. They spent one night near an old Cree medicine lodge that served as a landmark on the trail, and on June 3 they reached their staging area at a place they called Kootenay Plains, where Finan

McDonald and his canoe party were already camped.

This was a pleasant spot, and Thompson gave the people and horses a couple of days to rest. He reset his watch (it had lost time), observed for latitude (52° 2' N), and hired two men from the eastern Ojibway tribe who were trapping in the area to hunt for him. On June 5 he and the voyageurs continued on upriver, leaving the women, children, and livestock with Finan McDonald at Kootenay Plains, "as this was the last & only Place, where Pasture could be found for the Horses, or animals for the People for Food."

ABOUT EIGHTY MILES upstream from Rocky Mountain House, in the midst of the first big rise of the mountains, the Saskatchewan River canyon opens out into the broad, gently undulating parklands of Kootenay Plains. It's like a piece of the prairies lifted up into the hills, and this pocket of abundant grass attracts birds and animals in large numbers. Humans have followed game to this spot for at least ten thousand years; in more recent times, it was known as a camping ground to Kootenai hunters from across the mountains, a safe place on the edge of the dangerous Piegan Blackfeet lands. Bands of Cree, Sarcee, and Stoney Assiniboine also have traditions of using Kootenay Plains in one way or another. Jaco Finlay and his family lived there for a time, as did other hunters and horsekeepers of Thompson's era. North West Company agent Alexander Henry camped on these plains in the winter of 1811:

> I observed near the foot of the rocks behind the plain the remains of an old Kootenay camp, where the wood of the tents was still standing ... the greater part were built to be covered with pine branches and grass, and some were made of split wood thatched with grass. Formerly that nation frequented this place to make dried provisions, for which purpose it must have been

very convenient, as buffalo and sheep are always more numerous than in any other place. Moose and red deer are also plenty; jumping deer, grizzly bear, and other animals peculiar to this country are also found here.

On the morning after my own camp-out on Kootenay Plains, I found myself drawn to the benchlands west of the river. Long ridges of stone stepped up from the flats, thickening in color as they ascended from the gravelly grays of the watercourse—yellows and oranges added row by row up to a final band of deep rust that glowed at the snowline. My route pulled me into a thicket of lodgepole pine that closed off the daylight like a dark house. Under the trees, elk leg joints and knobby tire tracks, leftovers from last fall's hunting season, littered the ground beside fresh droppings. Someone had tied bits of white, red, and green sheet around in the pines, flags that surprised me every time I came upon one. Only when I reached a steep cut that broached the terrace did it occur to me that the rags might mark a trail.

It was a rough climb, over car-sized boulders and spindly deadfall pines. The line of rags disappeared at the cliff top, a couple of hundred feet above the flats, and for a while I followed an indistinct path along the brink of the precipice. Below me Kootenay Plains opened out into meadows quilted with the trembling greens of aspen. Many of the chalky white aspen trunks were scarred black up to the height of an elk's reach, rubbed raw by shovel teeth.

When the trail petered out, I veered into the open woods along the bench. The colored rags soon reappeared, all tied the same way, but now pointing in an obvious direction. They ended at a simple fire circle, placed so that anyone tending a blaze would have a view out over the cliffs. In a small clearing below, a freshly built shelter stood in plain sight: a lodge woven from standing aspen boughs, leaves still attached, perhaps head high. The boughs were bent in at the top and joined so as to form an open circle in the hut's roof. From my high vantage, the opening looked too wide to keep the rain out, but now I wasn't certain it was meant to be a shelter at all. Three much longer poles rose up out of the hole and were tied together with strips of cloth. As with the fire circle, the impression they left was formal, symbolic.

When I scanned the border between flats and pine forest again, other wickiups emerged one by one from the terrain. All except the first had lost their foliage. Some still showed off a neat lattice framework of saplings. More leaned in on teetering sticks, spiky abstract creations on the verge of collapse. All that remained of others was a charred fire ring at their center. I stared down at the angled lodge poles, wondering what kind of ceremonies had gone on at this place over the years. I thought of those old Kootenai lodges that Alexander Henry had described, and the Cree medicine lodge that David Thompson passed on his way to this spot. I thought about pictures I had seen of sun dance lodges, with those same hooped circles in the roof, and remembered the shirtless young man who had pumped gas across from me at a service station a few days before. He had two fresh scars high on his pectorals, and must have just taken part in the initiation rite; he had touched the wounds over and over with his free hand, gingerly tracing the puffy scabs.

A breeze stirred down on the flat, rattling the aspen leaves. Uneasy, I stepped back into the shelter of the woods; a spruce grouse thumped up from beneath my feet, and I froze in my tracks. The bird circled me in a slow crouch, puffing out a velvety black belly. Its bright display sacs and fleshy eyebrows pulsed with the colors of blood.

AFTER LEAVING Kootenay Plains, Thompson and his party traveled upriver for a day and a half until they reached a fork. Here they left the main branch of the Saskatchewan and turned up a smaller river (now called the Howse) that flows in from the southwest. After four miles the braided channels became too shallow for the canoe. This was where the horse trail began, but the snow was still too deep for them to follow it. Thompson sent everyone except Bercier and two other men back to Kootenay Plains to wait for some snow to melt, then pitched his tent on a knoll beside the river. They were camped right in the lap of the Rockies, in a broad bowl ringed with craggy peaks and glacial headwalls. The weather immediately turned nasty. Thompson occupied himself stalking the moose whose footprints he kept seeing in the thick woods, while three days of mixed rain and snow created perfect conditions for a rash of spring avalanches.

> June 15 Monday A fine Day, stormy Afternoon, flying clouds. Went across the Rivulet and split out 130 small Boards for Boxes for the Goods. The Snows that have fallen in the Mountains these 3 days past are in many places rushing down with such a Noise, that we can hardly persuade ourselves it is not Thunder – we hear them every Hour, sometimes oftener.

During the next week the surveyor and his men listened to more avalanches and sewed the thin fir boards together to make boxes twenty-three inches square and eight inches deep. Into these they packed most of their goods, and then they waited for the latest snow to melt. By the third week in June, Thompson could stand the delay no longer and convinced Bercier to try a scouting trip up the trail. They started out early on June 22 on two good horses, following Jaco Finlay's route of the previous summer, and by midmorning they had reached the pass (later known as Howse Pass) and crossed the Continental Divide, "where the Springs send their Rills to the Pacific Ocean; this Sight overjoyed me." Grass was springing up on the other side, and trees were beginning to leaf out. It was time to fetch the people and horses from Kootenay Plains.

Two days later the entire party gathered at Thompson's

campsite on the banks of the river and finished packing. There was quite a bit of gear left over, and Finan McDonald stayed behind to tend to the extra baggage until the men could come back for it. At 3:30 the next morning, the surveyor "started the men"; by 6:00 they had the fir boxes, the kegs of gunpowder and wine, and the rolls of tobacco loaded onto the pack animals and were climbing toward the pass. They stopped at midmorning to refresh the horses near the Kootanae Pound, a narrow strip of grassland that led up to a sheer precipice. Kootenai hunters had long used this place as a buffalo jump, herding animals up the slope and then driving them over the edge of the cliff.

While everyone else was resting, Thompson spotted five white mountain goats up on the cliffs of the pound and went off after them. The goats took a high, craggy route of escape, and in hot pursuit Thompson loosened a large boulder, which in turn unleashed a landslide that passed so close to him that he "was obliged to keep hold with my nails and feet to prevent myself sliding down." It was almost noon by the time he recovered his breath and rejoined his waiting party. Even so, they easily made it to the Divide, which Thompson called the "Height of Land," by early afternoon and stopped to camp in a marshy meadow beside Howse Pass.

The next day was not so easy, as their route down the west side of the mountains zigzagged back and forth across the Blaeberry River. Summer had arrived, and the warm weather made for increased snowmelt: "The water descending in innumerable Rills, soon swelled our Brook to a Rivulet, with a Current foaming white, the Horses with Difficulty crossed & recrossed at every 2 or 300 yards, & the Men crossed by clinging to the Tails & Manes of the Horses, & yet ran no small Danger of being swept away & drowned."

If the crossings were hair-raising for the men, they must have been doubly so for Thompson's three children, all under six years old. He described how he rode on a "capital" horse, sounding out the fords and trying to choose the safest ones,

but the animals were still almost carried away at times. At the
end of the day, the two Ojibway hunters Thompson had
brought along hadn't killed anything, and he was beginning
to worry that the 220 pounds of pemmican he had packed
would not be enough to keep everyone fed. "Gave the men a
large Dog for supper for want of better, of which they made a
Hearty Meal."

For the next week, the party continued to cross and re-
cross the heavy current. When the men weren't fighting the
river, they were fighting the trees. There was seldom any
semblance of a trail, and when one did appear it was often too
narrow for the horses' wide pack loads. It took three days to
cover two and a half miles, with most of the time spent chop-
ping trees and clearing deadfall. The men consumed huge
amounts of pemmican, and not until the fourth day did one of
the hunters shoot an elk. Thompson was concerned about the
scarcity of game, and with good reason, for with the arrival of
warm weather, the big grazing animals had dispersed
throughout the mountains in search of summer forage.

On the afternoon of June 30, the Blaeberry's unruly
course ended at a large river. Here the party quickly set up
camp and spread everything out to dry; Thompson lamented
that water had once again gotten to his small hoard of sugar.
But that was the least of his worries: his stock of pemmican
was way down, his man Beaulieu lay mysteriously incapaci-
tated, the hunters still weren't having much luck, and no fish
were biting in the river. The calking gum that Jaco Finlay had
left for them wasn't fit for use, and worse, the canoes he had
laid up were not big enough to haul their supplies. By this
time Thompson was thoroughly put out with Jaco, as he reported to the partners:

> From what has been said of the Road on the Portage, it
> is clearly seen that Jaco Finlay with the Men engaged
> last Summer to clear the Portage Road, has done a mere
> nothing . . . and it is the opinion of every Man with

me, as well as mine that Jaco Finlay ought to lose at least half his wages for having so much neglected the Duty for which he was so expressly engaged at 150 £ per year, besides a Piece of Tobacco & Sugar, & a Clerk's equipment.

Finlay's map work, on the other hand, had been quite accurate so far. The little party was camped on a big river that ran through a valley between the Rockies and another range of snow-covered mountains to the west, exactly as shown on Jaco's sketch. At this point Thompson had no idea where this big river came from, or where it went. His calculations told him that he was in latitude 50° 59' N. He knew George Vancouver's location for the mouth of the Columbia was very near the 46th parallel, far to the south and several meridians west, whereas the river he had struck was flowing almost due north, straight toward the area where Alexander Mackenzie had met the Tacoutche Tesse fifteen years before. Thompson had no way of knowing that he was actually on the long-sought Columbia River, and that it ran north for another two hundred miles before bending abruptly back for its south-westerly run to the sea.

He did know that he needed some help in coping with this utterly unfamiliar country, and on July 2 he sent off Bercier in one of the light canoes to try and find some Kootenais. He was particularly anxious to find a man he called the Old Chief, who was probably the same chief who had given him the foxskin cap and yellow horse back in 1800 and had taken La Gasse and Le Blanc across the mountains with him. Bercier had met some of the Kootenais while he was working with Jaco the previous summer and knew that one of their bands had a camp on a lake not too far south. He paddled that way, upstream, in search of the Old Chief and sustenance.

Thompson sent Michel Boulard and three other men back across the Height of Land with the packhorses to get

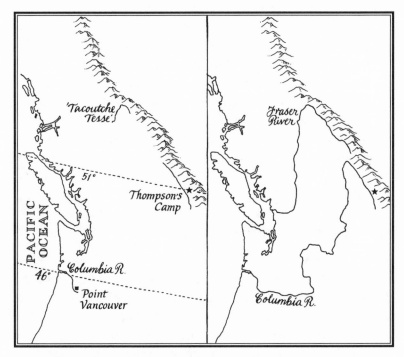

WHAT THOMPSON KNEW / WHAT HE DIDN'T KNOW

Finan McDonald and the rest of the baggage. Beaulieu was
still too sick to work, so the surveyor and Augustin Boisverd
went out to search for bark and wood to build a big canoe.
Everybody was hungry, and the pemmican was all gone. The
two Ojibway hunters had not produced much, and now
Thompson sent them word that he was going to eat one of
their horses if they did not deliver some food to the campsite
soon. Half a deer and a small beaver appeared forthwith. On
July 8 Bercier returned with enough meat for a proper meal
and three Kootenai boys to help hunt. That same morning
Thompson had a chance to exercise his medical skills:

> Beaulieu has been these ten days so very ill that he could
> not help us & at length so much so, that we despaired of
> his Life – his Complaint a violent Cholic & Pain under

his ribs on the Left. This Morning, perceiving a small Swelling close under his left Rib, mid of the side to be enlarging – he was feeling it with attention, & by his finger feeling something rough he sent for me. It appeared to be a small splinter – I extracted it & to our great surprise found it was a porcupine Quill, that had made its appearance from the inwards, it was of the short thick ones on the Rump & Tail of the Porcurpine. it can be accounted for only by supposing that when he eat part of the Dog the day we passed the Height of Land, he had in eating the Meat swallowed the Porcurpine Quill in the Meat, as he is a voracious eater.

West of the Divide nobody was eating voraciously. When Finan McDonald and his helpers arrived with the rest of the goods two days later, Thompson wrote that he "shared the last morsel with the men." The next day, fasting, they finished the big canoe. On July 12 Thompson sent the Ojibway hunters back east with a letter to James Hughes at Fort Augustus, and was loading his boats when the three Kootenai boys arrived with part of an elk. The explorer divided the meat among his men, distributed hooks and lines so everyone could fish along the way, and led off upstream in the small canoe. Nobody caught any fish, but they did shoot nine swans on July 13. On the 14th they went hunting but shot nothing; on the 15th they found a few gooseberries for dinner; on the 16th they came upon a small Kootenai camp, whose occupants could offer only a few pounds of venison. Thompson explained that his people were starving, and gave the Kootenais some tobacco and ammunition. "Two of them went a hunting & killed 3 Swans, which like a Hog they devoured without giving us a mouthful."

On July 18 the canoes reached the lake known today as Windermere, a promising location. The woods had given way to hilly grasslands, natural pastures for wild horses that had escaped from the Kootenai herds. There were berries along the shore, which the travelers soon devoured. In the after-noon, nine men from a Kootenai camp they had passed brought them half a *chevreuil*. (When Thompson said *chevreuil*, he meant deer, and from his usage it could be any-thing from a large mule deer to a white-tailed deer to a small pronghorn antelope. He figured that a small *chevreuil* yielded about the right amount of food for one meal for ten of his meat-hungry men.) The Nor'Westers finished off the meat the Kootenais had brought, then set out nets to catch some of the small fish they had spotted in the lake.

Michel Boulard, meanwhile, had been leading the horses upriver, and now he arrived with only three of the twenty-four mounts entrusted to him, "having left all the others behind from the badness of the Roads & his own laziness." This was a serious handicap, for the men needed horses to haul trees for buildings and to go hunting and exploring. Disturbed by these unexpected problems, Thompson had to cancel his plans to push farther south:

> From the State of the Country & the Situation of my Affairs I found myself necessitated to lay aside all Thoughts of Discovery for the present & bend my whole aim to an establishment for Trade etc.—and as our pressing necessities did not allow Time for Thought upon Thought, I set off to look out for a place where we might build, that as soon as I saw the Property in safety & a mode of living for the People I might be at liberty to seize every favourable opportunity of extending my knowledge of the country.

The next morning he and his men pulled in their nets, found them empty, and began looking for a good building site. After much searching they settled on a high bluff above the river where there was a small grove of trees. While scout-ing around, they came upon the body of a wild horse the Kootenais had killed the day before. Even though "a strong taint pervaded the whole carcase," they decided to cut off some of the meat and test it. They brought a sample back to camp, boiled it over the fire, and "shared a small piece to every Man who joyfully eat it, in hopes of its being portable in the Stomach. Hunger is an excellent Sauce, we found the Taste tolerable good." Thinking they had just found a few days' groceries, three of the men hurried back to the carcass to "dispute with the wolves" and carried into camp a hundred pounds of meat. But about two hours later, they all became violently sick to their stomachs. Thompson optimistically concluded that this had nothing to do with the innate quality of wild horseflesh, only its advanced state of putrefaction.

That evening he called together the few Kootenai men camped near the lake. They told him that the Old Chief and most of their people were hunting to the southward, but that they should be at the lake in about ten more days, along with a large band of Flatheads, their allies and neighbors to the south. Thompson engaged three of the Kootenais to take some tobacco to the tribes to let them know he had arrived, and to ask the Old Chief to hurry up. Writing to the partners that night, he muddled through a list of worries until "Sleep at last relieves me from a Train of anxious thoughts."

Having settled on a spot for the post he called Kootanae House, Thompson applied his energies to the situation at hand. He ordered men out to find birch wood to make handles for their axes and other tools and sent Boulard to stay with a nearby camp of Kootenais and encourage them to hunt. He traded with some Kootenais for a few beaver and four beautiful white mountain goat skins, then hafted a dart for spearing fish in the river and sent Finan McDonald, "who is the most clever," to try it out. The clerk returned with two small fish that Thompson called mullet and herring— probably a bull trout and a small rainbow.

The men began felling trees, but the wood was heavy and hard to cut, and Thompson pronounced it the worst he had ever tried to work. "July 22nd Wednesday. A very fine Day. Nothing in the Nets but 1 Mullet – began the Walls of the

Warehouse 16 ft. by 16 ft. – got it half way up – Men are so weak for want of Food, that they cannot work." That evening Boulard arrived with the meat of two *chevreuil*. A few days later the warehouse was finished and the goods were all stored inside. Thompson continued to worry about feeding the thirteen men and women and six children under his care, and decided to construct a weir across the river to trap fish. About that time two new Kootenais arrived. One of them was the Old Chief's brother, whom the voyageurs called Capot Blanc (White Coat). Capot Blanc told the furmen that the water was too high for a weir, but Thompson set his men to work anyway. They got the barrier about halfway finished before the current washed it away.

At that point Thompson began listening to Capot Blanc, who plainly stated that the new post was not in a very good spot—it was too far from water and vulnerable to attack by the Piegans, who could be counted on to come and raid horses at least once a year. He helped Thompson find a better place a mile downstream from the mouth of the lake, and the surveyor drew neat plans in his journal for three buildings arranged around a yard that backed onto the river. He fiddled with their dimensions and placement, squeezing dwellings and storehouses together until only three-foot pathways separated them—a tight, defensible arrangement.

As the Nor'Westers busied themselves cutting more trees, other Kootenais began to filter into their nearby camp, bringing in occasional kills of *chevreuil*, elk, and bear, but certainly not the consistent flow of food that Thompson wanted. He complained that they spent more time gambling than hunting, and sounded quite cross in early August when five tentfuls of hunters arrived and did not generously share their supply of dried meat. Thompson was now short a hand, because Michel Boulard's contract had run out. Boulard was a "half-engaged" or "half-free" man, which meant that he signed an agreement to work for the company for half the year, then spent the other six months trapping as a "free

hunter" for his own account. There was also a beverage
shortage at Kootanae House: the keg of high wine (180-proof
whiskey) they had brought across the pass was almost empty.
In his *Narrative*, Thompson wrote that he had vowed to keep
alcohol away from the west-side tribes, "and thus be clear of
the sad sight of drunkenness, and its many evils." But the
voyageurs expected their daily ration, and the surveyor had to
admit that "a dram had often done us much good."

The men struggled to complete the living quarters and
began another warehouse at their new location. Some of
them went upriver and split out boards for a rough floor, then
floated them down to the site. The water level in the river
had begun to drop, and the Kootenais suggested that now
would be a good time to build a weir. On August 13, while a
couple of old men directed four of the voyageurs at that task,
a message arrived at the Kootenai camp that occasioned such
crying and shrieking that Thompson, certain an attack was at
hand, called his men to arms. After the lamentations died
down, the furmen learned that the new arrivals had come
from the south, where the main band of the Kootenais had
been hunting with the Flatheads. They reported that a large
group of Piegans, Bloods, and Blackfeet had crossed the
mountains to talk peace, and the parley had gone well until
one of the Piegans stole a horse. In the ensuing fracas, the
Old Chief's son had been killed, along with several Flatheads
and a dozen Piegans. The Old Chief and his Kootenais were
now on their way home, but most of the Flatheads, whom
Thompson had been so anxious to meet, had decamped to "a
military Post of the Americans." The news of Americans anywhere in the region was a surprise. There were forty-two of
them, according to the Kootenai messengers, including two
members of Lewis and Clark's expedition, and they were
building a post somewhere to the south. It was impossible
for Thompson to pinpoint the location of this unexpected competition, but wherever they were, his reaction in
his report to the partners was philosophical:

This establishment of the Americans will give a new Turn to our so long delayed settling of this Country, on which we have entered it seems too late; but in my opinion the most valuable part of the Country still remains to us & we have nothing to obstruct us, but the difficulty of getting goods from Fort des Prairies, & the still more formidable poverty of the Country in Animals. Time & Perserverance will show what we can do, & if worth our Expence & Trouble.

During the third week in August, the summer run of salmon arrived. So did twelve young Piegans, who had come across one of the passes that led from their hunting grounds to the Kootenai country. They said that their war chief Kootanae Appee had heard a rumor that the white men were building a house on the west side and had sent them "to see the Truth of the Matter." Thompson had been expecting such a visit, for he knew that the Piegans would be upset when they learned he was supplying arms to their old customers the Kootenais and their old enemies the Flatheads. The Piegans told Thompson that they were "pleased" with his new post, but he did not believe them. "What their future Intentions are Heavens knows – we hope for the best, as it is in their Power to be very troublesome to us." While Finan McDonald went out at night with a flambeau and speared salmon weighing up to twenty-six pounds ("tolerable good, but having come so far had lost all their fatness"), the Piegans hung around, worrisome to Thompson because he thought they must be the scouts for a larger party. But no more showed up, and after a week the visitors got hungry and broke camp, stealing three horses on their way out. Two Kootenais tried to chase down the horse thieves, and the ruckus put the camp into such a state of alarm that the Kootenais repitched their tents right next to the trade house and put all their valuables under the white men's protection.

The next day three new Piegans came to visit, all familiar

to Thompson from the east side and all proclaiming peace-able intentions. Not knowing how long these intentions would hold, the Nor'Westers quickly put up two heavy fences from their compound to the steep bank of the river. When thirty more Piegans arrived, led by two chiefs of Thompson's acquaintance, he went out and met them for a smoke but would not give them any rum or let them inside the yard.

Meanwhile, Bercier had gone to see what was keeping the main band of Kootenais and returned with news that they had been stricken by a "violent Distemper." One of the sick men arrived at the camp next to Kootanae House late that evening: "They sang around him all night, he says that many of them are very sick & several Children dead, it seems by the Hooping Cough." During the next week, more sick Kootenais straggled in, and Thompson administered doses of Turlington (an elixir of balsamic resin) from the supply he had brought with him. The Piegans, unalarmed by the sick-ness, stayed on.

At this point Thompson rehired Michel Boulard, reflect-ing that "he is useful in many respects more than another & many respects much less so – upon the whole he is a cheap bargain." Thompson had complained about Boulard's laziness and irresponsibility in the past, but the man was a good inter-preter, and Thompson was feeling the need for someone with a knack for language. It had been twenty years since his winter with Saukamappee, and the Piegan he had learned then was not sufficient for the present situation. The tongues being spoken in his camp included English, French, Piegan Blackfeet, Kootenai, and Charlotte Thompson's Cree; the Flatheads traveling with the Kootenais spoke yet another dis-tinct language. In a letter to the partners a few months later, Thompson described his difficulties: "What I say in French is to be spoken in Blackfoot, then in Kootanae, then in Flat Head etc. etc. so that the sense is fairly translated away before it arrives at the person spoken to."

With Boulard to help him interpret, Thompson had a talk

with the Piegans, who were finally getting hungry enough to think about leaving. As an inducement for them to decamp peacefully, he presented each chief with a foot of tobacco and five rounds of ammunition, and the other men with two inches of smoke and a paper of vermilion, the powdered red clay that the natives valued for body paint. After they were gone, Thompson heard a rumor that they were only waiting for the right occasion to plunder his post and drive him from the country. Two Piegans had stayed behind to gamble with the Kootenais, and Thompson called them in for a reckoning. They confessed that several of the young men had been looking to start trouble, but that the elders wanted to stay on good terms with the white men and had calmed things down for the time being. "I told them that we were well prepared for the worst that could happen, & that if any Trouble was given us, it was a very easy thing to build out of their Power, & where they would never get a pipe of Tobacco from us."

Three days later a more congenial group arrived—a dozen Flat Bow men and one woman, carrying small packs of furs on their backs. These people were a band of the Kootenais who lived to the south and west, and they had never seen white people before. They told Thompson that no elk or moose lived in their country, but sturgeon and berries were plentiful, and beaver abounded. They had brought beaver, bear, cat, otter, and fisher skins to trade, with a little sturgeon oil and a bushel of berries thrown in, which they exchanged for some ammunition, axes, and a kettle. Among the Flat Bows were two old men who "spoke much to the purpose on all questions I asked, & after drawing a Chart of their country & from thence to the Sea, & describing the Nations along the River, they assured me that from this House to the Sea & back again was only the Voyage of a Summer Moon; but from the number of Falls etc. it does not appear easy to go without a Guide." Thompson tried to talk the Flat Bows into taking him on a quick trip south to see whether the large river flowing through their homeland might possibly be the Columbia. But the old men told him that it was too late in the fall and that besides, he would have to wait for their chief, Ugly Head, "as he alone was capable of protecting us in distant Countries."

While Thompson was smoking and talking with the Flat Bows, dogs were also on his mind. The Kootenais had often warned the Nor'Westers not to let their dogs eat raw salmon flesh, but no one had paid any attention. For the past two weeks, however, several of the camp dogs had been very dull and lethargic, "always lying down in some lonesome place and sleeping, refusing all food, & scarcely lifting their Head even at the voice of their Master." On the evening of September 18, three of their best pups "made their exit."

On September 23 Finan McDonald and five voyageurs headed back across the mountains to drop off the summer's furs and pick up more supplies. Because of their horse short-age, Thompson was obliged to buy one from the Kootenais, who charged him a gun and a foot of tobacco for one sorry animal. These were black market prices for the explorer—back at Rocky Mountain House, he had purchased two good horses for five pints of rum—but the trip had to be made. Along with the pelts, Thompson sent off his report on the summer's adventures, a request for an extra man for the coming year, and a strange letter he had received from a Kootenai messenger. Dated July 10, 1807, at "Fort Lewis, Yellow River, Columbia" and signed "Zachery Perch, Captain and Commander, and James Roseman, Lieutenant, U.S. Army," the letter addressed itself to "Foreigners who may at present be carrying on a Traffic with the Indians within our Territories." It listed rigid mandates concerning liquor sales, flag raising, and trade practices, then ended with a sweeping American claim for the entire Northwest—including the Columbia River and all its branches, "of which we have now taken possession and on which we are now settled down to the Pacific Ocean." This epistle must have come from the same Americans whom the Kootenais had told him about earlier, and although Thompson did not record his reaction, he had learned enough about the area to deduce that the authors were either outrageous liars or had seriously misplaced the Pacific Ocean. As far as anyone knows, he did not honor the officers with a reply.

Two days after Finan McDonald departed, the long-awaited Old Chief of the Kootenais arrived, accompanied by the Flat Bow chief Ugly Head, so named for his curly hair. They told Thompson that during their peace parley with the Blackfeet tribes a few weeks earlier, they had heard that a party of Bloods and Blackfeet had pillaged Fort Augustus on the Saskatchewan during the summer. They did not know whether anyone had been killed, only that the raiding party had gotten away with guns, ammunition, tobacco, and the clothes off the traders' backs. This was alarming news to Thompson, for Fort Augustus was the residence of his colleagues James Hughes and McDonald of Garth and the destination of Finan McDonald. There had been other violent episodes with the Blackfeet tribes on the Saskatchewan, and Thompson knew just how vulnerable his little outpost would be if the trouble spread. All but three of his voyageurs had gone east with Finan McDonald, and even if they made the trip safely, it would be weeks before they returned. As it turned out, the men at Fort Augustus were safe, but the Hudson Bay Company's South Branch House had been overrun and the chief trader there killed.

When Ugly Head offered to guide Thompson to his country for a quick visit, the surveyor juggled his concern about an attack with his desire to investigate the course of the river on which the Flat Bows lived. On October 2 he made up his mind and, leaving his family and Kootanae House under the care of his three remaining men, he set off with Ugly Head and his wife, communicating by signs and a few words. With snow gathering on the mountaintops, they headed south on horseback from Windermere Lake and around a second lake, then crossed over a short portage to a large river that swept south out of the Rockies. They rode downriver on a well-used path through open woods and grassy meadows. Thompson had spent the summer feeling frustrated about his lack of exploration, but now that he was on the move, he couldn't stop worrying about the Blackfeet tribes. After two days he had seen enough of the river to know that it was navigable, and when the horse trail cut inland he told Ugly Head that he needed to get back. They turned around and retraced their steps—up the river, across the portage, and, unbeknownst to Thompson, right beside the headwaters of the Columbia River.

COLUMBIA LAKE, the actual source of the river, lies only a few miles upstream from Windermere Lake in southeastern British Columbia. It is long and narrow, hemmed in on the east by the ponderous, bare-shouldered Mount Sabine and on the west by the Purcell Range. There is no sign of rushing streams or a birthing spring; instead, the lake seems to ooze up from a shallow basin, and swords of sedge grass peek up far offshore. A few years ago the hills along the west side were blackened by a forest fire, and now summer finds them rife with charcoal spikes of Douglas fir and new pink fireweed. Along the lake's shoreline, white hoodoos catch the sunlight, their fluted columns intricately carved by wind and water. A little camping park called Thunder Hill overlooks the south end of the lake, and I was poking about there when a park ranger drove in to pick up the trash.

Unlike a Stateside ranger, this one didn't wear a uniform or ride in an official vehicle. He drove his own pickup, an older, squeaky-clean Dodge, and he was eager to talk. "Oh yes, the fire. Four summers ago, on the hottest afternoon you've ever seen. We sweated it out for a while, but you can see how it just nipped past us. She burned a lot of fine timber, quick and hot. They've found a way to mill a lot of what's left standing. The bad part of it is, though, they've had to cut it all as quick as they can. In four years I reckon they've fallen what it would have taken them twenty if they'd just cut it on their regular cycle. Threw their plans out of whack a bit. But you should see all the elk coming back in on the new growth now."

We looked out over Columbia Lake, and the ranger explained to me how the Columbia River bubbled up here and flowed north. He pointed down at Canal Flats, an open plain about one mile in breadth, which separates the Columbia from another big river that sneaks out from behind Mount Sabine and runs south. This south-flowing river is the one that Ugly Head had shown to David Thompson. At first Thompson called it the Flat Bow, but later he renamed it McGillivrays River in honor of his bosses Duncan and William. Today it is known as the Kootenay River in British Columbia and the Kootenai in Montana and Idaho. Looking down on Canal Flats from Thunder Hill, it was hard not to be amazed at how this one small strip of land in the middle of the entire Rocky Mountain Trench divides the headwaters of the Columbia from the Kootenay. I understood for the first time how David Thompson could make the switch with an easy portage and zip down into what is now the United States. The ranger nodded enthusiastically; he knew he was the steward of a good place, even if most fishermen shunned it.

"Nobody fishes Columbia Lake much. It's what we call a coarse-fish lake—trout, bass, sucker, kokanee, all mixed up together. The sportsmen run up to White Swan. That's because we killed that one out three years ago and fresh stocked it with rainbow trout. But I've heard this lake here used to be something else. There's an old-timer around who remembers salmon coming into the lake. Salmon! And seals too, he said. Seals."

The ranger saw my eyes widen—a harbor seal fourteen hundred miles upriver did sound a little outrageous—and backed off a bit: "That's just what the old-timer said now, couldn't prove it by me. I can see salmon maybe, before the dams. But seals—that's hard to swallow. That's what the old-timer said, though. Salmon and seals. And he was a lot closer to it than we are now."

Later, I got lost up in the eerie landscape of the burn. Scaly outcrops of rock tilted up like furrows in a giant field, and to walk at all I had to keep my eyes on the ground. When I did look up, there was wilderness all around: the massive Rockies across the river to the east, the craggy Purcells straight above me to the west. As I followed the outcrops back and forth, trying to make my way out of an island of charred blackness into the vast ocean of greenery that ringed the mountains, the notion of an animal from another time didn't seem so amazing. The Old Chief told David Thompson a story about a creature who lived up in these woods, an animal that stood eighteen feet tall and could never lie down, but had to lean against big trees to catch a nap. The Kootenais thought this was because it had no joints in the middle of its legs, but they couldn't say for sure since they had never been able to kill one and examine it. "Nurses Fables," Thompson called the tales, and got the Kootenais to admit that they had "rarely or never" seen one. Thompson had heard similar fables from other tribes, and whenever I read one of these tales I couldn't help thinking about woolly mammoths. Weren't mammoths supposed to stand almost eighteen feet tall? And didn't they sleep on their feet? Natives in the East told Thompson that in the old days mammoths lived all over their country and fed on other animals, including people. Eventually the Great Spirit grew tired of their ravenous ways and brought out his thunderbolts to kill them all. One big bull survived the onslaught and, with an enormous leap, escaped the wrath of the Great Spirit. He had run away to the West, they said, and lived there still. I liked the idea of an old kneeless bull leaning up against one of these trees above the Columbia while seals swam around in the lake below. Even more, I liked the fact that David Thompson occasionally found room in his daybooks for the fabulous.

WHEN THOMPSON got back to Kootanae House on October 6, he found Boulard, Buché, and Boisverd busy cutting pickets for a stockade. The surveyor sent the women out to dig watap for tying the logs together and began standing up the heavy posts. Work speeded up two weeks later when word arrived that the Blackfeet and Bloods had declared war on the Kootenais for supplying arms to the Flatheads, and on Thompson's post for supporting the west-side tribes. So far the Piegan bands had not joined their kin in the hostilities, but there was no way to know what might happen. Everyone prepared for an attack; the Kootenais tied their horses to their tents, and the white men quickly put up a bastion. On October 26, working together, they completed the stockade, then held a council to decide on a course of action in case they were attacked. They all agreed to "give them battle the moment they appear," and Ugly Head set off to alert the other bands of the danger. During the next six weeks there were sporadic reports of gunfire and war songs from across the lake, but no war parties materialized.

The salmon run was over now, and the shores were littered with dead fish. The men harvested trout and an occasional loon from their nets and hunted the swans that were gathering on the lakes to winter. Snow in the mountains was pushing the big game back down into the valley, and Kootenai hunters like Chien Faux (Deceitful Dog) and the Gauche (Left Hand) brought in fresh elk and *chevreuil* on a regular basis. In early November Finan McDonald and his crew returned safely with supplies from the east side. In addition to the regular array of trade items and new clothes for the men, Thompson's order included a keg of French brandy, two blank notebooks, a pair of brass candlesticks, a pound each of cinnamon and cloves, a bottle of "Eau de Luce" (toilet water), twenty pounds of marbled soap, twenty-four bottles each of peppermint (for digestion) and Turlington, two papers of black ink powder, and six black lead pencils.

With the warehouse full of fresh goods, Thompson was anxious to trade. He sent Boulard out to encourage the Kootenais to hunt beaver while their winter pelage was at its prime, for these thick pelts brought the best prices at the London markets. But winter was traditionally a time of relative leisure for the Kootenais, because game was concentrated in the valleys and the bands could gather together to socialize. In mid-November the families tenting near Kootanae House were all busy accumulating meat for a big dancing feast, and Thompson had the Old Chief deliver a "Harangue" for them to break camp and get after the beaver.

By December there was plenty of snow in the passes to keep war parties away, and things had calmed down enough for Thompson to get some bookwork done. On December 11 he noted that he had "Transcribed Capn Lewis's account of his journey to the Pacific Ocean." This account was actually a long letter written by Meriwether Lewis about his expedition to the Pacific. Finan McDonald must have brought it back from the Saskatchewan on his supply run, but no one has ever discovered how it fell into the hands of the North West Company. Wherever it came from, Lewis's letter provided information of great interest to Thompson, including a summary of Lewis and Clark's route up the Missouri River, across the Rockies, and down to the Pacific. From the account Thompson would have learned that the lower Columbia beyond the mouth of the Snake River was navigable to the sea.

Thompson copied Lewis's letter into the same notebook in which he had entered extracts of Vancouver's *Voyages* six years earlier, then turned to the lighter task of repairing a hand-cranked barrel organ that had been knocked to pieces on its trip over the pass. During the next week he built a desk, caught up on his accounting, and finished arranging the "Barrel of Music." On December 18 five Piegans came across the mountains with a welcome update: the Blackfeet tribes were now embroiled in a war with the Crees on the east side and no longer had any intention of bothering anyone on the west side of the mountains. During the next few days, a Flathead chief and four of his men arrived, then the Old Chief and four tents of his people. The Flatheads and Kootenais got together with the Piegans to smoke and talk peace, and spent Christmas night in dancing. The next day the Piegans left for home, and Thompson made arrangements with the Flatheads about collecting beaver for trade in the spring.

It was probably this same group of Flatheads and Kootenais that brought in a second note from the mysterious American military officers. This one was dated September 29, 1807, and addressed "To the British Mercht trafficking with the Cotanaiss." It was signed by "U.S. Lieutenant Jeremy Pinch," whose name looks suspiciously like the Zachery Perch who had signed the first letter. Pinch rebuked Thompson for his failure to respond to the Americans' original proclamation and stridently demanded that he retreat from his position: "We have more powerful means of persuasion in our hands than we have hitherto used, we shall with regret apply Force . . . You will see Sir the necessity of submitting and with good grace." The letter ended with complaints that marauding Piegans had wounded one of the American soldiers, and that British furmen ought to stop supplying these scoundrels with weapons and ammunition.

Thompson chose to answer this threat, and on December 26 he sent off a calm reply to "your polite favor of the 29th Sept." He noted that he was not politician enough to settle boundary disputes, but that it was his understanding that George Vancouver's initial exploration of the lower Columbia gave Great Britain claim to the river. He assured the Americans that he would forward their demands back East for consideration by the North West Company. Thompson sent a copy of the note to his partners, adding his own assessment of the affair: "not one of these petty officers but what has as much arrogance as Buonaparte at the head of his Invincibles."

Western historians have driven themselves to distraction trying to figure out the origin of these letters. There are no records of U.S. military expeditions anywhere near the Northwest during this time, nor are there records of any officers in the U.S. Army that match the three names signed on the two letters. The best guess seems to be that they came from a party that left St. Louis in April of 1807, led by independent furman Manuel Lisa. An ambitious man often surrounded by intrigue, Lisa did have forty-two men in his party. He did pick up two veterans of the Lewis and Clark Expedition on his way up the Missouri. He did meet up with a Canadian trader at the Mandan village who could have mentioned Thompson's expedition to the Kootenais. Some of his men did have trouble with the Piegans. But Lisa's fort was on the Yellowstone River, on the east side of the Divide, and quite a ways to the south; it was nowhere near the Columbia as claimed in the letters. The only things that can be said for certain about this incident are that whoever they were, the Americans had their sights on the big river, and wherever they were, the native tribes were keeping track of them and the other newcomers in their territories over thousands of square miles.

January of 1808 found Michel Boulard making an ice house, or "glacier," in which to store the abundance of fresh meat that Chien Faux and other Kootenai hunters were hauling in. Thompson's new year did not get off to such a happy start: he sprained his knee on an icy bank and had to limp around on a crutch for the entire month. While his men made birch pipestems for smoking with the chiefs and gathered aspen wood for a sled, he "arranged the desk for papers and drawing etc." On clear nights he took observations on Kootanae House (latitude 50° 32' 12" N, longitude 115° 56'

15" W) and on clear days he measured the elevations of local landmarks, especially one impressive peak that loomed behind the western shore of Windermere Lake. He named the uplift Mount Nelson, after the admiral whose heroics at the Battle of Trafalgar two years before had thwarted Napoleon's plan to invade England.

At his desk Thompson recopied the long lists of compass courses from his field books into a neat table, arranging them in columns alongside the coordinates from his observations. Many days were then spent reworking mistakes and inconsistencies. When it was finally time to draw an actual map, he used these numbers to re-create the curves of a given river between his fixed points of latitude and longitude. He penciled in the outlines and then inked, tinted, and shaded the topography onto a series of foolscap sheets that measured sixteen by thirteen inches each. Laid together, these sheets filled in a few more sections of the wilderness.

The surveyor also made time to go horseback riding almost every day, the better to learn his new territory. He found the weather on the west side of the Divide mild compared with what he had grown used to in the East—so mild, in fact, that the birch rind growing there was too thin to make good canoes. He hunted elk and antelope and tried going after the mountain goats up in the hills, but without much success; the Kootenais told him they were wicked animals that kicked down stones on hunters.

Aside from his daily entry of "Drawing, etc.," the events that Thompson chose to record over this first winter at Kootanae House almost all took place during the day, and out of doors. But he was living in a latitude that gets barely eight hours of sun in the winter months, and even allowing for his nocturnal observations, the great majority of his time must have been spent indoors. Fur trade journals did not usually dwell on personal matters, and Thompson's was no exception. There is no hint of Charlotte's role. There are no descriptions of furnishings, utensils, or of playing that odd barrel organ. There is no comment on what it was like to work out several hours of trigonometry by a grease lamp with three kids playing on the rough floor of a small cabin. There is no mention of how his men were entertaining themselves during the long evenings, although his supply order for this season had included a request for two decks of playing cards.

Whatever was going on inside Thompson's stockade at off hours, there was no mystery about how the Kootenai men were spending their spare time.

> Febry 6th   Saturday   Rode 4 Hours – Drawing – Netmaking . . . After a long gambling Match, one Kootanae has gained near the whole. His gains are 17 Red Deer Skins – 24 Chevreuil – 1 Gun – 3 Axes – 10 Knives – 350 Balls – 7 lbs. of Powder – 6 Horses & Saddles – Saddle Stuff etc. – 1 Robe – 1 Blanket & many small Articles besides 2 good Tents. The others have only their Wives, Children, and old leather clothing left.

On March 1, half a dozen Piegans arrived from across the mountains, carrying with them letters that had been sent from Fort Augustus three months earlier. Thompson quickly wrote answers, which the Piegans carried with them when they returned to the east side two days later. Of the hundreds of letters Thompson sent off during his career, copies of the two missives he entrusted to the Piegans are among the very few that have survived. One was a "public letter," addressed to James Hughes, Donald McTavish, and John McDonald of Garth but meant for the eyes of all the partners. Here Thompson tries to explain that the west side of the mountains is "utterly different" from anything they have ever experienced, and says he has had a terrible time finding food over the summer due to a lack of fish and especially rabbits ("Were these plenty I should be at my ease, as I yield to none in the country in the art of killing them"). He has also had trouble convincing the Kootenais and Flatheads that he would rather receive beaver skins than the horses and berries that are their own favorite items. Yet the natives look upon his arrival as a godsend, and if he can induce them to hunt beaver, he is certain the company's investment will pay off. He speaks highly of the prospects of the country he has seen so far and thinks it would be a good idea to send over ten or twelve good Iroquois free hunters to help trap. He hopes he can make thirty packs of furs this season and asks for a two-year trial period on the west side, saying that if his efforts don't show a profit by then, he will be willing to give it up. He closes his letter with a request for a forge, a blacksmith, two good hoes, and some extra blue beads.

Thompson's second letter was addressed to Donald McTavish, an agent in the Athabasca district whom he must have come to know well during his own years there. Thompson thanks his friend for his support, revealing his awareness that other partners of the company are set against his whole enterprise across the mountains. He rails at their short-sightedness and at his own lack of knowledge about the "fluctuating politics" within the company. But he also conveys his excitement about the possibilities of the west side: "I wish to heaven you could be transported by some Geniis to see how this Country is formed and the pains and trouble I have taken to carry on our Business." He adds up all the expenses so far on his expedition to the shilling, tallying the cost of provisions and the men's wages, and figures that he just might come out of it with a profit at the end of the year. "You know that I do nothing without calculation, so that I know fairly what I am about."

Near the end of his letter to McTavish, Thompson makes a personal request: "I must now again beg of you to take my little child under your protection and if possible to get him from his mother . . . you might send him to Fort Augustus or contrive some way or other to put him in my hands – at least see him well clothed and of course charge it to my account." The mother that he refers to cannot be Charlotte, since she is at Kootanae House with him. Apparently at some point

Thompson had a child by another woman in the Athabasca district and left them both behind. This was not an uncommon practice among the furmen; what is unusual is his attempt to get custody of the child. Having asked his favor, Thompson tells McTavish that the Piegans who brought the letters are in a hurry to be off, and bids his friend adieu.

Two days later a North West Company clerk named James McMillan rode in behind a dog team, bringing Kootanae House more news and supplies from the east side. The surveyor dashed off another batch of correspondence and five days later sent it back to the Saskatchewan with McMillan, transported by dogsled. Thompson was trying to keep in close touch with a world that seemed very far away.

CHAPTER FIVE

BORDER CROSSING

SPRING 1808–WINTER 1809

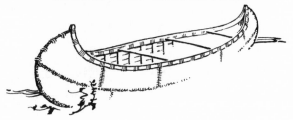

B Y MID-APRIL of 1808, the willows around Kootanae House were leafing out, and Thompson was ready to continue the trip he had started with Ugly Head the previous fall. Leaving Finan McDonald in charge of the post, he retraced his route south along the two source lakes and across the Canal Flats portage to put into the Kootenay River. While four voyageurs paddled the canoe downstream, Thompson the geographer was hard at work, listing compass directions and distances as usual. He noted the location of rapids and shoals, the mouths of tributaries, and good camping spots. And all the time he was scanning the surrounding terrain, studying the way the country was put together.

As they moved south, the explorer remarked on the new leaves of gooseberry and aspen, and the appearance of Douglas fir among the mix of trees. He saw elk and *chevreuil*, a few wolves, and many ducks. When they put up to camp on the second evening, one of the men shot a goose and got eight eggs out of her nest. Thompson wrote glowingly of the country's prospects: "April 22nd Friday Morning a little

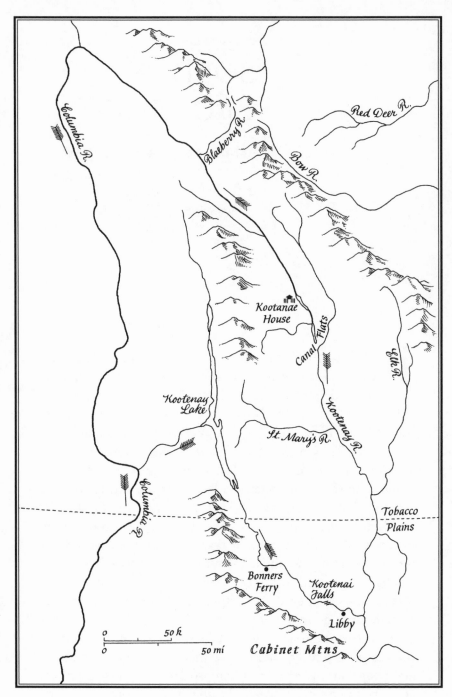

Columbia R.

Red Deer R.

Blaeberry R.

Bow R.

Kootanae House

Canal Flats

Elk R.

Kootenay Lake

Kootenay R.

St. Mary's R.

Columbia R.

Tobacco Plains

Bonners Ferry

Kootenai Falls

Libby

0   50 k
0   50 mí

Cabinet Mtns

EXPLORING THE KOOTENAI COUNTRY

Cloudy but clear in the afternoon ... the River in general has a very smooth easy Current with a sufficient depth of Water & where we are camped the Points of fine Meadows & the first ground I have seen that I think has sufficient moisture to farm a Garden for Herbs."

It rained the next day and they stayed in camp to re-gum the canoe, which had been badly scraped on some shallow rapids. When the rain stopped, they floated on past the mouth of the St. Mary's River, which was as far as Thompson had made it the previous October on his quick trip with Ugly Head. He had been remarking on the scarcity of beaver sign ever since he left Columbia Lake, but on this stretch he spotted some lodges and set out traps every evening in hopes of catching a meal. The nights were frosty and the current of the river picked up, keeping his senses on alert; he was mesmerized by tiny whirlpools on the surface of the river that made "a hissing noise as if they were full of small icicles."

As they slipped below the 49th parallel on April 25, the canoe began taking on water again, and they stopped to camp in one of the beautiful meadows that lined each side of the river. "This is the place where the Indians speak so much of growing their tobacco; and we named them on that account, the Tobacco Meadows." The Kootenais had told him about this area, and about their practice of burying a dead fish beneath each tobacco seedling at planting time. Looking through his telescope, Thompson could see that the grasslands continued up onto the hills to the east. Now known as Tobacco Plains, these open hills were prime habitat for bitterroot, a low-growing pink flower whose root was an important vegetable food for many western tribes. Bands of Kootenais gathered here every summer, and the women fanned out across the dry hillsides with their pointed willow digging sticks to twist up great mounds of the fleshy bitterroot bulbs. They spread the roots in the sun to dry, then ate them boiled or stewed with meat.

Thompson had made plans to meet some of the

Kootenais here and sent two voyageurs off to look for them. They found a few tracks, a trail leading downriver, a place where six lodges had recently been taken down, and one skunk, which they killed and brought to camp. The men spent the next few days hunting and repairing their canoe while they waited for the Kootenais. Just before they landed, Thompson had remarked on what he thought would be a fine location for a trade house, but he couldn't do much scouting because he had sprained his knee again. He did attempt to go hunting, but was so lame that he needed a stick to walk. "April 30th Saturday A fine Day – Gale at South – visited our traps – nothing . . . our Subsistence this day was a Dram of Rum & half a Partridge [grouse] per man."

The next morning they heard a man calling from across the river. It was Le Monde, a Kootenai who had hunted for them at Windermere Lake, and the Nor'Westers fetched him and his family in the canoe and gave him some balls and powder for hunting. Thompson spent part of that night observing for longitude, but had to skip the next one because he had already used up most of his candles. Two days later Le Monde killed a mountain lion, "His Tail 2 ft. 10 in. – Coulour of a Fawn – Belly white very strong Legged & sharp Claws . . . very good Food & yields as much meat as a Chevreuil."

Thompson decided that he must have missed his rendezvous with the Kootenais and tried to hire Le Monde to go south as their guide. But Le Monde did not want to leave his family, so the furmen continued downriver on their own. Along the way they emulated a common native practice by setting ground fires to clear the brush and attract game to the new growth that would follow. By evening they had left the grasslands behind and passed into a rich forest of big trees; Thompson measured one tamarack that was 13 feet around and 150 feet clear to its first branch and noted what fine masts such trees would make for the Royal Navy. Another day of paddling brought them to an abrupt westward turn in the river's course. The wooded hills began to close in on them, the banks turned to steep cliffs, and within twenty miles they came upon the cataracts of Kootenai Falls thundering through a tight, S-shaped canyon. The only portage they could find around the falls was a long and treacherous animal trail three hundred feet above the river. "The least slip would have been inevitable destruction, as the steepness of the rock allowed no return; or, in once falling, to stop till precipitated into the river."

The men put on two pairs of shoes, but the rocks soon cut them to pieces. Each trip across the portage took over an hour, and it was nightfall before they got all the packs over the path. They made a light supper from the last of their provisions and next morning faced the daunting task of fetching the canoe. Two voyageurs usually carried one boat, but even with some of the timbers removed, it was all four men could do to maneuver the canoe around the cliffs that edged the narrow trail, and "it was with difficulty preserved from breaking against the rocks."

ON THE MUGGY summer day when I happened along, that same nasty portage had the Montana Department of Highways out in force, trying to make a more secure shelf for the road between the towns of Troy and Libby. They had blasted thousands of tons of rock down onto the old roadbed, and flaggers were allowing traffic to creep through the construction zone only once every two hours, day and night. While motorists swore and sweated, yellow bulldozers and front-end loaders pawed away at the bedded purple stone that forms the tumultuous landscape around Kootenai Falls.

I got out of the car to stretch and watched the vehicles stack up behind me. A pickup truck pulled a shiny boat, probably headed for some kokanee fishing on a dammed-up section of the Kootenai River. A muddy logging truck groaned under the weight of big Douglas fir and tamarack.

The twin trailers of a mule-train ore truck were ferrying milled earth from somewhere deep underground to a smelter across the Canadian border. David Thompson had fished the eddies at the base of Kootenai Falls and pointed out the marketable timber as he paddled downstream, but he had no premonition that the rocks that shredded his shoes and tore at his canoe would ever be in demand by anyone. Within seventy years of his passage, however, a mad gold rush was luring the first white settlers into the area. The gold played out long ago, but in the years since, copper, silver, lead, zinc, and vermiculite have all taken their turns at fueling the local economy.

I wormed my way through the roadwork and on into downtown Libby, where I caught up with Terry Webster just finishing lunch. "I figured you were sitting out there waiting for the pilot car," he grinned. "Everybody else is." Terry works for the Hard Rock Division of the Montana Bureau of Lands, which oversees permits on all mining jobs in the state, and he was in town that day to check on a couple of big mines—one slowly winding down, the other just starting up. He filled me in on the details as we drove down Main Street past the Stitch 'n' Shoot, a needlepoint and ammo supply shop, then over to the office of the Kootenai National Forest. Terry talked with a couple of foresters there, then made sure that I heard the story of the local Howard brothers. Grubstake miners from Libby's earliest days, the Howards got advance word that the railroad was headed their way and came down from their mining claim to stake out the area where they guessed the tracks would have to pass. Railroad officials moving ahead of the track crew arrived in the valley to find a sea of flagged ground and figured the Howard boys had them by the shorts. After long negotiations, the brothers bargained the railroad slicks right out of a pair of round-trip tickets to Chicago, with sleepers, on the first passenger train that steamed out of town.

Back outside the office, Terry pointed up toward a huge

carved hill that dominated Libby's landscape like a stairstepped Mayan temple, roaded and sculpted over time. "That's where we're headed," he said: "Vermiculite Mountain." After almost a half century in operation, the company that had mined the mountain was shutting it down, and for the rest of the afternoon we wound through a maze of muddy tailings and freshly planted fir seedlings as Terry checked on the progress of their reclamation efforts. By the time he finished his inspection it was late in the day. His next appointment was early the following morning in the opposite direction, and he had planned to get a head start by camping out along the way. We drove out of town and soon turned south onto a washboarded Forest Service road that led up into the Cabinet Range.

The Cabinets lie directly south of Libby and the Kootenai River—they are the "right tolerable snowy mountains" that David Thompson faced as he paddled from Tobacco Plains toward Kootenai Falls. The crest of this range was set aside as a National Wilderness Area several years ago, and as we bounced along Terry caught me up on the controversy now swirling around its peaks. Deep beneath the mountains lies a mammoth deposit of copper and silver ore. Many people thought that wilderness status would squelch any plans for extracting it, but an old mining claim on a neighboring ridge provided a foothold in the area, and a consortium of U.S. and Canadian companies called Montanore had obtained a permit to drill an exploratory tunnel. "*Quite* a deal," Terry said. "You can imagine the screaming and yelling over that piece of paper."

We were riding on what would be a main access route for the proposed mine, and Terry kept waving one arm out the window to describe changes of immense proportion: electrical power lines roping through the forest here, the backup from a three-hundred-foot impoundment dam there. Near the top of the drainage, though, his conversation veered away from the effects of the Montanore project and onto which twisted side road he might be able to negotiate with his pickup. "How's that one look? Too scraggly . . . too many tire tracks . . . ah, I'm gettin' hungry . . . what the heck—let's try this one."

He banged his Ford across the gravel pile of some gold prospector's old sluicebox operation, bucking mightily to reach a flat area at the end of the track, and backed up to a spot of tall grass beside the stream. We hopped out and walked a circle around the pickup. "Looks good to me," Terry said. "Let's set up."

Terry doesn't camp out quite like anyone else I know. He clambered into the bed of his pickup and shoved out a wooden picnic table that had spent the day holding down a sizable piece of green canvas. While I got the table roughly leveled, he rolled back the tarp and produced canvas folding chairs, a two-burner propane stove, a milk crate packed with utensils and condiments, a pair of Army-issue air mattresses, two battery-powered lanterns, and three sacks of groceries. "Bring on the grizzly bears," he chortled as a package of hamburger tumbled onto the ground. The next thing I knew, he was revving a little orange chain saw and wading into a patch of beetle-killed pines. Within ten minutes he had whacked out enough firewood for a night's stay in the bush. He switched off the saw, tossed out a rusty double-bitted ax head he had found inside the copse, and then stepped back into the clearing to survey his handiwork. Once again, he approved.

"Some people," he said, "just don't understand how to get set up."

Next morning Terry and I drove farther up Libby Creek to Montanore's base of operations. A section of rough hillside had been completely stripped of timber and enclosed with a tall cyclone fence; an access road carved into the steep hill switchbacked down to a flat area crowded with heavy equipment and wet, fractured rock. Terry swept his arm around the enclosure. "Yep," he said. "Some old-timer patented this forty acres as a claim years ago, and it ends up as a little piece of private land in the middle of the national forest. Now there's your wilderness area right up there." He pointed across to the spine of the Cabinets, where long outcrops of bare rock folded up to form the crown of each summit; the one called Elephant Peak shimmered like a dancer in the blue air above the scene.

"So Montanore comes along and—you've got to picture this now—and they figured that if they start right here"—he held one fist out and lined up his knuckles with the trio of big peaks directly in front of us, then wormed a finger sideways between two of the knuckles to the opposite, hidden side of his hand—"and bore this tunnel for about three and a half miles under the mountains over there, they think they'll run smack dead into their ore body." While I took in the crust of trees and dirt and crumbling talus, Terry's eyes drilled straight into the bedrock.

"So here's the deal. We gave them a permit for one exploratory shaft. Now *if* they manage to hit the right spot, and *if* they decide the stuff has a high enough ore content, and *if* there's enough of it, *then* they've got to prove they can pull this off without screwing up the wilderness area."

Already big mounds of rock were windrowed along the entire lower edge of the fence line—not surprising, noted Terry, since the shaft had to be big enough to accommodate an oversized dump truck alongside the conveyor belt that was carrying the mountain's innards out to the parking lot. A battered crew-cab pickup rolled in through the gate, its driver giving us the once-over as he eased past. Terry told them he was with the State, just taking a couple of samples, and his words worked their usual ambiguous magic. The pickup eased down the roller-coaster road to the shaft entrance and its crew slumped out to begin their day. The big conveyor was already going, dropping rocks onto the ground with a steady beat. One of the new arrivals cranked up a front-end loader and started pushing the tailings farther away.

"Yep, it's that second permit that's going to be the bitch," Terry said, and went on to explain that the plan called for two more tunnels under a low ridge to the north—one to haul out the ore and the other to carry wiring and plumbing inside to the digging equipment. "This is going to be a room-and-pillar mine—that's where you hollow out the mountain except you leave a few pillars of rock to hold the whole thing up." Terry paused to consider such a structure, describing vast chambers of empty underground space.

"Anyway," he continued, "it's going to be a big deal. One hundred million tons of tailings. Major impact. We're hearing from a lot of people about this one."

I had seen the way people looked at Terry when he told them he worked for the State. I had been to enough town meetings to know the sort of tug-of-war that goes on around new mining permits. I knew that Terry had worked for private exploration companies before, and I also knew that he took his present job as a watchdog for the State very seriously. I was curious to know what he thought about this situation.

"I don't know," he said, shaking his head. "The thing is, *nobody* really asks the right questions when it comes to a deal like this. I mean, everybody just funnels down into their own little crack and that's as far as they can see. The wildlife guys, they're all upset about the dynamite scaring the grizzly bears. The botanists, they've got some plant that's gonna get run over by a bulldozer. The mining guys, they want to get their hands on that ore. Then the folks down in Libby . . . they've got one mine closing down already, and they see jobs. What're they supposed to do? It's hard to know what's the right thing. And I guess I'm just as bad as any of them—I want to find out where the water's going and base every other little thing on that."

Terry is a hydrologist, and he spends a lot of time visualizing the flow of water through rock. Much of his thinking is done out loud, and now he began muttering, half to himself, half to me, as he sent his mind underground, down through the strata of Precambrian rocks beneath the peaks. There was one place in particular that made him a little nervous: on the far side of the crest, the tunnel would pass ticklishly close to a fault. Just above that fault lay a deep alpine lake. "You never know," he said. "They could all come paddling out of that tunnel in a rowboat."

We walked over to the mouth of the exploratory shaft, and I watched the conveyor belt roll while Terry talked to the foreman. The opening was larger than a warehouse, and its blackness swallowed up the puny efforts of the people scrambling around it. Noise, trucks, lights, men, the long conveyor itself, all faded quickly into the gaping hole. When I stepped back outside, the stature of the surrounding peaks seemed to have diminished.

I looked up to the line of flatiron peaks around the Elephant. There were no visible signs of the machines eating their way in among the roots of those giants, but at my back, quite distinctly, I could hear the sound of big rocks plopping down off the conveyor onto the growing pile.

BY NOON on May 7, Thompson's men had bumped their canoe past the last of the rocks on the Kootenai Falls portage trail and set off again. They ran the rest of the canyon, plowing through "violent Eddies that threatened to swallow up the Canoe and People." At one point they put ashore and found a dead *chevreuil*, half eaten by eagles. Ignoring their experience with the wild horse, they loaded the remains into their canoe. "It smelt strongly, but as we were without Food, we were glad to take what remained, altho' we could hardly bear its Smell." They put back in the river and bore the smell while Thompson jotted down twenty-three more river courses before making camp. They boiled the deer for dinner, then spent a sick and sleepless night. Later Thompson theorized that, "had we had time to make charcoal, and boiled this with the meat, the taint would have been taken from the meat."

Early the following day, as the river emerged from the

narrows and calmed itself between broader banks, the furmen spotted a Kootenai man on shore. He climbed aboard to float downstream a short distance to his camp near the present location of Bonner's Ferry, Idaho. The ten lodges gathered here were recovering from a recent scuffle with some Piegans, and as Thompson listened to the details, he realized that two of his men had been involved. At the end of March, he had sent Michel Boulard and Augustin Boisverd south to find the spring camps of the Flatheads and Kootenais and encourage them to work beaver. Somewhere along the way the two voyageurs had met a group of Piegans, who had followed them to the Old Chief's camp. The peace the tribes had agreed to at Kootanae House the previous Christmas did not hold, and a fight had broken out. Three Piegans had been killed, and three Kootenais wounded, including the Old Chief, who had taken a bullet through his thigh. The surviving Piegans had gotten away with thirty-five Kootenai horses, and the turmoil had completely disrupted the spring hunt.

The people at the Kootenai camp were short of food—all they had to offer were a few suckers and some of their moss bread. This "bread" was made not from moss but from the black goatsbeard lichens that hang from old Douglas fir and tamarack trees. The hair-like lichens were cleaned, soaked, roasted on hot stones, then mashed into cakes. Thompson found the bread "of a slightly bitter taste, but acceptable to the hungry . . . I could never relish it, it has just enough nourishment to keep a person alive." Things looked up the next day when a hunter brought in a *chevreuil*. Then Ugly Head arrived and agreed to go south and fetch the Flatheads with their furs.

Thompson spent a day trading at the Kootenai camp, passing on eight tanned beaver hides to his men so that they could make themselves some new shoes. While waiting for Ugly Head to return, he continued downstream toward Kootenay Lake in search of a good site for a trade house. The wide, lush valley at the base of this lake was the home of the

Flat Bows, so named by the Blackfeet after their particular style of bow. The Kootenai word for this group translates as "the marsh people," and Thompson sometimes called them the Lake Indians. Their language was the same as that of their upriver Kootenai relatives, but their lifestyle was quite different. Although individual members occasionally went east on buffalo hunts, for the most part these people relied on their local resources. Instead of tipis, they lived in lodges covered with mats woven of rushes from the surrounding wetlands. Dried fish was their staple food, supplemented with other meat when they could get it. They had a Fishing Chief who supervised the construction of weirs, as well as a Duck Chief and a Deer Chief to orchestrate communal hunts. They didn't have many horses, for the long-legged animals were not very useful in their wet, woody country. Dogs with miniature saddlebags served as pack animals, and on water they traveled in distinctive pine-bark canoes with elongated ends that sloped back from the waterline. This design made the boats more stable in the wind-driven waves that often swept the shallow lake, and the Flat Bows claimed that the jutting chins tracked better in swift river currents. In a memorandum dashed off on an odd page of his journal, Thompson noted: "Legs of the Lake Indians crooked inwards by sitting cross-legged in their small canoes."

The Nor'Westers had not been on the lower river long before they met four of the Flat Bows riding in one of their sturgeon-nosed canoes, who stopped to trade a few skins. The Flat Bows also had some moose and sheep meat to offer, "but it was too much putrified"—apparently the furmen had finally learned to stay away from meat of a certain age. The next day, May 14, Thompson and his crew paddled through their first mosquitoes of the season into the long shoestring of Kootenay Lake. As they wandered among a series of marshy side lakes in search of anyone who might have some skins to trade, Thompson's compass read NE. When he stopped to observe for latitude, his calculations told him he was at

49° 17' 44" N: he had navigated a long U since leaving
Windermere Lake. If he had continued north along the western shore of Kootenay Lake, he would soon have reached the
Kootenay River's outlet, and from there it was only fifty miles
farther west to its juncture with the Columbia.

But they were fifty long miles. From a letter that he wrote
to the partners later that summer, it is clear that Thompson
realized where he was. The Kootenais had told him that a
series of waterfalls and five portages—one of them twenty
miles long—lay between him and the big river. Even though
the passage sounded unnavigable, Thompson wanted to go
and explore it in person, "but my time and the weakness of
my men prevented me." So the surveyor made the pragmatic
decision to tend to business first. He finished his trading
along the lakeshore, then headed back to meet the Flatheads;
along the way he bought four bows for the personal collection
of Duncan McGillivray.

When he got back to the Kootenai lodges, he found his
old campsite under water and learned that the route south to
the Flathead country was also flooded. Thompson had been
counting on the Flathead hunt to meet his projections, but
now no one from those bands would be able to make it to him
with their furs. He had been expecting Boulard and Boisverd
along with the Flatheads and the main band of Kootenais, but
had heard nothing from them. Thompson tried to make
arrangements to go himself to the Flathead country, but no
one would lead him. He couldn't wait for things to dry up,
because he had a shipment of pelts waiting at Kootanae
House that had to be delivered across the mountains, ". . . &
thus all my fine hopes are ruined."

With few alternatives left, he set up a makeshift post near
the Kootenai camp and left Beaulieu to man it. Thompson
knew his canoe would never make it back up the canyon
during high water, so he bought a few horses from the
Kootenais and loaded the three packs of furs he had managed
to collect. He hired a young Kootenai to lead his party

overland and, possibly anticipating a rugged trip, decided to
leave his precious sextant behind. "May 19 Thursday A fine
Day – arranged the Skins, Goods etc. & got ready to set off
with our Kootanae Guide." All the paths that the Kootenais
usually followed to Tobacco Plains and Windermere Lake
were flooded, and after two days of floundering through thick
forest, their guide abandoned them. Thompson could still
barely walk with his bad knee, and he sent Lussier and another man back to the Kootenai camp for help. Time hung
heavy for Thompson for the next two days, and on Tuesday
he came back after wandering about "in sad reflections" to
find that his men had returned with Ugly Head himself
to guide them. For his services, Thompson agreed to pay
the chief one belted jacket, a yard and a half of red wool
cloth, one large knife, one small ax, ten balls, and a quantity
of powder.

Even with Ugly Head's local knowledge, it was not a good
time of year to be traveling. Bushwhacking along steep moun-
tainsides, "the broken rocks has cut the Legs of the Horses to
Pieces, so that we can often trace them by the Blood only –
poor Animals." Entire days were spent throwing down trees
to bridge the torrents of meltwater; at several crossings, they
laboriously chopped down big spars only to watch them be
sucked into the current and swept away as if they were jack-
straws. They lost one fur bundle and Lussier's personal belongings while trying to line them across a roaring stream.
But Ugly Head was able to kill an occasional antelope and elk
to vary their diet of moss bread ("which gave us all the belly
ache"), and after twelve days brought them out of the dripping wilderness back on the upper Kootenay, not far from the
Columbia Lake portage. Here the men helped Ugly Head
strip out a new canoe, and on the afternoon of June 5 they
"bid a kind adieu to our humane Guide, without whose
Perseverance & Attention, we had certainly not been able to
have reached this Place."

By the time Thompson got back to Kootanae House, it

was time to head east with the season's fur packs. Finan McDonald had already started downriver in the big cargo canoe with the women, children, and furs. When the surveyor caught up with them on June 8, he learned that "they have fared but poorly at times & have eat most of the dogs." Thompson canoed on downriver while the rest of his men brought the horses through the woods. At the beginning of the portage trail, they cached the canoes and loaded the horses, substituting pack saddles made out of well-smoked leather for the standard wooden frames. Thompson was trying to pamper his pack animals, and had also made belly bands for them out of some linen cloth, because when the old leather straps got wet they cut the horses' sides severely. It was mid-June, and although spring runoff had swollen the river, there was still snow in the woods. The trail up Blaeberry River had not improved since the previous spring, and Charlotte was well along in another pregnancy. Game remained scarce, forcing them to kill some of their horses for meat. As they neared the Divide, Thompson had a scare: "One of my horses nearly crushing my children to death with his load being badly put on, which I mistook for being vicious, I shot him on the spot and rescued my little ones." They stripped the meat from the dead horse, then pressed on. The next day they marched up very close to Howse Pass:

> June 20th Monday A frosty Morning, but very fine Day. by 6½ A.M. we were ready and set off . . . unloaded our Horses to refresh them & ourselves – at 3 P.M. we reloaded, but missing my little Daughter & nowhere finding her, we concluded she was drowned & all of us set about finding her – we searched all the Embarrass [logjams] in the River but to no purpose. At length Mr. McDonald found her track going upwards. We searched all about & at length thank God at 8½ P.M. found her about 1 Mile off, against a Bank of Snow.

This would have been either seven-year-old Fanny or, more

likely, two-year-old Emma. These perilous days on the way up the Blaeberry mark two of the very few appearances of Thompson's children in the field journals.

With no further mishaps, the pack train made its way over the pass the next day and on to Kootenay Plains, where it was met by James McMillan and five Iroquois free hunters. Following Thompson's suggestion, the partners had hired the Iroquois to hunt beaver across the mountains and had equipped them with two steel traps each. Steel traps were a relatively new innovation and, when baited with castorum from a beaver's musk gland, had proved a deadly efficient way to capture beaver. Thompson accepted some fresh sheep meat from the Iroquois, then arranged to take their boat as well when he found that winter snows had crushed his own cached canoe beyond repair. The Saskatchewan was running fast, and as they flew downstream, Thompson had to give up all attempts at taking compass readings. He did note that the women went ashen as the voyageurs ran the canoe through the swift rapids.

They stopped to shoot a bison and enjoyed their first meal of fresh buffalo in over a year. On June 25 they camped just below the empty Rocky Mountain House, where they found Jaco Finlay tenting across the river. Jaco was working the area as a free hunter, and whatever grievances Thompson harbored about the trail work of the previous summer, he was always willing to buy furs. By the next evening, he had arrived at Boggy Hall, a new post in the Fort des Prairies Department—trade houses seemed to spring up like mushrooms along the Saskatchewan.

Charlotte's brother Patrick Small was working at Boggy Hall, so Thompson dropped his family there and kept right on going east. By August 2, sometimes paddling all night, he and his men had made it all the way down the Saskatchewan and through Lake Winnipeg and Lake of the Woods to Rainy Lake House. The North West Company had set up this supply depot for the far-flung Athabasca canoes, which could

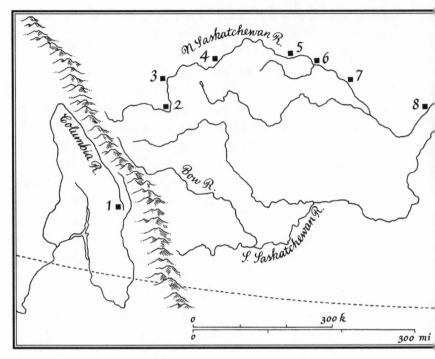

SHIPPING THE FURS EAST

never make it back and forth to Fort William during the open
season, and now it would also service David Thompson's
newly designated Columbia Department. Thompson's friends
Donald McTavish and James Hughes were already at Rainy
Lake when he arrived, along with several other North West
partners. Here, if he hadn't heard about it already, Thompson
would have learned of the death of Duncan McGillivray the
previous April. Less than forty years of age, McGillivray had
been one of the most vigorous proponents of Thompson's
Columbia venture and had spent the last few months of his
life petitioning the British government to send a ship to the
mouth of Columbia to protect the North West Company's interests. In a letter written shortly after he heard the news,
Thompson said that he had named the Flat Bows' river after
William and Duncan McGillivray, "in honor of the family

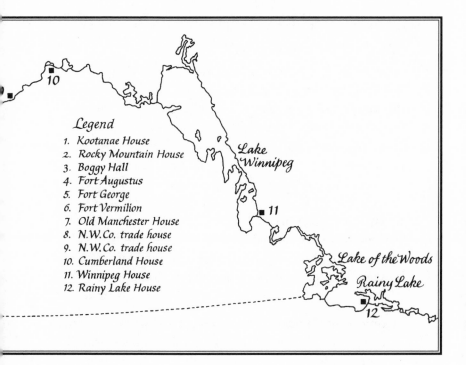

Legend
1. Kootanae House
2. Rocky Mountain House
3. Boggy Hall
4. Fort Augustus
5. Fort George
6. Fort Vermilion
7. Old Manchester House
8. N.W. Co. trade house
9. N.W. Co. trade house
10. Cumberland House
11. Winnipeg House
12. Rainy Lake House

who may be justly attributed the knowledge and commerce we have of the Columbia, one of [them] as is now no more, yet sacred be his memory." The surveyor didn't say what he did with the four Lake Indian bows he had brought with him for Duncan's artifact collection.

Thompson stayed at Rainy Lake for two days, just long enough to unload his furs and pack up new trade goods. By October 3 he and his two supply canoes had made it back to Boggy Hall, where Charlotte had recently given birth to a baby boy, named John. The family did not travel west with Thompson that fall; it was obviously easier for them to remain on the Saskatchewan with Charlotte's brother than to labor across the pass again. Trying to beat the onset of winter, Thompson left Boggy Hall after another two-day stop and moved quickly upriver. While his men dragged the loaded canoe upstream, he hunted ahead on horseback, and one day he brought down a big cow elk.

> As she was dying the Canoes came up, the Men began skinning her, and one man cut off her head, upon this the Deer arose and for half a minute stood on her feet ... The Men became Frightened, said she was a devil, and would have nothing more to do with her ... I cut a piece of meat for my supper, put it in the Canoe, and marched on; when we camped, I expected my piece of meat for supper, but found they had tossed it into the River, and my servant said to the Men, "Does he wish to eat a piece of the devil, if he does, it is not me that will cook it." Instances of this nature are known to the Indians, who call them Seepanee, that is strong of life.
>
> *Narrative*

Strong of life himself that season, Thompson pressed on through rain and sleet and the season's first snowstorm. The bad weather forced the party to lay by for a day, during which the men made socks, mittens, and winter jackets for themselves. The next morning they cleared the snow off the canoes and tracked on up the river, but layers of ice began to form on the birch bark, turning the boats into "unwieldy Masses of Snow and Ice." Finan McDonald and James McMillan came to the rescue with horses from Kootenay Plains, and after a day's shuffling of supplies the weather moderated and the pack train set off. A pair of buffalo cows ambled ahead of the party all the way up the Howse River and across the Divide, and the Columbia brigade made it back to Kootanae House by November 10. Their supply run to Rainy Lake, a round trip of over three thousand miles, had taken a little more than five months.

The day after their arrival, Thompson was hanging new doors on his warehouse when Jaco Finlay and his family stopped by with the five Iroquois free hunters. They had already trapped eight packs of pelts, and after James McMillan took some rum to their camp that evening, "they drank and fought the whole night" in celebration. Thompson spent the next two weeks refurbishing the post: he mended the chimneys, put up his bed, and whitewashed his room. Finan McDonald and four voyageurs had gone down to the Kootenay Lake country to set up an auxiliary post for the winter trade, and in late November the clerk returned with discouraging news: his canoe was frozen fast in the ice on the Kootenai River. He rounded up a dozen horses and went back south with two men to try again. They made it only as far as Kootenai Falls before the horses were "knocked up" in the deep snow, and they decided to set up two leather tents and hunker down for the winter nearby.

For his part, Thompson passed the cold months of 1808–09 at Kootanae House in a state of relative tranquillity. "My mode of passing the day is to 10 A.M. writing my journal, calculations etc. To 2 P.M. Exercise in walking, Riding etc. From thence Indian & horse affairs – in the evening my Letters on the Country." He made drawings of the east slope of the Rocky Mountains and found time to indulge his interest in the local bird life. He watched magpies gather around open holes in the frozen lake in search of fish fry, "of which they make great havock." The men were working on another ice house for meat, the ravens "most cordially helping them finish." On a clear sharp day in January, Thompson walked over to a large gully and came upon a flock of what, from his description, sound like pine grosbeaks: "the Cocks of a beautiful brick Red in the Head Back breast & Belly & some parts of the wings – with stripes of white in the wings & lower part of the Belly – Thighs and the rest a blueish color – three claws before & 1 behind." He watched the wary trumpeter and tundra swans that wintered around the lakes and succeeded in bagging one of each. "The former is a large species . . . weighing thirty-two to thirty-five pounds; the inside fat filled a common dinner plate."

Thompson also spent time chasing after some of the feral

horses that grazed in the foothills above the lakes. The Kootenais told him that these horses had once belonged to the many members of their tribe who had been wiped out by smallpox. The French Canadians called them *marrons* (chestnuts), their slang word for something domestic gone wild. Upon learning that Jaco Finlay had captured and tamed eighteen of them, Thompson and Bercier decided to try their luck. On the first excursion they tracked the *marrons* with their most long-winded horses on "a wild steeple-chase, down hills and up others." The next day they again dashed after them on their swiftest steeds. Two of the mustangs fell dead, but they were able to hobble a third. "I passed my hand over his nostrils, the smell of which was so disagreeable that its nostrils and the skin of its head became contorted." On the third day he led the mustang back to the fort, where it was broken to the bit and saddle and before long came to find the smell of its captor's hand agreeable.

On the same day that Thompson caught up with his first *marron* stallion, Michel Boulard and Augustin Boisverd arrived from the Flat Bow country, where they had been trading. They brought with them a letter from Finan McDonald and must have also carried the sextant that Thompson had left at the Kootenai camp the previous spring—on the next clear night, the surveyor was out taking observations for the first time in months. Boisverd had accumulated a handsome total of eighteen packs of furs, and apparently had acquired a Kootenai wife as well. Most of the voyageurs had native wives—they were the ones taking care of the endless busywork that kept the operation going—but they were rarely mentioned in fur trade journals. Boisverd's "country wife," however, would become well-known to both natives and whites over the next few years.

HER STORY BEGINS down in the Flat Bow country around Kootenay Lake. Her given name was One-Standing-Lodge-

Pole-Woman, and she was apparently a healthy girl, large and heavy-boned. In the 1930s, Kootenai elders told anthropologist Claude Schaeffer that as she reached maturity she wanted to marry, but no man showed any interest in her. They said that Lodge-Pole-Woman was a teenager when white traders first came to her country, and when they left she went away to live with one of them. Her people thought that the girl soon grew unhappy and was ready to return home, but it was more than a year before she reappeared at her tribal camp. This part of her story fits with Boulard and Boisverd's visit to the Flat Bow country, and with David Thompson's memory of his first meeting with the woman as Boisverd's wife. When he wrote about her two years later, he did not remember her fondly—her conduct had become so loose, he said, that he had asked Boisverd to send her back to her friends.

When Lodge-Pole-Woman did return to her own people, she announced that her white husband had transformed her into a man. She changed her name to Gone-to-the-Spirits and began to dance out the story of her sexual transformation for everyone she met. She wore men's shirts, with leggings and breechcloth; she began to carry a gun along with a bow and arrows. It wasn't long before she was claiming to possess great spiritual power. In the Kootenai scheme of the world, a person might claim such power but would not use it without a need. Some of the Kootenai people believed that she had lost her mind, while others, especially the younger women, grew afraid of her.

The voyageurs used the word *berdache* to describe a person who chose to live out the role of the opposite sex. The notion was not an unfamiliar one to the North American tribes, but almost all of the recorded berdache stories deal with a man living as a woman. Now Gone-to-the-Spirits declared that since she was a man, she wanted to marry a woman. She approached several available girls and was rebuffed each time. Some people mocked the berdache, but stories began to circulate that she would use her new powers to harm any girl who might refuse her.

After a time Gone-to-the-Spirits found a woman who had been abandoned by her husband and was willing to share a tent. The two became constant companions, and curious Kootenais tried to catch the new "wife" alone to discover the intimate details of their relationship. Gone-to-the-Spirits' companion only laughed at these intrusions, but a rumor went around that the berdache had stitched together a leather phallus. There was also talk of jealousy and unfaithfulness. Loud arguments were heard between the two, and soon Gone-to-the-Spirits was openly beating her wife. The berdache had taken up gambling, and in one costly session she lost a bow, quiver, and canoe. Her wife, upset at the loss, picked up a bow that lay nearby, shot an arrow through the side of the canoe, and left her "husband" for good.

Around that same time, Gone-to-the-Spirits accompanied her brother on a raid to capture horses. The party made a long trip without locating the enemy camp they were looking for. Over the course of their journey, they had to cross several streams and creeks, and they would always undress for the crossing and carry their clothes across on their heads. The berdache's brother noticed that his sister was holding back at each crossing, and hid himself to watch her at the next ford. In the middle of the stream he saw his sister standing in water well below her waist. She was clearly still a woman. When she noticed her brother, Gone-to-the-Spirits quickly squatted down in the water to hide herself, pretending that her foot was twisted between two rocks. A while later she caught up with the raiding party, complaining of a sprained ankle.

When the party arrived at their home camp, Gone-to-the-Spirits announced that she was changing her name once again. Her injury had forced her to sit down in the stream, she said, as her own brother had witnessed. From this day on she wished to be known as Qánqon kámek klaúla (Sitting-in-the-Water-Grizzly). Her brother said to his friends that he was going to call her Qánqon instead, a derisive nickname that referred to the squatting posture she had assumed when he spied her in the middle of the stream.

Shortly after the raid, Sitting-in-the-Water-Grizzly found a woman from the marshlands around the south end of Kootenay Lake who was willing to be her new wife. They hadn't lived together long before the berdache became jealous, and one night the two began to quarrel. The quarrel turned into a noisy beating that roused the berdache's brother from his nearby lodge. He came out and denounced her to the village in a loud voice, saying that he knew her sex had not been changed, and that was why he would only call her Qánqon. After her brother's revelation, all the Kootenai people called the woman Qánqon, but she endured their ridicule and continued to camp with her tribe. She associated with a number of other women, but there were no more stories of arguments or beatings. Finally she took a long journey with one of her companions, and was gone from her people for several years.

WHILE RUMORS about Qánqon circulated around the Kootenai country, the man who had booted her out of his trade house was himself the subject of discussion on the other side of the Divide. James Bird, the Hudson's Bay Company agent at Edmonton House, next door to Fort Augustus, kept an eye on the rival furs that floated past him and an ear to the whispers of the voyageurs. Bird had been trying to decide whether to risk sending a party of his own across the Divide, and followed Thompson's movements with interest. He was not quite sure what to make of the latest reports: "The expedition across the mountains does not seem to be quite relinquished by the NW Co [North West Company] though their success last year appears not to have been encouraging."

In February of 1809, North West Company trader Alexander Henry, wintering near Bird on the Saskatchewan River, offered an updated reckoning of his partner's position in a letter of his own:

We have not heard from Mr. Thompson since last
October when he was taken in the Ice in the first ridge
of the Mountains about a month's journey short of his
wintering ground. He was then preparing to proceed
with the property on horses and was in hopes of reaching his destination in due time. The snow in the mountains is the only obstacle he had to surmount; once over
that he comes to a warm climate & a fine country, when
all his troubles are at an end. He gives us great hopes of
making at least 40 packs of beaver.

Forty packs of beaver, almost two tons of furs, would be a re-
spectable haul—enough to attract the attention of James Bird
and the Hudson's Bay Company. Henry remarked that:
"Should the Philosopher David Thompson succeed in
making good returns in Beaver on the Columbia, we may rest
assured that Bird will attempt sending them the ensuing
summer."

When Henry spoke of David Thompson as the
"Philosopher," he was paying tribute to his unusual status
among the furmen. Thompson was an explorer, making a historic push west. He was a trader, bent on good returns. And
he was also a philosopher—that is, in the usage of the time,
someone well versed in a particular area of natural science,
such as botany, zoology, or, in this case, astronomy. He was a
man who could navigate by the stars and chart a course for
others to follow.

CHAPTER SIX

TOUCHING
THE CIRCLE

SPRING 1809–SPRING 1810

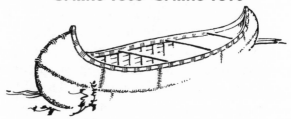

A S MIGRATING TUNDRA swans passed above Kootanae House in March of 1809, Thompson finished drawing Mount Nelson and began preparing for spring. He sent men out on the never-ending search for good birch rind and dispatched James McMillan down the Kootenay River to help Finan McDonald bring up his winter trade. He gave Boulard and his wife supplies and sent them south to pass the summer with the Flat Bows at Kootenay Lake. While his men pulled meat out of their glacier to make pemmican and began pressing the furs into packs, he put a handle on his hoe and planted some turnip seeds. Everything was almost ready for their trip east by late April, when their final preparations were interrupted by sickness in the camp.

> APRIL 24 MONDAY A very fine hot day...Passed a sad
> night with Lussier's wife, who is dying.
> APRIL 25 TUESDAY A fine day. At 2 A.M. it pleased
> Heaven that Lussier's wife should depart this Life –
> she has left four small Children – the youngest only 6

months old, which much distresses me. At 1 P.M. the men returned & we buried the poor woman & take the best care we can of her Children.

A few days later the Nor'Westers left Kootanae House with their fur packs. On the way to the Blaeberry River, they stopped at Jaco Finlay's camp and made arrangements to leave Lussier's children in the care of Jaco and his wife. Thompson spent the next two weeks ferrying horses down-river to the portage trail and sowing turnip seeds at promising sites along the way. He set up camp near the mouth of the Blaeberry to wait for Finan McDonald, and there he met Martin and Jacques, two of the Iroquois who had spent the winter trapping with Jaco. They had been "on discovery," looking for beaver to the north on a section of the Columbia that Thompson had not yet seen. Martin and Jacques reported bad rapids, few beaver, and generally unfavorable country. They traded Thompson a good beaver and some bear fat, then collected the pelts they had stored at Jaco's camp and brought them back to Thompson's tent. He gave them part of their payment in rum, and somehow an argument ensued. "Martin insolent & dislocated my right thumb in thrashing him which will render me incapable of doing anything for a few days."

Two days later he was able to use his thumb enough to hobble horses and write a little, and that evening Finan McDonald and James McMillan finally arrived from the south, carrying thirty-two packs of good furs. These, combined with twenty-two packs from around Kootanae House plus a half-pack of the skins of white goats, swans, and a large grizzly bear, meant that the Columbia Department had more than met Thompson's projection, and he was pleased: "Thank God for this great Success."

He set off as soon as possible for his trip across the mountains, topping Howse Pass with relative ease and arriving at Fort Augustus in late June. James Hughes was manning the post, and Charlotte and the children must have been in residence there with him. Hughes was family now, for his daughter had married Charlotte's brother Patrick Small. In the flurry of drying and re-pressing furs, finishing out two new canoes for the trip east, and giving the men a dance, it was three days before Thompson discovered that over the course of the winter he had somehow lost a day. "June 27 Tuesday. A fine day . . . The Gentlemen here hold this to be 28th June Wednesday."

Thompson sent James McMillan on to Rainy Lake with the fur packs and spent the next three weeks at Fort Augustus, visiting with his family and catching up on news. Here he probably learned that the previous summer, Simon Fraser had completed his run down the Tacoutche Tesse (later named the Fraser River) to its mouth just above the 49th parallel—three full degrees too far north to be the Columbia River. Alexander Mackenzie's dotted line had been wrong: the Tacoutche Tesse and the Columbia were not the same river after all. The Tacoutche Tesse would not work as a trade route, either—its lower canyon was even wilder than the upper section that had turned Mackenzie away. Any hope for a navigable path to the sea now lay with the still unexplored Columbia. But apparently the North West Company no longer considered tracing that river a high priority. As Thompson later summarized the situation: "1809. The Partners of the Coy. allow of no further discoveries but only trading posts upon a small scale, and I have means for nothing else."

But Thompson was to prove himself a master at working within tight limits. As a partner in a profit-sharing company, he had to bring in furs, and his movements for the next year combine the rounds of a determined trader with an explorer's steady advance. During his two years across the Divide, through assiduous questioning and many stick-drawn maps, he had gleaned information from every tribe he met. He had shaped a coherent sense of the tangled geography of the

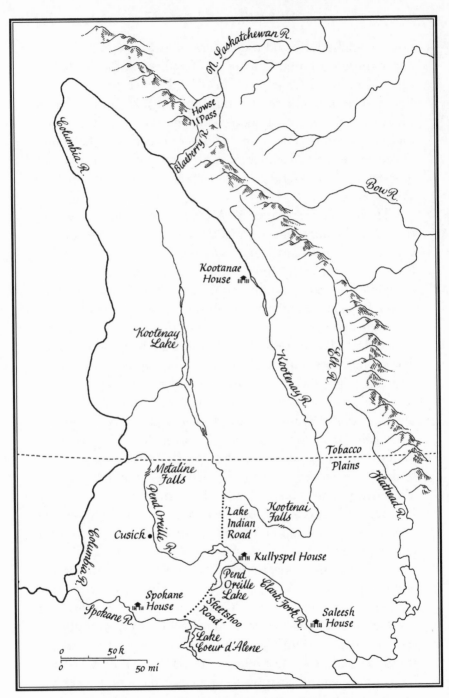

TRADE ROUTE OF THE COLUMBIA BRIGADE

region, and knew where he wanted to build new posts to expand the trade and prove to the partners that the Columbia Department was economically viable.

Hoping to get a jump on winter, Thompson and Finan McDonald left Fort Augustus in mid-July with a few supplies and headed west on their familiar route up the Saskatchewan. A few miles above the old Rocky Mountain House, the surveyor experienced "a violent palpitation of the Heart" and had one of his men bleed him for relief. They traveled on through Kootenay Plains and soon afterward met Joseph Howse of the Hudson's Bay Company, returning from a quick scouting trip up into the mountains. As Alexander Henry had predicted, the Bay Company was preparing to make a move. Thompson breakfasted with his rival, gave him a letter to deliver to James Hughes back at Fort Augustus, and continued on his way. Just across the Height of Land, the Nor'Westers met Jaco Finlay and his wife and children, all traveling on foot. Two weeks earlier a group of Piegans had crossed the mountains and raided their camp near Kootanae House, robbing them of their whole string of horses and most of their personal property. Thompson loaned Jaco a few horses to carry his family, and the Finlays turned around and continued down the Blaeberry with the Nor'Westers.

The surveyor had decided to abandon Kootanae House for the present and concentrate on the more populated area farther south. Moving quickly, he and his men passed by the empty trading post, portaged across Canal Flats, and launched their canoe in the Kootenay River again. As they traveled downstream, they frequently noticed places where the Piegan horse thieves had forded the river with Jaco's animals only a few days before. Their tracks finally turned east at the Elk River, which marked one of their "War Roads" across the mountains; after that, Thompson and his party breathed a little easier. At Tobacco Plains they stopped to check on the progress of a garden Finan McDonald had planted the previous spring; they found "nothing of the Peas, the turnips only in Leaves & their very small roots worm-eaten." Five or six stalks of barley were faring well.

Near the top of Kootenai Falls, the men stayed for a day waiting for Michel Boulard, who had spent the summer in the Flat Bow country and was supposed to meet them here with horses to carry their cargo around the falls. When he didn't show up, Finan McDonald went off to search for him and instead found several Kootenais who agreed to come and help them across the portage. After working their way through the tight canyon, the party continued downriver to a trail they called the "Great Road of the Flat Heads," where Thompson dispatched a man to find some horses to carry them overland. A week later sixteen Flathead men arrived with mounts to collect the furmen and their baggage. Everyone got busy widening the "Great Road" and headed south.

On September 9 the pack train arrived at present-day Pend Oreille Lake, where a large camp of several different tribes welcomed the Nor'Westers with berries, fresh *chevreuil*, and dried salmon. The next day Thompson and two Flathead men explored around the lake until they found a location that he deemed acceptable for a trade house, even though "the soil was light, and had no blue clay, which is so very necessary for plaistering between the logs of the house and especially the roof." His crew got to work setting out fishnets in the lake and digging postholes in the rocky ground while he traded with the natives who kept arriving with quantities of furs. The men dubbed the new post Kullyspel House, after the local people's name for themselves (spelled Kalispel today). The French Canadians called this tribe the Pend Oreilles, while Thompson sometimes referred to them as the Ear Bobs or Ear Pendants. According to several sources, Finan McDonald married a daughter of a Kullyspel chief.

When Jaco Finlay and his family wandered into the new post on September 21, the men were hauling in trout and getting ready to roof the warehouse; Finan McDonald hung the doors in the middle of a thunderstorm. A week later, leaving his men to frame a second floor in the warehouse, Thompson set off west on horseback: "My view was to see if we cannot change our Route to cross the Mountains, as at present we are too much exposed to the incursions of the Peeagan Indians." By this time, the surveyor had figured out the general course of the upper Columbia and knew that he had built Kootanae House either on the big river itself or on a main branch of it. Now he hoped to find a route that would follow its northerly loop and bypass the country frequented by Piegan raiders. Accompanied by his man Beaulieu, he rode across the top of the lake and followed a good trail down the Pend Oreille River through yellowing leaves, taking meals from among the migrant ducks, geese, swans, cranes, and plovers that covered the water. The second day out, the surveyor pulled out his compass and found that the glass had fallen off and the needle had been lost; for the rest of the trip he had to eyeball their courses.

After four days they reached the extensive marshy plain around the modern town of Cusick, Washington. The friendly Kalispel Indians camped there were so completely untouched by white culture that they lacked iron tools of any sort, even an ax. There were plenty of beaver about, which the Kalispels killed for their winter clothing, but they had nothing more than pointed sticks and snares to hunt them with. One of their elders presented Thompson with dried salmon, a basket of camas bulbs, and two cakes made from camas roots that had been pounded to a pulp and then baked on hot stones. The surveyor reciprocated with tobacco and a steel and flints for starting fires. Then he asked his usual question: "I enquired of the Road before me. They say there is only another Fall to go to the Columbia of which they drew the Chart." This was good news, and very different from what he had been told by the Flat Bows, who had described a series of heavy falls that required a long portage of one and a half days. Thompson indicated to the Kalispels that he would like to go and have a look for himself.

They told him that the trail downstream along the Pend
Oreille was no good for horses, but they did offer to loan him
a pine-bark canoe and a guide. Thompson, Beaulieu, and the
Kalispel guide put in the river next morning in a drizzling
rain, in what turned out to be a very leaky canoe. At first the
river was wide and placid, but as they proceeded it narrowed
and picked up speed. Around midmorning on the second day,
Thompson asked how far it was to the falls, and the guide
confessed that he had never been on this stretch of water
before. The surveyor reluctantly turned around, his appointment with the Columbia postponed again.

"THAT'S WHAT I like about those old guys," said Steve
Zender from the bow of the canoe. "They'd take off down
some unknown river to see where it was going, and I mean a
bedroll and a compass was about it. We go out for one night
and fill up a truck with air mattresses and hot dogs and—
whoooa, look out to your right there. Deadhead."

Zender feathered his paddle to ease up on a fat fir log that
was bobbing vertically in the water. It slipped away from his
oar and dawdled in the current, pogoing up and down in the
murky Pend Oreille River. Steve is the state wildlife biologist
for northeastern Washington, and he was out to check a bald
eagle nest on one of the river's grassy islands. From my seat in
the stern he had a dark, compact presence, and he approached
his job with dogged concentration. Leaning forward on his
knees, he studied the deadhead to see where the river's slow
current was pushing it.

We had put in just below Cusick, near the spot where
David Thompson had his first taste of dried camas roots.
Camas flowers still turn these bottomlands blue each May,
and the pumping gulps of bitterns fill up the low, marshy ex-
panse. The wildest of the downriver canyons that stopped
Thompson's progress toward the Columbia have been

dammed, and the edges of the river are dotted with pilings for yarding up sawlogs. Some of the disused poles are topped with the ragged twigs of osprey nests or nesting cans set up for Canada geese. Steve looked downstream and pointed to a cluster of spars where a handful of cormorants, sharing the oily creosote color of their perches, stood on tiptoe and spread out their stubby wings to dry.

"Don't you wonder what these pole-sitters did before we stuck poles in the mud?" he asked. "I mean, do you think they really belong here?" As a matter of fact, cormorants have always been a part of the local scene. The Kootenais attributed weather-changing powers to these long-necked birds. During hard winters, they said, you could shoot a cormorant through the head, fetch the body and dip it in an unfrozen pool, then throw water from the pool three times to the sky. If after all that the dead bird was thrust into a snowbank, warm chinook winds were sure to blow up soon.

The eagle nest Steve wanted to check was a bulky pile of sticks atop a tall yellow pine. While the male sat in a roosting tree about a quarter of a mile off, the female flew circles between nest and roost and us. We tied up our canoe and, using an alder thicket for cover, quietly worked our way close enough to watch one jet-black chick stand up for a look around. We stared through our binoculars until we were sure there weren't two chicks, then quickly backed away to stroll down the gravelly shore of the island and see how the ospreys at the south end were faring. On the way we smelled dead suckers—David Thompson's carp—along the beach, and Steve commiserated with the explorers who had to eat such ugly fish. A male bobolink uncoiled its long, metallic song across the field above.

When some willows blocked our way, we scrambled up onto a rolling field of timothy grass well beyond the whistling eagles. There was raven noise coming from a stand of cottonwoods ahead, so we aimed for the trees and talked about where we were. Steve said that later in the summer, when the

Corps of Engineers drew the river down, the island's owner could drive a tractor over from the mainland and cut the grass for hay. The place was not a full-time island, but it stayed separate and safe at just the right time for the eagles.

Then we walked right up on a spotted fawn in the grass. Dry and pretty, it lay so still that at first we thought it was trusting its camouflage to protect it. When it finally stretched up on its front legs, afraid, the line of spots on its neck winked like eyes. It bawled a bit, then got quiet. When we looked around we could see where it had been flopping through the timothy, and that it was exhausted from pulling itself along by the forelegs. Its hind legs didn't work at all. The only sign of injury was a slash beneath its left hip. Steve guessed it had gotten caught on a fence, but I spent some time imagining an eagle attack. Either way there was nothing for it: the fawn was paralyzed, and the ravens were all around. Steve snapped off a stout fir branch and whacked the little deer across the snout. It went down immediately, breathing easy, and I knelt on its chest the way trappers do when they want to protect a pelt.

Canoeing back across the river, we came up on the deadhead again, still wallowing in the middle of the current. Steve thumped at the butt end of it with his palm and considered the fiberglass body of his canoe. "This thing's dangerous," he announced. "Think she'll pull?"

We managed to loop a line over one end, then found that we had harnessed ourselves into a very awkward paddle, with the current dipping and snapping the log against the weight of the boat. Steve joked about good deeds, but the hard row reminded him of those early fur traders again, how they lived out here, all year, with nothing extra.

"Those guys amaze me," he repeated. "Do you think they were that much tougher than us? I mean, I like being out as much as anybody, but after a few days I'm ready to go home and get a hot shower."

SCRUBBING UP was a luxury that occasionally occupied David Thompson's mind as well—his supply order for the previous season had included twenty pounds of soap, "for without soap, there is no effective cleanliness; this we know very well, who too often experience the want of it." One of the things that impressed him about the tribes he had met on the west side was that they were "as neat in their persons as circumstances will allow." He found the ones around Kullyspel House industrious as well. When he and Beaulieu got back to their new post on October 6, Finan McDonald had just finished trading with a band of Coeur d'Alenes (Pointed Hearts) for three horses and almost two hundred pounds of good furs.

By the end of October, Thompson had met James McMillan coming from Fort William with trade goods and led him back to Kullyspel House. The surveyor had decided that the Flatheads to the east (whom he also called the Saleesh) needed a post of their own, and that it would be a good idea to reach them before the Bay Company or the Americans did. Leaving Finan McDonald in charge at Kullyspel House, he and McMillan led a pack train up the Clark Fork River along the "Saleesh Road to the Buffalo" to a location near the modern town of Thompson Falls, Montana. There, opposite the mouth of a fine creek, they built Saleesh House. The surrounding open country promised plenty of game, but during that first week in November nobody could find any food. The weather was rainy, and when McMillan and Thompson did get out, they didn't do much to improve their situation.

> November 12th Sunday. A fine mild day – As we are all quite hungry and much in want, Mr. McMillan, Forcier and myself went a hunting but without Success. By the accidental going off of his Gun Mr. McMillan had both

the forefingers of his Hands shot through by a Ball &
much lacerated with the Powder, both of his Fingers are
broke & seemingly will with difficulty be kept from
falling off – I dressed them the best I could.

Two days later Jaco Finlay and his wife showed up with
twenty-eight beaver tails and forty pounds of dried meat.
Steady work on Saleesh House resumed, and eight daily entries about meals and construction matters passed before
Thompson returned to the matter of his clerk's damaged
digits. "Mr. McMillan's forefinger of the left hand having a
bad appearance & no hopes of its joining with the stump I
separated it."

Saleesh House was on a route used by several tribes on
their way to hunt buffalo or trade with the Flatheads, and it
proved to be a magnet that attracted its own diverse community. Thompson was still unpacking his baggage when a man
whom the voyageurs had nicknamed Le Bon Vieux (Good
Old Man) stopped by with his band, on their way to join a
large hunting camp upriver. Ugly Head arrived with his com-
patriots Large Kidney and Deceitful Dog at the end of
November, and all three stayed to hunt for the company.
Several groups of Kalispels and Kootenais stopped to smoke
and trade on the way to their winter camps in the Flathead
Valley. Six free hunters, independent trappers who had
crossed the mountains on their own and were working beaver
in the area, came in to get supplies. Hoping to bring in tribes
from even farther afield, Thompson sent Boulard and
Beaulieu to spread the word of his new trade house.

The rest of the men continued to work on the post compound. While they covered the walls and roofs of the buildings with clay, Thompson built himself a desk, fashioned a
cupboard, and put in paper windowpanes for want of the
parchment skins he usually used. On December 19 the men
split out rough planks for their beds and slept in their own
house for the first night. Over the next few days, warm

weather brought rain, and all the buildings started to leak. Thompson traded for some mats that the local women wove out of rushes and covered the roofs with them, but they didn't do much good. "December 24 Sunday – not withstanding the Matts the Rain is so incessant & smart that the Houses drip everywhere, especially the Warehouse in which hardly anything is dry. Our Matts flew off with the Storm."

Thompson found the bands that clustered around his post most compatible; they in turn dubbed him Koo-koo-Sint, Star-Looker, and he gained a reputation among them for both integrity and curious interests. One of his interests was their language; he made a long list of English words and phrases and began filling in his phonetic approximations of the Flathead equivalents:

What do you say?	*Stem soon annouer*
Where is my horse?	*Chane sin chits arks kar*
I speak the truth	*Oa na uf*
Where are you going?	*Et chin oo e*
You have lost it	*Host a*
What do you call it?	*Stem thloo, tarn oo*

Among the families tenting near Saleesh House were two tribal leaders—Thompson called them Cartier and the Orator—who often came over in the evening for a smoke. In his *Narrative*, Thompson tells of a February night when the two chiefs entered wearing such grave expressions that he asked if there were rumors of war afoot. In reply, the Orator asked if the white men knew that his people's penalty for adultery was death for both parties. It turned out that the Orator had a married daughter, and one of the furmen had apparently been bringing beads and rings to her while the men of her family were out hunting. Thompson looked around in surprise at his voyageurs—"the men and myself were every day too much fatigued to think of women"—then noticed that one of them had slipped from the room. The surveyor told the Orator that he wouldn't think of protecting the offender, that the chiefs could deal with him however they thought fit. But if they killed him, he would need a strong warrior as a replacement to return east with him and pick up more guns and steel. The chiefs looked at each other and said that they could not send one of their men so far away among strange people where he might be killed. Thompson replied:

> Very well, then if you kill my man I cannot return to you, but shall stay with the Peeagans, your enemies; then what is to be done exclaimed the Orator. I replied, let him live this time, and as you are noted for being a good gelder of Horses; if this Man ever again enters your Tent, geld him, but let him live; at this proposition they laughed . . . after smoking they retired in good humor.
>
> *Narrative*

Toward the end of February, Thompson and Michel Boulard started out on a winter sojourn in search of birch bark for two canoes. Along the way they stopped to visit the Old Chief and his Kootenai band, who were hunting in the valley where the Clark Fork and Flathead Rivers meet. A few days later word came that Thompson was needed at a large Flathead camp nearby. He and Boulard immediately set off and arrived to find a group of white free hunters and several Kootenais waiting for them. These men had with them the property of an American trapper named Courter who had recently been killed in another Piegan attack somewhere in the vicinity. Thompson took responsibility for settling affairs as best he could, giving out credits to one Kootenai for rescuing Courter's body and to another for helping with the burial. He purchased all of the trapper's furs that had been brought in, even though they were of poor quality, and paid the hunters who had loaned horses to the rescue effort. But beyond saying that Courter was an American, Thompson provides no information on what had happened. Some historians think that Courter must have been Charles Courtin, a French Canadian naturalized as an American citizen who was known to have trapped with other American free hunters far up the Missouri River. In his *Narrative*, Thompson added that he had spent the rest of the afternoon with the Flatheads, asking about birch rind and discussing the fatal folly of those American trappers who were hunting around the headwaters of the Missouri. They had a habit of wandering about in Piegan and Blackfeet territory alone or in small parties and setting their traps without asking permission, imagining that "the Natives of the Plains were all skulkers in the woods, and never dared shew themselves on open ground, and they suffered accordingly, being frequently attacked in open ground and killed."

Thompson was not so naive about the Piegans, whom he characterized as "those ever watchful people, ever alive to what is passing," and whom events of the last five years had caused him to consider as adversaries rather than friends. He never underestimated their strength or volatility, but he knew that much of their power lay in intimidation, and he encouraged the west-side tribes to stand up to them. The second week in March found him on another visit to the big Flathead camp, and while he was there Jaco Finlay rode in to report a suspicious-looking group of horsemen nearby. A hundred men quickly gathered up their new guns and iron-tipped arrows and rode off to do battle. The invaders turned out to be the Old Chief with a Kootenai hunting party, but Thompson was gratified by the quick response of the Flatheads.

He was also gratified by the results of his trading that winter. He had chosen a good location for Saleesh House, in a rich beaver area where several tribes traditionally wintered. He had found natives he could work with and trust, who had kept him supplied with dried meat and pemmican. The growing number of free hunters in the area had helped him accumulate an impressive haul of furs. Thompson liked this rich territory, especially the stretch to the east, along the Flathead River:

> The impression of my mind is, from the formation of the country and it's climate, it's extensive Meadows and fine Forests, watered by countless Brooks and Rills of pure water, that it will become the abode of civilized Man, whether Natives or other people; part of it will bear rich crops of grain, the greater part will be pastoral, as it is admirably adapted to the rearing of Cattle and Sheep.
>
> *Narrative*

FROM THE TOP of a lookout ridge above that same section of the Flathead River, I scanned the slopes for animals poised in the grass. At my feet, sharp sunbeams lit up a woolly slope of balsamroot sunflower; to the northeast the ice-scraped walls of the Mission Range shimmered in the summer air. This is a good place to watch for hawks or whistle up a ground squirrel. It's also a good place to get a feel for just how close the country looks today to the way David Thompson predicted it would almost two centuries ago. The land remains under the care of the Flathead Indians, and over the years the tribe has bucked several proposals for dams within its territory. The river still flows freely through the flats, and beside it farmers grow oats and barley. The hills that roll up in huge swells are dry but grassy, spotted with cattle and sheep.

Along the western base of the ridge, a little tributary named after Jaco Finlay creeps secretly in the shade of cottonwoods and willows, then bursts with reflections as it meets the Flathead River out in the open. Together they wind west across the foot of the reservation to pour into the Clark Fork forty miles downstream. That was the trade route, a path Jaco must have followed many times: a day's canoe ride east to Saleesh House, then another day or two downstream to the Kullyspel post.

Back in my car, I drove the other way, along the main road north, and soon passed a giant sign announcing the many attractions of Doug Allard's Flathead Trading Post. The parking lot crawled with tourists and revelers on their way to the annual Pow Wow of the Confederated Salish and Kootenai tribes—a grouping that includes most of the peoples who lived around David Thompson's west-side trade houses. Doug Allard sat on a wooden bench on the front porch of his substantial peeled-log structure, comfortable in his position between a poster commemorating the Declaration of Independence and another announcing the Pow Wow Rodeo Finals. His long ponytail shone raven in the sun; the broad features of his face complemented his powerful bronzed hands. A big eagle chain-sawed from a yellow pine butt guarded the rail beside him, its vanilla scent still hanging fresh in the air.

At the moment Allard was talking about farming. A friend of his had just spent a whole week trying to make hay, riding the back of a baler fiddling with knotters that refused to tie. "Couple hundred bales for a whole week's work," he laughed. "Pitiful." Allard flashed his teeth as the stream of people flowed past. A stretch van with Washington plates slid up to the railing and deposited a contingent of native women. Allard began hooting about their homeland on the Spokane Reservation before they were clear of the van. Five of the ladies mounted the boardwalk and approached Allard in a swirl of fawnskin, and when he noticed that one of them brandished a huge roll of raffle tickets, he slapped his forehead and turned away, pretending to look for a place to hide. Then he turned back to greet each of them by name, deferring to age, before he started moaning about the

unreasonable demands on proper braves and small business-
men. As I backed out of my parking place, I saw one of the
Spokane women stuff a sizable loop of tickets into Allard's
shirt pocket.

The Pow Wow at Arlee was just hitting its stride when I
got there late in the evening. License plates from every western state filled the rodeo ground's mammoth parking lot,
which was dotted with cardboard signs giving directions and
cautioning that a prohibition against alcohol would be strictly
enforced. Many of the vehicles were large and made for living
in; I eased in next to a bubble-windowed conversion van and
picked my way through the tipi village near the gate.

In the center of the grounds, three long tents shaded a
group of stick game players. Two lines sat facing each other in
folding chairs, enmeshed in the same guessing game that used
to exasperate David Thompson so. The idea of the game is
very simple: the leader of one side shuffles short sticks behind
his back, then holds out his closed fists for the other side to
guess left or right. The guessing team sings a special song
that helps them visualize which hand holds the prize, and if
they are right, they collect the wager and then take their turn
at hiding the sticks. I watched a few rounds, yet I never could
see exactly who was holding the sticks, or what the guess had
been, or even who had won. But it was impossible not to
bounce to the rhythms of the family chants. Two women with
their eyes closed, an ancient grandmother, giggling sisters, a
pimply teenage boy, a man in overalls—their voices trembled
like aspen leaves in a breeze, gradually rose in pitch and in-
tensity, then suddenly dove to a halt. When they stopped, I
thought I saw one poker-faced elder in a faded Stetson make
the merest twitch of his left forefinger. His brethren beside
him broke into cheers. While the old man calmly lit a cigarette, the line opposite him launched into *their* song, and the
winds blew through another many-leafed tree.

Behind the stick game was a marketplace of exotic booths.
The crowd in the dusty pathways moved slowly, stopping to

examine strips of leather, little cylinders of colored beads, trays of jewelry. A bunch of boys gathered around a hide seller to rub their hands along a black skunk pelt hanging from a pole, then moved on to a pile of wolfskins. As the boys thumbed through the stack, oohing and aahing at the swirls of wolf pelage, I found myself studying their profiles, looking for the kind of oddly clipped Welsh nose that David Thompson was supposed to have had. Although most historians write about Thompson's lifelong faithfulness to Charlotte, rumors about his time at Saleesh House have circulated among the local people. In the 1930s Duncan MacDonald, a man of mixed blood who grew up in the area, told a newspaper reporter that "David Thompson was a great man. He lived among my people . . . He had a woman among the Salish. His descendants still live on the reservation." Duncan's sister Christine told another interviewer that Thompson had a daughter by a Pend Oreille woman. Neither Duncan MacDonald nor his sister ever identified any descendants, however, and Thompson's own writings contain no hint of any involvements on the west side of the mountains.

Across the way from the booths, tiers of bleachers surrounded a covered pavilion, which rocked with the furious rhythms of the Pistol Creek drummers. Two or three hundred dancers of all ages and attires jostled around the ring. There were toddlers and grandfathers, a blond modern dancer in Los Angeles garb, and a high-schooler wearing a plain black cowboy shirt. Feathered headdresses and elaborate animal masks were everywhere. A warrior with an armband of beaten tin shook his eagle-claw medicine stick playfully in my face. I had missed the performance by the Fancy Dancers, but several of the little girls bounced around the ring with the crowd, their fringed buckskin dresses and entry numbers flapping with each move.

The Pistol Creekers put down their sticks, and the caller cleared the ring and ordered up the five finalists for the Clown Dance competition. The crowd hooted lustily when the first contestant, Ms. Canada, pranced out. She was a big, muscular woman with wild black hair, and she wore a deerskin dress, swiped with grease, that stretched from her shoulders clear down to the ground. A few snatches of lewd, showy bumps evoked a round of catcalls from the grandstand. A small boy crawled out from under the bleachers at my feet; he was crying, and clambered up my sock. I picked him up and toted him around in back of the crowd until a woman tapped me on the shoulder to claim him. As I returned to my place, the last dancer was being announced: I-Am-a-Horny-Person. She entered the sawdust ring as a whirling mass of burlap, lumped in all the wrong places and clanking with several beer can belts and bandoliers. She shrieked like a witch and let her long hair fly; she ground her wide hips; she mocked the mocking crowd for the time of a rodeo ride and then backed away to furious applause. It wasn't until Ms. Canada was announced as the winner half an hour later, and a healthy young man in blue jeans and a T-shirt strutted out to collect his trophy, that I understood the dance's sexual inversion and could laugh along with the crowd. As the grinning Ms. Canada held his prize up for approval, the Pistol Creekers burst into a fanfare of rimshots and staccato shouts; the victor answered with a twisted kick.

DAVID THOMPSON finished gathering furs from the Flathead and Kootenai camps in late March, just as the first foals were born in the valley. The tribes were preparing to pitch away for a place they called the Root Plains to dig the first of the season's bulbs, but many of them were sick "with a violent Cold which generally ends in a Rash breaking thro' the Skin. A Purge of Salts with a little Paregoric Elixir soon eases them entirely." Spring snow squalls hindered the furmen's trip back to Saleesh House, and by the time they arrived, many of them were also ill.

At the post, Thompson found he had too many furs to fit into the warehouse, so he stored the surplus in his own quarters and moved outside into a tent. Within two weeks he had pressed and packed his winter take and headed west to Kullyspel House, where he arrived in time for an uncharacteristic journal entry: "April 22nd Sunday. A very fine Easter Sunday – rested all day." The next morning he dispatched Finan McDonald to manage Saleesh House while he was away. He had recently rehired Jaco Finlay "in his old Capacity of Clerk & Interpreter" and now gave him orders to follow the "Skeetshoo Indian Road" southwest to a busy salmon-fishing camp on the Spokane River. Thompson wanted Jaco to build another trade house there, to serve the Colville and Spokane tribes as the next link in his supply line. Once it was completed, his network of posts would cover the main native routes in the region, and the traders would be able to visit them all in two weeks' time. He would also be one step closer to the Columbia River.

Thompson now had a clear picture of how that big river arches far to the north, then suddenly turns back on itself to rush almost straight south before bending toward the sea. He now understood how the Kootenai's neat horseshoe nests into the long parabola formed by the Flathead–Clark Fork–Pend Oreille system, which he had the good sense to call simply the Saleesh River. He now knew how both of those large tributaries oddly mirror the Columbia's course as they flow south from the Rockies, then twist north and west to meet their mother just above the 49th parallel. Like an astronomer who factors in the invisible effects of gravity, he had made his deductions about the country by keeping the elusive Columbia on a tangent to his expanding circle of trade.

Thompson had arrived at Kullyspel House with a little time to spare. Still hoping to reach the Columbia and pioneer a more northerly route back across the Divide, he sent Le Bon Vieux to buy him a pine-bark canoe so that he could make another try at navigating the Pend Oreille's northward swing. With a different guide this time, he probed deeper into the canyons, but kept getting penned in by steep rocks until he was finally stopped cold by the sudden drop of Metaline Falls, thirty miles from the spot where the Pend Oreille spills into the Columbia. His Kalispel guide explained the difficulties of the portage in clear detail: "Highly dangerous & passable only to light active men & they obliged to go on hands & Feet up the steep Crags, which he assured us was continued for a distance of 2½ days." The Kalispels only came to the falls to gather red ochre, he said, and never went far beyond them. Leaving his canoe, Thompson scrambled up a mountain that offered a view to the north. From there he could see exactly how the big river was flowing down to intersect his route, and he couldn't do a thing about it.

> I now perceived the Columbia River was in a deep valley at the north end of these rude Hills, and its west side the high rolling lands of Mount Nelson, round which it runs. Attentively surveying the country, and considering all the information I had collected from various Indians, I concluded that we must abandon all thoughts of a passage this way, and return by our old Road, till some future opportunity shall point out a more eligible road.
>
> *Narrative*

The guide described a path overland through the Colville Valley that his people followed to reach the Columbia, but Thompson had no more time to scout it out; once again, his pendulum of duty swung east. He turned back toward Kullyspel House and on the way passed his fortieth birthday without remark, his dinner "a good Meal of swan, Geese, and Roots." A day's ride from his trading post, he came upon Beaulieu and Boisverd splitting wood. "Boisverd is very ill, having been ruptured by a violent Fall from a Horse 3 days ago, & his foot hanging in the Stirrup the Horse hauled him a considerable distance before he could be extricated. He has thrown up much blood which has relieved him considerably."

With Le Bon Vieux helping to transfer packhorses, Thompson left Kullyspel House on May 9 to begin the trip along his established route north to Kootanae House. On May 17th he had a set-to with one of his men, who "declared himself unable to do his duty & upon my attempting to oblige him, deserted." Left short-handed, the surveyor had to send back the cargo of one of his canoes for later delivery, but he still had such a load of furs that it took the men five trips each to portage around Kootenai Falls. As they shuttled back and forth, Thompson stopped to watch a dipper, or water ouzel, that worked the swift water:

> He was in the Cascades of the Brook plunging & fishing for Worms boldly – often letting himself drive upon the foaming little Waves of the Brook & seemed always quite at his Ease – his plunging was always while he kept firm foot on the bottom – the moment he lost his footing he dove down, but in an instant always brought himself up with amazing dexterity & agility – he brought for his young a small Kind of Insect out of the Water something like a very small frog – his food seemed to be in plenty, he is not in the least web footed – & with all his plunging in the little Cascades his Feathers never in the least appeared either Wet or ruffled.

Farther up the Kootenay River, at another rapids, one of the voyageurs took a dunking, and when they tried to coax the horses across the river, several were swept away and nearly drowned. All the cargo went into the water. The time that was lost drying things out and re-gumming the canoes turned out to be a stroke of good luck, for at Canal Flats they found the fresh tracks of Piegans and an aspen branch that had been broken and stripped of its bark only a few hours before—had Thompson's canoes arrived a little sooner, there might have been a much longer delay. Pausing only for a quick shave and wash, "of which we stood in much need," the men put into Columbia Lake and paddled past Kootanae

House toward the ascent of Blaeberry River. At the beginning of the portage trail, they stopped at their "Hoard"—a stout hut constructed of logs and covered with pine bark, where they had cached saddles and dried provisions. Inside they found a wolverine: "He had cut his way thro' the door of our little House & eaten 25 pounds of Pemmican, ½ a dressed Skin, 3½ pairs of Shoes, & cut to pieces 6 or 7 large Saddles." They caught the carcajou and killed it, then made do with a swan and a goose for dinner.

CHAPTER SEVEN

OMEN OF THE RED STICK

SUMMER 1810–SPRING 1811

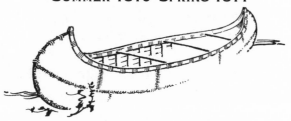

T HE NORTH WEST Company had a policy of giving its wintering partners a furlough every few years, and in 1810 it was David Thompson's turn to "go down on rotation." He left James McMillan to bring the fur packs and a parcel of his books over the pass and sped east in a light canoe with Augustin Boisverd and two other voyageurs. On June 23, running downstream on the Saskatchewan, they crossed paths with a pair of well-stocked Hudson's Bay Company canoes under the charge of Joseph Howse, bound for the west side: the Bay Company was finally making its move over the mountains. Thompson paddled on, docking that same evening at New White Mud House, a post that had just been completed by Alexander Henry and James Hughes near the present-day city of Edmonton.

Henry and Hughes had passed a rough winter. The Blackfeet tribes were still at war with the Crees, and traders on the upper Saskatchewan found themselves caught in the middle of the feud: both sides wanted the furmen to quit selling guns and ammunition to their enemies. Hughes had begun the year in charge of Fort Augustus, while Henry manned another establishment downstream, but repeated threats against both posts, plus news that Henry's scalp was in great demand by a band of Crees, had convinced the men to consolidate their forces at a central location. The neighboring Hudson's Bay Company traders, equally frightened, followed the Nor'Westers, and the two companies built their posts side by side within a single stockade. This show of force had prevented violence so far, but the situation remained tense. Alexander Henry's journal entry for the day after Thompson's arrival captures the mood:

> We got an alarm from the Children taking up a lock of horse hair, tied to a piece of Red Cloth and Feathers, that was found drifting down the river, and four of them at the same time declared they saw a human arm tied to a log pass down the stream. I sent a boat in pursuit of it, but to no purpose . . . Dumont's woman arrived and declares she saw a party of Indians concealed in the Woods, who had made a fire and were drying their Buffalo robes. All this spread a great alarm at this place.

Some of Thompson's children were probably among those who saw the phantom arm, since his family had moved up to White Mud House along with James Hughes. During the five days Thompson spent at the new post exchanging news and information, Alexander Henry would have told him what he knew about another recent Blackfeet attack on the upper Missouri: "They fell upon a party of Americans, murdered them all, and brought away considerable booty in goods of various kinds, such as fine cotton shirts, beaver traps, hats, knives, dirks, handkerchiefs, Russian sheeting, tents, and a number of banknotes, some signed New Jersey and Trenton Banking Company." This incident sounds similar to one that the Flatheads later related to Thompson, involving a Piegan attack on an American fort near the headwaters of the Missouri. On the subject of Americans, Henry also may have loaned Thompson his copy of Patrick Gass's newly published *Journal* from the Lewis and Clark expedition, which included a day-by-day account of the Americans' trip down the lower Columbia.

On June 28 Henry reported that "Mr. Thompson embarked with his family for Montreal in light canoe with five men." At this point the surveyor's family included Charlotte and three children: Samuel, six; Emma, four; and John, two. Their oldest daughter, Fanny, was already in Montreal attending a boarding school. The Thompsons passed a typical trip down the Saskatchewan, paddling through buffalo herds, rain, and relentless mosquitoes. In mid-July they stopped at the company post on Lake Winnipeg, and "here I left my little Family with her Sister in Law to the care of good Providence." Apparently Charlotte and the children were not going on to Montreal with Thompson for his furlough.

While the surveyor had been herding his fur packs and family across the continent, Finan McDonald had taken off from Saleesh House on a different mission. Before leaving his Flathead post, Thompson had asked his clerk to lay in a large supply of dried buffalo meat for the next winter. When the Flatheads and other neighboring tribes began gathering for one of their summer hunts, McDonald and two French Canadians went along. As always, the Flathead bands were on alert for enemy scouts, and they were barely across the pass when they met up with a party of Piegans. In a battle that lasted all day, the three Nor'Westers fired off many shots of their own ("I have noticed that the Indians allow no neutrals," wrote Thompson), and the losses at sundown tallied seven Piegans and five Flatheads. The west-side peoples counted this as a great victory, whereas the Piegans were mortified. The balance of tribal power was shifting again.

ON JULY 22 Thompson arrived at Rainy Lake House, where something happened that changed his plans to continue on to Montreal. Only a few days before, at their annual meeting in Fort William, the partners had reappointed him as the proprietor in charge of the Columbia Department for the upcoming year. There are no surviving minutes from that meeting and no record of any specific orders to Thompson, but in a letter written a few months later he explained that "the critical situation of our affairs in the Columbia obliged me to return." The critical situation involved New York entrepreneur John Jacob Astor, who was dispatching parties by land and sea to establish a fur-trading base at the mouth of the Columbia. Astor had done business with the North West Company before and, realizing the importance of Thompson's interior posts, had offered it a stake in his latest enterprise; the partners gathered at Fort William had voted to accept a one-third interest in the American's project. The partners forwarded a copy of their resolution to Thompson at Rainy Lake, and they must have also sent a dispatch asking him to finish exploring the Columbia down to the Pacific. They were planning to send their own supply ship around the Horn the following year and needed to make sure there was a workable route from the coast to their inland posts.

Some historians have inferred that Thompson was supposed to race Astor's men to the coast, but in that case, the partners would surely have sent Thompson ahead and put someone else in charge of ferrying the trade goods west. Thompson's journals are of no help here, because no notebook survives for the three months following his arrival at Rainy Lake. Judging from his later comments and from an 1811 letter written by William McGillivray, it seems clear that his mission was to cross the mountains and distribute his trade goods as usual, then tackle the Columbia. Given the absence of any field notes between his arrival at Rainy Lake on July 22 and the end of October, Thompson's only account of the fall's events is in his *Narrative*, and there he completely

ignores the breaking political situation. Instead he describes
an incident involving a woman he had encountered some six
years before in the Muskrat Country, who was now in the
possession of a marvelous long stick.

> The day after my arrival a Lady Conjuress made her ap-
> pearance. She was well dressed of twenty five years of
> age, she had her Medicine Bag, and bore in her hands a
> conjuring stick about 4½ feet in length 1½ inches at the
> foot and three inches at the top, by one inch in thick-
> ness, one side was painted black, with rude carved fig-
> ures of Birds Animals and Insects filled with vermilion;
> the other side was painted red with carved figures in
> black, she had set herself up for a prophetess, and gradu-
> ally had gained by her shrewdness, some influence
> among the Natives as a dreamer, and expounder of
> dreams, she recollected me, before I did her, and gave
> me a haughty look of defiance, as much as to say I am
> now out of your power.
>
> *Narrative*

This woman and her conjuring stick were apparently involved
with a religious cult of the Ojibway tribe who lived around
Rainy Lake, but without recording any of her prophecies,
Thompson got directly back to work and by the end of his
next paragraph had loaded four supply canoes and paddled off
up the Saskatchewan.

Alexander Henry noted in his journal that the explorer
made it back to White Mud House on September 6, 1810:
"At 2 O'clock Mr. Thompson arrived from Lake la Pluie in a
Canoe with six men, bound for Columbia. He brings us the
long-wished-for news from the civilized world, for which we
have been anxiously waiting for this some time past." Much
of the news from the civilized world was unsettling. Napoleon
was trying to isolate Great Britain with economic blockades.
The Royal Navy was impressing sailors from U.S. merchant
ships into its own service, and the Americans appeared ready

to fight over the matter. There was also sentiment in the United States to try and drive the British out of Canada, and tensions at the fur posts on the Great Lakes were running high.

None of these international crises affected Thompson's plans. When his three other canoes arrived the next morning, Henry had his blacksmith put up his bellows to make iron tips for their poles, then hosted a dance that lasted until daybreak. It was late the next afternoon before Thompson directed his voyageurs on upriver. A couple of days later, he followed on horseback with two Iroquois hunters and Alexander's cousin William Henry, who was on his way north to a post on the Athabasca River. According to Thompson's *Narrative*, they killed three elk about a day's ride above Rocky Mountain House and camped beside the river to dry the meat while they waited for the canoes. The next morning the oldest Iroquois stared at the drying racks and announced: "I have had bad dreams, this meat will never be eaten." He then saddled his horse and rode off. The voyageurs were overdue for their rendezvous with Thompson, who, somewhat worried, sent William Henry and the remaining Iroquois to look for the boats. What they found was a camp of Piegans only a few miles downstream. When Henry returned with this news, Thompson deduced that the Piegans were on the lookout for his party, and fearing that a rifle shot had revealed their whereabouts, the three men took off cross-country at daybreak in a fall snowstorm.

> We rode on through the Woods until it was nearly dark, when we were obliged to stop; we remained quiet waiting our fortune, when finding all quiet, we made a small fire, and passed the night with some anxiety; my situation precluded sleep, cut off from my men, uncertain where to find them, and equally so of the movements of the Indians, I was at a loss what to do, or which way to proceed.
>
> *Narrative*

Meanwhile, Alexander Henry was traveling upriver from White Mud House to reopen Rocky Mountain House for trade with the Blackfeet tribes, who wanted to avoid any contact with the Crees at the trading posts downstream. Relations with both nations were still strained, and the traders were making every effort to keep peace on the river. When Henry approached the supposedly empty fort on October 5, he was surprised to see smoke rising from chimneys within the stockade and to find Piegans and white men standing at the gate. The white men turned out to be voyageurs from Thompson's Columbia brigade, who had been stopped by a group of Piegans a few miles upstream and told that they could go no farther upriver. The Piegan Blackfeet, upset about their summer defeat by the Flatheads, had determined not to allow another shipment of guns and ammunition across the mountains to their enemies. The voyageurs reported that the group that detained them had been cordial but had kept them under an unrelenting watch. The voyageurs also told Henry that they had decided to return to Rocky Mountain House in hopes of finding Thompson, whom they had not seen since he parted from them to go hunting on horseback over two weeks before. "Sadly perplexed to know whether Mr. Thompson was above or below," Henry broke open the trade goods and began to placate the Piegans with rum.

It wasn't until the following day that Henry had a chance to walk around the post. To his distress, he found that the Piegans had dug up the graves of two Crees who had been buried on the premises a few years before and scattered their bones—"a certain Omen of their bad intentions." That afternoon more Piegans came in to trade and informed Henry that four tents of their tribesmen were keeping watch on the river a day's ride upstream, in order to make sure that no traders got past. Next evening several Piegans from the blockade arrived on horseback, and Henry recognized one of Thompson's steeds among them. When he asked about the

horse, the Piegans replied that they had found it at a camp
upriver, along with a pair of blue leggings that Henry knew
belonged to his cousin William. The Piegans said that they
had tried to follow tracks leading away from the camp, but
that a snowstorm had buried them. Henry pretended noncha-
lance, saying that the horse and pants must have belonged to
a party of free hunters after beaver. From the information on
hand, Henry had to assume that Thompson was somewhere
upriver from him, probably at Kootenay Plains, and he determined to send the supply canoes on up to him as soon as possible. But "this could not be done while any Indians were at
the fort; they are suspicious of our every movement.
However, I kept everything in readiness, until a favorable opportunity should present."

On the sixth afternoon all the Piegans departed, and the
canoes were about to launch upriver when a group of horsemen was sighted in the distance. Henry quickly instructed the
voyageurs to paddle downstream a ways, as if they were going
to another post for supplies, then tie up and wait until midnight to sneak back upstream, "when whatever Indians might
arrive I would keep dead drunk." He kept his word, and by
2:00 A.M. the canoes had lined their way past the fort and the
group of Blackfeet were snoring in Henry's tent.

The next evening, cousin William showed up. Henry
"was astonished to hear that he came from below," *downriver*,
from a campsite he and David Thompson had set up after
fleeing the Piegans. Thompson had already sent an Iroquois
messenger up to Kootenay Plains to tell Bercier, who had
been waiting there with horses for the portage, to bring the
horses down to him by a trail through the woods on the north
side of the river. Alexander Henry quickly sent a man upstream to stop the canoes, and the next morning he paddled
down himself to see Thompson.

At 4 Oclock arrived at the spot where Mr. Thompson
was camped on the North side of the River, upon the
top of a Hill about 300 feet from the level of the water,

where tall Pines stood so thickly planted that I could [not] see his tent until I came within ten yards of it. Here he was starving, and waiting for his people – both his own Canoes and those men who were coming down with his Horses. This affair of his Canoes being stopped by the Peagans has induced him to alter his route and endeavour to open a new road . . . It is therefore determined that the Canoes should be ordered to return below in as private a manner as possible, to avoid all misunderstanding with the natives.

Henry returned to Rocky Mountain House and, three nights and several quarts of rum later, accomplished the re-doubling of the cargo back downstream: "As the Piegans were roaring drunk, the canoes got away unperceived & my Cousin went with them . . . I was happy to get clear of those canoes, that had caused me so much worry and anxiety ever since my arrival." A few days later a Cree hunter arrived from across the mountains with the news that the Piegans had also set up a blockade across the pass; even if Thompson had somehow gotten his canoes around the barricade on the Saskatchewan and made it across the Divide, he would have been stopped by this second blockade. His oft-expressed desire to find a way around the Piegan Blackfeet had now become imperative.

For years Thompson had been thinking about some alternative route, and he and Henry had both heard about a pass near the headwaters of the Athabasca River. The upper Athabasca River runs about eighty miles north of the Saskatchewan and roughly parallel to it; the country between them is wooded and marshy, and the Blackfeet tribes seldom ventured that far north. Though pioneering a new route this late in the year would require precious time, Thompson obviously felt he had no choice but to try—not only did he have the exploration of the Columbia to complete, but he also had men at three trade houses waiting for supplies. By the time his next journal notebook resumes at the end of October, Thompson has reassembled his men, gathered twenty-four

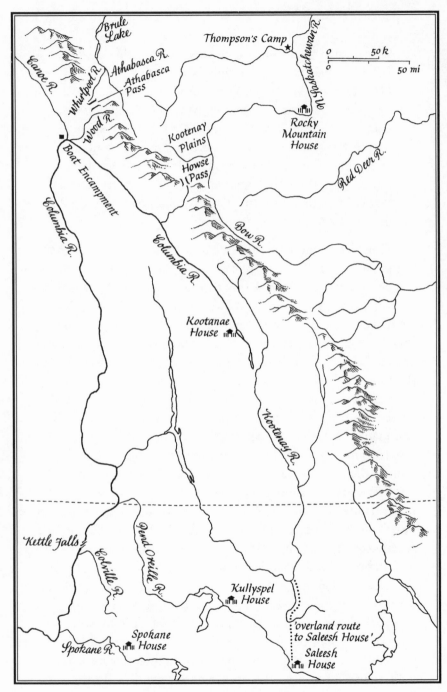

CROSSING ATHABASCA PASS

horses, and signed on a pair of Iroquois hunters. He sent two men to a post downstream to obtain dogs that could pull sleds over the pass. He found another Iroquois, named Thomas, who professed to know the way over the Athabasca River pass. On October 29 the revamped expedition set off for the Athabasca along an old hunting trail.

A week later two of the voyageurs made their way back to Alexander Henry at Rocky Mountain House with a request for more supplies, and their account of the journey so far prompted Henry to express concern about Thompson's well-being: "They had left him on his way to the Waters of the Columbia, cutting his road through a wretched, thick, Woody country, over Mountains and gloomy Muskagues, and nearly starving with Hunger, Animals being very scarce in that quarter . . . in fact, their case is pitiful."

Thompson's case was not so pitiful that he meant to waste his winter on the east side of the Divide. By the first week in December, he had reached the Athabasca River and followed it to the foot of the mountains. He stopped at Brule Lake and quickly built sheds for provisions, then scattered his men in search of birch trees to make snowshoes and sleds. A few of the men had brought their wives this far, and Thompson assigned them to cutting line and netting snowshoes. He complained that the women made an awkward job of it, but did allow that the temperature had not risen higher than twenty below zero for several days. From this campsite, just before Christmas, Thompson wrote a letter to Alexander Fraser, the old friend whose post had been his first stop when he joined the North West Company almost fourteen years before. Fraser had recently retired from the field and was living in Montreal, where he had visited Fanny Thompson.

21 Dec. 1810, Athabaska River
Foot of the Mountains

My Dear Fraser,

I received your esteemed favour the 9th Sept. and am

obliged to you for the traits of civilized life and the information of my daughter. She costs me 62£ 10s. at present, and I think 50£ a year would do her all the good that the present sum costs me. It is my wish to give all my children an equal and good education; my conscience obliges me to it, and it is for this I am now working in this country.

I intended to have paid you a visit at Montreal last summer, but the critical situation of our affairs in the Columbia obliged me to return. The Americans, it seems, were as usual determined to be beforehand with us in the Columbia in ship navigation. As the Peagans killed an officer and 8 soldiers out of a tribe of 12 ditto, if this accident has not drove them back, they will probably get the start of me.

My canoes were also drove back by the Peagans, but no lives or property lost and I have changed our route from [illegible] to the Athabaska River and am now preparing in this hard season to cross the mountains and gain my first post near the head of the Mississourie [Saleesh House], a march of about 34 days, and a part of it over a dangerous country for war. I hope good Providence will take care of us and bring me safe back again.

I am always in such distant expeditions that I cannot write to my friends regularly . . . I am getting tired of such constant hard journeys; for the last 20 months I have spent only bare two months under the shelter of a hut, all the rest has been in my tent, and there is little likelihood the next 12 months will be much otherwise.

Your humble servant,
David Thompson

On December 29 Thompson left his Brule Lake camp with twelve men and eight dogsleds loaded with over seven hundred pounds of supplies. Four horses carried two hundred pounds of pemmican, thirty-five pounds of grease, and sixty pounds of flour. A temperature of minus thirty-two degrees made for solid sledding, but they had a rough climb ahead. On January 1 the dogs could not pull their loads, and Thompson stopped to cache a third of his goods. The men frittered away most of the day repacking, "during which time they cooked twice a four gallon Kettle of Meat, which they devoured, although they had had a hearty breakfast . . . upon my reproaching some of them with their gluttony, the reply was 'what pleasure have we in Life but eating?'" Most of these voyageurs were new to Thompson and to his methods of travel; even before they reached the mountains, several had shown that they did not share his zeal for exploration.

That evening the hunters brought down two buffalo bulls and a mountain sheep, so the party stopped for a day to split and dry the meat. When they started again, they forked off to follow the Whirlpool River, moving among thick, stunted trees and marshy lakes. The horses, helpless in the deepening snow, were left to fend for themselves in a small meadow around some little ponds. But the heavy snow did not impede all animals; soon afterward the men came across a set of tracks that gave them quite a start: each footprint had "4 large Toes, about 3 or 4 inches long & a small Nail at the end of each; the Ball of his Foot sank about 3 inches deeper than his Toes; the hinder part of his Foot did not mark well. The whole is about 14 inches long by 8 inches wide." At the time Thompson surmised that the track must have belonged to a big grizzly bear, although his hunters had a different idea. In his *Narrative* he remembered their qualms: "Strange to say, here is a strong belief that the haunt of the Mammoth is about this defile, I questioned several, none could positively say they had seen him, but their belief I found firm and not to be shaken."

It was Thompson's habit to travel for a few hours every morning before stopping to eat, but on the march up the Whirlpool his crew continually exasperated him by cooking breakfast before they set out. On January 8 the voyageur Du Nord beat one of his dogs senseless, and tossed it to the side of a trail with a broken sled. "He is what we call a 'flash' man, a showy fellow before the women but a coward in heart, and would willingly desert if he had the courage to go alone." The next day the temperature climbed to thirty-two degrees, and the snow turned to slush: "Very bad hauling: the Sleds I may say stuck to the Snow." Despite the conditions, the party made its way above timberline and began the final ascent to the Divide. Just short of the pass, Du Nord refused to haul his sled any farther. Thompson had had enough of the man's obstreperous behavior and ordered him back down the trail. But Du Nord apologized and the surveyor allowed him to continue "although, in my opinion, he is a poor spiritless wretch."

That afternoon they crested Athabasca Pass and made camp on the west side. Thompson went out to look at what lay before them, and when he returned found his crew probing the snow with a twenty-foot pole, trying to measure its depth. There was too much to clear away, so they had to build their fire on top of the snowpack. That night a storm blew through, and the few logs they had brought with them for firewood were soon consumed.

> In this exposed situation we passed the rest of a long night without a fire, and part of my men had strong feelings of personal insecurity. On our right about one third of a mile from us lay an enormous Glacier, the eastern face of which quite steep, of about two thousand feet in height, was of a clean fine green color, which I much admired . . . My men were not at their ease, yet when night came they admired the brilliancy of the stars, and as one of them said, he thought he could touch them with his hand.
>
> *Narrative*

Thompson and the Iroquois Thomas led the way down

the Rockies' western slope along the Wood River, which the surveyor called the "Flat Heart" in memory of his men's low spirits. Several members of the crew continued to balk at the task before them. They seemed to find comfort only in food, and in thirty-six hours consumed fifty-six pounds of pemmican. One morning Du Nord went out hunting for a couple of hours and when he returned chastised the cook for not having any moose meat ready for him. "What, said he, do you take me for a Horse to go for so long without eating?"

The snow was waist deep, and the warmer west-side temperatures made for slushy, wretched traveling. When Thomas shot two moose, the expedition halted again for a day to dry the meat. Thompson, short on paper, scribbled a letter to the partners on wooden boards. Their guide had completed his job, and on January 13 he set off with another man to start the message on its journey east. In the face of the continued mild weather, Thompson decided that in order for the dogs to get down the mountain he would have to further lighten their loads. He stripped his supplies down to the bare essentials, hung up the rest to come back for later, and set off through the wet snow. "The Courage of part of my Men is sinking fast. They see nothing in its proper Colour – the soft Weather is a thing, it seems, they never felt before . . . but when Men arrive in a strange Country, fear gathers on them from every Object."

On the 18th of January they camped within a mile of the Columbia, close to the mouth of the Canoe River. In heavy rain, Thompson pushed the party south toward the refuge of Kootanae House. After three days they had made only twelve miles, and some of the men refused to go on. Thompson knew that he was more than two hundred miles north of his post and decided to retreat back to the Canoe River to wait for breakup. There Du Nord and three others, "having long been dispirited & useless as old Women, told me he would return." The surveyor gave the deserters forty-five pounds of pemmican for provisions and gladly let them go.

The handful of remaining men built a twelve-by-twelve hut and settled in for a long winter with few amenities. Thompson found a big birch knot and carved himself a bowl, "as I have no Kitchen Furniture other than a Kettle." He had happened into the midst of a big snow winter, in a forest that contained the largest timber he had ever seen—cedars up to thirty-six feet in circumference, larches just as large that "rose full two hundred feet without a branch, and threw off very luxuriant heads . . . on the west side we were pigmies; in such forests what could we do with Axes of two pounds weight?"

What they had to do was build a canoe. For several days he and his men searched for birch bark without finding any thick enough to make even a dish. In early March they decided that they would have to fabricate a wooden boat. Thompson drew up a plan, then they threw down a cedar three feet in diameter and split out nine timbers thirty-one feet long. The next five weeks were devoted to a maddening process of trial and error, as they transformed those rough cants into a twenty-five-foot clinker-built canoe. Frozen boards had to be thawed for the drawknife and carefully scraped down. The men had to keep redesigning the frame as they went along, sometimes replacing sections of boards that had ended up too thick or too thin. They overlapped the planks like clapboard and sewed them to the frame with spruce watap that they dug out of the icy ground. Cracks from their auger holes ran too far in the brittle wood, ruining whole pieces. Often the cedar turned out to be too green, and they had to unsew their day's work and redry it by the fire. One version of the boat broke in half under its own weight.

The trials of this project inspired Thompson to name the place Boat Encampment, but finally, on April 16, the tedious job of heating gum and calking the seams was almost finished, and he was busy packing. He had made a cedar box for his sextant and another for his clothes and papers, but there wasn't much else to load: "We have abt. 3 pieces of Goods, 180 lbs. of poor dried Meat & 30 lbs. of Grease – 10 lbs. of

Pemmican & a little Flour." They left behind the hides of seventeen moose they had killed for food; "all the skins were useless, there being no woman to dress them."

The Canoe River flows into the Columbia right at the tip of the big river's northern elbow, just as it turns decisively to the south. Thompson knew where he was, and in his *Narrative* says that he toyed with the idea of going straight down the river, but it would have been foolish to take off with only three men over several hundred miles of unfamiliar water in a jerry-rigged canoe. So he resolved to pole and track his way up the Columbia toward his trade houses, where he knew he could find more voyageurs.

The first night out, a storm dumped heavy snow on the four men as they slept under the canoe, and Thompson thanked Heaven that the cedar boards didn't split under the drift. Fighting through five feet of snow around the portages, or dragging their outfit on a makeshift sled across iced-over sections of river, it took them three weeks to cover the two hundred miles to the mouth of the Blaeberry River. When they met a canoe of free hunters along the way, Thompson hired an Iroquois named Charles to go south with him as canoe foreman on the Columbia trip. All the hills and mountains were still completely snow-covered, and the late thaw kept the river at the lowest level Thompson had ever recorded. What elk and mule deer they managed to shoot were in very poor condition due to the persistent winter, and at Columbia Lake the surveyor sampled one of the black cormorants that had just arrived for the breeding season: "They are very fishy tasted and their eggs almost as bad as those of a Loon."

From Columbia Lake he crossed Canal Flats and headed down the Kootenay River. Near Tobacco Plains he found a group of Kootenais and free hunters, including another Iroquois named Ignace who had traded at Saleesh House. Thompson knew Ignace to be a skilled canoe hand and hired him to serve as his steersman. One of the Kootenais told the surveyor that Finan McDonald, after a dispute with some Piegans, had abandoned Saleesh House and built another post twenty miles farther down the river. The Hudson's Bay Company agent Joseph Howse had also had trouble with the Piegans; during a short winter of trading near Flathead Lake, he had been so harassed that he and his party returned to the east side for good. Howse reported to James Bird at Edmonton House that the Piegans had warned "that if they again meet with a white man going to supply their Enemies, they would not only plunder and kill them, but that they would make dry meat of his body."

It was a wary group of Nor'Westers who continued on overland to Saleesh House, expecting to find a letter from Finan McDonald giving them his new location.

> May 27 Monday A cloudy Day and much heavy Rain in the afternoon & Night. I examined the old Ho[use] – but found no Letter nor writing of any kind to inform me what had become of the people who had wintered there – wrote a few Lines in Charcoal on a Board in case the Americans should pass – purporting that we had left the Ho[use] on account of the War with the Peeagans – Killed a Mare for Food – Killed 2 Rattlesnakes – I was near treading on one of them.

It is unclear for whom the surveyor intended his charcoal note—it might have been for the independent American trappers in the region, but he might also have been thinking of the expedition that John Jacob Astor had sent west from St. Louis that summer, bound overland for the Pacific. In either case, Thompson himself kept moving. He and his men rode west to Kullyspel House, which was also deserted, then continued down the Pend Oreille River to the camas plains near modern Cusick. There they found a group of Kalispels preparing for war. "Every warrior puts white Earth on his Head as a kind of Mourning for those who are to fall & Penance for himself, that the Great Spirit may give him success." The Kalispels reported that Finan MacDonald had joined Jaco Finlay on the Spokane River, and Thompson sent word that he needed horses. While he waited, Le Bon Vieux dropped by with twelve mullet and some elk meat.

Finan McDonald and Michel Boulard arrived on June 12 with a string of pack animals and led Thompson's party south to Jaco's new post, nicely situated on a yellow pine flat beside the Spokane River. Thompson spent his first day there calculating its position (latitude 47° 47' N, longitude 117° 27' W). He traded for some carp from the Spokane families camped nearby and sent gifts to the neighboring chiefs. Then, since the Spokane River was unnavigable downstream from Spokane House, he rode north on a trail through the Colville Valley with his voyageurs. On June 18 they met two Canadian free hunters living in the valley. Thompson shot a curlew near Blue Creek, then moved on toward his rendezvous with the Columbia.

CHAPTER EIGHT

WANAPAM

JUNE 19–JULY 14, 1811

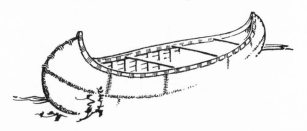

THE COLVILLE RIVER empties into the Columbia just below Kettle Falls, and David Thompson reached their junction on June 19, 1811. Near the falls he found a village of square cedar sheds, built from boards split out from driftwood cedars and roofed with rough shakes and woven mats. The interior of each hut was criss-crossed with poles for drying salmon. The natives here (known today as the Colvilles) set up big woven baskets at the bottom of the falls to capture fish, and Thompson called both the place and its inhabitants "Ilth koy ape," a local phrase meaning kettle trap or net.

After all of his detours and delays, Thompson had finally made it to a launching point for the Pacific; now all he needed was a canoe to get him there. The ponderous local boats, made from burning out half a drift pine or cedar trunk, would never do, so he fanned out his men with some villagers to look for clear cedar or serviceable birch bark. They searched for two days without success and finally backtracked seven miles up the Colville River to a hummock of branchy cedar they remembered from the ride up. The wood was of poor quality, but they managed to piece together the parts for a boat from several trees.

The Nor'Westers had gotten to Ilthkoyape Falls at the beginning of the first salmon runs of the summer, only a few days too late to witness the ceremonies and dances that ushered in the fishing season. For several days after they arrived, a single spearman worked alone from the rocks, although there were enough fish to keep many spears busy. "The salmon are about from 15 to 25 to 30 pounds weight here, well tasted, but have lost all their fat, retaining still all their meat. Their flesh is red and they are extremely well made." Later on, once the Salmon Chief announced that the prescribed number of salmon had ascended the falls, other men set out nets and baskets to begin the harvest in earnest.

Thompson studied the complex rituals that these people attached to one of their most important food sources—"Deep attention is paid by them to what they believe will keep the Salmon about them." He was intrigued by the salmon's mysterious ability to switch from fresh to salt water and then back again for their spawning journey, and he cut open stomachs to confirm that none had eaten anything on their long trip from the sea. He puzzled again over the fact that dogs, which could eat other fish, were poisoned by the flesh of raw salmon. He grappled with the natives' explanation of the salmon's birth, migration, and death: "It is the popular belief that all the Salmon that enter the River die and not one ever returns – this is perhaps almost true of all those that go to the very sources of the River to spawn, when exhausted by their long Journey, weakened by spawning, they become so emaciated as to have no strength to return and die in great numbers of very weakness." He had witnessed the hordes of dead salmon around Windermere Lake at Kootanae House but found it hard to believe that this phenomenon was repeated lower on the Columbia. "But this is only at the very sources of the River as all the water of the River is perfectly clear, and were the whole to die, their amazing numbers would cause such a putrid odor as would soon bring on a pestilence to cut off Mankind."

The Colvilles told Thompson that the salmon had an aversion to any water tainted by humans or animals, and could taste if others of their kind had been cleaned in the water. The explorer watched them sweep the river's edge of all debris and clean their catch well away from the banks; he saw how fish parts down to scales and drops of blood were kept strictly away from the river. One morning the appointed spearman, on the way to his post at the falls, passed near the skull of a dead dog. He immediately returned to his hut, for "to have speared fish with such unclean Eyes would have driven all the Salmon away, and he purified himself with a decoction of the scraped Bark of the Red Thorn [hawthorn]. Thus cleansed he proceeded to work."

Thompson thought this and other taboos pure superstition until one of his men carelessly tossed a horse bone into the river after a meal, and all the salmon instantly spooked back downstream. One of the villagers took to the water and dived for the bone, bringing it up within a few minutes, but fishing was done for the day. The more Thompson watched, the more he became convinced that there was more to these practices than hocus-pocus: "Experience has taught them the delicate perceptions of this fish."

THE CANADIAN artist Paul Kane visited Kettle Falls thirty-five years after Thompson. In his painting of a fall salmon run, fish leap straight up at a series of cataracts that pour over the bedded pitches of rock. On the river's edge three spearmen stand waiting while a fourth man, out on a ledge, leans forward to club a nice-sized chinook that seems to dangle from a short cord attached to the point of his lance. Woven traps, supported by trussed tree limbs and twisted lines, are set up in three different eddies. People are gathered on the columns of stone that edge the falls, but they are not in a fishing frenzy—they stand or sit quietly, eyes on the great numbers of salmon that flash up from the white water. At the edge of the painting, one man lies belly-down on the stone, his head propped on his forearms in the posture of a sphinx. He studies the fish.

A hundred years after Thompson's visit, the Colville and other tribes still gathered at Kettle Falls to capture and prepare salmon in much the same way. A Colville woman named Mourning Dove wrote about camping out at the falls early in this century at her family's traditional place, on the west side of the river. She describes the big fishing baskets they wove from red willow with rims of limber serviceberry. She details spears made with detachable deer-horn prongs held in place with pine pitch and secured by a line; when a salmon was struck, the point came loose, allowing the spearman to play the fish and bring it close to shore for a deathblow. Only men could catch the fish; it was the women's job to split and dry the salmon for winter food.

Mourning Dove says that her great-grandfather, See-whehl-ken, was Salmon Tyee when David Thompson came on the scene. The people of See-whehl-ken's band had never seen a white man before, but they had heard stories of Lewis and Clark from people downstream, and welcomed the strangers. The Salmon Tyee's job was to distribute the salmon caught each day, and Mourning Dove maintains that her grandfather gave the whites the finest fish caught. She says that Thompson couldn't pronounce her grandfather's name very well, so he called See-whehl-ken "Big Heart."

WHILE THOMPSON ate salmon at Ilthkoyape Falls, he tried to find out everything he could about the rest of the river. The Colville people told him that the Columbia upstream was quite rocky, with sparse trees, and that hunting was poor except in the winter months. Of the world downstream they knew little beyond the next village, whose people were called the San Poil. During the week that it took to put the new canoe together, he watched as people from all over the area gathered at the village, "a kind of general rendezvous for News, Trade, and settling disputes." On June 27 five San Poils arrived from a weir they had set up nearby, along with his Kootenai friend the Old Chief and a free hunter from the Flathead country. They presented the surveyor with a bushel of roots, and that wasn't all. "They brought me also from Boisverd's wife a present of 2 pieces of Iron, 5 dressed Skins, 1 Beaver skin & 2 Horses to be paid for when I see her." Thompson does not say whether this is the same wife of Boisverd whom he had sent home from Kootanae House and who later became known to her people as Qánqon. Nor does he explain why this woman would be sending him presents, or where he expected to see her again.

By the first of July, the voyageurs had finished their canoe and were rendering gum to take with them. The men had tired of their salmon diet, and Thompson ordered a horse butchered for provisions along the way. The tribes for some distance downstream spoke languages of the same Interior Salish group as the Colville, Kalispel, and Flathead peoples, and a young San Poil couple fishing near the falls agreed to go along and help interpret for the first part of the trip. The explorer's crew also included a French Canadian free hunter, two of the voyageurs who had come over Athabasca Pass with him, the Iroquois canoemen Charles and Ignace, and his old hand Michel Boulard.

"July 3rd Wednesday After arranging several small affairs, we in number 8 Men with 2 Simpoil Indians set off on a voyage down the Columbia River, to explore this River, in order to open out a Passage for the Interiour Trade with the Pacific Ocean." As the Nor'Westers floated south from Ilthkoyape Falls, the comfortable humpbacked mountains faded behind them, and they watched the landscape dry up before their eyes. Beyond the mouth of the Spokane River,

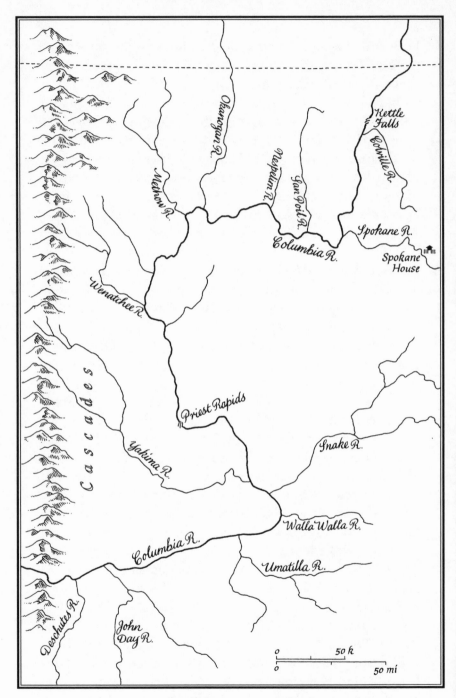

THE MIDDLE COLUMBIA

the Columbia turns west to make its big bend, passing through country that varies from scattered stands of ponderosa pine to open sage rangeland to vast flows of basalt scoured bare by a series of glacial floods. Powered by the runoff of the same deep snows that had dogged the furmen all winter, the canoe flew downstream for that whole first day. From his vantage in the boat seat, Thompson had time to note little more than "high rocks on the right" and "high rocks on the left." Later he described steep cliffs of columnar basalt, with deep ravines and monstrous stacked rocks "often in step like Stairs." Voyageurs traditionally loved fast water and fewer portages, and Thompson let them run while he plotted courses in his notebook as best he could: "The Courses are not so correct as I could wish. The strength of the Current caused many eddies and small whirlpools which continually toss the canoe from side to side so that the Compass was always vibrating. I hope by the mercy of Heaven to take them much better on my return."

This part of the river was totally new to white men, and Thompson made a point of stopping at every little fishing camp he passed in order to introduce himself. It was a practice that slowed his progress but, as he pointed out in his *Narrative*, seemed politically astute: "My reason for putting ashore and smoking with the Natives, is to make friends with them, against my return, for in descending the current of a large River, we might pass on without much attention to them; but in returning against the current, our progress will be slow and close along the shore, and consequently very much in their power ... "

The party spent the first night at the home village of the San Poil, a poor but friendly tribe who lived in pole huts covered with rush mats. They subsisted mainly on salmon, roots, and berries; they possessed no stone or clay pots for storage, no forged tools or weapons. Thompson passed out tobacco and sat down for a session of smoking and speechmaking— first the chief, then Thompson, who delivered a message through his two interpreters that he would repeat many times over the next ten days: "I then explained to them my object to know how this River was to the Sea, and if good, very large Canoes with Goods of all kinds would arrive, by which they would be supplied with Clothing and all they wanted if they were industrious hunters." The San Poil, like nearly all the tribes he sat down with, were very responsive to his offer of trade. After matters of state were taken care of, a man asked if the women could bring the furmen a small present. Thompson consented, on condition that the present didn't include any *eetoowoy* roots. These eetoowoys were probably camas lily bulbs, which at other times the surveyor enjoyed but at the moment had most of his party doubled over with colic. The women proceeded to shower him with baskets full of eetoowoy and other assorted roots, and the voyageurs asked for a dance. The San Poil, without any musical instruments beyond their expressive voices, performed so eagerly that they raised a cloud of dust that "often fairly obscured the Dancers, tho' we stood only about 4 feet from them."

The next day, July 4, Thompson and his men stayed in the San Poil camp talking and taking observations until noon, then put back into the river. Late in the afternoon, they stopped to scout a rapid, and the voyageurs decided to portage their cargo and ride down in the empty canoe, "but in doing this they run too close to a drift Tree on a Rock, which tore part of the upper lath away & struck Ignace out of the Stem of the Canoe – Altho' he had never swam in his Life he swam so as to keep himself above the Waves, 'till they turned the Canoe around & took him up." That night in camp Thompson bled Ignace to help him recover from his dunking, then got busy splitting a driftwood log to make replacements for the two paddles they had broken during the day.

Afloat again next morning, the Nor'Westers stopped to parley with the Nespelim, a prosperous group with many horses. The elders presented the furmen with five horses, five roasted salmon, three bushels of roots and berries, and four small dried animals that Thompson thought must be marmots but declined to taste. He also declined another basket of eetoowoy bulbs. He repaid the gifts with three feet of tobacco, ten plain and four stone rings, eighteen hawk's bells, a fathom of beads, four papers of vermilion paint, four awls, and six buttons. In return the Nespelims performed a dance to wish him luck on his journey. An old man sang for the dancers, who seemed to jog in place along a curving line. Both men and women wore decorations of brilliant white shells—armbands, bracelets, headbands—and a few had copper baubles hanging from their clothing, ornaments brought from far away through an active trade relay. While they were exchanging presents and smoking together, Thompson counted a chief and sixty men. It was his custom to number the men who showed up to pass the pipe, then multiply by seven for an estimate of the size of the band, thus providing a consistent first census for the native peoples he encountered.

The next tribe downstream was the Methow, who greeted the white men with another dance. Afterward the women sat down outside the circle of men and joined in the smoking. Thompson noted that the ladies were entitled to only one puff, whereas the men got between three and six. The Methow said that they didn't have any knowledge of the river beyond their nearest neighbors, and the travelers didn't tarry. That afternoon, as the river curled south through the rude, wild country around the base of the Cascades, they saw the first mountain sheep and rattlesnakes of the trip; they killed two rattlers but missed the bighorn.

"July 7th Sunday A fine day but cloudy Morning . . . We came to a large Band of Indians at 10½ A.M. – They received us all dancing in their Huts, one of which was about 80 yards long and the other 20 yards." These were the Wenatchee people, a large tribe of about 120 families. They had heard of the white men but had never seen them before. One of their elders came and sat beside Thompson to feel his shoes and

his legs, "gently, as if to know whether I was like themselves."
Many of the Wenatchee wore shells in their noses and
sported fine goat-hair blankets. In the mountains to the north
they were able to hunt goats as well as sheep and mule deer,
and Thompson pronounced them hearty in health. Their settlement marked the last of the tribes who belonged to the
same language family as the San Poil; the Columbia Plateau
tribes to the south spoke Sahaptin tongues. By chance a chief
of one of the Plateau bands was visiting the Wenatchee, and
he offered his services as interpreter. Thompson accepted,
and the chief and his wife replaced the San Poil couple in the
canoe.

It was still early in the afternoon, and despite much pleading to stay the night, Thompson was determined to push on.
As he paddled away, the Wenatchee people stretched their
arms heavenward in a prayer for his safe return. A few hours
later the furmen entered country that was "all steep rock and
fine low meadows. It is curious to see fine meadows as it were
springing out of the feet of steep rocks, and spreading along
the river, at times fine knolls of sand." That night proved
fitful, with mosquitoes and a high wind.

In the morning the men decided to take advantage of the
breeze and rigged up a mast and sail. They had made only a
few miles under their sheets when they came to the high
waves of Priest Rapids and shot through them. There was a
sizable native camp at the bottom of the rapids, but the current was so strong that the canoe was a half-mile below it
before the paddlers could put ashore. A chief from the camp
rode down to investigate, followed by "an old white headed
man with the handle of a tea-kettle for an ornament about his
head. He showed no signs of age except his hair and a few
wrinkles in his face, he was quite naked and ran nearly as fast
as the horses. We could not but admire him." When
Thompson wrote up this meeting in his *Narrative*, he focused
on the chief rather than the athletic old man: "The chief on
horseback now rode down to examine us, he appeared very

much agitated, the foam coming out of his mouth; wheeling his horse backwards and forwards, and calling aloud, who are you, what are you?"

IT WAS HIGH noon, midsummer hot, when Gene Hunn and I knocked on the door of James Selam's modest house on the Yakima Indian Reservation in central Washington. As we waited for an answer, the fragment of a bird call drifted around the corner of the house. "Oriole?" Gene asked, corking his head around for a better listen. The grating blackbird notes sounded out again, in series this time, and he affirmed his guess with a nod. "Oriole. James has a pond back there."

Gene is an anthropology professor at the University of Washington in Seattle with a serious side interest in birds. I had first watched him in action on a frigid November afternoon in an apple orchard not far from where we now stood, as he cheerfully explained to half a dozen bewildered people peering through binoculars that they were looking at a wayward yellow-headed parrot. "Has to be," he had said. "See how it's flying with its fingertips?" Gene had been living on the Yakima Reservation at the time, studying the Plateau tribes' view of the world as revealed through their language and natural history. Now, two decades later, he continues to make frequent trips to the Columbia Basin, still mapping out the Plateau culture. James Selam is a tribal elder who has served as Gene's main contact throughout his study.

After a few more knocks on his door, James ushered us inside to a room lit only by the glow of a television. Gene was excited to see his friend and began rattling off plans for the weekend. James punched off the television with a grunt and nodded occasionally at Gene's flow of words, but did not voice his thoughts. His blue jeans were new and stiff; so was his geometrically patterned rayon shirt and brown bandana marked with yellow arrowheads. Only his dark brown cowboy boots seemed seasoned and comfortable. He had the soft, round face of an old woman, coppery smooth with a broad expanse of cheek and forehead. A sparse mustache prickled out from beneath his generous nose. His silvery temple hairs were plaited into pencil-thin braids that fell down over his shoulders and were in turn plaited into two thicker and darker braids pulled forward from the back of his head. These pigtails disappeared inside the bandana tied cowboy-style around his neck, then reemerged from beneath the flap to fall down over his chest to his ample belly.

Gene handed James a compact camera he had brought for him; James touched all the prominent buttons and took two pictures of his wall. As Gene introduced me, mentioning my interest in David Thompson's trip through the Plateau country, James moved over and carefully chose a black baseball cap from a collection on a dresser. It was only when we bumbled together in the narrow doorway that he spoke to me.

"David Thompson, huh? I remember that guy. I remember David Thompson." James pursed his lips into an oval and let his deep eyes flash—not exactly a smile, but an expression that allowed Gene and me to smile. "You ready to go?"

We drove east, away from the Yakima Reservation and up over the Rattlesnake Hills, then down into a vast desert basin. For their latest project, Gene and James were working on a map that would cover the range of all the various tribes of the Sahaptin language group, detailing their traditional place names and cultural sites, and this area had yet to be thoroughly covered. As Gene drove, he kept looking down at an old book balanced on his lap, written by a reporter named Click Relander who had befriended several local Sahaptin clans during the 1940s. With one hand on the wheel and one eye on the road, Gene flipped to marked pages, scattering questions out to the horizon. Was there any special legend connected with that low ridge to the south? Do you know of any word that sounds like this? What could he have meant by this spelling? James burped out a small laugh as he took a picture out the window with his new camera. "I don't know, Gene," he said. "It all depends on how you pronounce it."

Sailing dreamily into the heat waves, we cut across one corner of the Hanford Nuclear Reservation and slowed to a crawl as we approached the Columbia River at Vernita Bridge—Gene didn't want to miss any shorebirds that might be out wandering after their nesting season. Across the bridge we turned upstream, making for the Priest Rapids Dam. A road runs across the top of the huge dam, and when we arrived there in early afternoon, a work crew had parked a crane directly in our path. We got out to walk around on top of the dam, and James directed our sight to the base of the fish ladders, where a lone sturgeon flapped idly against the current. Then we lifted our eyes to stare downstream at the deep channels cut into the ancient layers of basalt by river and wind. Except for sage and rabbit-brush and a green swipe down each side of the river, the land looked entirely empty. This was once the hunting and root-digging territory of the Wanapam tribe; today it is mostly the domain of the U.S. Government. Downstream lies the Hanford Nuclear Reservation. To the east stretches an expansive national wildlife refuge. To the west the Yakima Firing Range occupies another large tract, set aside as a bombing range for the military.

The crane moved, and we crept over the dam and down into a narrow, dusty flat squeezed between the river and a rugged basalt ridge. This was the village of Priest Rapids, home to a remnant of the Wanapam tribe that chose to stay on the river rather than live on a reservation. We had come here to find an elderly woman named Margaret and her nephew Lester Umtuch, who had helped Gene identify local plants some years before. A handful of prefab houses surrounded a Quonset hut that served as longhouse and community center, and it took only a couple of minutes to walk their circle. No one answered the door at Lester's house or at Margaret's. We were wondering what to do when a young boy rode up on his bicycle and started petting a tired dog that lay beneath a planted spruce tree, one of the few green things in the village. The boy wore a T-shirt with a yellow number 77 on it and allowed Gene to engage him in conversation. The dog was either his or Margaret's. It had just had eight or ten puppies. He either had one or none or all of the puppies for his own. He had no idea where Lester or anybody else was.

The boy's attention drifted to a group of wasps around the drip of a hose in Margaret's yard. We followed him over and examined the insects as they touched down in the wetness, honeybees and yellowjackets and dirt daubers and one all-black solitary wasp. The boy had a keen eye for the different patterns on their backs and could follow a single wasp's flight across the yard. It was a sweltering day, and Gene decided that Margaret wouldn't begrudge him a drink. He traced the hose over to a faucet, turned it on just a tad, and walked back toward the trickle. Number 77 made his own way to the faucet and, the moment Gene put the hose to his mouth, turned the water on full blast. Wet and sputtering, Gene pointed the hose at the boy, who immediately cut back the pressure. Gene put the hose back to his mouth, and Number 77 cranked it back on. James and I howled as the game went on for several rounds, until finally Gene grabbed up a loop of the hose and ran straight at Number 77. *"I can't get wet!"* squealed the boy with delight. *"I can't get wet! Don't touch me! Momma told me I can't get wet!"*

Lester Umtuch heard the commotion and came out of his trailer to talk to us in the sun. He was a wide man of perhaps fifty years, with an imposing head and teeth that glowed brightly when he grinned. His crow-black hair was cut close to the scalp, and he frequently reached up to rub the little spikes with one big palm. James stepped forward and tried to explain to Lester about the information he and Gene were after. Gene pitched in with a little encouragement, pointing down the river. Lester shuffled and touched his hair.

"Well, I dunno, ya know, I went away from here when I was just a little fella. They moved us off our regular campsite, so I went to White Swan School on the reservation from the third grade on. I remember twice riding the buckboard from White Swan through Moxie spending the night at the old windmill—sleeping on some people's kitchen floor—and then riding on up here to our family's campsite."

Lester shook his head and picked at his teeth; Gene asked a couple of gentle questions that only made him shake his head more.

"I don't really know much about that kind of stuff, I didn't see it after I went off to reservation school. I remember after I got my license, driving my grandmother around to visit, and she would be singing the songs and then trying to explain to me the meanings behind the songs and I'd be down here listening to the radio"—Lester leaned forward and reached his right hand out to fiddle with imaginary knobs—"and her words went *poof!* In one ear and out the other. I remember lying down on the bed beside my grandfather and maybe plucking his whiskers or something while he would tell me his stories and he'd talk for a while and then he'd say *tsup tsup:* we go on from here tomorrow or whenever."

After each memory, Lester backed off and opened his mouth wide for a burst of laughter. Gene stood facing him with his hands cradled around his book, rocking on his heels. James only nodded. Lester kept on swearing he couldn't remember, then stepping back to touch his burry head, and then stepping forward again.

"My grandmother said how they used to go up to the swallow nests and pick out the naked baby birds even before they had grown their feathers and roast them under the ground—*tamaksh*—and then pop them in their mouths whole. They didn't even have no bones yet, it was all still gristle you might say, and man she said them was good—you could hear their fat just dripping into the fire while they was cooking down there."

He licked his lips and began to talk about the rock pictures that had been buried by the dam, how they were all up and down the river: "They saved a couple of those rocks I guess, you can see 'em up in our graveyard. But there was lots more. Man, we used to watch them pictures when we was kids. Some of those things would change overnight you know. I saw 'em. I was little and I'd go out there at night and look, go back out there again the next morning, and they'd be changed."

Lester laughed at the charmed foolishness of children. He remembered a kid who was out digging roots with his aunts and saw the Little People—impish little beings that inhabit Sahaptin mythology—and came screaming back to camp. "If he just could have kept it to himself," Lester said. "If the boy hadn't talked about Them out loud, he would have been able to use some of their power.

"That's like me," he continued. "When I was a little fellow we was camping up in the Naches and my father gave me two buckets and told me to get some water and I went up to the spring and a frog there told me *Go away* that was *his* water and I couldn't have any. If I hadn't gone back to camp with two empty buckets and talked about the frog as an excuse, maybe he might have shared some of his power with me. Huh?"

Big grin. Lester waved at some people in a station wagon that had just pulled up, but they stayed in their car, invisible in the glare of the sun, leaving Lester free to ferret through his mind for another memory. This time he came up with a special white clay from the other side of Saddle Mountain. His uncles used it like putty to secure sticks and feathers, or to chew on—nibble-chalk, they called it. Lester smiled, and then stopped as one of the station wagon's doors popped open. He shook his head without any smile. "Oh well," he said. "Now I guess you got to talk to this guy for a while."

A tall, lean man with long, black braids rolled out of the car and stomped straight over to us, a can of beer in one hand. The arm that held the can bulged with veins and sinewy muscles. He addressed himself directly to Gene.

"What you want, man?" he asked, his face inches away from Gene's. Behind heavy black-rimmed glasses his eyes were bleary, as if he had been crying. He had on a red T-shirt with a small photograph of Chief Joseph and letters that spelled out WANAPAM: LAND OF THE COLUMBIA. He looked to be around thirty years old, but it was hard to tell for sure.

"I said what the hell you want, man?"

I suddenly wished that Gene hadn't chosen to wear his new red Audubon Bird Ambassador cap to the village, but he calmly met the man's gaze and said that he was working on a map project and wanted to see if Lester could help him.

"I'll tell you what you want," interrupted the Wanapam, supplicating toward the rock cliffs with his arms. "You want our names. And why should we give you all our names? What do we get out of that?"

Gene clasped his hands together at his belt, still holding his book. He cocked his head to look at his adversary, but kept quiet.

"I'll tell you what we get. We get nothin'. And we ain't telling you nothin'. Those names, them's the only things we got left. Why should we give those away? You tell me that. Why?"

Gene coughed to clear his throat and tried saying that he certainly didn't want to take anything away, but the Wanapam wasn't listening. His tirade grew loud and profane. He was drunk, but lucid—he knew all about Gene, and about his research. Gene coughed a couple more times without attempting a sentence, simply taking the abuse. He held his head up, his eyes locked on the man.

"And this old man here," the Wanapam said, pointing at James. "What you got him up here for? He wants our river and we ain't giving it to him. *Our* river. These Yakima want everything when they already got everything. Why should we give them something when we don't got nothing except that dam right there, and that bomb factory down there? We're the ones that live here! We're the ones who know this place! I know what's here and *I ain't tellin' you*. Go home, old Yakima man."

"He's Warm Springs," Gene said, as the Wanapam swept his beer can through the air. "Not Yakima."

The Yakima were the most populous of the Sahaptin-speaking tribes in the Columbia Basin; James Selam had been born into the smaller Warm Springs tribe. While it was true that James did not live in the Priest Rapids area, his dad had been raised just downstream and had told young James many stories about the land and its people.

James offered none of this information out loud, and Gene heeded his cue to keep quiet. The Wanapam looked hard at both of them as he shouted on.

Lester had disappeared inside his trailer soon after the drunk man arrived. Now James evaporated also, back to Gene's van. Gene stood his ground, assuring the Wanapam that he didn't want anything that the people didn't want to give, that he was after simple knowledge.

"Forget your knowledge," said the Wanapam. "Look what you done for us so far." He waved again, at the dam that changed the river. The cliffs where jets flew too close to the ground. The big factories that leaked death.

His companions began honking the horn of the station wagon. A new person emerged from the trailer beside Lester's and made a beeline for our depleted circle. He was about the same age as the Wanapam but larger, with a bigger belly, and dressed all in black. He faced up to Gene, his face even closer than the Wanapam's had been. He held that pose for several seconds, then burst into words: "*Gene Hunn!* Haven't seen you in a while, man." He shook hands, clasped fingers, tweaked thumbs with Gene, then moved on to me. "Donald Blackbird," he announced. I shook, clasped, and tweaked with Donald before he continued on to the station wagon to see what the horn-honking was all about.

The Wanapam raged on. "You ain't gonna get nothin', man. You stand here with your stupid books and notepads and you don't know nothin'. Now Click Relander, he knew. Click listened when we said something. He wasn't afraid to put down the truth."

This was an odd turn in the stream of invective, and for a moment I thought I was hearing things—Click Relander was the white reporter whose book Gene had been quoting from all day. Now Gene simply unclasped his hands and held up Relander's book, *Drummers & Dreamers.* The Wanapam stepped back in surprise. In the silence that followed, Gene told him he had every right to be angry, and that he agreed with much of what he had said. The Wanapam listened for the first time since his arrival and stood quietly for a moment. He turned in a half circle and started back toward the station wagon, then stopped and reversed the maneuver to replant himself in front of Gene. "So," he said, not as loud this time. "I'm going to get myself a sip of whiskey from the car. Need one for yourself?"

Gene rocked on his heels. "No thanks," he said. "I guess I'll hold off for now."

ONCE THOMPSON'S Sahaptin interpreter assured the foaming chief at the Priest Rapids camp that all was well, the men of the village collected for the usual smoking and talking. After one dance the Nor'Westers took their leave, heading due east now at the base of the Columbia's Big Bend. Late the same afternoon they put up at a camp of about 150 men belonging to the Yakima tribe. The salmon these people offered as gifts showed a little fat, and peering into the kettle, Thompson saw that traces of fish oil had risen to the surface of the water—something he had not seen happen with any of the salmon he had eaten upstream. He thought this camp had a very favorable situation and promised to build a trade house on the site sometime in the future. When he went out during the night to make some observations, he discovered that his sextant had been shaken out of adjustment in the rapids.

On July 9 Thompson's canoe arrived at the mouth of the Snake River, where the Columbia again turns west for its final run to the sea. This was the point at which Lewis and Clark had entered the big river, and Thompson knew where he was from his knowledge of Meriwether Lewis's letter and Patrick Gass's journal. Both of these accounts clearly noted that the Americans had named this large tributary Lewis's River, but Thompson chose to call it the Shawpatin River after the people who lived in the vicinity. Near the front of his notebook, Thompson had copied a short memorandum from Gass's journal that gave Lewis's calculation of the latitude of this point as 46° 15' 14" N. Thompson took his own reading at the junction and came up with the slightly more southerly conclusion of 46° 12' 35" N. This was the farthest south the surveyor had ever been; he was now in the same latitude as the mouth of the Columbia.

At the confluence of the two great rivers, the surveyor put up a small pole with half a sheet of paper tied around it, claiming the territory for the British Crown and stating that the North West Company merchants "do intend to erect a factory at this place for the commerce of the country around." Five miles farther downstream he came upon the claims of the United States in the form of a miniature American flag in the possession of Yellepit, a chief of the Walula tribe. Yellepit wore a peace medal decorated with Thomas Jefferson's portrait, also given to him by Lewis and Clark in 1805. Thompson found the chief "intelligent, he was also very friendly, and we discoursed a long time." Yellepit complained that his tribe had been accustomed to travel across the Blue Mountains to hunt buffalo, but in recent years the Snakes had chased them off. He was very willing for the Canadians to come and supply his people with guns, and he and Thompson decided that the place where the Snake met the Columbia would be an excellent spot for a trading post.

When the Nor'Westers put back in the river after their talk with Yellepit, they faced up to one of the afternoon gales for which the Columbia is famous. Even though they were moving with the current, the men had a difficult time making much headway against the wind. During the course of their struggle, they had their first sight of one of the Cascade volcanoes, probably Mount Hood, a "conical mountain right ahead alone and very high, seemingly a mass of snow." Thompson's journal for the day ends with an offhand sentence sandwiched among observations of Antares and Saturn: "Passed in all about 80 families in small straggling camps." These were bands of Umatilla people, and when he sat down to write his *Narrative*, that simple statement touched off the memory of an unsettling encounter:

> We embarked and proceeded thirty two miles down the River, and passed about eighty families in small straggling lodges; at one of which of ten families we put ashore to smoke with them, but they were terrified at our appearance. My men stayed on the beach, and I went forward a few paces unarmed, and sat down with a pipe and stem in my hand; they sent forward two very old Men, who lying flat on the ground and in the most pitiful manner; crawling slowly, frequently lifted their heads a little as if imploring mercy; my Native Interpreter would not speak to them, and all the signs I could make gave them no confidence; close behind the men three women crawled on their knees; lifting up their hands to me as if supplicating for their lives; the men were naked and the women nearly the same, the whole, a scene of wretched destitution, it was too painful, they did not smoke with us, I gave to each of the

men two inches of Tobacco, and left them. They appeared as if outcasts from the others . . . when I spoke to
the Interpreter when we camped to learn the state of
these people, he gave me no answer, and both himself
and his Wife did not wish to be spoken to about them.

Lewis and Clark recorded a similar incident at a small encampment some miles below the mouth of the Snake, very
near where Thompson stopped. Clark had landed at a group
of lodges and had been greeted by silence. When he entered
one of the huts, he found three dozen people hiding inside,
"in the greatest agutation, Some crying and ringing there
hands, others hanging their heads." When his interpreters arrived, they learned that the frightened people had seen Clark
shoot a flying sandhill crane and thought that the white men
had come from the clouds and were not human. Only the
presence of the young Shoshone woman Sacajawea in one of
the canoes finally assured them that all was well.

The next day Thompson stopped at a camp near what is
now called the John Day River for a more familiar reception.
He counted another eighty families here and measured a
dugout canoe thirty-six feet in length by a full three feet wide.
He noticed that in addition to setting seine nets to capture
salmon, this band had crafted long poles with hoop nets on
the end. When the furmen put back into the river, another afternoon gale had blown up and "the water was swept away
like snow." Forced ashore, they spent the evening watching
the most dexterous curved-line dances they had seen so far.
Dance, song, and step were measured out by an old chief, and
all the young people of both sexes took part. Thompson's
journal for this day ends with the line, "Heard news of the
American ship's arrival." John Jacob Astor's men, coming
around the Horn, must have already made it to the coast.

On July 11 the Nor'Westers came to a long set of rapids
called The Dalles, or the Narrows, a famous fishing and
trading spot for far-flung tribes, as well as the rough bound-

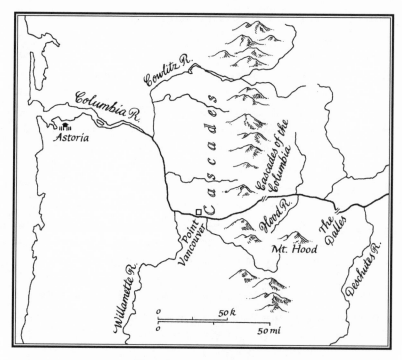

THE LOWER COLUMBIA

ary between the Sahaptin-speaking tribes of the middle river
and the Chinookan groups of the lower Columbia. Near the
top of the rapids the furmen almost cracked up on a big rock,
and when they put ashore to drop off their Sahaptin interpreter, they were surrounded by hordes of large crickets.
Thompson and his crew camped at the top of the portage
with over three hundred families, and that evening they were
treated to a dance that almost got out of hand: "The re-
spectable men among them had much trouble to reduce them
to order, and they were the least regular in their way of behavior of any we have yet seen – at Night they cleared off
with difficulty & left us to go to sleep."

The next day the furmen had to make the long portage
around The Dalles on foot, since the horses that the natives
had promised the night before never materialized. At the

bottom of the rapids, they came upon bunches of harbor seals chasing after the migrating salmon—a sure sign that the ocean was near. They fired a few shots at the seals, but missed. Sixteen miles later they floated into the tight, luxurious growth of the Columbia Gorge, and everything about the countryside changed. As they passed through veils of hanging clouds, the men saw their first extensive forest since the Spokane country, gigantic trees, more harbor seals, and smoky huts filled with curing salmon. The local Chinookan people who came out to greet them babbled English words, "some of them not the best," learned from trading ships. Thompson worked at picking up phrases of their language and listened as they described to him the five species of salmon that annually passed by on their way upriver.

On the evening of July 13, the Canadians camped for the night "a little above Point Vancouver." This was a landmark whose name Thompson had copied into his notebook at Rocky Mountain House during the winter of 1800 as he and Duncan McGillivray planned their trip to the western sea. Twelve years later Thompson knew that he was finally drawing close. The next morning he recorded a tidal fall of two feet overnight, then pressed on. "July 15th Monday A very fine day, somewhat cloudy. Staid 'till 6:25 A.M. shaving & arranging ourselves, when we set off . . . the Fog all along prevents me seeing well."

CHAPTER NINE

SITTING IN THE WATER

JULY–SEPTEMBER 1811

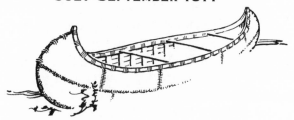

O NE YEAR EARLIER, at about the time David Thompson departed from Rainy Lake House, a large birchbark canoe had swept down the Hudson River toward New York City. The paddlers were all Canadian voyageurs, fresh recruits for John Jacob Astor's Pacific Fur Company. One of the passengers was Gabriel Franchère, the son of a Montreal merchant, who had signed on with the company as a clerk. Sensing that he had hooked into an adventure, the young man kept a journal of the trip: "The Americans took our voyageurs for Indians ... we sang as we rowed, and our singing, along with the sight of the bark canoe, drew a crowd of people to the wharves." Another new clerk, an opinionated Scot named Alexander Ross, had left behind a teaching job in Upper Canada for "the gilded prospectus of the new Company." Ross had already traveled south and was on hand for the dramatic arrival of the voyageurs in their birchbark canoe. He too had a pencil in hand.

The appearance of this unusual kind of craft on the

American waters, with the cheerful chantings of its crew, their feathered caps and sylvan appearance, as they approached the gay city of New York, attracted such a crowd of spectators of all classes around them, as left but little space to land; but what was the astonishment, when, in the twinkling of an eye, two of the crew were seen to shoulder their craft, capable of containing two tons weight, and to convey it to a place of safety on terra firma. Mr. Astor, who happened to be present, was so delighted with the vivacity and dexterity of the two men, that he gave them an eagle to drink his health.

On September 6, 1810, as David Thompson and his Columbia brigade beached their canoes in front of Alexander Henry's post on the upper Saskatchewan, Astor's ship the *Tonquin* set sail from New York Harbor, bound for the Pacific via Cape Horn. The expedition leaders were all from Canada, as were most of the twenty-nine voyageurs, clerks, and artisans under their charge; several were former employees of the North West Company. Alexander Ross wrote that they were scarcely out of port when the captain threatened to "blow out the brains of the first man who dared to disobey his orders." His bluster incited a running feud that percolated for the rest of the journey. During a stopover in the Sandwich (Hawaiian) Islands to take on supplies, several crew members deserted. When the *Tonquin* left Hawaii in early March of 1811, she was loaded down with an extra complement of islanders, plus a variety of livestock and chickens to help feed the new post. Two weeks out, huge seas washed most of the animals overboard, and cold winds coated the rigging with ice. When they finally reached the mouth of the Columbia, it was a cloudy, stormy day, and the ship lost a dory and five men before making it across the river's notorious bar and into safe harbor. When they touched land, David Thompson was still more than a thousand miles upstream, struggling to finish his cedar plank canoe at Boat Encampment.

Once ashore, expedition leaders Duncan McDougall and Robert and David Stuart took charge. By mid-April they had chosen a spot for their intended fort a few miles in from the bar and put their men to work hacking at the thick coniferous forest. Gabriel Franchère reported that "the weather was superb and all nature smiled. We imagined ourselves to be in an earthly paradise—the forests looked like pleasant groves, the leaves like brilliant flowers . . . we set ourselves to work with enthusiasm and in a few days cleared a point of land." Alexander Ross was less enthusiastic—the way he tells it, it took four men two days to chop down each tree, and it rained constantly. In his opinion they had landed in the worst spot on the planet for an establishment. He was sick of boiled fish and wild roots, and McDougall, whom he dubbed "the great pasha," did not meet with his approval: "He was a man of but ordinary capacity, with an irritable, peevish temper; the most unfit man in the world to head an expedition or command men." McDougall's journal is more evenhanded—among the routine business of building shelters and keeping his crew fed, he reports meetings with leaders of the local Clatsop and Chinook tribes and outbreaks of venereal disease among his men; he also tries to sort out a variety of rumors about the presence of white men in the unknown territory upriver.

Franchère, Ross, and McDougall do agree that by the end of May the men had laid the foundation for a storehouse and had named their rudimentary post "Astoria." The three of them also reported that an unusual pair of visitors arrived on June 15. According to Franchère, "some natives from up the river brought us two strange Indians, a man and a woman. They were not attired like the savages on the river Columbia, but wore long robes of dressed deer-skin, with leggings and moccasins in the fashion of the tribes to the east of the Rocky Mountains." The man spoke some Cree and was found to be carrying a letter, which McDougall promptly perused. Dated April 5, 1811, it had been sent by a Mr. Finan McDonald from Spokane House and was addressed to Mr.

John Stuart, Estekakadme Fort, New Caledonia.

This was a curious occurrence. John Stuart was a partner with the North West Company, working on the Fraser River in the section of British Columbia then known as New Caledonia. There was no fort called Estekakadme there, but Finan McDonald was a most adventurous speller and could have scrambled any number of words to come up with the name. At the time there was no charted route between New Caledonia and the Columbia country, so Finan McDonald could not have given his messengers very detailed instructions, but he certainly would have indicated to them that Stuart's post was several hundred miles to the northwest of Spokane House. Yet here was his letter in Astoria, which was decidedly southwest. All the letter-bearer had to say was that he and his wife had lost their way and had ended up following a big river down to a falls, where they had learned that there were white men farther downstream. Assuming that the addressee would be among them, the pair had continued on.

The message that Finan McDonald was trying to communicate to John Stuart remains unknown, for Duncan McDougall did not record its contents in his journal, only his puzzlement at the messenger: "We cannot make out the motive of his journey hither either from his conversation or the tenor of the letter he brought." By the next day McDougall was beginning to suspect that the "inland stranger" was a spy for the North West Company. Alexander Ross thought that the husband "was a very shrewd and intelligent Indian, who addressed us in the Algonquin [Cree] language, and gave us much information respecting the interiour of the country." So encouraging was this information that David Stuart immediately began planning a trading expedition upriver. A month later, on July 15, Gabriel Franchère reported that preparations were almost complete:

> All was ready on the date planned, and we were about to load the canoes, when, toward midday, we saw a large

canoe, carrying a flag, rounding what we called Tongue Point. We did not know who it could be . . . The flag she bore was British, and her crew was composed of nine boatmen in all. A well-dressed man, who appeared to be the commander, was the first to leap ashore; and addressing us without ceremony, he said that his name was David Thompson, and that he was one of the partners of the North West Company.

By all accounts the unexpected callers were well received by the Astorians. Franchère speaks of "the usual civilities" and says they invited Thompson back to their quarters at one end of the warehouse, where he told them all about his winter's travails. McDougall noted the arrival of the Nor'Westers in his straightforward manner, commenting only on the unusual construction of their cedar canoe. Alexander Ross sounds a more discordant note, wondering if the surveyor was not being treated a little too kindly: "M'Dougall received him like a brother; nothing was too good for Mr. Thompson; he had access everywhere; saw and examined everything; and whatever he asked for he got, as if he had been one of ourselves."

As far as Thompson knew, there was no reason why he shouldn't be greeted like a brother—not only were many of these men fellow Canadians and former Nor'Westers, but he had left Rainy Lake in the belief that the North West Company held a one-third partnership in Astor's Columbia venture. According to McDougall, Thompson told the Astorians "that no doubt remains with him, but ere now a coalition of the two companies had taken place, regarding which he handed us an extract from a Letter on the same subject." That letter was a copy of the resolution passed by the North West partners at Fort William the previous summer, giving their consent to the deal with Astor. Thompson had no way of knowing that Astor's agreement with the North West Company had disintegrated months before. McDougall and the Stuarts should have learned about this before they sailed from New York, but if they shared the news with Thompson, none of the witnesses mentions it. Maybe the partners' letter convinced them that the deal was still viable. This would actually have been good news for the head Astorians—as British citizens working for an American company, they were all very much aware of the hostilities brewing between the United States and England, and they knew that Astoria would be an easy target for the King's navy if war did break out. In that event, it would certainly be to their advantage to be allied with the Nor'Westers.

For whatever reason, all four of the leaders acted as if the deal were still on, and at some point on the day he arrived, Thompson wrote the sort of formal letter that would serve as an official notice of intent. He congratulated the Astorians on their new establishment and expressed his hope "that the respective parties at Montreal may finally settle the arrangement between the two Companies which in my opinion will be to our mutual benefit." The next day McDougall and the Stuarts responded with an almost identical letter, seconding Thompson's wish "that final arrangements may take place to the mutual satisfaction of both parties, which would inevitably secure to us every advantage that can possibly be drawn from the Business."

Alexander Ross, who tended to see intrigue all around him, theorized that there was a double-edged game of cunning going on:

> How could we account for the more than warm and unreserved welcome Mr. Thompson met with from Astor's representative. Unless, as some thought at the time, M'Dougall was trying to pay Mr. Thompson back with his own coin, by putting on a fair face, so as to dupe him into an avowal of his real object. This is more than probable, for in point of acuteness, duplicity, and diplomatic craft, they were perhaps well matched.

There is no doubt that hidden sentiments lurked between the lines of the two high-minded epistles written that day. At the end of their letter, the Astorians stated that when Thompson arrived they had just been preparing to go upriver and meet their expedition coming from St. Louis. Since the overland party was not due for at least three months, this was an outright falsehood. But if the Astorians' attempt to disguise the true mission of the boats being readied by their wharf was disingenuous, so were Thompson's exaggerated descriptions of "the dangers and difficulties" of conditions inland. His efforts to keep the Astorians from going upriver were quite transparent to Franchère: "The description this gentleman gave of the interior of the country was not calculated to leave with us a very favorable impression, and did not perfectly accord with that of our two Indian guests."

The two guests, Finan McDonald's stray letter-carriers, were still at Astoria when Thompson arrived, and at some point they caught his eye. According to Ross's account, "Mr. Thompson at once recognized the two strange Indians and gave us to understand that they were both females." Franchère echoes the schoolteacher: "He [Thompson] recognized the two Indians, and told us that they were two women, one of whom had dressed herself up as a man in order to travel with greater security." This woman dressed as a man was none other than the Kootenai berdache called Qánqon, the former wife of the voyageur Boisverd—the same woman Thompson had asked to leave Kootanae House three years earlier for her loose conduct, and a woman that he had obviously heard more of after he sent her home:

> The Kootanaes were also displeased with her; she left them, and found her way from Tribe to Tribe to the Sea. She became a prophetess, declared her sex changed, that she was now a Man, dressed, and armed herself as such, and also took a young woman to Wife, of whom she pretended to be very jealous; when with the Chinooks,

as a prophetess, she predicted diseases to them, which made some of them threaten her life.

Narrative

Qánqon and her "wife" had been camping at Astoria for a month when Thompson arrived, and had caused Duncan McDougall considerable anxiety during their stay. Apparently the berdache had been claiming to possess "the power to introduce the Small Pox" on her trip downriver; since epidemics of the pox had already swept the Pacific Coast, such a declaration terrified the natives. Qánqon, so ridiculed at home, must have intended to impress these people by boasting of supernatural powers, but she had seriously miscalculated the effect of her message. Several times the Chinook and Clatsop chiefs had demanded that McDougall turn over the two "inland visitors" to them for slaves; he had repeatedly refused, saying that he wanted to keep them as his own slaves. McDougall knew that the pair would be killed if they fell into the hands of the chiefs, and he wanted to save their lives so that they could guide David Stuart and his party upstream. The berdache had drawn several maps of the interior for Stuart and had been anxiously waiting to leave under his protection when the unexpected appearance of David Thompson delayed their departure.

Thompson's own journals for his stay at Astoria contain no word of surprise at finding Madame Boisverd in disguise at the fort, and no wonderment as to why Finan McDonald would have entrusted a letter to the berdache. There is no thrill at the historic import of his arrival at the mouth of the Columbia, or any expression of disappointment that he did not get there first. There is no puzzlement about the fate of an important deal, no hint of deception in dealing with the Astorians. Rather, his entries for the week, minus his usual survey notes and astronomical observations, sound like nothing so much as a man on holiday:

JULY 15TH MONDAY . . . At 1 P.M. thank God for our safe arrival, we came to the House of Mr. Astor's Company – Messrs. McDougall, Stuart & Stuart – who received me in the most polite manner, and here we hope to stay a few days to refresh ourselves.

JULY 16TH TUESDAY A fine day. Observed for Latitude, Longitude & Time – Latitude 46° 13' 56" N . . . Longitude 123° 48' ¼" W.

JULY 17TH WEDNESDAY A very fine day, if we except an appearance of Rain with a few Drops of ditto. A steady Gale from the Sea as usual.

JULY 18TH THURSDAY A very hot calm Day. I went across to the Indian Villages with Mr. Stuart and my men – after visiting the Houses, we went up a great Hill where we gratified ourselves with an extensive view of the Ocean and the Coast South'd.

JULY 19TH FRIDAY A fine hot day.

JULY 20 & 21 SATURDAY & SUNDAY Fine weather.

THE WEATHER AROUND the mouth of the Columbia is hardly ever fine; it is too powerful a place, too wild a conjunction among the peaks of the Cascades, the draining waters of the whole Inland Northwest, and the massive weather systems that spiral across the Pacific. Below the modern town of Astoria, the river still races to meet the ocean head-on; wide and rough, its reeking sea smells steal attention from the sodden green land. Tongue Point licks out into the current just east of the port, a narrow lacework of hemlock that reclines steeply to the river. In the lee of the point, a marshy flat has been transformed by river dredgings into fennel-covered fields and the town sewage ponds.

As I walked toward Tongue Point along a railroad track that parallels the river, white wooden buildings began to emerge from the green curtain of trees, the nucleus of a Job Corps center and Coast Guard installation. Where the steep slope meets the water, a pier juts out from the shade of the hemlocks, forming a second forest of creosoted pilings spotted with tool shacks, incandescent lights, and ramps for rescue boats. Lined up along the pier, rolling like king-sized amphoras from some ancient dig, red navigational buoys awaited repair.

Two teenage boys in shorts came toward me on the track. They were barefooted, and choosing steps between the splintery ties and sharp gravel had them hopping like chickens. Still, they managed to swagger a little bit. One of them carried a belly-board with two fins, as if he were getting ready to fight his way through the cold outgoing tide that lapped at the riprap beneath us. We grunted to each other, and I asked them if the walking wasn't a little rough today. My voice might have been lost in the wind; they stared back without answering, then padded on.

As I continued down the tracks, an outgoing freighter appeared from around the point. It was of a modern design, with bulbous bow and stern, and slid through the water like a melon-headed beaked whale. Its wide-mouthed stack puffed out a plume of diesel smoke that hung in the hemlocks above the Coast Guard station. The Columbia's dredged channel angled the ship in toward the railroad tracks; as she came closer, I watched her sprout wiry antennae and the clear eyes of bridge windows. Then she straightened out her course for the Pacific, and I spelled out the huge white letters spaced down the length of her black hull—D A I O   P A P E R.

The leviathan glided toward me in utter silence. Gulls and cormorants on nearby pilings sat tight, watching the wake from her shapely bow slap up against their perches. Her great bulk obscured the clearcuts across the gray river, and only when the vessel was right upon me could I hear the clanks and grinds of her inner speech. She plowed right past me and then was gone, off for the Far East with a belly-load of logs from western forests, plying the same trade route that Alexander Mackenzie and the McGillivray brothers all dreamed of, and that David Thompson inaugurated when he scraped ashore at Tongue Point that July day of 1811.

"JULY 22 MONDAY A fine day. Arranged for setting off for the Interior . . . I pray Kind Providence to send us a good journey to my Family and Friends. At 1:24 P.M. set off in company with Mr. David Stuart and 8 of his men. They are to build a Factory somewhere below the Falls of the Columbia [The Dalles]." Apparently McDougall and David Stuart had dropped their pretense about meeting Astor's overland party and replaced it with a half-truth about building a post on the lower Columbia. According to McDougall's journal, however, Stuart's party intended to accompany Qánqon and her companion at least as far as a river they called the "Wahnaaihye," which was probably the Wenatchee and was certainly much farther upriver than The Dalles.

Alexander Ross says that the Astorians had decided to travel upriver in company with the Nor'Westers "for the sake of mutual protection and safety." Ross and two other clerks were among Stuart's crew, and they embarked with style: "After our canoes were laden, we moved down to the water's edge—one with a cloak on his arm, another with his umbrella, a third with pamphlets and newspapers for amusement, preparing, as we thought, for a trip of pleasure." The wind was brisk and sails went up, but Stuart's two dugout canoes proved unwieldy to his paddlers. Loaded with over a ton of trade goods, the heavy boats began to take on water and soon ran ashore on the rocks of Tongue Point. The men lugged baggage and dugouts across the narrow isthmus to the other side, where Thompson's men, having successfully negotiated the point in their cedar canoe, sat waiting. The Astorians loaded up again and made a few more miles before a sandbar

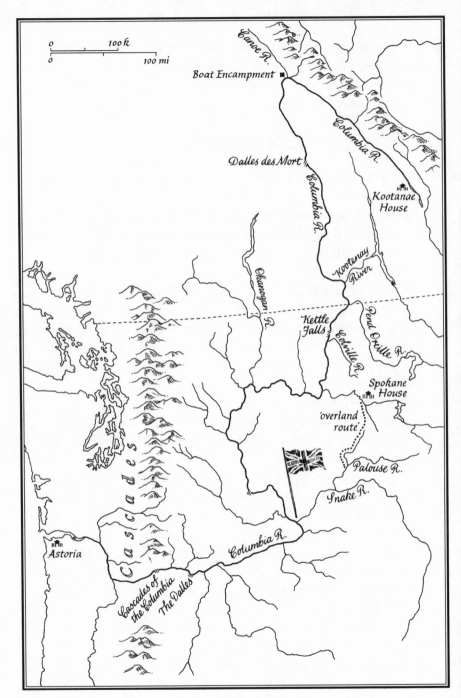

Scale:
0 — 100 k
0 — 100 mi

Canoe R.

Boat Encampment ■

Columbia R.

Dalles des Mort !

Kootanae House

Columbia R.

Kootenay River

Okanogan R.

Kettle Falls

Pend Oreille R.

Colville R.

Spokane House

'overland route'

Palouse R.

Snake R.

Columbia R.

Astoria

Cascades

Cascades of the Columbia

The Dalles

CLOSING THE CIRCLE

arrested Ross's boat: "Down came the mast, sail, and rigging about our ears . . . cloaks and umbrellas, so gay in the morning, were now thrown aside for the paddle and carrying strap, and the pamphlets and newspapers went to the bottom."

The two parties made better progress on Tuesday, but as evening came on, they couldn't find a place to camp. Thompson wrote that at seven o'clock "on a very steep Shore, we put up; with difficulty we could place the Goods, & all slept as I may say standing." They found more comfortable campsites for the rest of the week as they sailed and paddled toward Columbia Gorge, stopping occasionally to dry out baggage or trade for berries and more salmon. Thompson charted the river's courses, fretting now and then that his distances were off or that he couldn't get his bearings because the sail was in his way. One afternoon they passed eight canoes seining for salmon and tried to buy some of their catch, but the fishermen were "inhospitable" and refused to sell any. On Saturday evening, soon after the parties stopped for the night, two natives brought a blind chief from a nearby village to their camp for a smoke. As they were passing the pipe, two more canoes paddled by on their way to a village upstream; David Stuart called out and asked if they would bring back some salmon, to which they agreed. When they never returned, Thompson began to worry that some sort of treachery was afoot, and through the night he kept his canoe loaded and ready to shove off.

No one bothered him until very early the next morning, when the Kootenai couple, who had been riding with the Astorians, appeared at the door of his tent. Qánqon, still dressed as a man, was carrying a bow and a quiver of arrows. She must have lost faith in David Stuart's ability to defend her and her companion, because she asked Thompson for his protection. He does not say whether he made room for the couple in his canoe, only that his party set off at 5:50 A.M. and rowed half a mile through rapids. At the top of the shoals, they spied four men who offered to share some of their salmon. The canoes put ashore, and while the fish were boiling, the four fishermen approached Thompson. Giving the berdache a stern look, they "enquired about the Small Pox, of which a report had been raised, that it was coming with the white Men & that also 2 Men of enormous Size [were coming] to overturn the Ground." Thompson assured the men that there was no truth to this tale and that the Great Spirit would continue to watch after them and their grandchildren. They appeared to be relieved, he wrote, but "I saw plainly, that if the man-woman had not been sitting behind us they would have plunged a dagger in her."

With breakfast concluded and Qángon safe for the moment, the men faced up to the long portage around the boisterous flume of the Cascades of the Columbia. Lewis and Clark called this series of rapids the Great Shute; to Thompson it was the Great Rapid. His seven voyageurs had no problem scurrying over with their minimal load, but the Astorians needed some extra manpower, and Stuart hired several men from a nearby village to help. Most worked with goodwill, while others were more interested in seeing what was inside the small mountain of packs and parcels that emerged from the boats. Several flaunted short, double-edged daggers, reminders of the coastal tribes' long contact with European and American trading ships.

By midafternoon the goods were across the portage, and as the porters gathered around to be paid, so did a number of men who had served only as spectators. Stuart, who could not distinguish those who had helped from those who had not, wound up passing out a great deal of extra tobacco. Thompson wrote that some of the natives remained "highly discontented; they all appeared with their 2 pointed Dags, and surrounded us on the land side, their appearance very menacing." Several of them pulled out whetstones and began sharpening the blades of their long knives and waving them in the white men's faces. Thompson grew impatient with their posturing and drew his pistol; the troublemakers quickly dispersed, but there was no way of knowing if they would return with reinforcements.

Since the Nor'Westers had already gotten their canoe to the top of the rapids, they probably could have escaped an attack, but Stuart's dugouts were still back at the other end. They were too heavy to carry, and none of the local men would help him drag them across until he promised them better pay. Thompson "spoke to the Chiefs of the hard usage they gave Mr. Stuart, & reasoning with them, they sent off all the young Men." Eventually Stuart got his boats over, and they all paddled upstream a short distance to camp. Recapping the day's events in his journal, Thompson concluded: "These people are a mixture of Kindness & Treachery. They render any Service required, but demand high payment, & ready to enforce their demands, Dag in hand. They steal all they can lay their Hands on, & from every appearance only our Number and Arms prevented them from cutting us all off." Canadian and American travelers up the Gorge would write variations on these sentiments for years to come; the proximity of a native village and the logistics of this portage provided a frequent stage for conflict between residents and visitors.

THE COLUMBIA GORGE, where the fully formed river makes a tight squeeze through the Cascade Range, has always been a bottleneck. Tens of thousands of years ago, when the ice dam of glacial Lake Missoula crumbled, the Gorge absorbed an incredible torrent of floodwater. And it was only a few centuries ago, within the memory of man, that a huge landslide crashed down from Table Mountain into the heart of the Gorge, temporarily plugging the river and giving rise to a wealth of local myths such as "The Bridge of the Gods." In one version of this legend, demons from the mountains were at war against the river spirit, and erected a stone dam to block the course of the river. The river spirit cut a long tunnel through the barricade, creating a stone archway that people who lived on opposite sides of the river used as a bridge. A bloody war between these peoples caused the demons and spirits to band together and destroy the Bridge of the Gods. In another story, Thunderbird murdered five of Coyote's sons. Coyote in turn killed Thunderbird, and it was the mangled body of the monstrous bird that formed the rapids.

The same topography that worked for Coyote, that made this spot such an ordeal for generations of boatmen, also made the Gorge at the base of Table Mountain an ideal site for a hydroelectric dam. In 1934 the rocks of the Cascades of the Columbia became the foundation for one of President Franklin Roosevelt's first big WPA projects: Bonneville Dam. On this lower stretch of the river, the politics of salmon carried weight even back in the thirties, and public pressure forced the Corps of Engineers to keep an eye on the fish when they designed the dam. Beginning well below the main structure, a long series of fish ladders winds upriver, skirting the concrete buttresses at the outside base of the dam and the humming turbines within. The original fishway consists of even cement stairsteps, mossy and black with age. On the July morning that I stopped to visit, I had to stand at the bottom of the ladders and stare into the water for several minutes before I could discern any silver ribbons moving along the slabs. The fish drew me up a path into a newer, more random system of groins and vaults designed to mirror the rocks of a real river bottom. A set of stairs mounted to a catwalk that ran above the ascending waterway; from above, the protruding groins looked like letters in a concrete alphabet, no two alike, each one subtly altering the swirls of water. At the base of each letter were eddies where introduced shad steadied themselves comfortably, noses to the current. The walkway ended atop an observation deck with a view out over the surrounding landscape. There was Table Mountain on the

Washington side, dominating the whole scene; there was a spot where the old portage trail might have started; there were the deep pools where harbor seals used to strike at the circulating fish.

I took an elevator down into a basement viewing room, where a thick wall of glass glistened with more shad. At first I could see nothing beyond them but a rainbow of spume. Then a couple of big steelhead muscled their way through the tanks, shiny missiles that whipped smoothly from section to section up the line. A shadow that lingered for a moment in the green darkness was part of a wave of summer king salmon. I followed one of them for the length of the aquarium, through all four tanks, until I was stopped by a wall at the end of the room. Behind a door in the wall was a separate cubicle reserved for the Game Department's official fish counter. In shifts around the clock, employees sit in a chair in that special room and tick off the species as they come through: chinook, coho, sockeye, chum, steelhead. A chart outside toted up the count for each kind of fish for yesterday, and last week, and for the whole season so far.

As I turned away from the chart and back to the fish windows, I saw the raspy mouth of a lamprey eel clasped against a lower corner of the glass. The water rippled past the comb-toothed ridges on its lips while the rest of the creature, all tail, swung out into the bubbles. These eels that are really fish also return upstream to spawn, using their sucker mouths to grip the rocks and pull themselves against the current. The tribes along this part of the Columbia have long made good use of the lamprey, gathering them alongside the salmon; James Selam's friend Elsie Pistolhead still runs poles across the rafters of her garage in the summer to dry their snaky bodies for winter food. When David Thompson compared the taste of rattlesnake meat to that of eels, he was paying the land serpents a compliment.

THOMPSON ATE BREAKFAST with the Astorians on Wednesday, July 31, two days upstream from their troublesome portage around the Cascades of the Columbia. They were in the general area where David Stuart had said he intended to build a trade house, and Thompson prepared to take his leave. He left behind Qánqon and her companion, as well as the voyageur Michel Boulard, who had been part of his crew off and on ever since their first foray into the mountains to meet the Kootenais eleven years before. In his *Narrative*, Thompson explains that he had arranged with Duncan McDougall to swap the forty-year-old Boulard, "well versed in Indian affairs, but weak for the hard labor of ascending the River, for a powerful well made Sandwich Islander" called Coxe. Boulard's experience in the country would make him very useful to the Astorians, whereas Thompson intended to send Coxe to Montreal and then on to London to act as interpreter on the North West Company supply ship that was supposed to sail to the Columbia the following year. Alexander Ross, in his account, added that Coxe "was looked upon by Mr. Thompson as a prodigy of wit and humor, so that those respectively acceptable qualities led to the exchange."

With David Stuart tagging along to scout The Dalles a short distance upstream, the Nor'Westers paddled through thick smoke from a local grass fire until they reached the base of the big rapid at around eight-thirty in the morning. On their way downriver they had been kept awake by the rowdy camp here and had not been able to get horses for the five-mile portage, but this time their interpreter was back in time for lunch with plenty of horses and fresh salmon, and everything went smoothly until they reached the end of the carrying place. There they heard a rumor that one of the chiefs was gathering men to come and steal their guns. Thompson defused the situation with some "sharp words," then asked for another dozen salmon. He presented most of them to David Stuart, and the two men parted ways.

Traveling against the current, Thompson had time to notice much that had flashed past on the way downstream. Early on the morning of August 1, the Nor'Westers came upon a burial island near Celilo Falls. "There were many sheds under which the dead bodies were placed, all of which I wished to examine, but my Interpreter begged of me not to do it, as the relations of the dead would be very angry." The surveyor turned his curiosity instead to the eroded basalt pillars and fractured bluffs along this part of the river, whose shapes he compared to castles and pipe organs. They stopped several times during the day to smoke at friendly camps, and Thompson noted that the river level had fallen at least ten feet in the three weeks since they had passed. Back in the desert now, they had trouble finding enough wood for a fire to boil their salmon. The wind was blowing, and everything was full of sand. After a rattlesnake crawled into one voyageur's bedroll on a cool evening, the men learned to leave their blankets in the canoe until the dew was on the ground and they were certain the serpents were down in their holes.

Near the mouth of the John Day River, the furmen bypassed by a couple of small villages and pushed on upstream. When they stopped to line the canoe up a rapid, Thompson had a chance to measure one chinook salmon at four feet, four inches in length and over two feet in girth. They stayed to eat the fish and were about to reembark when two fishermen crossed the rapids to see them. "They seemed hurt that we did not stop at their villages and give them the news of our voyage, of which they are all very fond." From then on he made sure to stop and smoke with the natives he had met on his way down and recount the events of his trip: "Every trifle seemed to be of some importance to them, and the story of the Woman that carried a Bow and Arrows and had a Wife, was to them a romance to which they paid great attention and my Interpreter took great pleasure in relating it."

The evening of August 5 found Thompson back at the mouth of the Snake River. Months before, he had sent a letter to Alexander Henry requesting that his winter trade goods be sent across Athabasca Pass for an October 1 rendezvous, and now he would have to move smartly to meet them. He was out of gum to patch the leaks in his canoe, and there were no trees around to tap for more. Since the Columbia's Big Bend would take him well out of his way to the west, the surveyor decided to try a shortcut. He sent a messenger off for Spokane House to tell Jaco Finlay to bring packhorses south to meet him, then left the Columbia and ascended the Snake River for two days to the "Shawpatin and Pilloosees Road," a trail that led north into the Spokane country. The Nor'Westers put ashore near a camp of Palouse tribesmen, who "danced till they were fairly tired and the Chiefs bawled until they were hoarse. They forced a present of 8 horses on me, with a war garment." Thompson insisted on leaving an IOU for the horses, then he and his men took off riding through the rough scablands of the Palouse, choking on dust from the fine volcanic soil. On August 13 they reached Spokane House; Jaco and his horses turned up that evening, having missed them on the trail.

ON THE SAME evening that Thompson pulled into Spokane House, the Astorians made camp near the mouth of the Snake River. When Alexander Ross and his companions arose the next morning, "what did we see waving triumphantly in the air, at the confluence of the two great branches, but a British flag, hoisted in the middle of the Indian camp, planted there by Mr. Thompson as he passed." Ross was not amused at this symbolic gesture, especially when the chiefs at the big camp indicated that they would not let the boats pass any farther up the Columbia,

> saying that Koo-Koo-Sint—meaning Mr. Thompson— had told them so, pointing at the same time to the south branch [the Snake], as if to intimate that we might trade

there. The chiefs likewise stated that Koo-Koo-Sint had given them such and such things and among others, the British flag, that they should see his commands respected, but if Mr. Stuart would give them more than Koo-Koo-Sint had done, then he would be the greater chief, and might go where he pleased.

It is hard to know just what Thompson was up to here. He had obviously suspected that the Astorians' talk about building their post below The Dalles was a ruse, and maybe this was his way of suggesting to his new partners that a fair division of the business would be for them to turn up the Snake and trade in the territory Lewis and Clark had explored, while leaving the country he had charted to the North West Company. But he was certainly not so naive as to think that a British flag was going to turn them on their heels. Under the rules of joint occupancy, American and British companies had equal rights to the lands west of the Rockies known as the Oregon Territory, and the Astorians could build trading posts wherever they chose, no matter how many Union Jacks Thompson planted in their path. After a council with the chiefs the next day, Stuart's boats continued up the Columbia.

According to Alexander Ross, Qánqon shadowed the Astorians all the way, but not from any seat in a dugout canoe. She and her companion, "bold adventurous amazons they were," shot ahead or hung back from the main party like pups on a hunt, and were "the objects of attraction at every village and camp on the way." It was only later that Ross discovered the reason for all this attention. It seems that Qánqon had judiciously altered her prophecies, and was now showing off a letter (probably Finan McDonald's original note) and claiming that she and her mate

had been sent by the great white chief, with a message to apprize the natives in general that gifts, consisting of goods and implements of all kinds, were forthwith to be poured in upon them; that the great white chief knew their wants, and was just about to supply them with everything their hearts could desire; that the whites had hitherto cheated the Indians, by selling goods in place of making presents to them, as directed by the great white chief.

This new prophecy, though it might make David Stuart's life awkward in the future, helped make the berdache and her companion very popular figures among the Plateau peoples, "who loaded them for their good tidings with the most valuable items they possessed—horses, robes, leather, and higuas [shells]; so that, on our arrival at Oakinacken [the Okanogan River], they had no less than twenty-six horses, many of them loaded with the fruits of their false reports."

DAVID THOMPSON had no such distractions to impede his fall business. After only three days at Spokane House, he was off again, this time on horseback, carrying the fur packs that Jaco Finlay had collected. Back north through the Colville Valley he went, meeting Le Bon Vieux on the way to Kettle Falls, where he paused for twelve days to build yet another clinkersided cedar canoe. His old acquaintance Cartier was there with his band of Kalispels, ready to present him with a basket of dried berries. On September 2 the Nor'Westers put into the water above Kettle Falls and set out on the only stretch of the Columbia left uncharted. The first night they camped with the Old Chief and his Kootenai band, in country surrounded by hills of hard white limestone. Over the next three days, they poled and paddled their way around the mouths of the two big tributaries that Thompson had spent the past four years exploring: first the "Saleesh River" (the Pend Oreille, just north of the 49th parallel), then "McGillivray's River" (the Kootenay, near Castlegar, British Columbia). Here the men were relieved to buy some fresh fish, because their diet of dried salmon and berries had made all of them somewhat ill, and Coxe very much so. A few nights later they witnessed a celestial event: "Observed a Comet this evening, we had seen it these few nights past, but having a cloudy hilly horizon took it for a misty cloud then. Its place is nearly in a right line with the 2 guide Stars at 8:25 P.M." Within another week the party had lined its way up the Dalles des Morts (near modern Revelstoke), one of the most treacherous rapids on the whole river. Thompson knew he had almost closed the Columbia's circle, and along the way he watched as Coxe absorbed a whole new world:

> He had lived wholly on an Island, and knew it's extent, but had no ideas beyond it, as we proceeded up the River, and passed the great branches, the stream became lessened, and not so wide, as he did not know from what cause, every day he expected to get to the end of it; as we approached the cold increased, and the first shower of snow, he was for some time catching in his hand, and before he could satisfy his curiosity it was melted: the next morning thin ice was formed, which he closely examined in his hand, but like the Snow it also melted into water, and he was puzzled how the Snow and ice could become water, but the great Mountains soon settled his mind, where all became familiar to him.
>
> *Narrative*

It was September 18, 1811, when Thompson reached the Canoe River and revisited his winter hut at Boat Encampment, thereby completing his end-to-end survey of the Columbia's sinuous course. He had proved that the Great River of the West did run from the mountains to the sea after all, and the route that he pioneered across Athabasca Pass and down the Columbia to the Pacific served as the Northwest Passage for the rest of the Canadian fur trade's reign.

CHAPTER TEN

ROOM
TO FEED

FALL 1811–SUMMER 1812

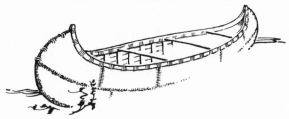

WHEN WILLIAM HENRY arrived at Boat Encampment with Thompson's fresh trade goods, he brought word from the North West Company's annual meeting three months earlier. There the partners had decided to send out a new agent to handle the business of the Columbia Department, "intending by this arrangement that Mr. David Thompson should be left to prosecute his plans of discovery on the west side of the Rocky Mountains towards the Pacific." Thompson did not record his reaction to the news that now that he had surveyed the entire course of the Columbia, the company was going to give him time to do it.

Winter was coming on as he began his first trip downstream from Boat Encampment on October 19. Two days later he came upon a herd of eight caribou resting beside the river: "They were not at all shy and had the place been good we might have killed several." His hunters had told him that these animals lived in the area, and he had noticed some of their tracks in the sand on his way upstream but had not actually seen what he called "reindeer" since his posting on

Hudson Bay. He thought this herd must be a different species, and his intuition turned out to be correct: he was looking at woodland caribou, close cousins to the barren ground species of the far north.

The furmen arrived back at Kettle Falls without incident on October 30. The native village there, so full of life when Thompson had passed through on his way to Astoria, was now entirely deserted, and there was no sign of the horses he had sent ahead for, either. He waited one day, then walked the seventy miles south through the Colville Valley to Spokane House. There he left the Hawaiian Coxe with Jaco Finlay and set off with packhorses for the Flathead country. Near Kullyspel House he met Bercier, who reported that the Flat Bows were doing more gambling than trapping and that there had been another Piegan raid near Kootanae House—this time two Kootenais had been killed and three Iroquois hunters robbed and left naked on the trail. Word had it that the Piegans had been planning to ambush Thompson's supply canoes, which they had expected to come by the southern route over Howse Pass, but had gotten tired of waiting.

Thompson pushed on through snow and sleet to Saleesh House, and when he arrived on November 19, he found the post "in a Ruinous condition." The roofs and floors all needed repairing, and the men's house was such a mess that they had to pitch a tent inside in order to stay dry. There was nothing to eat. Finan McDonald had left a note saying that he had gone to the Flathead camp for food, but he didn't come back for days and days, and in his journal entries Thompson sounds a bit testy about the whole situation. A week later his clerk did return with an ample supply of provisions, and on the same day James McMillan arrived from the Saskatchewan with John George McTavish, the man slated to succeed Thompson as supervisor of the Columbia Department. Within two days the supplies they brought had been sorted and McTavish was headed west to Spokane House to assume his duties. On his own again, Thompson concentrated on repairing the buildings at Saleesh House so they'd last, especially the roof. Le Bon Vieux brought in a nice *chevreuil* at an opportune moment and loaned Thompson three horses to take a short trip up the Clark Fork. The weather was a sloppy "glush" that made a mess out of everything.

January of 1812 began cold and clear, with only a skiff of snow on the ground, and Thompson took sick with a sore throat and feverish cold. Too puny to work for a couple of days, he couldn't eat or sleep, and measured his pulse rate at 120. As he began to mend, he laid out plans for a sledge with wheels on it and designed a mousetrap. A very sore eye troubled him through the latter part of January, but did not keep him from using his wood-bending skills to craft some snowshoes for Finan McDonald. The men started work on a cargo canoe, and Le Bon Vieux's wife braided seventy fathoms of cordage to sew it together. When cold weather stalled the boat project, two of the voyageurs set up a kettle of ashes and boiled them with water to make lye, which they then mixed with animal fat for a supply of soap.

In mid-February the surveyor and Finan McDonald pointed two canoes upriver, intending to trade at the various winter camps for furs and provisions. There was strong shore ice in many places along the Clark Fork, and at one point they had to plow through eighty yards of frozen river. Their first stop was at the tents of the Kalispel chief Cartier, who provided them with some dried meat. Next day, hungry again, they shot "a poor Chevreuil that was run down and much torn by the Wolves," and Cartier followed along with them to the large Flathead camp at the junction of the Flathead and Clark Fork Rivers. Here Thompson counted sixty tents of families and noted that so many of the men had been killed in recent battles with the Piegans that there were another twenty tents of widows.

While Finan McDonald handled the trade, Thompson hired the Gauche, a Kootenai who had hunted for him in the past, to guide him on an excursion. The Gauche led him from

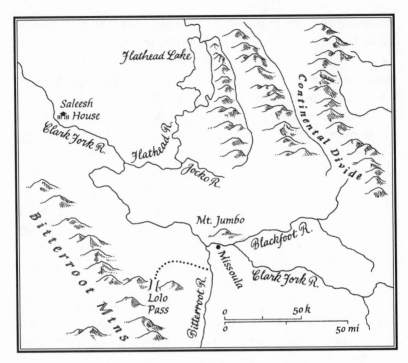

the Flathead River south along a ridge trail and down into the valley where the modern town of Missoula lies. The day was clear and good for viewing; Thompson climbed the round hill now called Mount Jumbo and looked out at the surrounding valleys. With information he had gathered from local people and his knowledge of Lewis and Clark's journey, he was able to retrace the Americans' path along the Bitterroot Valley to Traveler's Rest, then across the mountains through Lolo Pass. It was a lot of geography to take in, but the surveyor knew exactly what he was looking at: "The route Capn. Lewis & Party were from the Misserourie, behind those blue Hills to the above Branch & down it to the Brook of the Defile that leads to the Salmon." With that vision Thompson closed one long seam in the scheme of his big map, and from the mountaintop it all made sense.

Thompson made a rough sketch of the rivers and hills, then he and the Gauche climbed down from Mount Jumbo into the narrow river canyon known as the Hell Gate, a favorite rendezvous spot for Piegan war parties gathering to attack the Flatheads. Thompson called this cleft "the Defiles of Courter" in memory of the American trapper who had been killed two years before somewhere in the vicinity. He would have liked to look around some more, but their horses were worn out from struggling through the deep snow and it was beginning to storm: "Very bad Weather all of the Evening & Night & no shelter, I passed much of the Night standing leaning against a Tree – Kingfishers about."

On their way home the next day, they passed the bones of a horse beside the trail. Thompson noticed that the skull was carefully positioned in the center of the skeleton, and the Gauche told him that its nose pointed to the grave of its master—both warrior and horse had been killed in a battle on this spot. "The ridge of the Nose was marked with 7 Stripes of red signifying the number of Enemies he had slain with his own hand in Combat, on one side of the Head were marked 1 red Stripe, on the other side 3 red Stripes, signifying the number of Wounds he had received in former Battles. The Nose was all marked with red, signifying his End."

The pair made it back to the Flathead camp by noon, where Finan McDonald had been trying unsuccessfully to dry some meat underneath a linen tent. Two days later Thompson was invited to a council of the Flatheads and their allies, who had gathered to discuss a recent peace offer from the Piegans. As he related the story in his *Narrative*, not everyone thought peace was a good idea; one old man said he felt much safer with the Piegans as enemies than as friends:

> Who is there among us that has not cut off his hair several times, and mourned over our relations and friends, their flesh devoured, and their bones gnawed, by Wolves and Dogs. A state of peace has always been a

time of anxiety, we were willing to trust and sure to be
deceived ... Do as you please, I now sleep all night,
but if you make peace I shall sleep in the day, and watch
all night.

Some of the other elders spoke in favor of calling a truce,
while many of the younger men wanted to use their new guns
to avenge their dead. When the chief Cartier asked
Thompson for his opinion, he listed the different tribes east
of the mountains and their approximate sizes. He pointed out
that the bands and allies of the Piegans were numerous and
not under a single chief's control: "My advice is, that you do
not make peace with only one Tribe, and leave yourselves exposed to the inroads of all the others, and let your Answer
[be] that you claim by ancient rights the freedom of hunting
the Bison, that you will not make War upon any of them but
shall always be ready to defend yourselves." After much discussion the tribes at the parley decided not to make peace,
but to cross the Divide only in parties large enough to defend
themselves. If harassed by the Piegans again, they vowed to
fight, and the chiefs dispatched messengers telling all of their
allies to prepare for war the next summer.

Directly after the council, the surveyor reengaged his
guide the Gauche and rode north. They passed the Old
Chief's winter camp and then "came smartly on trot & hard
Gallop to 1:25 P.M., when we alighted on the top of a bare
Knowl, commanding a very extensive View of the Lake &
Country far around." They were looking across Flathead
Lake, "a fine sheet of water . . . the haunt in all seasons of
aquatic fowl." While the surveyor sketched the lake and some
of the surrounding landscape, the Gauche pointed out a wide
gap in the mountains to the east; he said that his people and
many other west-side tribes used to follow a trail through this
gap on their way to the plains to hunt buffalo, but no one
had gone that way for several years because of their fear of
the Piegans.

Back at the Flathead camp the next day, Thompson loaded his canoe with the meat and furs he and Finan McDonald had traded from the various hunters and started for Saleesh House with his voyageurs. On their way they camped through a violent storm: "Heavy gust of Wind about Midnight tore up the Tent, tossed the Canoe over & over, split it in several places & we often thought to be buried under the trees." They were able to repair the canoe and get to the post the next morning, where they started packing for the long haul across the mountains.

By March 12 everything was ready, and while the men gummed two canoes, Thompson made a last-minute sketch of the view of plains and hills to the north. The next day they started downriver and immediately damaged both boats in the rapids of Thompson Falls. After half a day for repairs, they continued on through sleet and snow. At another big rapid they passed a cluster of wooden crosses that the voyageurs had erected in memory of a free hunter and his family who had drowned there the previous summer. They stopped for a barrel of gum at Kullyspel House, then took the overland route to the Spokane post. The pelts collected there amounted to 122 fur packs, weighing almost 11,000 pounds. The Columbia trade was steadily increasing, much as Thompson had hoped it would in the letter he had written to the partners four years before.

He and his crew started north toward Kettle Falls on horseback and a few days later camped near a stand of decent cedar along the Colville River. While they split out timbers for canoes, a steady flow of visitors came and went: a group of free hunters who had been trapping on the Okanogan River; Bercier, leading eighteen horses loaded with gum and furs; Jaco Finlay, who stayed to help build four new boats; a voyageur with ten rolls of watap; Martin, the Iroquois who had helped Thompson dislocate his thumb two years before; three-fingered James McMillan and newcomer John George McTavish. By the evening of April 21, Thompson had collected six canoes at the falls, gummed and ready to go. He divided the baggage and then went out to observe for the latitude and longitude of the Ilthkoyape Falls one more time (48° 37' 22" N, 117° 54' 58" W). At noon the next day, the heavily laden Columbia brigade moved upstream. They portaged around the Dalles des Morts, negotiated the Columbia's hairpin loop at Boat Encampment, then switched to horses for the climb over Athabasca Pass. Thompson, walking ahead on bearpaw snowshoes in ice-crusted snow, sprained his right ankle and limped to the summit.

"AH, ATHABASCA PASS," said the park guide when I asked him about the trail. "Gonna make a slog for yourself, eh?"

"It's nice up top," he allowed. "They have the brass plaque at the Committee's Punchbowl, where the fur traders used to clink a toast every time they crossed. And you'll get a good look at Scott Glacier. But down in the woods, it's just a lot of walking. And you won't see much game. Elk OK. Goat. Moose here and there. A few sheep if you glass the slopes. Maybe caribou up on the ridges. Grizzly, of course. If you're lucky a wolf—there was a wolf pack working that area when I made my wildlife count. But mostly it's a long slog."

A long slog was just fine with me that day. I started up a hill on a wide gravel track that wound through some bog-lands, then narrowed to a horse trail and took to the trees away from the noisy course of the Whirlpool River. Mosquitoes wafted up in clouds from a rich understory of berry bushes and ferns, and there were miles to put in with only occasional glimpses of river. Old-growth spruce and lodgepole pine blotted out the sky, and the trail turned soggy as the gravel faded to sodden hoofprints. But even with the skin curling off my toes from the constant wetness, I could see how this path made sense to David Thompson. The river lay far to the north of his Piegan troubles, and the rolling benches made for a gradual ascent.

About halfway through the thirty-mile trek up to Athabasca Pass, the trail breaks out of the timber onto the wide, silvery promenade of the Whirlpool River's floodplain. A few miles ahead, the icy jumble of Scott Glacier pours from a saddle between two massive peaks. Buffalo of former times ascended this drainage during their late-summer searches for cool air and fresh grass, marking out a course that hunters could follow, then Thompson and his voyageurs. Bison and furmen liked those long, even slogs.

The open flat beside the river ends in a steep, wooded headwall; after that it's all rocks and intricately carved cascades as the trail climbs through a dense subalpine forest to top the Divide. It was somewhere around here that David Thompson had seen that big set of footprints on his first trip over this pass—the tracks his hunters had insisted belonged to a "large unknown animal." During his next trip the men reminded him of the tracks and pointed out a mountain where the creature was supposed to live: "On the top of the eminence, there was a Lake of several miles around which was deep moss, with much coarse grass in places, and rushes; that these animals fed there, they were sure from the great quantity of moss torn up, with grass and rushes; the hunters all agreed this animal was not carnivorous, but fed on moss, and vegetables."

It's hard not to be intrigued by this account. The Whirlpool drainage does have an Ice Age look about it, and it has the room, the vast empty spaces that it would take to harbor an outsized relic. Rich bogs and lakes lie pocked all along the watercourse, many of them surrounded by dense, wetland vegetation. The thought of such good coarse grass, of sedges and rushes torn up by roving tusks, of sphagnum moss trunk-fed by the bucketload into some gaping maw . . . but Thompson never saw a mammoth, and his hunters admitted that not one of them had ever seen one either.

I reached the incline late in the afternoon and didn't feel

like getting swallowed up by the woods again, so I set up my tent at a campsite right there. I wandered around a little bit, in and out of the trees, until I stepped in a huge, berry-rich bear flop. I returned to the tent, unlaced my pack, and gobbled everything I could find inside it to eat. After supper I was still filled with the restless exhaustion that had dogged me all the way up the trail. I wanted to be looking for some of those fourteen-inch footprints, but I couldn't seem to keep my mind focused on the ground.

Three days before, on another steep trail in the woods, a Frenchman walking ten feet in front of me had keeled over with a heart attack. I hadn't known the man—we were part of a group of tourists on the way up to look at some fossil beds—but I couldn't shake the image of the awkward twist in his shoulder as he had turned to speak, or the way dribbles of liquid had leaked from his red plastic water bottle as it rolled down the hill into my hand.

My campsite on the Whirlpool stared straight at Scott Glacier, and I thought I would ford the river and hike over for a closer look. The water didn't look more than waist deep, but it was running fast enough that I could see round rocks rolling along its bed. I took off my boots and pants and knelt down on the bank to test the water, so loud and cold. My knees nestled into the smooth skipper rocks along its edge.

He had seemed healthy enough, a middle-aged man on vacation. He had brought along his tripod to take pictures of the fossils. He had a thin, curved nose, and porcelain skin that looked almost translucent. After he collapsed onto the ground, the dirt and needles that stuck to his face had made it seem as if he were sinking into the forest; his last breaths had drained away into the vast mountains, and within a few minutes he was gone.

Down on my knees by the Whirlpool, gooseflesh covered my legs. I stood up and stepped into the current, feeling for the rocks with my toes. The water rushed about my knees. My arms flapped in the air, grasping for balance. As I worked my way across, the crags of Scott Peak hovered directly before me. "The passage to the other World, the Indians suppose to be by a high Crag. Their grandfather lends them a hand up it – if good he brings them safe to the top. If bad, he when half way up lets them fall to the bottom, where a mist forever blinds their Eyes." So reads a brief note in the back of the daybook that David Thompson carried with him across Athabasca Pass in 1812.

On my way back down from the pass, I was caught in a violent hailstorm and took refuge on the front porch of a forestry work cabin. Propped up against the wall was a neat cross-section from an old lodgepole pine. The tree slice, about as big around as a logger's chest, had 206 tight little growth rings, and someone had counted backwards from the outside of the circle, marking dates and events with an ink pen in a long winter count. Thin blue lines showed the year of Canada's independence from the Crown, World Wars II and I, and the bad winter of 1886–87. Near the center was a dot for the year Thompson first passed this way. The tree had been a mere sapling then, not even big enough to chop for firewood. I ran my finger around the little ridge of raised grain, barely a hair's thickness, and then followed the circles on out, feeling the layers that had gradually buried the winter of 1811 inside the tree. I thought about how David Thompson had struggled that season, and during most of his others, with the elements and with the Piegans; I thought about his close calls with rapids and blizzards, starvation and sickness. Yet as far as I could tell, during all of his distant expeditions, the surveyor never lost a single man under his command.

"MAY 8TH FRIDAY A very fine Night & Day – did not freeze much. At 3½ A.M. set off – held on up the Banks, very bad walking . . . could find no water 'till 8½ A.M. when we breakfasted – At Height of Land tried to observe, but the Sun was past the Meridian. Took a pipe [with] men." The surveyor worked his way down from Athabasca Pass for the last time and steered his canoes east, picking up Charlotte and the children, including a year-old boy he had never seen, somewhere along the way. Upon retirement many of the furmen left their native wives and offspring in the field and married again in eastern Canada or England, but Thompson was taking his family with him.

By the time they arrived at Fort William in July, war had been declared between the United States and Great Britain. Although this was obviously a subject of great concern, the partners had hopes that the conflict would not completely disrupt their business. William McGillivray was in London, where he was fitting out a merchant vessel for the mouth of the Columbia; in a letter that his emissary Donald McTavish delivered to Fort William, he wrote that he was waiting to launch the ship until he heard whether David Thompson had found a practical route for transporting the supplies to his interior posts. Thompson indeed had, and the partners at the rendezvous recognized how much he had accomplished during his five years of unbroken work. After setting in motion a range of plans to develop the surveyor's new Athabasca-Columbia route, they placed before the meeting "a resolve entered into that David Thompson now going down on Rotation shall be allowed his full share of the Company's profits for three years . . . that he is to finish his Charts, Maps, etc. and deliver them to the agents in that time."

A couple of days after the wintering partners approved the measure, a vessel arrived at the fort carrying news that the American fort at Mackinaw had fallen. Fearing live action on the Great Lakes, Thompson and his family got back in their canoe and dashed along the north shore of Lake Superior to the narrow straits that lead into Lake Huron, where they had to scrape the U.S. border. Once through, they were safe to cut north for the Ottawa River and float on to Montreal.

CHAPTER ELEVEN

THE SMELL OF
CAMAS ROOT

1812–1857

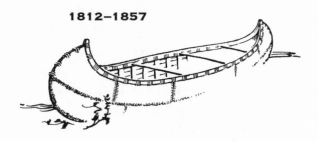

W HEN THOMPSON arrived in Montreal in the fall
of 1812, he walked down a city street for the first
time in twenty-seven years. He seemed to take to the settled
lifestyle straightaway, purchasing a house and a farm in the
village of Terrebonne, north of the city. He was still arranging his family in their new home when he resumed his daily
journal, using the same fur company format that he had
learned as a teenager on the Saskatchewan. "October 20th
Tuesday A white frosty morning, but charming day...en-
gaged a House Keeper at 10 Dollars per month...Sent for
writing desk Hinges." In early entries, he recorded the latest
news of the War of 1812 and observed for the latitude of his
new abode (45° 40' 59" N). On October 30 he called in a
minister and solemnized his vows with Charlotte. The next
day he was commissioned as an ensign major in the
Sedentary Militia under former North West partner
Roderick Mackenzie and immediately set about getting the
guns in good order for the local troops. There were several
retired furmen living in the area, and the rest of the fall reads

like a typical Thompson blur of work mixed up with an established couple's social schedule: the surveyor bought a milk
cow and danced till midnight; he built wooden bedsteads for
the children and dined at the priest's house after attending
high mass; he copied out his Columbia journals and took in a
holiday ball; he was rousted out of bed by a troop alert and
went for a ride in his new cariole. Just before Christmas he
made the four-hour drive to Montreal, where he had dinner
with William McGillivray and then brought Fanny home
from boarding school for the holidays. During January he
nursed Charlotte and two of the children through a bad case
of the measles and made a model of a cannon cart for the war
effort. But what Thompson really concentrated on, from the
moment he was settled in Terrebone, was his map work.

Building on the sheets he had begun to ink in years
before, and adding information forwarded to him from other
traders, Thompson settled down to his ambitious cartography
project. Within seven months he had sent McGillivray a
sketch of the Oregon Country, and soon afterward he mailed
a representation that incorporated all of the territory from
Hudson Bay west to the Pacific. This second large map was
hung in the dining hall at Fort William, on a blank wall
across from oil paintings of Admiral Nelson and the Battle of
Trafalgar. For many seasons Thompson's map guided travelers who passed through on their way west. On the Pacific
Slope of these first two maps, he penned in a watercourse he
called the Caledonia River, which he showed rising just west
of his Boat Encampment and curling southwest to enter the
Pacific between the Fraser and the Columbia. No such river
exists, and Thompson corrected this mistake in the next version of his work. But the original maps were reproduced several times without his permission, and the phantom river
serves as a marker that traces uncredited editions of the surveyor's work. In 1814, Thompson delivered yet another chart
of the West to his partners, an even more accurate version
that didn't get a public viewing for another thirty-five years.

THOMPSON'S BIG map of 1814 is on permanent display at the Provincial Archives of Ontario in Toronto. At ten by six-and-a-half feet, the chart covers an entire wall at the entrance of the archive's reading room. It is enclosed in a specially designed glass case and further protected by a dark curtain that rolls away when you press a button. To prevent excessive light from damaging the paper and ink, the drape automatically rolls back after one minute.

The first thing I saw as the curtain opened was color: the sheets of rag linen paper have darkened with age to a varied, autumnal hue that in another two centuries might approach the orange back side of good birch rind. The writing ink of Thompson's day was rendered from oak apple galls, boiled together in a recipe that included lumps of iron sulfate and gum arabic. It flowed jet black from the goose quill, but over time mellowed into its original oaken tones, and now spreads a web of sepia across the linen continent. Around the periphery of his chart, the heavily inked squares that delineate degrees of latitude and longitude glow with the umbers of a deep forest night.

When he assembled the twenty-five individual sheets of his project, Thompson allowed himself plenty of overlap; where the folios join, his mucilage glue forms a wide strip that's lighter than the single layers and often damaged or blurred. One of these glue strips follows the 49th parallel, and there are tears and gaps along the crease; light brown repair marks obscure parts of the upper Okanogan country, Kettle Falls, the Kootenay River between Bonner's Ferry and Kootenay Lake, and the territory east of the Tobacco Plains.

Thompson used several sizes and styles of script to conjure different levels of information from the map. All-capital block letters designate mountain ranges and major rivers. Brooks, rivulets, and native trails he labeled in smaller, cursive script. A swirled "NWCo" appears wherever a trade house existed. There are snippets of information, the sounds of the surveyor whispering to himself: he deems the Colville River "Unnavigable," and at the mouth of the mighty Fraser he remarks, "To this place white men have come from the sea." He laid neat feather plumes beside each watercourse to denote the direction of flow, and along these arrows the furmen's journeys of discovery move again. Alexander Mackenzie's short portage across the upper Rockies makes sense. Ram Rivulet is clearly delineated, and no matter what a charlatan the Rook turned out to be as a guide, you can see that he was very close to being on the mark. Thompson used the local names for many of the rivers; Howse Pass and Athabasca Pass are simply "Heights of Land."

It's an amazingly accurate and at the same time idiosyncratic piece of cartography. Thompson laid the ink on as an artist might, with delicate nuances of shade and texture that indicate the width of a river oxbow or the elevation of the Eagle Hills in the midst of the prairies. The Rocky Mountains look like a twisted chain, with separate loops linking the big peaks north and south in an effort to convey timberline, glaciers, height, and mass all in an instant. Thompson deviated from this bird's-eye perspective only once, right above his Kootanae House at the headwaters of the Columbia. During the two winters he spent there, he developed a special regard for the peak he named Mount Nelson, "which stands alone in native grandeur." He went outside over and over again to measure its height and sketch its profile, and on his big map he inscribed a circle in the range west of Kootanae House, then drew in a side view of the peak. It's the only construction like it on the whole chart, one nod to the mountain that stood at the center of all his western movements.

AS THOMPSON sat in Terrebonne, tending his garden and transcribing points and courses from his field notebooks onto his maps, the situation on the Columbia was anything but calm. In August of 1812 a visitor to Fort Astoria told the Americans that their supply ship *Tonquin* had been overwhelmed by angry natives off the coast of Vancouver Island and blown to smithereens. The vessel's loss left the American post defenseless in a time of war, and when Thompson's successor John George McTavish paddled down the Columbia from Spokane House in the summer of 1813, he negotiated a deal with Duncan McDougall to buy Fort Astoria for the North West Company and place its men under British protection. The following March the Nor'Westers' merchant ship *Isaac Todd* arrived from Portsmouth, accompanied by a frigate from the Royal Navy that had orders to wipe out any American settlements in the region, but the Union Jack was already flying over Astoria. The *Isaac Todd* provided the post with all the trade goods it needed and offered some company veterans an opportunity for a comfortable ride back around the Horn to civilization. On a sloppy May evening in 1814, two of Thompson's old cohorts, Alexander Henry and Donald McTavish, left a farewell party and stepped into the dory that would ferry them out to the vessel, which lay anchored off Tongue Point. The Columbia's dark currents capsized the little boat, drowning all hands on board.

That same year David Thompson was visited by personal tragedy.

> January 11th Tuesday. A fine cloudy day. My poor dear little John passed the Night with great difficulty of breathing, but quiet thro' extreme weakness, and at 7 A.M. it pleased the Almighty God to take him from this World – had a Coffin of Oak made for him. He is 5 years 4½ months old – measures 3 ft. 9 in. and still appears a beautiful Boy. This loss has plunged us in deep affliction, especially his poor Mother.

A few weeks after John's death, Thompson traveled to Quebec to obtain a license as a land surveyor. When he returned to Terrebonne after riding all night, he found two of his daughters ill with roundworms, a common affliction of that time. Twelve-year-old Fanny soon recovered, but seven-year-old Emma grew worse. For the next week Thompson tirelessly nursed the little girl who had crossed Howse Pass with him as a toddler, dosing her with calomel, Carolina pink root, and castor oil. On February 20 he recorded hopes of her recovery. Over the next two days, however, she relapsed, and on the evening of February 22, she died. "February 24 Thursday. A very fine Morning - at 10½ A.M. smart Rain came on & continued with Sleet all day - at 9 A.M. sent off the Body of my poor Emma. At 10 set off myself and at 1½ P.M. buried my poor little Daughter close touching her little Brother John in the same Grave. God Almighty the Saviour of the World, bless them both."

In 1815 the family moved to Glengarry County, Ontario, and the next year Thompson mailed a prospectus to a London bookmaker that described an ambitious atlas he had in mind. It stretched "from the east side of Lake Superior, and Hudson's Bay, quite across the continent to the Pacific Ocean." It would include the territory of each of the Indian nations, and all the trading posts as set out by the Hudson's Bay and North West Companies. It would be accompanied by a sister chart, marked with the important mountains and drainages, on which he would superimpose the "position and extent of the Coal Mines; of the various Beds of different kinds of Stone and Rock; of the great Meadows and Forests; the limits of the countries on which the Bison, Elk, Red Deer, Wild Sheep, etc. are found; the line of the position of the Countries, over which, is the most constant appearance and greatest brightness of the Aurora Borealis."

Referring to himself in the third person, Thompson strived to give his potential buyer some idea of what had gone into the making of such a project, and promised delivery within three years: "Nothing less than an unremitting perse-verance bordering on enthusiasm could have enabled him to have brought these maps to their present state; in early life he conceived the idea of this work, and Providence has given him to complete, amidst various dangers, all that one man could hope to perform." The publisher was not so impressed, and turned down the proposal.

Around this time Thompson accepted a post as astronomer with the International Boundary Commission. From his new position he guided the official U.S.-Canadian survey of the border from Saint-Régis, Quebec, west through Lake of the Woods, then down to the southeastern corner of Manitoba. This kind of baseline survey constituted a life's work in itself, and he traveled many of the routes exactly as he had during his days with the North West Company, directing a handful of voyageurs in a small boat and recording his positions neatly in a daily journal. On the Great Lakes they fought heat and mosquitoes, wind and heavy surf. In many areas flat land and thick woods made observation points hard to establish; the men would fell trees and erect pole stations, then clamber up live trees at the next stop and try to spot the poles.

In the summer of 1819, on the western end of Lake Erie, the surveyor and his crew entered an area of miasmic swamp and soon all came down with sweats and fever. One of the men lay delirious in the bottom of the boat, and the rest of the crew had trouble getting up the strength to row. "August 8th Heavy showers with close sultry weather and we camped on a wet sand with everything dripping wet. Myself in fever: pulse 101 to the minute. 2 men very ill of the fever and the rest complaining at times." His daybook entries for the month sound a lot like those from his first difficult summer on Windermere Lake, except that in this case the local inhabitants were Dutchmen who sold the party milk and loaves of bread, and when Thompson's crew pulled out of the field in early fall, they ferried across Lake Erie in a steamboat: "The rolling of the vessel and working of the engine, made us all sick."

In 1820 William McGillivray held a dinner for all present

and former North West Company partners at his palatial house in Montreal. It was a gala affair, attended by many members of Montreal society. One of the guests was a young scientist named J. J. Bigsby, who found himself seated beside the explorer David Thompson: "He was plainly dressed, quiet and observant. His figure was short and compact, and his black hair was worn short all around, and cut square, as if by one stroke of the shears, just above the eyebrows. His complexion was of a gardener's ruddy brown, while the expression of deeply furrowed features was friendly and intelligent, but his cut-short nose gave him an odd look . . . "

Since there are no known photographs or portraits of Thompson, this description is the closest contemporary likeness of him that exists. At the time of McGillivray's dinner, the surveyor was fifty years old, still at work in the field for the Boundary Commission. Bigsby later got a job with the commission himself and, while traveling with Thompson, had the chance to hear some of the surveyor's tales: "He can create a wilderness and people it . . . or climb the Rocky Mountains with you in a snowstorm, so clearly and palpably, that only shut your eyes and you hear the crack of a rifle shot, or feel the snow-flakes melt on your cheeks as he talks." Bigsby also recorded Thompson's practice of reading, "in the most extraordinary French," three chapters each of the Old and New Testaments to his men during their spare time.

David Thompson served ten years on the Boundary Commission, the last four as sole chief astronomer—his calculations were one of the few things agreed upon by both sides. When the project degenerated into a political dispute in 1826, he resigned and retired back to Glengarry County to live as a farmer and businessman. His neighbors included some of his former fur-trading partners, but by this time William McGillivray's North West empire had collapsed. The Hudson's Bay Company had merged with its former nemesis in 1821, and the terms of amalgamation were not at all favorable to the North West Company. McGillivray died in 1825, and two months later his company declared bankruptcy; its substantial debts included the sum of four hundred pounds owed to David Thompson.

At the end of 1826, Finan McDonald joined the enclave of retired Nor'Westers in Glengarry County. His career had extended all over the Northwest, where he had become known as a faithful family man and good-hearted giant with a quick temper; every traveler of the period tells a story about him. Jaco Finlay kept a lower profile, taking over Spokane House when it was abandoned by the Hudson's Bay Company shortly after it assumed control of the business. Jaco lived there peacefully with his family until his death in 1828.

Another of Thompson's former acquaintances did not fade so quietly. The Kootenai berdache Qánqon, the messenger-prophetess who had paced Thompson and the Astorians up the Columbia in 1812, apparently told her story of white men who would come bearing gifts as far north as the Shuswap Indian territory in New Caledonia. Despite rumors of her death there, Qánqon reappeared some years later in the Kootenai country as a translator and shaman. Her fame spread south, and trade journals from western Montana's Flathead Post make mention of her in 1825 and again in 1837, when, according to a missionary's account, her attempt to broker peace between some Flatheads and a Blackfeet raiding party finally led to her demise.

Modern Kootenai people provided anthropologist Claude Schaeffer with a fuller version of the berdache's death. Apparently Qánqon, though no longer a young woman, had gone out with a raiding party of young Kootenai warriors. As on her first raid, the party was unable to locate any enemy bands and was returning to its home camp under relaxed guard when it walked right into a Blackfeet ambush. One brave, traveling toward the rear of Qánqon's party, managed to hide himself in thick brush, where he listened to the successive war whoops of the Blackfeet, each one signaling the end of another Kootenai warrior. He heard a woman's yell and recognized Qánqon's voice. Her screams seemed to continue for a long time before he heard a final Blackfeet whoop.

Over time, details of Qánqon's death filtered back to her people. Members of the war party said that she sustained several gunshot wounds before they could subdue her. Then she was held in a seated position while the warriors methodically slashed at her midsection with knives. But each new wound closed up as soon as the knife was withdrawn. Apparently this healing occurred several times, but Qánqon gave no more cries. Finally one warrior opened up her chest and ate a piece of her heart, a coup de grace that was reserved for the most tenacious enemies. Qánqon was unable to heal this wound and died, after half a day of torture—a measure of the great strength of her spirit protector. It was said that when the Kootenai burial party arrived some time later, no wild animals or birds had disturbed her body.

BETWEEN HIS SHARES in the North West Company and his position with the International Boundary Commission, David Thompson made considerable money over the course of his career. But in the years after his retirement, it began to slip away. William McGillivray's bankruptcy hurt, and several of Thompson's children made poor business decisions with their father's backing. The collection of petty local debts, which within the scheme of the fur trade he had accomplished so efficiently, proved more difficult back in civilization; even the town church defaulted on a note to Thompson. The last of David and Charlotte's thirteen children was born in Glengarry County in 1829, and that winter he made an unfortunate contract to supply the British army with cordwood that cost him the rest of his capital. His notebook for 1833 begins with a page entitled "A List of Accounts due to D. Thompson, 30th January 1833," but the debts were for paltry sums, and by the end of the year, he had lost all his landholdings to creditors. At about the time his personal finances dwindled to nothing, his journal comments were concerned with a dry summer that seemed to reflect his own situation: "No Pigeons and very few Ducks Geese etc. very few Rooks or Birds of any kind except in the depth of the Forest in July, and August, almost all the Wells dried up and the Fields were destitute of Herbage even the Clover when cut had no under-grass but appeared as if the ground had been exposed to a burning sun. Butter very scarce and fever – frequent winds."

Over the next three years Thompson undertook a variety of routine surveying jobs, measuring out canals, township boundaries, and land grants. May of 1837 found him inter-viewing, at age sixty-seven, for the job of clarifying the Muskoka-Madawaska River route from Georgian Bay to the Ottawa River. A Captain Baddely was a member of the gov-ernment panel who heard the interview, and he wrote to the Surveyor General about it:

> Mr. Thompson dined with me yesterday . . . he is highly qualified for the duty in point of scientific and profes-sional requirements . . . I think it is necessary, however, from the confidence which has been placed in me, and my desire to see the service properly conducted, to ac-quaint you that there are rumours abroad that Mr. T. is not trustworthy as to reporting of facts. This I mention without knowing what degree of credit to attach, al-though I must confess that there is something in his conversation which I do not like and which makes me suspect his candour.

Apparently the rumors that clouded the surveyor's reputation involved Canadian resentment over several decisions made by the International Boundary Commission, on which he had held a prominent position—an ironic smear, since Thompson was highly critical of some of the political decisions that were being made concerning Canada's boundary with the United States. In any case, the commission hired Thompson for the Muskoka job.

The surveyor began by rejecting Captain Baddely's recommendation for a tin canoe, listening instead to his voyageurs and spending two weeks in the construction of a more seaworthy cedar vessel. Once out, he searched the somewhat barren landscape for more than simple points on the map, thinking, as he often had in the West, of the possibilities for human settlement. In a vigorous stand of hardwoods he "bored the Soil for 2 feet a good dark grey loam, with about 2 or 3 in. of rich vegetable Mould on the top. Appears very good for Agriculture."

When he had time apart from his surveying work, Thompson kept tinkering with his sheaf of maps, and in 1843 he mailed the final, perfected set of his atlas to officials in England. These five large sheets, each one four feet by ten feet, contain much of the detailed information promised in his 1816 proposal. That same year the Canadian government decided to purchase a version of all his maps of the country. Arrowsmith of London, still the world's premier cartographer, was asked to set a fair price. It was decreed that Thompson would receive 150 pounds, a pittance for the amount of work he had invested in the project. Arrowsmith then borrowed from the set to clarify its own maps, which were soon published as a Hudson's Bay pamphlet without any credit to Thompson.

Thompson's maps were important documents—Britain and the United States were still arguing about the location of their border, and his explorations and surveys constituted a legitimate stake to a large part of the Oregon Territory. During the negotiations Thompson wrote several letters to the officials involved, once suggesting a boundary along the 47th parallel from the Rocky Mountains to the Columbia, then down the center of that river to the sea. This would have awarded to Canada what is now northwestern Montana, the Idaho panhandle, and most of Washington State. In another letter Thompson described how he had crossed the Rocky Mountains in 1801 and 1802 to begin the exploration of the region. Whether he misremembered the date by five years or was fudging to establish precedence, his efforts came to nothing. The Americans held firm in their demands for the entire region, and in 1846 the British government ceded its claim to all lands south of the 49th parallel. Thompson was outraged, and for the rest of his life he felt that "blockhead" politicians had given away to the Americans some of the best of the country he had explored—especially his old trade route from Saleesh House west to Kullyspel and Spokane Houses.

Shortly after the 1846 boundary settlement, Thompson's vision failed. Apparently the eye that he had damaged as a teenager, during his frantic winter of learning with Philip Turnor, had never fully recovered, and finally his other eye weakened enough to leave him unable to practice his trade. Thompson and Charlotte moved in with one of their daughters, and this was the time when he decided to write an account of his adventures in the fur trade. A decade earlier, the American writer Washington Irving had tried to purchase the rights to all of Thompson's personal notebooks for use in writing *Astoria*, but Thompson had refused to sell, preferring to tell his own story. Certain that the public would be interested in his far-ranging travels, he began paging through his old field journals.

DAVID THOMPSON'S surviving notebooks, all seventy-seven of them, are grouped by number in a series of green archival boxes in Toronto. They are old and fragile, and before I could look at them I had to slip on a pair of soft cotton gloves. Each of the daybooks is ten inches wide and fourteen inches tall, large enough that it took a lot of steady writing to fill one up. Inside their marbled covers, some of the pages are smeared with mud and marked with dark splotches of lamp oil. Circles of mold range in color from dove brown to a beautiful mauve. A note fell out of one journal volume into my gloved hand; it had been written by a conservator who had inspected the molds and decided that they had probably stopped growing some time ago.

The script in Thompson's western field journals does not have the elegance and versatility of the lettering on his maps, but it is for the most part still clear and readable. As I sat in the reading room of the Provincial Archives, within sight of the curtain that hides his monumental map, I could see how his writing clenched up as he grew old. By the time he had penned four drafts of the *Narrative*, his fluid stroke had grown very shaky. Some historians have tried to connect Thompson's faltering hand with a dimming of thought, in the way that his brother-in-law, John McDonald of Garth, expressed it when he tried to dictate his own adventures at age eighty-five: "It may naturally be expected that, at that age, the memory is gone." But David Thompson's memory was far from shot. He had nursed the idea of a book about his travels for many years, perhaps ever since he copied out pages of Samuel Hearne's explorations at the frigid trade depot in Churchill when he was fourteen years old. While working on the *Narrative* he had his copious diaries before him, and they formed a mother lode of original data. For long stretches Thompson stuck right with the daybooks, reeling off events almost exactly as he had originally set them down. At other times a simple journal entry sparked deeper memories.

On a fall day in 1809, Thompson had stopped at a bend in the Pend Oreille River to smoke with a small group of Kalispel Indians led by a good-natured old chief. In his diary it amounts to nothing more than a brief exchange: "The oldest man according to custom made a speech & a Present of 2 Cakes of Root Bread about 12 lb. of Roots & 2½ dried Salmon . . . " The Kalispel chief had presented the surveyor with his first basket of roasted camas bulbs. They would become one of his trail staples, a food that made his belly grumble but kept it full. Thompson had saved some of these roots, and from his desk in 1847, when he was seventy-seven

years old, he could take time to savor the moment, to focus
his rheumy eye on a few small tubers.

> These Roots are about the size of a Nutmeg, they are
> near the surface, and are turned up with a pointed Stick,
> they are farinaceous, of a pleasant taste, easily masti-
> cated, and nutritive, they are found in the small mead-
> ows of short grass, in a rich soil, and a short exposure to
> the Sun dries them sufficiently to keep for years. I have
> some beside me which were dug up in 1811 and are now
> thirty-six years old and are in good preservation . . . but
> they have lost their fine aromatic smell.
>
> *Narrative*

As he sniffed the camas roots, Thompson transported himself
back to the blue-petaled meadows of the Pend Oreille, and
the shriveled relics on his desk brought back the taste of the
whole place.

STORIES HAVE BEEN passed down about David
Thompson's pitiable later life—how at age seventy he applied
for a clerk's position with the Hudson's Bay Company, only to
be rejected; how, blind and penniless, he was forced to pawn
the instruments of his trade and on one occasion even his
winter coat. But there are other stories, such as the one about
him taking his grandchildren out at night and teaching them
the names of the stars. His daughter Mary also set down a
series of memories from this period that don't sound so terrible. She said that a Montreal oculist, much to everyone's
amazement, managed to restore clear vision to both of her aged
father's eyes. She remembered how Thompson remained particularly neat in his dress and appearance, his only complaint
being a pair of very tender feet, and his only indulgence being
the accumulation of a great variety of slippers and shoes. At
the age of seventy-five, when he was immersed in writing his

Narrative, "he seemed to live his life over in talking to himself aloud over some anecdotes and jokes they played on each other in his travels with his companions. We would hear him laugh heartily over them with tears streaming down his cheeks." She remembered one story that he delighted in telling, about a particularly hungry winter journey across the mountains. He and his men became so desperate, he said, that they decided they would have to kill one of their dogs for breakfast the next day. But when they awoke in the morning, all their dogs had disappeared, and they didn't see them again until they were twenty miles down the trail. Mary said that her father became quite absent-minded and once completely filled his niece's house with smoke when he left his sealskin cap and gloves on a hot woodstove. On another occasion he drove home from a friend's house with the wrong horse harnessed to his buggy, wondering all the way why his steed was acting so strangely. When everyone laughed at his mistake, "he enjoyed it himself and thought it a good joke."

Thompson died on February 10, 1857, two months before his eighty-seventh birthday. Charlotte followed him within three months and was buried beside him in the Mount Royal cemetery in Montreal. One of their sons sold the unpublished *Narrative* to a lawyer, and for years it languished in a drawer. Thompson's name faded altogether for thirty years, until the Canadian explorer and geologist J. B. Tyrrell plotted courses off some surprisingly accurate old maps during a survey of the Rocky Mountains. When he found out who had drawn them, Tyrrell researched David Thompson's original reports. He located and purchased the pages of the *Narrative*, then put together a manuscript from the four drafts that Thompson had never completely finished. In 1916 it was published in a limited edition by Canada's Champlain Society, causing a great stir among history buffs on both sides of the border. In 1927, J. B. Tyrrell raised a fluted column, with a sextant riding on top, as a monument over Thompson's grave.

EPILOGUE

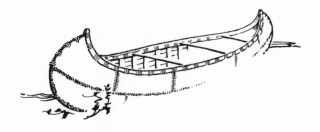

T HE SIXTY-MILE section of the Columbia River that courses downstream from Priest Rapids Dam is known as Hanford Reach. It is the last free-flowing stretch of the river in the United States, unchanged by dams or dredging. On the morning we chose to paddle through it, we had quite a load in our tubby canoe. I sat in the lookout seat in the bow and Gene Hunn took the stern, an unlikely steersman surrounded by books and binoculars. James Selam's son Willie, a coach at Wapato High School, took the middle seat alongside two coolers and a pile of life jackets. We had shoehorned James into a space directly in front of Willie, with his feet stuck straight out under my seat in the bow. The elder Selam remained motionless as we pushed cautiously out into the Columbia, negotiated the pilings of Vernita Bridge at a bit of an angle, then straightened out and glided smartly down into a landscape dominated on the west by Hanford's nuclear ziggurats. The huge compounds galvanized everyone's attention at first, and James said they reminded him of the mythical Swallowing Monster that according to Sahaptin lore dwells in the depths of the Big River.

In contrast with the complex structures on the nuclear reserve, the river's east bank stands absolutely empty. It was toward the east that Gene started looking as he leafed through Click Relander's book about the Wanapam people, trying to get James to help identify the local landmarks. "That ridge of hills that begins above Priest Rapids: Wahluke, 'rising up.' That means leaping or jumping, right James? You can see how it rises up off the plain."

James shook his head. "More like the rising of your spirit when you are dead, moving from stage to stage as it ascends." He let his outstretched hand float up from waist to shoulder.

"OK. And here Relander calls these points Na Nook? Ya Nook? Wa Nook? Does any of that make sense, James?"

"To me, maybe. I don't think to you."

Willie spotted some geese on a gravel bar downstream, and we ruddered to drift quietly toward them. The geese spooked while we were still well away, honking low and then taking off. Willie told us that when he was a kid, he would spend hours stalking honkers as they fed, moving a little ways on his belly, never looking at them directly with his eyes. When the sentry bird lifted its neck, Willie would pause and flatten himself on the ground until the birds all put their heads back down. He would shake his hair out over his face and peer at them through the strands until he thought it was safe to move another few feet.

As we drifted closer, we realized that the bar fluttered with other life as well. Stationary blue herons, horned larks, a mule deer nibbling at grass, mergansers in a backwater, spotted sandpipers at the waterline, cormorants bunched up along the point, and—what was that? Four white pelicans.

James had never seen a white pelican, so we paddled hard across the current to land on the lower tip of the gravel bar and sneak back for a look. James's feet had gone fast asleep, and Willie and I had to hoist him out of the canoe, then send him stumbling stiff-legged toward the birds. Much calmer than the geese, the pelicans contorted their necks and tucked their bills up under their wings. From hopelessly far away, James snapped a couple of pictures of the white bumps. The birds took off, and in slow motion one wheeled its black wingtips close around us. James whirled with his camera and caught it flat against the sun.

As we approached Coyote Rapids, James told how the Wanapam prophet Smohalla had led his dream and dance sessions at this site over a hundred years ago. Straight downstream we could see the point of the sacred hill, Laliik, where the Oriole came to Smoholla and infused him with the idea that the Plateau peoples should resist white encroachment and stick to the old ways; that a day would eventually come when the whole world would turn over, swallowing all the whites and those who followed their path. Then all the generations of honorable dead would resurface to live as people should live.

Gene had spoken often of the great paradox of this spot in the river, where Smohalla's prophecy of extermination might be bearing fruit on the nuclear reserve. We were hoping for a wild, frothy ride across the shoal, but the height of the water had reduced Coyote Rapids to a riffle, and we glided through with only a few burbles to waver our bow. "Those who are true shall pass through the earth," chanted Willie. "So spoke Smohalla."

Next we entered waters where some years before James and Willie had fished for salmon at night. For the rest of the afternoon Willie would spot a certain gravel bar or swirl of water and remember exactly how they had set their net and each fish that came over the side as they reeled it in. He said it had not been a profitable trip.

And yet on this day the fish were moving. *Whack!* A series of well-spaced, chinook-sized splashes kept our heads turning, but never quite in time to make out what they were. We eased through a left bend of the river, past a shoestring of an island, and headed straight for a line of creamy cliffs marked by strata of volcanic ash.

"The White Bluffs," said James. "My father camped here, and told me how they would look. Just like this. But I've only been here at night before, on our fishing boat."

We decided to stop as close to the cliffs as we could. The air temperature was 105 degrees, and Gene, Willie, and I flopped into the river as soon as we got the boat ashore. While the rest of us swam in the cool water, James waded gingerly in the shallows, trying to get some feeling back into his feet.

When we returned, he was picking up fist-sized river rocks and pitching them straight down on the shore one by one. After each toss he would bend stiffly down to retrieve the rock and feel the broken edge. He did this over and over, until finally he bobbed up with one that had cracked ragged and keen but kept a smooth round end that nested in his palm. "See?" he said. "Just right for scraping hides." A cursory search turned up several piles of similarly knapped flint along the shore, mixed up with iron wagon-wheel hoops and hubs, oak spokes, and the rings of many campsites. The bend at the White Cliffs had been a river ford since prehistoric times, and then the regular route of a cattle drive that pushed north to feed the prospectors in the gold rush on the Kootenay River. James picked up an iron rod, oddly curled at one end, and used it as a shepherd's crook while he patrolled the shore. It was at just such a place as this, he said, that Heron would stretch out his foot, farther and farther, until his toes reached the opposite shore, forming a bridge that his smaller animal kin could walk across.

After lunch we drifted downstream, and James nodded off in the parboiling heat. We entered a wide part of the river where for the first time we could see amber rocks on the bottom as we moved along at four or five miles an hour. I tumbled off the bow and floated on my back, toes forward, letting the current whisk me over the rocks. As I bobbed downstream, I kept thinking of how David Thompson recorded only cool, cloudy days on this stretch of the desert, whereas here we were, in the same month, under a most relentless sun.

A roar of voices went up from the canoe, an explosion that seemed to lift the pattern of sunlight off the surface of the water. Stunned, almost afraid, I rolled over on my belly to stroke a wide circle, searching across the water's surface for a sign. The river seemed to have turned black and opaque. Willie was hollering to me about a big fish; Gene suggested with much laughter that the Swallowing Monster was after me and I might want to get out of the river. I curled my toes under and swam for the canoe, hard, trying to keep my eyes peeled all round. There was nothing to see, but when Willie leaned forward to give me a hand up out of the water, he reeled me in with the extra strength of adrenaline.

"It was a sturgeon," he stammered."It came up head first. I could see its nose, and then its eyes, those beady eyes, and then its mouth—it had a big mouth. And then those plates on its back, it came up so slow, and it just kept rising and rising..." With his hands Willie tried to describe the head of a man-sized fish. When he got to its mouth, he opened his fingers up wide.

"I think it was a whale," offered Gene. "Spyhopping."

"Spying on us."

"Looking," said James. "Looking for the Wanapam."

"It was right next to the boat. It was three feet from the boat. It could have eaten a paddle."

"A sturgeon," said Willie. "They live on the bottom. Sturgeon don't do that. I've been fishing all my life and I've never seen a sturgeon roll up to the top like that."

THE SUN WAS mercifully setting by the time we landed and shuttled the canoe back around to Vernita Bridge. Everyone was tired and hungry, but James asked that we form a small circle before we drove away. "Let us stand together here for just a minute," he said, "and think about what we have seen today."

He pointed away from the hazy sunset. "Today the fathers were talking to me, telling me the old things because when I heard them the first time, as a child, I was listening. I couldn't see them outside today, but I could hear them inside. I could feel that they were there. You talk about David Thompson. I've seen what he said. I've read Lewis and Clark. These men saw how the Indian had stored up food, and could provide for their needs. You think about the things that your explorers did not see."

James lifted his head, and said it again. "Think about these things."

CHRONOLOGY

Date	Event
1607	English colonists found Jamestown, Virginia
1608	Samuel de Champlain and French colonists found Quebec
	Telescope invented
1610	Henry Hudson explores Hudson Bay
1670	Hudson's Bay Company chartered in London
1673	French explorers explore Mississippi River, reach mouth of Missouri River
1730	Mirror sextant invented
1752	Benjamin Franklin flies kite in electrical storm
1754	Anthony Henday travels west from Hudson Bay onto Plains, meets natives on horseback and sees Rocky Mountains
1763	Treaty of Paris officially ends French and Indian Wars and gives Great Britain control of Canada
1770	David Thompson born in London
	William Wordsworth born in Cockermouth, England
1771	Captain James Cook completes his first voyage around the world
1772	Samuel Hearne explores Coppermine River to Arctic Ocean
1775	Daniel Boone leads party of settlers into Kentucky
1776	American Revolution begins
	Spanish establish mission at San Francisco
1777	David Thompson enters Grey Coat School
1778	Spinning mule invented to spin multiple strands of yarn
	James Cook trades for sea otter pelts in Nootka Sound
1779	James Cook killed by Hawaiian natives, cutting short his search for Northwest Passage
1781	Smallpox epidemic begins to sweep northern Plains
1783	Treaty of Paris ends American Revolution
	North West Fur Company established in Montreal
1784	David Thompson begins apprenticeship on Hudson Bay
	Dr. Samuel Johnson dies in London
	James Cook's journal of his last voyage published in London

1785   Introduction of power loom in England for weaving cloth
1787   David Thompson winters with Piegans near Rocky
          Mountains
1789   French Revolution begins
          Alexander Mackenzie reaches Arctic Ocean
          David Thompson learns surveying from Philip Turnor
1790   Benjamin Franklin dies in Philadelphia
          British Captain George Vancouver begins his three-year
          survey of northwest coast of North America
1792   American Captain Robert Gray discovers mouth of
          Columbia River
          George Vancouver's Lieutenant William Broughton
          explores Columbia 100 miles upriver
1793   Alexander Mackenzie reaches Pacific Ocean at Bella Coola
          David Thompson surveys Muskrat Country west of
          Hudson Bay
1794   Jay Treaty establishes neutral commission to settle border
          disputes between United States and Canada
1796   Scottish explorer Mungo Park reaches headwaters of Niger
          River in what is now Mali, West Africa
1797   David Thompson leaves Hudson's Bay Company to join
          North West Company
1798   David Thompson travels to Mandan villages and charts
          headwaters of Mississippi River
          Napoleon invades Egypt; Horatio Nelson and British Navy
          defeat French at Battle of the Nile
1799   David Thompson marries Charlotte Small
          Alexander Mackenzie resigns from North West Company
          George Vancouver's *Journeys to the North Pacific Ocean*
          published in London
1800   Alexander Mackenzie joins XY Fur Company
1801   David Thompson attempts to cross Rocky Mountains
          Alexander Mackenzie's *Voyages to the Frozen and Pacific
          Oceans* published in London; Mackenzie knighted in
          honor of his explorations
1803   Thomas Jefferson completes Louisiana Purchase
1804   David Thompson works in Peace River country
          Lewis and Clark start up Missouri River
          Merger of the Northwest and XY Fur Companies
1805   Admiral Nelson defeats French at Battle of Trafalgar
          Lewis and Clark reach Pacific Ocean

1806   Russian-American Fur Company collects otter pelts from
Alaska to Spanish California

Mungo Park killed by natives on Niger River

1807   David Thompson crosses Rockies and builds trading post
at headwaters of Columbia River

Manuel Lisa winters on Yellowstone River

Zebulon Pike explores Southwest into Colorado

Great Britain abolishes institution of slavery

Thomas Jefferson signs bill banning all foreign trade
following British attacks on American shipping

1808   David Thompson explores Kootenai River

Simon Fraser follows Fraser River to the Pacific

Napoleon invades Spain

1809   President James Madison reinstates embargo on British
trade

Jean-Baptiste Lamarck's theory of evolution based on
acquired characteristics published in Paris

Tecumseh and the Prophet campaign to unite all native
Americans east of the Mississippi

Charles Darwin born

1810   David Thompson builds trade houses on Pend Oreille
Lake and Flathead River

Sir Walter Scott publishes *The Lady of the Lake*

1811   John Jacob Astor's Pacific Fur Company establishes
post at mouth of Columbia River

David Thompson follows Columbia to Pacific and finishes
charting entire length of the river

William Price Hunt, leading Astor's overland party,
explores Snake River Valley and much of future Oregon
Trail

1812   David Thompson retires to Montreal

War declared between United States and Great Britain

Napoleon retreats from Russia after burning Moscow

Baron Cuvier publishes first volume of his *Researches on the
Bones of Fossil Vertebrates*

1813   Jane Austen publishes *Pride and Prejudice* anonymously in
London

1814   David Thompson delivers his map of western North
America to partners of North West Company

Treaty of Ghent ends War of 1812

1815   Wellington defeats Napoleon at Waterloo

1817   David Thompson takes post as chief surveyor for
        International Boundary Commission
1821   Amalgamation of North West and Hudson's Bay
        Companies
1823   James Fenimore Cooper's *The Pioneer*, first volume of his
        Leatherstocking series, published in United States
1825   Spokane House closed; Fort Colville built at Kettle Falls
1836   Washington Irving's *Astoria* published
1839   American Elkanah Walker builds mission for Spokane
        Indians north of Spokane House
1843   David Thompson sends a set of refined maps to London
        The first of 300,000 American settlers follow Oregon
        Trail west
1846   David Thompson begins compiling a book about his travels
        Great Britain and United States settle long-disputed
        boundary of Oregon Territory
        United States annexes California after war with Mexico
1849   Alexander Ross's *Adventures of the First Settlers on the
        Columbia River* published in United States
1851   Gabriel Franchère's *Narrative of a Voyage to the
        Northwest Coast of America* published in Montreal
1853   Isaac Stevens surveys route for railroad across northern
        Rockies
1855   Stevens persuades tribes of Columbia Plateau to sign treaty
        ceding their lands and to move to reservations
        Flatheads, Kootenais, and Pend Oreilles sign treaty ceding
        25,000 square miles of territory
        Gold discovered on Pend Oreille River
1856   Bessemer furnace used to make steel in England
1857   David Thompson dies in Montreal
1916   Thompson's *Narrative of Travels in Western North America,
        1784–1812* published by Champlain Society in Toronto

FURTHER READING:
A SELECTED BIBLIOGRAPHY

PRIMARY SOURCES

Belyea, Barbara, ed. *David Thompson's Columbia Journals.* Montreal: McGill-Queens, 1994.

Bigsby, John Jeremiah. *The Shoe and the Canoe, or Pictures of Travel in Canada.* 2 vols. London: Chapman & Hall, 1850.

Bridgewater, Dorothy Wildes, ed. "John Jacob Astor Relative to his Settlement on the Columbia River." *Yale University Library Gazette* 24 (1949): 47–69.

Burpee, L. J., ed. "Some Letters of David Thompson." *Canadian Historical Review* 4 (1923): 105–126.

Coues, Elliott, ed. *New Light on the Early History of the Greater Northwest: The Manuscript Journals of Alexander Henry and of David Thompson.* 3 vols. New York: Francis P. Harper, 1897; reprint, 2 vols. Minneapolis: Ross and Haines, 1965.

Dempsey, Hugh, ed. "David Thompson's Journey to the Red Deer River." *Alberta Historical Review* 13 (1965): 1–8.

_____ "David Thompson on the Peace River." *Alberta Historical Review* 14 (1966): No.1: 1–11; No.2: 14–21; No.4: 14–19.

DeVoto, Bernard, ed. *The Journals of Lewis and Clark.* Boston: Houghton Mifflin Company, 1953.

Elliott, T. C., ed. "Journal of David Thompson." *Oregon Historical Quarterly* 15 (1914): 39–63, 104–25, 216.

_____ "David Thompson's Journeys in the Spokane Country." *Washington Historical Quarterly* 8 (1917): 183–87; 9 (1918): 11–16, 103–06, 169–73, 284–87; 10 (1919): 97–103.

_____ "David Thompson's Journeys in Idaho." *Washington Historical Quarterly* 11 (1920): 97–103.

_____ "David Thompson and Beginnings in Idaho." *Oregon Historical Quarterly* 21 (1920): 49–61.

_____ "The Discovery of the Source of the Columbia River." *Oregon Historical Quarterly* 26 (1925): 23–49.

_____ "David Thompson's Journeys in the Pend Oreille Country." *Washington Historical Quarterly* 23 (1932): 18–24, 88–93, 173–76.

Franchère, Gabriel. *Narrative of a Voyage to the Northwest Coast of America.* Edited by W. Kaye Lamb. Toronto: Champlain Society, 1969.

Franks, C. E. S., ed. "David Thompson's Explorations of the Muskoka and Madawaska Rivers, 1837." *Queen's Quarterly* 92 (1985): 348–363.

Glover, Richard, ed. *David Thompson's Narrative.* Toronto: Champlain Society, 1962.

Gough, Barry M., ed. *The Journal of Alexander Henry the Younger, 1799–1814.* 2 vols. Toronto: Champlain Society, 1988.

Hopwood, Victor G., ed. *David Thompson: Travels in Western North America, 1784–1812.* Toronto: Macmillan, 1971.

Howay, F. W., ed. "David Thompson's Account of his First Attempt to Cross the Rockies." *Queen's Quarterly* 40 (1933): 333–56.

Hudson's Bay Company Archives. Provincial Archives of Manitoba, Winnipeg.

Johnson, Alice, ed. *Saskatchewan Journals and Correspondence.* London: Hudson's Bay Record Society, 1967.

Kane, Paul. *Wanderings of an Artist among the Indians of North America.* 1859; reprint, Edmonton: M. G. Hurtig, 1986.

Lerette, Clarke E., ed. "David Thompson's Journal of the IBC Survey 1817–27 of Lake Erie." *Inland Seas* 44 (1988): 32–45.

McDougall, Duncan. "Astoria Journal, 1810–13." Manuscript. Rosenbach Museum and Library, Philadelphia.

McGillivray, Duncan. *Journal.* Edited by A. S. Morton. Toronto: The Macmillan Company, 1929.

Mackenzie, Alexander. *Journals and Letters.* Edited by W. Kaye Lamb. Toronto: Macmillan for the Hakluyt Society, 1970.

Mourning Dove. *Mourning Dove: A Salishan Autobiography.* Edited by Jay Miller. Lincoln: University of Nebraska, 1990.

Ross, Alexander. *Adventures of the First Settlers on the Oregon or Columbia River, 1810–1813.* Edited by Kenneth Spaulding. London, 1849; reprint, Lincoln: University of Nebraska Press, 1986.

Schaeffer, Claude. "The Kutenai." Manuscript. Special Collections, Glenbow Museum Archives, Calgary.

Thompson, David. "Journals." Manuscript. Special Collections, Provincial Archives of Ontario, Toronto.

Tyrrell, J. B., ed. *David Thompson: Narrative of his Explorations in Western North America, 1784–1812.* Toronto: Champlain Society, 1916.

_____ "David Thompson and the Columbia River." *Canadian Historical Review* 18 (1937): 12–13.

_____ *Journals of Samuel Hearne and Philip Turnor.* Toronto: Champlain Society, 1934.

_____ Miscellaneous papers. Special Collections, Fisher Library, Toronto.

Wallace, W. Stewart, ed. *Documents Relating to the North West Company.* Toronto: Champlain Society, 1934.

White, M. Catherine, ed. *David Thompson's Journals Relating to Montana and Adjacent Regions, 1808–1812.* Missoula: Montana State University Press, 1950.

Wood, W. Raymond, ed. "David Thompson at the Mandan-Hidatsa Villages, 1797–98: The Original Journals." *Ethnohistory* 24 (1977): 329–42.

SECONDARY SOURCES

Allen, John Logan. *Passage Through the Garden: Lewis and Clark and the Image of the American Northwest.* Urbana: University of Illinois Press, 1975.

Belyea, Barbara. "The 'Columbian Enterprise' and A. S. Morton: A Historical Exemplum." *B.C. Studies* 86 (1990): 3–27.

Campbell, M. W. *The North West Company.* New York: St. Martin's Press, 1957.

Chance, David. *People of the Falls.* Colville, Washington: Kettle Falls Historical Center, Inc., 1986.

Dempsey, Hugh. *The Indians of Alberta.* Calgary: Glenbow Museum, 1988.

DeVoto, Bernard. *The Course of Empire.* Boston: Houghton Mifflin Company, 1952.

Ewers, John C. *The Story of the Blackfeet.* Washington, D.C.: Bureau of Indian Affairs, 1959.

Hunn, Eugene S. *Nch'i–Wana: The Big River—Mid-Columbian Indians and their Land.* Seattle: University of Washington Press, 1990.

Innis, Harold A. *The Fur Trade in Canada: An Introduction to Canadian Economic History.* New Haven: Yale University Press, 1956.

Josephy, Alvin M. *The Nez Perce Indians and the Opening of the Northwest.* New Haven: Yale University Press, 1971.

McGregor, J. G. *Peter Fidler: Canada's Forgotten Surveyor, 1769–1822.* Toronto: McClelland and Stewart Ltd., 1966.

Masson, L. F. R. *Les Bourgeois de la Compagnie du Nord-Ouest.* 2 vols. Quebec: Cote et Cie, 1889.

Morse, Eric. *Fur Trade Canoe Routes of Canada—Then and Now.* Ottawa: Queen's Printer, 1969.

Newman, Peter C. *Company of Adventurers.* New York: Viking, 1985.

_____ *Caesars of the Wilderness.* New York: Viking, 1987.

Relander, Click. *Drummers and Dreamers.* Seattle: Pacific North West Parks and Forest Association, 1986.

Ronda, James. *Astoria and Empire.* Lincoln: University of Nebraska Press, 1990.

Schaeffer, Claude E. "The Kutenai Female Berdache: Courier, Guide, Prophetess, and Warrior." *Ethnohistory* 12 (1965): 193–236.

_____ *Le Blanc and La Gasse: Predecessors of David Thompson in the Columbian Plateau.* Browning, Montana: Museum of the Plains Indian for the U. S. Department of the Interior, 1966.

Smyth, David. "David Thompson's Surveying Instruments and Methods." *Cartographica* 18 (1981): 1–17.

Tyrrell, J. B. "David Thompson and the Columbia River." *Canadian Historical Review* 18 (1937): 12–13.

Waldman, Carl. *Atlas of the North American Indian.* New York: Facts on File Publications, 1985.

INDEX

Acton House, 51, 61, 80
Alcoholic beverages, 61, 65, 96; brandy,
    17, 105; high wine, 88, 96; rum, 13,
    31, 66, 69, 80, 81, 116, 133, 140, 169,
    170
Agriculture, 2, 44, 115, 143, 154, 253, 254
American Revolution, 9, 42
Americans, and Blackfeet, 78, 152, 152,
    164; claim to Northwest, 63, 100; and
    Thompson, 96–97, 100, 107–8. *See
    also* Lewis & Clark expedition
Antelope, 93, 109. *See also Chevreuil*
Arrowsmith, Aaron, 76, 254
Aspen, 108, 113
Assiniboine Indians, 13, 22. *See also*
    Stoney Assiniboine Indians
Assiniboine River, 43, 48
Astor, John Jacob, 166, 180, 204, 207
Astoria, fur post, 4, 209–15, 217, 247;
    modern day, 215–17
Astronomy, practical, 33, 138
Athabasca Pass, 176, 226, 229, 238–41
Athabasca River, 49, 171
Avalanches, 87, 88

Baddely, Captain, 253
Badger, 17
Barrel organ. *See* Music
Basalt, 189, 195, 224
Battle of Trafalgar, 109
Bears, 6, 95; grizzlies, 58, 85, 175, 238,
    240; pelts, 61, 140; polar, 14–15
Beaulieu (voyageur), 83, 89, 91–92, 126,
    145–46, 150, 160
Beaver, 11, 106, 111, 115, 153; as food,
    91, 113, 150; pelts, 10, 17, 23, 25, 31,
    60, 61, 99; trapping, 11, 65, 74, 106,
    111, 129
Bella Coola, 63
Beluga whale, 14–15
Bercier (voyageur), 83, 87, 90, 170, 232, 237
Berdache, 135–37. *See also* Qánqon

Berries, 19, 24, 55, 92, 93, 99, 113, 144,
    186, 189, 219
Bighorn sheep, 26, 58, 66, 85, 191, 192,
    238; as food, 83, 125, 129
Bigsby, J. J., 250
Birch rind, 53, 68, 109, 139, 152, 153.
    See also Canoes
Bird, James, 137, 138, 180
Bison. *See* Buffalo
Bitterroot (plant), 115
Bitterroot Valley, 234
Blackfeet Indians, 18, 21, 55, 65, 66, 73;
    and Americans, 78, 164; and
    Canadians, 101, 105, 163; and other
    tribes, 105, 107, 163–64. *See also*
    Blood Indians; Piegan Indians
Blaeberry River, 88, 89, 128, 140, 179
Blizzards, 43–44
Blood Indians, 19, 55, 80, 105. *See also*
    Blackfeet Indians
Boat Encampment, 208, 229, 231, 238, 244
Boggy Hall, 129, 131
Boisverd, Augustin, 83, 91, 105, 160, 124,
    126, 134, 163
Boisverd, Madame. *See* Qánqon
Bonner's Ferry, Idaho, 124
Bonneville Dam, 222
Books, 4, 10, 14, 49, 255–57; read by
    Thompson, 9, 14, 37, 41, 67, 75, 165
Boulard, Michel, 83, 90, 93, 124, 126, 150,
    152; on Columbia River voyage, 187,
    224; at Kootanae House, 95–96, 105,
    108, 134; as translator, 60, 61, 98–99
Bow River, 19, 65, 66, 73
Brazeau River, 67
Broughton, William, 63–64
Brule Lake, 173, 174
Buché (voyageur), 83, 105
Buffalo, 18, 19, 20, 51, 62, 66, 85, 239;
    hunting of, 17, 24, 62, 64, 88, 125,
    236; meat, 17, 43, 65, 69, 129;
    products, 19, 44, 48

ABOUT THE AUTHOR
AND THE ILLUSTRATOR

JACK NISBET is a field biologist and natural history teacher. A native of North Carolina, he has lived for more than fifteen years in the Inland Northwest. His book *Sky People* (1984) is a collection of stories based around the highlands of eastern Washington. Nisbet first became acquainted with David Thompson in the 1970s when he discovered Thompson's *Narrative*; he has been following the explorer's trail ever since.

JACK MCMASTER is an illustrator and graphic designer. His works include the re-creation of David Thompson's 1814 map, the "North-West Territories of the Province of Canada," which is on display in the Great Hall of Old Fort William, Thunder Bay, Ontario. Jack lives with his family in Lonsdale, Ontario.

Praise for Lancaster County Secrets

The Choice

"Fisher's writing brings that Amish sense of peace into your own world. *The Choice* brings an entirely new perspective to the Amish way of life. You will love it!"

> —Kristin Billerbeck, author of *What a Girl Wants*

"A story of endearing characters. . . . Fisher writes with a fresh mix of humor and depth, splashing raw emotion onto the pages. I guarantee your heart will be touched."

> —Ginger Kolbaba, founding editor of Kyria.com,
> former editor of *Today's Christian Woman*,
> and author of *Desperate Pastors' Wives*

"Fisher kicks off a refreshing new series, Lancaster County Secrets, with characters that are strong, both in body and spirit."

> —Romantic Times

The Waiting

"More than just a story of the Amish, *The Waiting* is the story of a woman, sometimes triumphant, sometimes struggling, carried through turbulent times by a plain faith."

> —Lisa Wingate, national bestselling author of
> *Tending Roses* and *Never Say Never*

"In *The Waiting*, Suzanne Woods Fisher takes the sweet story expected in Amish fiction and adds a kick of realism. I treasured my time with Jorie King and the whole Zook family, sharing their grief and laughter— what a lovely read."

> —Sarah Sundin, author of Wings of Glory series

The SEARCH

Books by Suzanne Woods Fisher

Amish Peace: Simple Wisdom for a Complicated World
Amish Proverbs: Words of Wisdom from the Simple Life

☙ LANCASTER COUNTY SECRETS ❧

The Choice
The Waiting
The Search

~ LANCASTER COUNTY SECRETS ~
Book 3

The SEARCH

A NOVEL

Suzanne Woods Fisher

Revell

a division of Baker Publishing Group
Grand Rapids, Michigan

Published by Revell
a division of Baker Publishing Group
P.O. Box 6287, Grand Rapids, MI 49516-6287
www.revellbooks.com

Printed in the United States of America

Library of Congress Cataloging-in-Publication Data
Fisher, Suzanne Woods.
    The search : a novel / Suzanne Woods Fisher.
       p.   cm. — (Lancaster County secrets ; bk. 3)
    ISBN 978-0-8007-3387-2 (pbk.)
    1. Amish women—Fiction. 2. Amish—Pennsylvania—Fiction. 3. Lancaster
County (Pa.)—Fiction. I. Title.
 PS3606.I78S43 2011
 813'.6—dc22   2010029611

Scripture used in this book, whether quoted or paraphrased by the characters, is taken from the King James Version of the Bible.

Published in association with Joyce Hart of the Hartline Literary Agency, LLC.

This book is a work of fiction. Names, characters, places, and incidents are the product of the author's imagination or are used fictitiously. Any resemblance to actual events, locales, or persons, living or dead, is coincidental.

11 12 13 14 15 16 17   7 6 5 4 3 2 1

For Steve,
who has been such a supportive and kind husband
that nobody would believe it if I were
to write him into a book!
Thank you with all of my heart.

1

*J*t was a June morning, hazy with summer's heat, and Billy Lapp was already bone tired. Only one person on earth could wear out an eighteen-year-old farm boy, and Billy happened to be her hired hand. For over two weeks now, Bertha Riehl had met him at the barn door of Rose Hill Farm with a to-do list that seemed to grow longer with each passing hour. Bertha's granddaughter, Bess, was coming for a summer visit, and Bertha wanted the farm so spic-and-span clean a body could eat off the barn floor. Which, Billy knew, meant he would be the one scrubbing that barn floor until it shone.

He didn't know why Bertha felt her farm needed sprucing up. So sauwer wie gschleckt. *It was as clean as a whistle.* The vegetable garden ran neat and tidy from the kitchen steps down to the greenhouse, beside the yard where she stretched her clothesline. Why, hardly a rose petal dared to wilt without Bertha flying out to the fields with a pair of pruning shears in her big hands. And besides that, folks visited each other all the time. But then Billy remembered that something was not quite right between Bertha and Jonah, her son, Bess's father. He had left years before. Billy didn't know what had caused the rift, but he knew enough not to ask. Bertha could be private like that, keeping her business to herself.

"Could you tell me something about Bess?" Billy had asked Bertha the other day as he helped her turn the mattress in the spare bedroom she was readying for Bess.

Bertha flipped her end of the mattress and let it slip into the wooden bed frame with a soft sough. "Like what?"

"Well, how old is Bess now?" He vaguely remembered a tow-headed, skinny wisp of a girl coming in from Ohio a few years back when Samuel, Bertha's husband, passed.

Bertha raised an eyebrow at him, as if she thought his motives were highly suspect. "Old enough," she said, lifting her big chin. "But too young for you."

Billy sputtered. "I wasn't asking for that. Besides, me and Betsy—" He stopped abruptly. He knew how Bertha Riehl felt about his Betsy Mast, and he didn't want another lecture about thinking with your head and not your nether regions, a comment at which he took offense. But that was Bertha Riehl for you. She didn't mince words and she didn't hold back her opinions. And she had plenty of both.

On this sunny day, Bertha handed him a broom. "When you're done sweeping out the hay loft, you need to clean out the ashes in the chimbley place." She bent over to pick up her favorite rooster, a fourteen-year-old leghorn named Otto, who followed her around the farm. Bertha tucked Otto under her arm, football-style, and headed up the hill to the farmhouse. Her left side was flanked by Boomer, a big black dog who had appeared one day and never left.

"You gonna finally cook that ol' rooster for dinner, Bertha?" Billy said, grinning.

"Been giving it some serious thought," she called over her shoulder, stroking Otto's feathers like he was a pampered house-cat.

Bertha was always threatening Otto was going to end up as Sunday's stew, but Billy knew better. Bertha Riehl was all bluff and bluster. Well, mostly bluff and bluster. He couldn't deny she had a way of intimidating folks that was a wonder to behold. It had happened to Billy only once, when he made the mistake of asking her if she was six feet tall. Bertha planted her fists on her deluxe-sized hips and narrowed her eyes at him. "I am five feet twelve inches." Then she stared him down until he was sure he had shrunk an inch or two, right in front of her.

From the kitchen door of the sprawling brick-and-frame farmhouse, Bertha turned and hollered at Billy. "Es is noch lang net faercih wann's yuscht halwe gedus is!" *Half done is far from done!*

He dashed into the barn and picked up where he left off, sweeping the concrete floor with a dash and a fury. One thing to be grateful for, he thought as hay and dust flew up around him, the day of Bess's arrival had finally come.

Jonah Riehl was seeing his daughter, Bess, off at the bus station in Berlin, Ohio. He handed her a ham sandwich for lunch and bus fare for the return ticket home. Bess would be spending the entire summer at his mother's farm in Stoney Ridge, Pennsylvania. His mother had written recently to say she had suffered through some female surgery and could Bess please come? She was in dire need of someone to help.

Jonah knew it couldn't be true that his mother needed help. Bertha had lived in Stoney Ridge all of her life and had plenty of sisters, cousins, and neighbors she could count on. Wasn't that what being Plain was all about?

And yet he couldn't rest easy telling his mother that Bess wouldn't come this summer. His mother was getting up there in years, and she was the type who had never been young to begin with. A few years back, Jonah's father, Samuel, had an accident while cutting timber. A big tree fell into a smaller tree, and the smaller trunk snapped under the weight, striking Samuel with terrific force in the forehead. He died seven days later. After his father's funeral, Jonah had invited his mother to come live with them in Ohio. She said no, she wanted to stay on the home place. Still, he knew his mother had a difficult time, losing her partner of so many years. Bertha Riehl did like she always did: she dug in her heels and made do with life as it was.

So, in the end, Jonah showed Bess the letter from his mother.

"The whole summer?" Bess shook her head. "I can't leave you, Dad. You need me around here."

He couldn't deny that. It was just the two of them rattling around in the house. He hadn't wanted to think of summer without his Bess—much less about the fact that she was growing up so quickly. It wouldn't be long before boys would start buzzing around her. Too soon, she would have a life of her own. It was the natural order of things, he knew, the way things were meant to be, but it still grieved him to think of it. So much so that he had written a letter to his mother to say he couldn't spare Bess.

That very afternoon, before he had a chance to mail the letter, Bess came home from school and announced a change of heart. She would go to Stoney Ridge, after all. "It's the right thing to do, and you're always telling me that we need to do the right thing," she said with a dramatic flair.

It still puzzled him why she had flip-flopped on the topic.

Now the loudspeaker was announcing the bus's departure, and Jonah's eyes got blurry. "Be careful, Bess," he said, "because—"

"—because you think I'm five, not fifteen." She smiled at him.

Jonah clamped his mouth shut. Bess teased him that each time he said goodbye to her, even as she left for school each morning, he would add the caution, "Be careful, because . . ." *Because . . . I won't be there to protect you. Because . . . accidents happen.* He knew that to be true. At any given moment, anything at all could happen. He brushed a few stray hairs from her forehead and gave her shoulders a quick squeeze, his way of saying that he loved her and would miss her.

As the bus pulled out of the station and Bess waved goodbye to her father, it was her turn for blurry eyes. She had visited Stoney Ridge only one other time, for her grandfather's funeral. That time, her father was with her. Now, it was just her. At the other end of the trip—Mammi. And no Daadi to soften her grandmother's rough edges. Bess had adored her grandfather. He came to visit them in Ohio every other year—as often as he could. He was a tenderhearted man, as lean and lanky as Mammi was wide and round.

As Bess watched the phone lines swoop up and down to each pole along the road, she remembered what wouldn't be there— no phone in the barn, like at home. No bicycles, only scooters. And no indoor plumbing. When she asked her father why her grandmother still used a privy despite knowing that their district allowed plumbing, he told her that his mother was a woman who held on tight to the old ways. "If it isn't broke, why fix it?" was her life motto, he said.

Hours later, when the Greyhound bus pulled into Stoney Ridge, Bess climbed down the steps onto the sidewalk. The driver yanked her suitcase from the belly of the bus and thumped it down next to her. There Bess stood at the end of the world with all her worldly possessions. Her suitcase and Blackie, her cat.

Blackie had traveled in a picnic hamper and spent most of the trip trying to claw his way out. As Bess set down the hamper and looked around, a small knot of fear rose in her throat. She assumed her grandmother would be here waiting for her. What if she had forgotten Bess was coming? What if no one came to meet her? How would she ever find the farmhouse? Maybe her grandmother had gotten even sicker since her female surgery. Maybe Bess had come too late and Mammi had up and died. Bess had to shield her eyes from the late afternoon sun, beating down on her. She was tired from the long, hot ride and briefly thought about getting back on the stuffy bus to head home. Home to her father, Ohio, and all that was familiar.

Bess sat down on top of her suitcase. These were the moments in life when she wondered if her mother was up there in heaven looking down at her now and maybe trying to figure out how to help her. She loved imagining what her mother was like, what she'd say or do. She never tired of hearing stories about her from her father. She hoped that she might be able to find out even more from her grandmother this summer. That is, assuming she could ever locate Mammi. She shaded her eyes to look as far down the street as she could.

Bess let out a sigh of relief when she saw a horse and a gray-topped buggy veering around the corner. The buggy tipped so far to the right, Bess worried it might topple right over. The horse stopped abruptly right next to Bess, and the buggy tipped even more sharply as her grandmother disembarked. Land sakes, but she was enormous. Bess hadn't seen Mammi in three years, and she was even bigger. Taller still with her large black bonnet. She had several chins with wattles like a turkey. She drew nearer to Bess till she blotted out the sun.

"Where's your father?" Mammi asked, looking up and down the platform.

"He didn't come," Bess said. "I'm old enough to travel alone."

For a long moment, Mammi stared at her. Then something passed through those dark brown eyes, something Bess couldn't quite make out. Irritation? Or disappointment, maybe? Whatever it was, she shook it off in a flash.

"Old enough, are you?" Mammi hooked her hands on her hips and looked Bess up and down. "You look like you need a dose of salts and a square meal." The picnic hamper in Bess's hand quivered and Mammi noticed. She pointed to it. "What's that?"

"Blackie," Bess said. "My cat."

"Hoo-boy," Mammi said. "Better be a good mouser."

With a powerful arm, she swung Bess's suitcase aboard the buggy, lifting it high as if it was a feather. "Well, make haste." She climbed into the buggy and Bess hurried to join her. A big black dog with a muzzle of white hair sat in the back and leaned his head forward to sniff Bess. He must have decided Bess passed inspection because he gave her ear a lick. "That's Boomer," Mammi said. "He showed up out of the blue one day after my Samuel passed."

"Boomer?" Bess asked, trying to push the dog back. "Where'd you get a name like Boomer?" The dog sniffed out the hamper with great interest. Blackie let out a hissing sound and Boomer drew back.

15

Mammi shrugged. "Wait'll you hear his bark. Sounds like a blast of dynamite."

Boomer settled down onto the buggy floor and fell asleep.

"A good guard dog," Bess said, trying to be friendly.

Mammi snorted, but she dropped a big hand to stroke Boomer's head. "The day that dog barks at anything worth barking at is the day there'll be white blackbirds in the sky."

"Mammi, do you want me to drive? You must not be feeling too well after your female surgery and all." Bess hoped she might say yes. She enjoyed driving horses. Some of her fondest memories were sitting with her father on the plow, holding the giant draft horses' reins in her small hands, his big hands covering hers.

"Female surgery?" Mammi gave her a blank look. "Oh. Oh! Had my teeth pulled." She opened her mouth wide and clicked her teeth. "Store-bought choppers. As good as new."

Then what am I doing here? Bess wondered.

Mammi slapped the horse's reins and it took off with a start, as if they were heading to a fire. But instead of turning down the road that would take them to Rose Hill Farm, Mammi steered the horse to a little bakery called The Sweet Tooth. She stopped under a shade tree and wrapped the reins on a low-hanging branch. "Bet you're hungry. Let's go get us something to eat." She turned to Boomer, who had a hope to go in with her. She waved her finger at him to say no. Boomer hung his head and settled back down for another nap.

Bess *was* hungry. The last few months, she had grown so quickly, she was always hungry. But it surprised her that Mammi was willing to shell out money to pay for premade food. Her father said that his mother's cooking skills surpassed most everyone in the county. And she was thrifty! Mammi never bought anything

16

new or threw anything away; even her letters were written on the backs of old bills.

Bess followed and waited in line behind Mammi at the bakery counter. An older woman standing at the counter gave a double take when she saw Mammi. The woman had a massive pile of braided hair, like a coiled snake, on top of her head. Bess wondered how she managed to sleep at night.

The woman recovered from her surprise. She put a hand to her chest. "Bertha Riehl, as I live and breathe."

"Dottie Stroot," Mammi said. "And I hope you are still living and breathing."

"Have you finally decided to let me sell your rose petal jam in my bakery?"

"I have not," Mammi said firmly.

Mrs. Stroot sighed. "Folks are asking me for it all the time, Bertha. They can't always find you to buy it up at the farm."

"I'm busy."

"I'd give you a generous cut."

"For my own jam?" Mammi stared her down, and Bess saw Mrs. Stroot start to crumble.

In a longsuffering voice, Mrs. Stroot asked, "Is there something you came in for today?"

"I want to talk to that one." Mammi pointed in the kitchen area, to the back of a girl in an apron and uniform who was putting a pie in a pink box, then carefully tying it with string.

Mrs. Stroot looked puzzled but called out, "Lainey. This lady wants you to wait on her." An oven buzzer went off and Mrs. Stroot quickly forgot Mammi to hurry to the kitchen.

Without looking up, the girl named Lainey called out, "Be with you in a minute." Bess saw her write something on top of the pink box and slip the cap back on her pen. The girl whirled around to face Mammi and froze. Then she stiffened up straight and swallowed hard. Bess was getting the feeling that people often had to swallow hard when they encountered her grandmother. She felt the same way.

"Bertha Riehl," Lainey said, faint and far off.

Bess had it wrong. Lainey wasn't a girl at all. She was a small woman, probably in her mid-twenties. She was very pretty. Her hair—nearly coal black—was cut short and curly. Her thickly lashed eyes were the color of blueberries that grew in her father's garden. Her complexion was perfection, as delicate as bone china.

"Lainey O'Toole," Mammi said flatly in return. "Last time I laid eyes on you, you were ten years old and so thin I could almost see the sun shining through you. You've gone and grown up."

Lainey swallowed again. "It's good to see you, Bertha."

"This here is Bess." Mammi indicated Bess with a thumb, without saying she was her granddaughter. Mammi never told more than the minimum.

Lainey gave Bess a brief nod, then turned back to Mammi. "I've been meaning to pay you a call since I came back to Stoney Ridge."

"Good. I'll expect you for Sunday noon dinner." Mammi looked through the glass counter. She pointed to a cherry tart. "You make those?"

Lainey nodded. "Just this morning."

"I'll have one. Make it two. And a cup of coffee." She glanced at Bess. "What about you?"

"A Danish please," Bess answered. "And a coffee too."

"Make it milk," Mammi said. "And best stick to those cherry tarts. If those are as good as I remember, you'd be a fool to miss 'em." She paid Lainey for the baked goods and took her coffee to a small table by the window.

18

Bess asked her grandmother how she knew her.

"Who?" Mammi asked, the picture of surprise.

"The bakery lady. Lainey."

"She grew up around here. Then she left."

Mammi didn't offer up another word. She ate with the fork in one hand, the knife in the other, polished off her two cherry tarts and then eyed Bess's. Bess quickly stuffed it into her mouth. It was the finest cherry tart she had ever tasted, with a crumbly crust and cherries that were sugared just right and still tart. Soon, Mammi was ready to go, and she looked at Bess pointedly. Bess guessed that when Mammi was ready, she'd better be.

That was another odd thing about Mammi—as big as she was, she could move like greased lightning. In a twinkling, she was at the door, pointing at Lainey. "Sunday noon, then." It was a statement, not a question.

The bakery lady looked a little pale but gave a nod.

Lainey O'Toole watched Bertha Riehl walk out the door and climb into the buggy. Bertha had always been a big, husky woman, now even bigger than Lainey remembered. Older, too, but she still moved along like a ship under full sail. And beside her was the young girl with platinum blond hair under an organza prayer cap that was shaped differently from the Lancaster heart-shaped cap. She had white lashes that framed her wide blue eyes. They made an odd pair. The girl turned back to wave at Lainey, as if she knew she was being watched. That young girl seemed as jumpy as a cricket. But those blue eyes—they were the color of a sapphire.

As surprised as Lainey was to see Bertha Riehl walk into the bakery, she was relieved too. She had wanted to see Bertha again and wasn't sure how to go about it. She'd already been in Stoney Ridge for two weeks and hadn't mustered up the courage to head to Rose Hill Farm. Bertha wasn't the kind of woman you could just walk up to and start asking personal questions. She could just imagine the way Bertha would stare her down, until Lainey's mind would go blank and she would forget why she was there. Like it did only fifteen minutes ago, when she turned and found herself face-to-face with her in the bakery.

Still, there were things only Bertha could tell her. It was the reason she was in Stoney Ridge in the first place.

Lainey had a plan. She was on her way to attend the Culinary Institute of America in upstate New York—she had scrimped and saved every penny for tuition since she was eighteen. She finally had enough money, was accepted, and was eager for her new life to begin. The school term didn't start until September, but she wanted to find a place to live and get settled. She thought she could pick up a waitress job to tide her over. Lainey liked planning her future. It was a trick she had learned years ago. Making plans gave her great comfort; she always felt better with a plan in place—like she had some control over her life.

Two weeks ago, Lainey packed up everything she owned and said a teary goodbye to her two best friends, Robin and Ally. She was going to make a quick pass through Stoney Ridge on her way to New York. At least, it was going to be a quick stop until her eleven-year-old VW Beetle sputtered to its death in front of The Sweet Tooth and she went inside to borrow the phone. Apparently, the bakery owner had just put up a sign for help wanted and assumed Lainey had come in to apply.

"Can you bake?" the owner, Mrs. Stroot, asked.

"Once I won first prize at the county fair for my cherry tart," Lainey said truthfully. She was just about to explain that she only came in to make a phone call, when Mrs. Stroot cut her off and gave a decided nod.

"You're hired," Mrs. Stroot said. "I'm desperate. My best girl quit this morning and my other best girl is out with bunion surgery. I'm busier than a one-armed wallpaper hanger. Here's an apron and there's the kitchen."

Lainey tried, several times, to inject that she wasn't going to be in town very long, but Mrs. Stroot was more of a talker than a listener. She pointed to a building across the street as she dialed the phone. "See that brick building across the street? The land-lord happens to be my very own sister—" she held a finger in the air when someone answered the phone—"Ellie? I found you a boarder for that room you got available. What's that? Turn your telly down." She rolled her eyes at Lainey and whispered, "She doesn't appreciate being interrupted during *General Hospital*." Ellie must have said something because Mrs. Stroot's attention riveted back to the phone. "A lady boarder. Uh-huh, uh-huh." She covered the mouthpiece. "Do you smoke?"

Lainey shook her head.

"No, Ellie. She doesn't smoke." Mrs. Stroot covered the mouth-piece again. "Any pets?"

Lainey shook her head again.

"Weekly or monthly?"

"Weekly," Lainey said. "Definitely weekly. I don't plan to be here long, you see . . . ." She gave up. Mrs. Stroot wasn't listening. She was asking her sister for today's update on *General Hospital*.

Lainey had to admit that God had a funny way of answering her prayers. As she set out on her road trip to New York, she had prayed that God would direct her path while she drove through Stoney Ridge. She wanted to visit only one person—Bertha Riehl. Here she was, just a few hours later, and she was employed—even

21

though she wasn't looking for a job. And it happened to be doing the one thing in the world that Lainey loved to do: bake.

Less than ten minutes after arriving in Stoney Ridge, Lainey had a place to live and a job to bring in some cash so she wouldn't have to dig into her culinary school tuition money. Her car, the mechanic said, was a lost cause. She thought that was God's idea of a joke. He directed her path all right. To a dead stop.

The house was painfully quiet. Jonah glanced at the clock in the kitchen and counted forward an hour. Bess would be in Stoney Ridge by now, probably at Rose Hill Farm. There were hundreds of reminders of his daughter throughout the house, more than he had ever been conscious of. Dozens of images of Bess at different ages rolled through his mind: taking her first wobbly steps as a toddler, dashing to the mailbox each afternoon to meet the mailman, running barefoot from house to barn and back to house.

Taking a sip of coffee from his mug, he lifted the pages on the calendar hanging by the window and counted off. Just twelve weeks to go and she'd be back.

He wondered how Bess and his mother would be getting along. He hoped Bess would let him know just how sick his mother was. He felt worried about her, and that was a new feeling for him. In the letter, his mother said she was pining for her grand-daughter and off her feed. It troubled him, that letter. It wasn't like his mother to pine. Or to be off her feed. She had a mighty appetite. He never remembered her ailing, not once, not even with a head cold.

He sighed. Something wasn't adding up. Either his mother's health was truly a concern or . . . she was up to something.

Just then, Jonah saw his neighbor and particular friend, Sallie Stutzman, coming up the drive with a casserole dish in her arms. He set down the coffee cup and went to see what Sallie had in that dish. It had been only a few hours since Bess had left, and he was already tired of his own cooking. And he was lonely.

Bess was a quick learner. After one buggy ride with her grandmother, she had already figured that she should hold tight to the edge of the seat so she wouldn't slide off and land on the buggy floor when Mammi took the curves. Her grandmother drove through those country roads like a teenage boy, the buggy leaning precariously to the side. She made a tight right turn and, suddenly, there it was: Rose Hill Farm.

The farm sat in a gentle valley surrounded by rolling hills, with fields fed by a secluded, spring-fed pond. The farmhouse—a rambling house with white clapboard siding and a brick foundation— was even prettier than Bess remembered. Three years ago, when she was here for her grandfather's funeral, she remembered being impressed by the neatness of the fields, the trimmed hedges, and the cherry trees that bordered the drive. It was the same today. Her grandmother may be ancient, but she had kept up the farm in good condition, that was plain to see.

A perfume wafted past Bess, and her eyes traveled to the fields that surrounded the house: acres and acres of blooming roses in what used to be pastures. The roses were at their peak. Pinks and reds and yellows and oranges blurred together to create a collage of color. Bess remembered that her grandmother had written awhile back that she had started a small business selling rose petal jams and jellies. But *this*—this was more than a small business.

Mammi stopped the horse under a shade tree next to a hitching rail. "We'd best get to work."

Oh no. Bess clutched her forehead. "On my first day here?"

Mammi lifted a sparse eyebrow. "Es hot sich noch niemand dodschafft." *Nobody ever worked to death.*

Boomer let out an ear-busting woof and leaped out of the buggy to run to the fields. Mammi hopped out of the buggy and reached a large hand to pull Bess forward by the arm. She stopped dead and aimed a stern look at Bess. "A little work might put a little muscle on them bones."

There were moments, like this one, when Bess thought it would be simpler to be English. On the bus this morning, a little girl wanted her mother to give her a snack, and when her mother refused she broke down and bawled. That's just what Bess would like to do right now, break down and bawl. Of course, she couldn't.

But oh! she was hot and tired from the bus trip and frustrated at what she had just figured out. She came to Stoney Ridge on a mission of mercy for her ailing grandmother, and the truth was that she was nothing more than another pair of hands—to pick roses. For an entire summer! Her father was right. Her grandmother was sneaky. Bess wished she had just stayed home and worked with her father on their farm. She missed him terribly. Far more than she had expected she would.

Bess heard Boomer bark again and she looked to see why the dog was causing such a ruckus. Boomer was standing on his hind legs, licking the face of a boy—or was it a young man?—and ended up knocking off his straw hat.

"That's Billy Lapp," Mammi said. "He's my hired help."

The boy pushed Boomer off of him and reached down to pat the dog's big head. Then he bent down and picked up his straw hat, knocking it on his knee a few times to shake off the dirt. Billy

Lapp looked to be about seventeen or eighteen years old. Man-sized. When he stood and his eyes met hers, Bess felt her heart give a simple thump. Clearly Amish by his clothes and haircut, he was tall, broad-shouldered, with curly brown hair and roguish eyes rimmed with dark eyebrows. Hands down, he was the best-looking boy Bess had ever laid eyes on. Her heart was beating so strangely now, she thought she might fall down and faint.

Things were looking up.

2

By the time Bess woke the next morning, she could hear Mammi banging pots and pans down in the kitchen. She dressed fast, already worried by yesterday's hints that her grandmother thought she had a lazy streak. She flew down the stairs expecting to encounter a hands-on-the-hips disapproving frown, but Mammi stood in front of the range at her usual place, on gray-speckled linoleum that was worn to the floorboards. With her thumb, she pointed to the table, already set with two places. Bess slipped into her chair and Mammi slid a belly-busting breakfast in front of her.

"How do you like your eggs poached?"

"Is there more than one kind of poached egg?" Bess asked.

"Runny, soft, or hard?"

Bess looked startled. "My yolks always end up hard."

Her grandmother flipped an egg timer. "Three minutes for runny, four for soft, five for hard."

"Dad and I poach eggs for fifteen minutes."

Mammi snorted. "A yolk like that could double for a rubber ball."

26

Bess grinned. Blackie had done just that with a yolk, patting it around on the ground with his paws. Her father had suggested Blackie be included in a game of kickball after church one Sunday.

Where was Blackie, anyway? He had disappeared the moment he was let out of that hamper and caught full sight of Boomer, head to tail. Mammi told her not to worry, that Blackie would find a place to live in the barn. Bess was horrified. She tried to explain that Blackie was a house cat and Mammi only scoffed. "Animals belong outside." Boomer apparently didn't qualify as an animal, because he had followed Mammi right into the house and stayed by her side like a shadow.

They bowed their heads and then dug into the meal. They ate in silence for a long while until Mammi asked, "What's your father got growing in his fields right now?"

Bess cracked the poached egg with her spoon and pulled off the shell in pieces. "He's leased out the fields to a neighbor."

Mammi broke up her egg over a piece of toast so that the yellow yolk oozed over it. "He's not farming?"

Bess looked up, surprised. "Well, his bad back made it too hard for him. So last year he started a furniture-making business and it's done well. He has orders piled up for months." Bess poured molasses into her oatmeal. She would have thought Mammi would have known such a thing. She seemed to know everything, often before it happened. But her grandmother was stunned to silence, a silence so thick that Bess could hear a wasp buzzing on the windowsill.

Mammi remained deep in thought. "It wonders me. To think of my Jonah without a farm to tend." She took off her spectacles and polished them. Then she reached into her apron pocket and pulled out a handkerchief to blow her nose. A loud honk that rattled the windows. "Allergies," she muttered, but Bess couldn't be fooled that easily. It shocked her, finding a tender spot in her grandmother. Mammi quickly recovered. She handed Bess a jar of pale pink jam. "Put that on your toast."

Bess spread some on it and took a bite. Her eyes went wide. "Oh Mammi. Oh my. Oh my goodness. Is this your rose petal jam?"

"It is," Mammi said. "It's the food of angels, if they have a choice."

Bess took more jam from the jar and spread it all over her toast, right to the edges. She took a large bite and chewed thoughtfully. It was the most delicate, delicious flavor she had ever tasted.

Mammi tried to hide a smile at Bess's rapturous expression with a swallow of coffee. "So what else is your dad doing?"

"Not much," she said, reaching for a spoonful of jam. "Well, except ... he's given some thought lately to getting married again."

Mammi raised an eyebrow. "About time."

She shrugged. "You know Dad. He acts like a sheep that spooks and runs off at the slightest mention of marriage. He says it's because his heart belonged only to my mother."

Mammi nodded.

Bess took a bite of toast. She took another bite, chewed, and swallowed, then frowned. "But there's a neighbor lady who's wearing down his matrimonial resistance." She hoped the glum note didn't sound in her voice.

"En grossi Fraa un en grossi Scheier sin kem Mann ken Schaade." *A big wife and a big barn will do a man no harm.*

Bess shrugged. "It's not that. I want Dad to find a wife ..."

She felt Mammi staring at her, hard. "What's wrong with her?"

"Oh, nothing. She's . . . real cheerful. And talkative. Cheerful and talkative." *Professionally cheerful.*

Mammi raised an eyebrow. "Our Jonah is a catch."

Bess knew that. Her dad was a fine-looking man. Even her friends said so. And he was young, only thirty-five. He was well thought of in their community, by men and women alike, and nearly every single female in their district—plus two neighboring districts—had set their cap for him. Cookies and pies, invitations to dinners and picnics, one father even boldly hinted to Jonah that his dairy farm would be passed down to his only daughter if Jonah married her. But Jonah never took the bait.

Until now.

That was half the reason Bess decided to come to Stoney Ridge this summer. Her father was spending time with Sallie Stutzman, a man-hungry widow with twin six-year-old boys—and the whole notion turned Bess's stomach inside out. Sallie had a heart of gold, everyone said so, but her very presence set Bess's teeth on edge. It wasn't that there was anything wrong with Sallie, other than the fact that she never stopped talking. *Not ever.* She even talked to herself if no one was around to listen.

Bess had a hope that her father would fall in love again, and she just didn't think he was in love with Sallie. That didn't seem to be a worry for Sallie, though. Bess saw how she was weaving her way into her dad's life. She asked him for rides to church and frolics, so often that other people assumed they were a couple since they always arrived together. Sallie stopped by every day with a casserole or cake or pie. The everydayness of it all was what made the difference between Sallie and other persistent female suitors. Even Bess found herself counting on Sallie's fine cooking. Sallie usually dropped broad hints about how it would be so much easier to cook for Jonah and Bess in their own kitchen.

About how their new cookstove was so much more reliable than her old temperamental one.

Her father always paled a little when Sallie dropped those hints. Sallie kept at it, though. Bess overheard her point out to her father that every girl needed a mother, and poor Bess—poor Bess, she always called her, as if it was one word—had gone without one far too long. She needed a mother's love before it was too late.

And what could her father say to that? Sallie's dogged determination was causing her father to weaken. Just last week, he asked Bess what she would think about having a little brother or two around the house.

The truth of the matter was that Bess thought it would be a terrible idea. Sallie's twins weren't like most Plain boys. Sallie's twins were as tricky as a box of monkeys. Their idea of fun was spreading Vaseline on Bess's toilet seat. But to her father, she only said, "Well, now, that's certainly something that needs serious thought." *Long and hard.*

Her father grew pensive at her response. And that was the moment when Bess decided to come to Stoney Ridge for the summer. She may not be able to stop a marriage with Sallie from happening, but she didn't want to watch it happen.

Bess suddenly realized that Mammi's gaze was fixed on her, and she was sure her grandmother could read the dark thoughts that were darting through her mind. Her cheeks grew warm and she looked out the window. Billy was coming up the drive and gave a wave to them before he disappeared into the barn.

Mammi smacked her palms down on the table. "We got us some roses to tend." She was on her feet now, making short work of the dishes.

Not ten minutes later, they joined Billy out in the rose fields. Mammi repeated the rose petal–picking instructions she had given out yesterday. Bess didn't interrupt her to say she understood; after all, her grandmother was older than the hills.

"The best time is in the late morning, after the dew has dried and before the strong afternoon sun." Gently, Mammi held a large pink rose with the tips of her fingers and pulled it off the base. "Trim the white sections with scissors—this will save you time." She quickly snipped the white part off of each petal and then let them shower into the basket by her feet. "Next, cut the stem to the next five leaves. That's where the next bud will form."

It amazed Bess to see Mammi's chapped, man-sized hands handling the roses like they were made of spun sugar. Her own hands looked like a child's next to her grandmother's. And she was embarrassed by how soft her hands were. As careful as she tried to be, thorns kept pricking her. Within fifteen minutes, her hands were covered in cuts and scratches. And how her back ached, bent doubled over!

When they had harvested a large basketful, Mammi gave a nod to Bess to come along, and they went to the barn. Boomer trotted behind, never more than a few feet away from Mammi. Inside, Bess stopped abruptly when she noticed that the cow stanchions and horse stalls were empty. There were no animals other than Frieda, the buggy horse. She had been so distracted by the sight of Billy Lapp yesterday that she hadn't even gone into the barn.

"What happened to the animals?" The last time she was here, this barn had been filled with horses, mules, cows, and even two ugly sows.

"Couldn't take care of them without my Samuel, so I sold them at auction," Mammi said matter-of-factly. "I buy milk from a neighbor. Still have my ladies, though." She meant her hens. She loved those chickens and called each one by name. She slid the door shut behind Bess. In the center of the barn were rows of sawhorses with screen doors laid on top. "This is how we dry the petals. Lay 'em out so they can air dry. No overlaps or else they'll mold. They need to get as crisp as cornflakes."

"Why don't you just put them out in the sun to dry?" Bess asked. "That's what we do with apricots and peaches. Apples, even."

"No. I keep them in the barn and out of direct sunlight."

"Have you ever thought about drying them in a warm oven?" Bess asked. "Once when it rained all summer, Dad put sliced up fruit in the oven to finish drying." She felt pleased with her suggestion. Maybe that was one way she could be helpful to her grandmother this summer: by pointing out ways to improve the farm. Being fifteen, Bess had some pretty good ideas about modernizing, and her grandmother had lived here since Noah's ark reached Mt. Ararat. She could use Bess's help with such things. *Like indoor plumbing.*

Mammi cast her a look as if she might be addle-brained. "Might work for fruit but not for my roses. You'll lose oil. Lose oil and you'll lose fragrance." She straightened and pressed a hand against the small of her back. "Go bring me another basketful." She handed the empty basket back to Bess. "Be quick about it. We can't pick flowers in the afternoon. It's gonna be hotter than hinges today."

Bess took the basket and went out to join Billy in the fields. Yesterday, he had left soon after she arrived so she hadn't had time to get acquainted with him. Mammi said he usually only worked a few hours a day, then needed to get home to tend to his father's farm. Bess was looking forward to getting to know Billy. She followed behind him as he worked. He culled roses from the right row of bushes, she from the left. She could see he was concentrating on the work. He kept peering at the roses as if he was learning something from them. She racked her brains for an interesting thing to say, but nothing bubbled up to the surface. Finally, Billy stopped for a moment to gaze at a golden eagle flying overhead and seemed surprised to discover she was there.

"So, Bess, where are you from?" he asked.

"Berlin, Ohio."

Billy went back to examining roses, so Bess hastened to add, "Some folks think it's Ber-Lin, like the place in Germany. But it's really pronounced Burrr-lin. Folks changed the way they pronounced it during World War I, so it would seem less German." She could tell Billy wasn't really listening. Silence fell again. She tried to come up with a topic that would create conversation. Something that would make him notice her and realize she was bright, intelligent, deep. Nothing came to mind.

He stopped at a bush and examined a few blossoms, then started picking them. "You sure don't look anything like your grandmother."

That was a good thing, in her mind. Mammi must be nearly six feet tall and half as wide.

He eyed her bright blue dress. "Is it different in Ohio? Being Amish?"

"What do you mean?" She shrugged one shoulder. "Amish is Amish."

He snorted. "That's like saying roses are roses." He put a hand on his lower back and stretched, looking out at the wide variety of blooms. "What color is your buggy?"

"Black." So maybe there were differences. Lancaster buggies had gray tops.

"Some folks think Ohio churches are more worldly than ours." He shook the basket so the petals spread out. "Can you ride bicycles?"

33

"Yes."

"Telephones?"

"Only in the barn."

"You drive a car?"

"Gosh, no." Billy looked so disappointed that she added, "Once I drove a neighbor's tractor, though. And I take a bus to the public school."

He whipped his head up. "You go to public school?"

"High school." Bess had just sailed through ninth grade and was in shooting distance of high school in Berlin. All that stood in the way was that dreaded algebra class. That was the other half of the reason she changed her mind about spending the summer at Mammi's. On the day she took her final exam for algebra, she decided Stoney Ridge didn't sound so bad, after all. And if she hurried about it, she could leave Berlin before report cards would be mailed home, which suited her just fine. That way, she wasn't being deceitful. She didn't know for sure that she had failed the class. She had a pretty good idea that she did, but until that report card arrived, there was a slight hope she had squeaked by. And had she failed, well, if she were in Pennsylvania, then she couldn't possibly attend summer school in Ohio.

She searched for something—anything—to pique Billy's interest. "My dad got arrested for letting me skip school," she blurted out. Then she clapped her hand against her mouth. Why in the world did she say *that*?

Billy spun around to look straight at her.

Oh my! but he was fine looking. Those dark brown eyes nearly undid her. She felt her cheeks grow warm. "Last September, Dad said I didn't have to go to school anymore. Kids in the county right next to ours had stopped going the spring before and no one bothered them, so a few families in our district decided to quit too. But it didn't work. The truant officer came knocking on the door and took Dad to the county jail."

"What happened then?"

"He was fined and let go. And now I have to go until I'm sixteen. Ohio law." Her dad wasn't going to mess with the law anymore, he'd said more than once when she tried to convince him to let her stay home. "I can't imagine stopping school at the eighth grade." She couldn't imagine it, but she sure would enjoy it. She had often thought she had about all the education she could absorb. Especially math.

A look came over Billy's face, as if he thought she might be a very dense child. "What makes you think an education has to stop?"

That was a new thought for Bess. She gave his backside a sharp look. A book stuck out of his back pocket. She never thought it any fun to be bothering about books when you didn't have to. "My teachers say you need a formal education to get ahead in the world." Now, why did she say that? Why did her mouth not seem to be connected to her brain today?

Billy took his time answering. He pulled a few more rose blooms, snipped the petals, and tossed them in the basket. Then he lifted his chin and looked at her. "I guess it all depends on which world."

They picked blossoms in silence for a long while. When the basket was full of rose petals, he picked it up and leaned it against his hip. "Have you followed the Wisconsin trial?"

"No."

He shook his head as if she had just arrived from the moon. "*Wisconsin vs. Yoder*. It's a big court case going on in Wisconsin right now. Might bring about changes for us."

She hated to seem ignorant, but curiosity won out over pride. "What sort of changes?"

35

"It's possible that we won't have to attend public schools. That we could have our own schools right in our districts. Schools that would stop at eighth grade."

Such a thought made Bess's heart sing with gladness. She . . . would . . . be . . . done . . . with . . . algebra!

He handed her the basket to take into the barn. She broke into a skip on the way there, so thrilled by the news of *Wisconsin vs. Yoder*.

Billy and Bess picked rose petals for a few more hours. The sun had already begun to punish them when Billy said it was time to quit.

"I'll be on my way," Billy told Mammi as he handed her the last basket. He put his straw hat back on. "But I'll be over tomorrow morning, first thing."

He nodded goodbye and tipped his hat slightly in Bess's direction, which made her knees feel weak. The boys in Berlin would never dream of tipping their hats to a girl.

Mammi watched him go and said to no one in particular, "He's a good one, that boy."

Bess wanted to ask Mammi more about Billy Lapp, but then she thought better of it. Mammi saved herself a lot of bother by not being the kind of person who answered nosy questions.

Mammi closed the sliding door of the barn to keep it cooler inside. "After lunch," she said, "we got us an errand to do."

A few hours later, Bess hurried to keep up behind Mammi as she breezed through the Veterans Hospital in Lebanon. On the bus ride there, Mammi told her they were going to pay a visit to her brother, Simon, who was seriously ailing. Bess had heard terrifying stories about Simon, bits and pieces of his life woven together from tales her cousins whispered to her at her grandfather's funeral. She knew he was Mammi's only brother, was the youngest in the family, had always been a black sheep, and—worst of all—that he had been shunned.

But Simon was nothing like Bess expected.

She had prepared herself for a hulking brute of a man, with eyes narrowed into slits and teeth sharpened into points and horns sprouted on his head. A monster.

Instead, before her was a tired, pale-skinned old man who looked as if he was weary of living and ready to die.

Bess and Mammi stood by Simon's bedside in the ward, trying to determine if he was awake or asleep. Bess had a fleeting thought that he might have passed.

She looked at her grandmother and whispered, "Should I get a nurse?"

Mammi ignored her and leaned over him. "Wake up, Simon!" she boomed, and the room echoed.

Simon's eyes flew open. "Oh Lordy. It's the town do-gooder." He glanced at the basket Mammi held in her hands. "Did you bring your jam?"

"I did," Mammi said.

"Homemade bread?"

"It's in there." She put the basket on his bedside table. "You always did take better care of your belly than your soul."

Simon squinted at Bess. "Who's that?"

"That's Bess," Mammi answered. She eased her big self into a hard-backed plastic chair.

"Jonah—your nephew—he's my father," Bess filled in. She shifted her weight awkwardly from foot to foot while standing at the end of the bed. There wasn't any other chair to sit in. "So I guess that makes you my great uncle."

Simon's eyes opened wide, full of mockery, as he looked Bess over. "Another holy howler." He looked at her long and hard with cold blue eyes.

She'd never seen eyes so cold. There was a touch of meanness in his thin smile. Bess felt a bead of sweat run down the valley between her shoulder blades.

Mammi was watching her. "Bess, en rauher Glotz nemmt'n rauher Keidel." *A rough log requires a rough wedge.* "Never forget that."

How could Bess remember it when she couldn't even understand it? Bess looked at her, confused, but Mammi had turned her attention back to her brother.

"Simon, you never did know beans from honey," Mammi said. "If you could put two and two together, you'd figure out by now that Bess is a relation."

"So?" Simon asked.

"So mebbe she'd be willing to get a blood test and see if she can help you out. Mebbe her bone marrow could be a match for you."

Bess's eyes went wide as quarters.

"If she's willing, that is," Mammi repeated, avoiding Bess's eyes.

The ride home on the bus was a silent one.

Mammi had been told by the nurse that since Bess was underage, the hospital required a parent's consent before her blood could be tested. Mammi hadn't expected that, Bess could tell. But Bess was thoroughly relieved. It wasn't easy to say no to Mammi, and yet she wasn't at all sure she wanted to have her blood tested. The blood test was pretty simple, she knew that, but what if she were

38

a match? Giving blood was one thing. Bone marrow was entirely different. She wasn't even sure what that meant and didn't want to ask. Her only experience with bone marrow was to cook up a pot of soup and simmer the bones for a good long while. Besides, even if Simon was her great uncle, he was not a nice man. He was downright mean-hearted. Maybe it all worked out just fine, Bess decided happily. Since she was only fifteen and her father was in Ohio—with no intention to come to Pennsylvania—there was no possible way she could have a blood test. Bess looked out the window and smiled. Things had a way of working out.

"Bess," Mammi asked, one sparse eyebrow raised, "have you ever driven a car?"

Bess shook her head. "Just a tractor."

Mammi gave up a rare smile. "Same thing. When we get back to Stoney Ridge, we got us another errand to do."

Lainey O'Toole reread the letter she had written to her friends one more time before licking the envelope and sealing it shut. She had written and rewritten this letter during her break today until it sounded just right.

Dear Robin and Ally,

A moment of silence, please, for the passing of my Beetle. It sputtered to a stop in a little town called Stoney Ridge, but it didn't die in vain. It took its final breath in front of a bakery called The Sweet Tooth just as the owner put out a help wanted sign. I kid you not! One thing led to another and . . . well, instead of hunting for a temporary job in upstate New York, circumstances dictate that I am going to spend the summer here. But do not worry! It is just a short-term turn of events.

Love you tons and miss you more.
Lainey
P.S. Did I ever mention that my mother and I had lived in Stoney
Ridge until I turned ten?

Satisfied, Lainey dropped the envelope into the mailbox before she crossed the street to head to her little rented room.

When the bus dropped Bess and Mammi off in Stoney Ridge, Mammi told her to keep up as she made her way through the streets. Finally, her grandmother found what she was looking for. She made a beeline straight to the sheriff's car, parked by the hardware store.

Mammi peered in the open window of the sheriff's car and saw the keys dangling in the ignition. She turned to Bess. "Come on, big talker. Show me what you know."

Bess's jaw dropped open. "Mammi, you don't mean . . ."

"I do." Mammi got into the passenger seat. "Sheriff won't mind a bit. We're good friends. I've known that boy since he was in diapers."

"Still . . ." Her father was forever warning her to avoid stepping into moral mud puddles, and here she was jumping headfirst into one of his mother's own making!

Mammi reached over and pushed open the driver's side door. Cautiously, Bess slipped in.

She glanced at her grandmother with a worried look. "Seems like there are rules . . ."

Mammi turned to give Bess one of her surprised looks. "Es is en schlechdi Ruhl as net zqwee Wege schafft." *It's a bad rule that*

40

doesn't work both ways. "Never forget that." She looked straight ahead. "Let's go."

Bess sighed and prayed God would understand. She turned the ignition and the car roared to life. She opened her mouth to try once more to talk her grandmother out of this notion, but Mammi only pointed down the road. "That way."

As if Bess was driving a car made of eggshells, she shifted the gear, took her foot off the brake, and the car lurched forward. This wasn't at all like driving a tractor in an open field. She was terrified she would hit something or somebody. She drove so slowly that a few shopkeepers came outside and stared at the sight of two Plain women inching a police car down the street.

"That'll do," Mammi said after one block. "Park it over there." She pointed to the curb.

Bess pulled over and shifted the gear to park. The car lurched to a halt and the engine died. She exhaled with relief. She knew she could start the car, but she wasn't quite sure about stopping it. Her grandmother's eyes were on the rearview mirror. On her face was another of those rare smiles. Running up the road was the portly sheriff, waving his fists in the air. Mammi opened the door and climbed out of the car, prepared to meet the sheriff head-on. Bess slowly stepped out, wondering how many years a car thief would spend in prison.

The sheriff slowed to a jog and reached them, panting heavily. "Miz Riehl! What the Sam Hill were you thinking?"

"Hello there, Johnny," Mammi said, friendly as anything. "Have you met my granddaughter?"

Still panting, the sheriff looked Bess up and down without a smile.

Bess stood there, nearly dying of shame.

41

The sheriff hooked his hands on his hips. "*Why* would you take my police car?"

Mammi looked unusually innocent. "Bess here is visiting from Ohio. She's driven a tractor before. We just got to wondering—"

We? Bess wondered.

"—if it seemed like the same thing . . . driving a car or driving a tractor. I don't know too many folks with cars. So I figured you wouldn't mind if we borrowed yours."

"Borrowed the car? Miz Riehl, what you did was to steal a police officer's car! That's larceny! I could have you arrested."

Mammi nodded agreeably. "So be it." She stretched out her hands so that he could handcuff her.

The sheriff looked down at her fists thrust in front of him, then looked up at her, bewildered. "Miz Riehl, I'm *not* going to throw a widder lady into the pokey."

"The law is the law," Mammi said. "But I get one phone call."

"Miz Riehl, I just don't want you moving my patrol car."

"Stealing," Mammi said. "You called it stealing."

The sheriff sighed, exasperated. "Seeing as how it was recovered and no harm was done, I'll just give you a warning this time." He got in the car, closed the door, and stuck his head out the window, jutting his round chin in Bess's direction. "I've got my eye on you, young lady. You should know I got E.S.P. Extrasensory perception. I see things before they happen." He glared at her. "I don't know what kinds of trouble Amish teens get into in Ohio, but you can't get away with those shenanigans in Stoney Ridge." He looked disgusted and shook his head. "Hoodwinking a sweet little old lady into taking a joyride. You oughta be ashamed."

Bess's eyes went wide with disbelief. *Mammi? A sweet little old lady?*

Mammi frowned. Then she marched through town and down the road that led to Rose Hill Farm. Bess hurried to keep up with her, wondering what in the world her grandmother was up to and how she could ever explain this to her father.

3

Dear Dad,

    Mammi and I are getting along fine, just fine. She seems to be fully recovered from her female surgery. I didn't realize that pulling a tooth or two would be considered female surgery, but she said it definitely falls under that category. And one thing I'm learning about her, it's best to just agree.

    Did you know Mammi's rose business is taking over Daadi's pasture land? Those roses of hers—they're something else. In full bloom! Lots and lots of rose blossoms. To handpick and hand trim. Each and every day. My hands have been pricked by so many thorns they look like a pin cushion.

    Love,

    Bess

Jonah was rubbing a final coat of stain on a picnic table ordered by Mrs. Petersheim. She was one of his best customers, and he had promised to deliver the table for a family reunion she had

44

planned this weekend. The humidity was working against him and the stain wasn't absorbing like it should. He put down the rag and opened the workshop door to let the breeze in. It had been a hot June. Even after thirteen years, he still wasn't quite used to the extremes of Ohio weather. Hotter in the summer than Pennsylvania and colder in the winter. He stood by the door, looking out over the fields of oats planted by his neighbor. It still ate at him, to not be able to work his fields anymore. He missed farming. Like his father, he had always marked his year by his growing crops. He planted alfalfa on the day after the new moon. Then oats and clover went in. Corn in April, when the sap was rising in the maple trees. The seasons turned like a wheel.

It used to give him great satisfaction to see crops growing in the fields, as if he was part of something bigger. But he didn't have the physical capability to farm anymore. He had tried to keep up for years now, but it was too much for him. He wasn't the same man he was before the accident. The doctor warned him he would end up in a wheelchair if he kept asking too much from his back. "Jonah," the doctor said, "if I were you, I would consider that limp a small price to pay for still being alive."

A small price to pay? What about losing the only woman you've ever loved? What about trying to raise a child alone? What about the fact that his daughter never knew her mother?

He had worked so hard to honor Rebecca's memory and raise Bess the way she would have wanted her raised. He created a new life for himself and Bess, and the Lord had blessed his efforts. When he finally decided to lease the fields and try his hand at furniture making, the business took off. So much so that he had taken on a partner, Mose Weaver. Mose was a lifelong bachelor, an older, quiet man who spoke with a lisp when he talked, which was seldom. Most knew Mose was silent as a tomb, a man of deep thoughts, none of them revealed. Some thought that was because he had no thoughts at all, but Jonah knew better. Mose lived with his parents, worked hard, and wanted for little. He was a fine business partner for Jonah. There was more than enough work for both of them.

Jonah had no complaints about his life. But with Bess gone this summer, and with the painful awareness that she was growing up, he knew that things were going to be changing soon. He never did like change.

And what would life look like after Bess was raised? Sallie was forever pointing that out, as if he didn't wonder about it himself.

Jonah wiped the sweat off the back of his neck. Sallie had been making loud suggestions lately about getting married. He was fond of Sallie, but the thought of getting married made his throat tighten up. There had been a time, four or five years ago, when Jonah had tried to find a new mother for Bess, but his heart wasn't in it. He wanted to love again the way he had loved Rebecca.

Sallie had different ideas about marriage. She had been a widow for less than a year and was already moving on with her life, eager to marry again. That was one thing he admired about her. She didn't hold on to the past. Just last night, she had told him that she never expected a second marriage to be like the first. "There's no feeling like that first love, when you're young and carefree and life seems filled with possibilities," she said. "But that doesn't mean that a real good friendship isn't a fine start for a marriage."

Sallie thought his ideas of marriage were unrealistic. And she should know—she'd been married twice before.

Her boys needed a father, she had told him frankly, and his Bess needed a mother. It made perfect sense, she said.

He picked up the rag and dipped it in the can of stain, ready to finish up that table for Mrs. Petersheim. Maybe Sallie was right.

The Sunday after Bess arrived in Stoney Ridge was an off-Sunday, so no church would be held. Earlier this morning, a chicken—whose pet name was Delilah—lost its head when Mammi had picked it out specially and wrung its neck off. It happened so fast that Bess felt woozy. Mammi was feeding her ladies by tossing cracked corn on the ground, making little clucking sounds at them. Suddenly, she reached down and picked up a chicken by the neck and spun it over her head, snapping its neck. Within seconds she had it on a tree stump. After plucking off the feathers and saving them in her pillow bag, Mammi dipped those chicken parts in buttermilk and bread crumbs, fried it, whipped up biscuits to mop up the gravy, added snap beans and sliced tomatoes from the garden. Bess was sure she'd never seen a chicken go from the yard to the table so quickly. It was record time.

Mammi asked her to set the table and get it all ready for Sunday dinner, so Bess took out three servings of utensils.

Without looking up from the fry pan, Mammi said, "Make it for four."

"Why four?" Bess asked.

"You never know," Mammi answered with an air of mystery. She tucked in a wisp of gray hair that escaped her cap. In English she added, "Mebbe I got extra-century perception like the sheriff."

So Bess set the table for four. What was the point of asking?

47

Jonah loved this time of year. On the way to pick up Sallie and her boys for church on Sunday morning, he passed by a neighbor's house and saw the straight rows of crops in the fields, tended lovingly. He loved summer best of all. The first fruits of summer gardens would be making an appearance for lunch after meeting: deep red beefsteak tomatoes, sliced thick; cucumber salad; a pyramid of pickled peaches; bowls of luscious, plump strawberries. Yes, this was a good time of year.

He was especially looking forward to meeting today. It had been nearly a week since Bess had left, and he was starting to talk to himself just like Sallie did, he was *that* hungry for company. He felt a familiar warm feeling spread over him as he pulled into Noah Miller's yard: dozens of buggies were lined up, shoulder to shoulder, like pigs at a feeding trough.

After meeting, the men and boys ate first at the set-up tables, then cleared out of the way so the women could eat. A softball game had been started by the big boys and Jonah watched for a while. He noticed Sallie's twins were sent off to the outfield to catch fly balls. They had been pestering the big boys until they were finally given a job to do and could be out of harm's way.

Jonah walked over to join Mose, standing with a few other men under the shade of a large oak tree. Jonah half listened to the men's grave analysis about the weather they'd been having. Too little rain, they worried, a drought in the making. But then, farmers always worried about the weather. He could hear the murmur of women's voices—including Sallie's laugh, for she was always laughing—through the open kitchen window, along with the clinking of plates and forks, the thumping of bowls and platters onto the tabletops to be taken home.

Young Levi Miller sidled up to him, kicking at the ground. Levi was an awkward boy, but he adored Bess, and for that, Jonah admired him. "Any word?" Levi asked in a low voice. He began to blush, a bright red trickling its way up from his collar to the middle of his ears. They were sizable ears. They stood straight out at the side of his head.

Jonah smiled. "Nothing yet. But I'm sure she's having a good summer."

Levi was crestfallen. "All summer? Bess is going to be there all summer?"

Jonah felt the same way.

Mose placed his large and gentle hand on Levi's shoulder and steered him to the softball game. He helped Levi find a spot in line to have a turn at the bat, then he jogged to the outfield to help Sallie's boys field balls.

Without a car, Lainey O'Toole had no option but to walk the entire way to Bertha Riehl's farmhouse. In her arms was a pink box—a lattice-topped gooseberry pie she had made last night at the bakery. She knew the way to Rose Hill Farm as if she'd been there yesterday. As she turned onto Stoneleaf Road, she slowed her pace and turned down the dirt lane that led to the cottage where she had lived with her mother and her stepfather. The cottage was set back from the road. When she saw it, her heart slowed and pounded. It had been fifteen years since she laid eyes on it. She squared her shoulders and approached the cottage. Her throat felt tight and a weight settled on her chest. She looked up at the worn clapboards, without a speck of paint, the rusted gutters, broken windows covered with nailed boards. It was even shabbier close up than it looked from the road. Like nobody cared.

She stopped for a moment and took her time looking. When she was little, she had tried to imagine it was pretty, but now she saw that it had always been just a poor man's house, with crooked shutters and a sagging front porch. The porch roof had a vicious slant to it, as if a strong burst of wind might carry it away. An old grape arbor, overgrown like everything else, sat at the end of a broken flagstone path. A crow shrieked in the distance and a few more answered back by telling it off. A mother deer and her baby were grazing under a tree and lifted their heads at the same time, startled to see someone in the yard. They froze, their stiff forelegs splayed out to the sides like stilts. They inspected Lainey with their black-tipped ears, worried she might be a threat. Then finally, deeming her harmless, they looked away and resumed grazing. Otherwise, the place looked lifeless.

She walked up on the front porch and tested the door handle. It wasn't locked, but she didn't go in. It was hard to even imagine walking through the door, so she stepped back and peered in the windows. There was nothing to see there, just an old, forgotten cottage, yet she had the strangest feeling about it. Like she was home.

She stepped off the porch onto the walkway and nearly tripped on a fallen-over For Sale sign. She tried to set it upright, then made her way through the weeds, back to the road that led to the Riehls' farmhouse.

Lainey smiled when she saw the old hand-painted sign hanging on Rose Hill Farm's mailbox: "Roses for Sale. No Sunday Sales." She'd forgotten all about that sign. It had always seemed odd to folks that a woman like Bertha Riehl—as tough as old boots—grew delicate roses to sell. Samuel Riehl was the tenderhearted one, most folks presumed. But Lainey knew better. Bertha Riehl might be tough on the outside, but she was as soft as a marshmallow on the inside.

She walked slowly past the leafed-out cherry trees that lined the long drive, mesmerized by the sight of endless rosebushes in full bloom. Those roses were the most glorious sight she had ever seen in her life. She felt sure that the path to the Pearly Gates of Heaven couldn't be any more inviting than the one leading up to Rose Hill Farm.

Lainey saw Bertha first. She was shaking out a wet dishrag to dry on the kitchen porch railing. Lainey stopped at the bottom of the porch steps and looked up at the big woman, wearing a shapeless plum-colored dress with a black apron stretched around her vast girth. "I've never seen such beauty, this side of heaven. It's like . . . God is showing off a little." She looked out toward the barn. "You've added so many roses. Doesn't your husband object to your converting his pastures to roses?"

"Samuel passed three years ago come October the tenth," Bertha said in a matter-of-fact voice. "I couldn't keep up the farm, but I could do one thing."

Lainey smiled. "Grow roses."

"That's right. And now I'm selling jam made from my mother's rugosas over there." She pointed to shrubs of pink, multiflowered roses.

"I remember those rugosas," Lainey said. "I remember your jam."

Bertha nodded. "I keep adding more and more stock. Filling the pastures with roses. I got a hired boy who has a knack for grafting roses, so he started grafting those rugosas onto heartier root stock." She nodded in the direction of a small greenhouse next to the barn. "Folks come from all over to buy my rosebushes and now they're after my jam and tea."

Lainey nodded. "Mrs. Stroot is hoping I'll talk you into selling some at The Sweet Tooth. She wants me to find out what you'd say to a barter arrangement."

51

"Such as?" Bertha lifted an eyebrow. She was interested, Lainey could see.

"Maybe you could have your pick of things from the bakery—like a credit—in exchange for letting her sell the jam and tea."

Bertha sized that up for a long moment. "Tell Dottie Stroot I'll think it over."

Lainey felt pleased. She had expected a flat-out no.

Bertha eyed the pink bakery box in Lainey's hands. "What's in there?"

"Gooseberry pie. Your favorite, if I remember right."

"You do." Bertha turned to go back to the house and Lainey took that as an invitation to follow.

Lainey was surprised to see the same young girl standing in the kitchen who had come with Bertha into the bakery the other day. Today she was steeping teabags in a blue speckled pitcher. "You're Bess, aren't you?" she asked. "Have you been working for Bertha for a long time?"

"Just this week, but it seems like forever and a day," Bess said. She held up a hand covered with Band-Aids. "She's wearing me to a frazzle."

Bertha looked unimpressed. "The poor child hardly knows a tea rose from a China rose."

Bess hooted. "But you're giving me a crash course on all things roses." She took out some glasses, filled them with ice, and set them on the counter, next to the pitcher. "Help yourself to the sugar. I like sweet tea, myself." She pointed to the sugar bowl.

"Too much sugar will make your teeth fall out like a picket fence," Bertha said. "I never have it, myself."

"Except for every day," Bess muttered.

"Mebbe just a little on Sundays," Bertha said, spooning heaps of sugar into her glass.

52

Lainey noticed Bess rolling her eyes and had to bite her lip to keep from smiling. When she first met Bess at the bakery, she thought she had seemed frightened of Bertha. Today, though, she was clearly at ease, gently teasing and joking with her. Lainey could tell Bertha enjoyed Bess's company too, though she would probably never say so. Bess was like a filly, all legs and arms. Watching Bess reminded Lainey of herself at that age, when she had grown several inches in one year and became awkward and clumsy, as if she couldn't get used to the new dimensions of her body.

Bess was pouring Bertha a second glass of iced tea when the kitchen door opened and in walked a very good-looking young man, straw hat in hand. He looked curiously at Lainey, then his gaze turned to Bertha. "Am I late?"

"Right on time," Bertha answered. "The very pineapple of punctuation." And with that, the glass slipped out of Bess's hand, shattered on the floor, and spilled tea everywhere.

Billy knelt down and began to carefully pick up broken glass. Lainey and Bess grabbed dishtowels to mop up the tea.

"Being barefooted, I ought not to help," Bertha said, sprawled in her chair, the picture of ease. "But I don't mind having a floor mopped clean, now that Bess's cat has moved in."

Lainey hadn't seen any sign of a cat, just a big dog sleeping in the corner and a rooster standing guard just outside the kitchen door.

As soon as the broken glass was picked up and the tea wiped clean, they sat down to dinner. The chicken was delicious, but Lainey had little appetite for it. Too nervous. She needed to have a talk with Bertha. How could she bring up anything private with Bess and Billy here? Bess, Lainey noticed, never gave up another word once Billy arrived. Lainey caught her studying Billy, aware of his every word and movement. Lainey fought back a smile. She was glad she wasn't fifteen anymore. Billy and Bertha seemed to be completely unaware of Lainey's anxiety or Bess's discomfort. They ate everything but the pattern on the plate.

Billy concentrated on his food until the subject of grafting roses was brought up, then he didn't stop talking. "Some rose varieties put on a lot of top growth and few roots, which makes them liable to be weak-wooded and short-lived," he said to Lainey with professorial patience, as if she had asked. "But we can graft that rose onto a better taproot so that it puts down a good deal of roots. Doing that makes a rose plant liable to be long-lived, grow better and bigger blooms, and be more resistant to stresses and strains, like a hard freeze."

"Where'd you learn how to graft roses, Billy?" Lainey asked when he finally stopped talking long enough to fill his mouth with roast chicken.

He shrugged and looked over at Bertha. "She told me if I could figure out how to graft, I could have a job. So I went to the library and read up on it and gave it a whirl." He spooned the rest of the pickled peaches onto his plate and looked around the table to see if there was anything left to polish off.

"Gave it a whirl?" Lainey asked in disbelief. "Why, I've heard people go to college to learn how to graft plants!"

"His mother was a Zook," Bertha said, as if that explained everything.

Billy looked embarrassed but pleased. "Roses aren't difficult to graft because they're compatible with nearly all other roses."

When Bertha served the gooseberry pie, silence fell over the table. Lainey started to worry that something was wrong until Billy looked up and said, "This is the best pie I've ever had. Better even than yours, Bertha, if you'll pardon me for saying so."

"Pardon accepted," Bertha said, helping herself to a second slice. "You're right. This pie is unparalyzed."

Bess's spoon froze, midair. She looked at Bertha, confused. Lainey swallowed a smile. Only Billy took it in stride, as if accustomed to Bertha's way of twisting English words around.

"I taught Lainey how to make a flaky pastry shell when she could barely reach over the counter," Bertha said.

Now it was Billy's turn to be surprised. He looked at Lainey, curious.

"It's true," Lainey said. "I used to live nearby. Bertha would let me come visit and help her in the kitchen. She taught me how to bake. Once she could get that black iron range fired up, she could do some serious cooking."

"Still can," Bertha said between bites.

They wolfed down the pie so quickly that Lainey knew it was good. Just as Billy had his eye on another helping, a horse nickered from the barn. Lainey looked out the window. A horse and buggy had turned into the drive, and Bertha's horse knew company was coming. Lainey had forgotten how horses always seemed to know things that people didn't.

Billy jumped up from the table. "That'll be my cousin, Maggie. She was coming by to get me for a youth gathering at the Smuckers' this afternoon."

"Good," Bertha said. "It will give Bess a chance to meet some other young folk."

Billy froze. A look of mild panic lit his eyes. He spoke hesitantly. "She seems awful young for a gathering—"

"I'm nearly sixteen!" Bess said indignantly.

Billy looked unconvinced.

Bertha waved that concern away. "Die Yunge kenne aa alt waerre." *The young may grow old too.*

That only confused Billy.

"Besides, your Maggie Zook is only twelve or thirteen and she's welcome," Bertha said.

"But . . . it's Maggie! You know Maggie. She's thirteen going on thirty. Besides, she's the bishop's daughter. Who's going to tell her she can't go?"

As Bess saw Billy's hesitation, her face clouded over. Bravely, she lifted her chin. "Actually, I had plans of my own this afternoon."

"Like what?" Bertha asked.

Bess looked around the kitchen until her eyes rested on a jar of homemade jam. "You were going to show me how to make rose petal jam."

"Can't," Bertha said. "It's Sunday."

Billy still looked uncomfortable. He scratched the top of his head. "She really shouldn't . . ."

"Sure she should," Bertha said, clamping her granite jaw. "Besides, Lainey and I got us some visiting to do." She shot him a deeply dangerous look.

Defeated, Billy slumped to the wall, plucked his hat from the peg, and held the door open for Bess. She grabbed her bonnet and brushed past him, head held high.

Lainey went to the window to watch them drive off in Maggie's buggy. When they were out of sight, she turned to Bertha, who was still seated at the table, halfway through a third slab of pie.

Lainey sat back down at the table. "There's something I'd like to tell you."

Bertha picked up the blue speckled pitcher and refilled their glasses. Then she added three teaspoons of sugar into her glass and stirred. "What's that?"

"I've never thanked you for helping me like you did, years ago.

You always made me feel welcome in your home, and you took an interest in me and helped me and my mother out. It's thanks to you that I'm a Christian today."

Bertha picked a loose thread from her apron front.

Lainey could have been talking about the weather. She tried again. "Bess is a lovely companion for you."

"She's a nervous little thing. Jumpy as a dog with fleas. But time will fix that."

Then quiet fell again. How could Lainey shift this conversation in the right direction without making Bertha suspicious? A stray thought fluttered through her mind, something she hadn't noticed before. She cocked her head. "When Bess left just now, she called you Mammi."

"So she did." Bertha took a sip from her glass.

"Isn't that the Deitsch word for grandmother? I . . . thought she was your hired girl."

Bertha snorted. "Not hired. Doubt I'd hire her—she oozes away like a barn cat when there are chores to be done." She looked straight at Lainey. "But she is my girl. My only grandchild."

Lainey was confused. "I thought Jonah and Rebecca and their daughter were in Ohio."

Bertha smoothed her skirt and pulled in her lips. "Rebecca died in that buggy accident, long ago."

"Oh no," Lainey said. That news was a shock to her. "I'm so sorry. I didn't . . . I thought she had survived it." She stood and went to the window, then turned to Bertha, confused. "So Jonah remarried?"

Bertha shook her head. "Not yet. Far as I know."

"Are you . . . ?" Lainey's voice cracked and she had to start over. "You can't mean that Bess is Jonah's daughter? That girl with the blond hair?"

Bertha nodded. "Bald as an egg until she was two years old."

Understanding flooded through Lainey and she felt her face grow warm as blood rushed to her head. She sat down in the chair to steady herself. "I never knew her name," she said in a faraway voice. "I knew Rebecca had her baby, but I never knew the baby's name. It was the same week my mother died . . ." The words got stuck in her throat and she couldn't continue.

Bertha leaned back in her chair and crossed her arms over her chest. "Jonah and Rebecca's baby was named Bess, so that's what he called this little girl." She took a deep breath. "That's what he called the little baby girl you switched on us, Lainey. Fifteen years ago."

Lainey felt as if her heart was pounding so loudly that Bertha must be able to hear it. She looked down at her lap and saw that her hands were trembling. It was such a hot day, but she was suddenly cold. For a brief second, the room started to spin and she thought she might faint. "How long . . . ?" Her voice drizzled off.

"How long have I known?" Bertha leaned forward, cool as custard, to take a sip of iced tea. "From the moment I arrived at the hospital, after the accident." She smoothed out the oilcloth on the table. "Think I wouldn't know my own grandbaby? And Mrs. Hertz told me—told the whole town—about your baby sister's passing and you getting shipped off to a foster home. Wasn't beyond my apprehension to put two and two together."

Lainey chanced a look at Bertha. "Samuel knew too?"

For the first time, Bertha seemed mildly distressed. She slipped off her spectacles and polished them. Then she blew her nose, loud. "That rain we had last night was hard on my sciences."

Lainey frowned. "Your what?"

"My sciences." She gave her nose a honk.

"I think you mean your sinuses."

Bertha huffed a small laugh. "That's what I said." She stuffed her handkerchief in her apron pocket.

Lainey tried again. "Did Samuel know?"

Bertha took her time answering. "No. The very week Rebecca had her baby, Samuel's brother in Somerset was laid up in the hospital for a bleeding ulcer. Samuel went to go help finish up spring planting on his brother's farm. He hadn't laid eyes on his own granddaughter yet. But he came back as soon as I sent word about the accident."

Lainey felt the words lock in her throat. "Why . . . why didn't you ever tell?"

"When Jonah found out that Rebecca had died, it was like the light had gone out of him. His back was broke to smithereens."

Lainey's eyes went round as quarters. "He's paralyzed?"

"No. His spiney cord wasn't hurt, but his lower back was broke. He had to learn to walk all over again. Knowing Bess needed him was all that kept him going."

Lainey stared at Bertha for a long time. She rubbed her forehead. "Are you saying that Jonah doesn't know?"

Bertha shook her head and looked away. "You know how fast babies change and grow. By the time Jonah was able to see her and hold her, she was already holding her head up and rolling over." She sighed. "But Jonah never knew. I planned to tell him. I meant to. But there never seemed to be a good time. And then weeks and months turned into years."

Lainey closed her eyes and squeezed her fists tight. She should have realized! She should have known! The color of Bess's hair—white blond—and those turquoise eyes. Simon's hair color. Simon's eyes. She looked at Bertha. "So . . . Bess . . . is my half sister?"

As Bertha nodded, a single tear fell on Lainey's cheek, followed by another and another, until she couldn't hold them back anymore. She covered her face with her hands and wept.

When Bertha Riehl invited Billy for Sunday lunch, even then, he felt a pang of unease. He should have known that she would have something up her sleeve. She had a reputation for doing the unexpected. He had been working for her for over two years now, and she had never once invited him for Sunday dinner . . . until today. Normally, he got a kick out of Bertha's unpredictable methods of getting what she wanted. But he had never been the object of her finagling. He liked working for her. She paid him well, and he knew she needed his help around Rose Hill Farm. But now he was stuck babysitting her granddaughter for the rest of the afternoon—a girl who acted as nervous as a cottontail and had a hard time stringing more than two words together that made any sense. He found younger girls to be tiresome: they giggled a lot and refused to take anything seriously.

A horrible thought darted through his mind. He hoped Bertha wasn't trying her hand at matchmaking. He was real fond of Bertha, even if she was crafty, and he didn't want to lose this job. It was more than a job to him. It was his future. This was what he wanted to do with his life. He could never work up much enthusiasm pushing a plow behind a team of mules, but this—experimenting to create a better plant—this felt like something he was born to do. He studied books about roses, he wrote away to experts and asked their opinions, and he kept precise records—something Bertha had no interest in. It was a sin to be prideful and he was careful not to indulge in it, but it did please him when folks said they drove long distances to buy rose stock from Rose

Hill Farm. Last week, an English lady came all the way from Pittsburgh because someone at Penn State told her this was the only place to buy a rose that smelled like one grown a hundred years ago. "The hybrids might be the rage," the lady told Billy, "but they have no fragrance. But these roses"—she scanned the fields—"you can tell they're grown with passion."

How his father and older brothers would laugh at that comment. They thought his ideas were nonsense, so he stopped doing experiments and bringing his horticulture books home from the library. But his mother had understood. She and Bertha had been good friends and neighbors. His mother must have told Bertha the kinds of things Billy liked to learn about, because at his mother's funeral, she asked him to come work at Rose Hill Farm.

But as much as he liked and admired Bertha Riehl, as much passion as he felt for the roses, he knew he would never be passionate about this skinny girl sitting on the buggy seat next to his cousin Maggie. He guessed Bess could hardly weigh ninety-nine pounds soaking wet. She had an unnaturally scrubbed look, like she'd been dipped in a bottle of bleach and came out with ultra blond hair and white eyelashes. And that anxious-to-please expression on her face made him nervous.

He was glad his cousin was with them. Maggie could talk to a brick wall and never notice it wasn't answering back. At least he was off the hook from trying to come up with any more painful attempts at conversation, like he had to do—just out of politeness—when Bess was out helping him pick roses.

Still, the least he could do was to be nice, for Bertha's sake, so he took the long way to the Smuckers to show Bess his favorite spot on earth, Blue Lake Pond. A little jewel of a pond with pine trees that lined the shores. It was deserted, just as he expected. That was another thing he loved about this lake. He stopped the horse, hopped down, and tied its reins to a tree branch. He took a few steps and then stopped to wave to the girls. "Well, come on."

"Not me. I'm going to stay here," Maggie said, pushing her glasses up on the bridge of her nose. "I don't want to get my shoes dirty."

"Suit yourself," he said. "What about you, Bess? Every visitor to Stoney Ridge needs to get acquainted with Blue Lake Pond."

Thrown that small morsel of encouragement, Bess leaped off the buggy and trotted behind Billy.

Down by the shoreline, he put his hands on his hips and inhaled deeply. "This is the best lake in the county. In all of Pennsylvania. I spend every free hour on these shores—swimming in the summer, skating in the winter. Fishing in between." He picked up a rock and skimmed it across the pond. He gave Bess a sideways glance. "Me and my friend Andy go skinny-dipping here every summer." He paused for her reaction.

Bess's eyes went wide and her cheeks flamed scarlet.

Billy grinned.

Clearly mortified, Bess turned away from him and walked along the shore. Billy kept skimming rocks. After a while, she stopped to look up in the treetops. "It's the quietest place in the world."

"Sure is. Quiet and peaceful."

"I didn't mean it that way. I meant it in a strange way."

He tilted his head. "What's so strange about a quiet lake?"

"There are no birds singing."

He searched the skies and the trees. "Huh. You're right." He shrugged. "Maybe it's the time of day."

She walked further along the shoreline. "You'd think there'd be some sign of wildlife. A loon or a duck or a goose. Even a crow or scrub jay." She looked all around. "Nothing."

Maggie hollered to them she wanted to get to the Smuckers' before the gathering was over, if they wouldn't mind, so they turned around to walk back to the buggy. Before Billy left the shoreline, though, he shielded his eyes from the sun and scanned the lake. He saw plenty of dragonflies skating over the surface of the pond, but he was looking for some sign or sound of a bird in the trees or skies. Not one.

Billy disappeared to join his friends the minute they hitched the horse at the Smuckers', but Maggie stuck to Bess like glue. She reminded Bess of a pixie, small and dark, with eyes darting here and there, forever watchful. She could talk a person to death. Bess didn't mind at all; she'd grown accustomed to half listening after being around Sallie Stutzman so much. As they walked around the yard and watched some boys pegging out a game of horseshoes, Maggie pointed out names and gave Bess the full rundown on each person. Bess nodded, vaguely interested, but she kept one eye on Billy the entire time.

Someone tapped Bess on the shoulder. "*Who* are you staring at?"

Bess whirled around to face a tall, shapely girl with sandy-blond hair and dark brown eyes. If it weren't for the fact that she was glowering at Bess, she could even be called attractive.

Maggie intervened. She hooked her arm through Bess's and pulled her along. "I should have warned you about Esther Swartzentruber. She set her sights on Billy awhile back and hasn't let go. Well, most every girl has her sights on Billy, but Esther is the only one bold enough to tell everyone. She watches him like a hawk." She looked back at Esther who was scowling at both of them. "With you here, Bess, I think it's going to be a real fun summer. Esther thinks she's got all the boys pining for her, but look at how they're sizing you up like a hog at auction."

Bess was absolutely sure no boy was looking at her, but such a loyal remark earned Maggie a spot in her heart.

Right at that moment, a buggy wheeled into the driveway and pulled to a stop. Out poured four girls. It was the fourth girl who caught Bess's eye. Actually, it was Billy's reaction to Girl #4 that she noticed. He stopped playing horseshoes and walked over to greet Girl #4, lingering over her. But who wouldn't? She was *that* pretty.

Maggie leaned over and whispered, "That's Betsy Mast. Every boy in Lancaster County is wild over her."

A wave of pure jealousy came over Bess, shaming her. She said nothing. She was afraid it might show in her voice.

"How could they not be?" Maggie continued. "Look at her big eyes and gigantic pouty lips. Her chest looks like the prow of a ship! I call her Busty Mast. Have you ever seen such enormous—" She clasped her hand over her mouth. "Oh, I *shouldn't* have said that! Jorie—she's my stepmom—she's always telling me to think before I speak. But my mouth does run away from me."

Bess looked down at her own flat chest and up again at Betsy Mast. She sighed.

"Fellows sure do seem to love the prows of ships. They're always talking about them." Maggie spoke in a wise, mature woman-of-the-world voice and patted Bess's shoulder. "I know these things." She gave a sly grin. "I have a gift for eavesdropping."

For the rest of the afternoon, Billy hovered around Betsy like a bee around a flower.

For hours, listening to crickets in the thick, muggy silence, Lainey lay in bed and stared at the ceiling. Bess was her sister. *Bess was her sister!* She still couldn't believe it. She never dreamed she would see her again. Her thoughts bounced back to that terrible night, when she made a snap decision that altered lives. She had made a bold promise to her mother, who lay dying just two weeks before, that she would take care of her baby sister, Colleen. But within a few days, Lainey was overwhelmed and exhausted. And sad. Terribly sad. She missed her mother. She had found a small amount of cash tucked in the back of her mother's dresser drawer, but that was disappearing quickly after buying two weeks of baby formula. By now, she had been sure Simon would have returned. She was starting to panic.

When she heard the screech of tires and the horse whinnying and then that horrible crashing sound, she grabbed her baby sister out of the cradle and ran outside to see what had happened. The buggy had flipped to its side. She bolted over to it and her heart lurched with recognition—Rebecca and Jonah Riehl. She called their names, but they didn't respond. They both looked pale and still. Rebecca was bleeding from her ear.

The truck driver who had hit the buggy climbed out of his cab. He walked up to Lainey in shock. "I didn't see them! It was so dark and I was trying to pass . . ." He looked as if he expected her to tell him what to do next.

Lainey took a deep breath. "Go down the street until you come to the intersection. Find the gas station and call for an ambulance."

The man just stood there, looking at the horse trying frantically to get up, panting heavily. Its leg was twisted grotesquely. Then the man looked at the buggy, at the bodies in it, as if he couldn't believe his eyes.

"Go!" Lainey shouted, pointing her small finger down the road.

The man backed up, staggering, then started to run down the road.

Lainey heard a sound and turned to Rebecca, whose eyes opened halfway. "Mein Boppli," Rebecca whispered. "Meine Dochder." *My baby. My daughter.*

Lainey looked around and found a small bundle, thrown from the buggy. She hurried to the bundle and felt her stomach reel. The baby looked nearly identical to her own baby sister—same size, bald like Colleen, the same wide blue eyes. The face was unmarked, but the baby's chest appeared to have caved in. Her eyes were wide open, showing no signs of life. There was no breath. She didn't blink at all, even when Lainey touched her cheek. She put her hand on the baby's tiny chest but couldn't find any heartbeat. She had seen enough of farm life to know that this baby was dead. She heard the horse whimper in pain and shock—she would never forget that sorrowful sound as long as she lived—and she looked back at the buggy, at Jonah and Rebecca, and then down at the dead baby. Nausea rose in her throat and she coughed, retching. There weren't many times she wished Simon were home, but she wanted him here now, to help her. She was frightened, so frightened, and didn't know what to do next.

Lainey heard Rebecca call out. How could she tell Rebecca that her baby was dead? Slowly, she walked back to the buggy and saw Rebecca's eyes flicker open again. Impulsively, hoping to give Rebecca comfort, she tucked Colleen into her arms. "She's here, Rebecca," Lainey lied. "She's just fine."

Rebecca's eyes tried to open, but Lainey could see she was fading. "Denki," she murmured. *Thank you.*

Lainey hoped that truck driver could figure out where the gas

66

station was. She stayed by the buggy, telling Rebecca and Jonah to hold on, that help was coming. When she heard an ambulance siren in the distance, she exhaled with relief. As she reached down to pick up Colleen, she had a heart-thudding moment. Her infant sister looked up at her with wide blue eyes, oddly serene and peaceful despite this gruesome scene.

A plan took shape in Lainey's ten-year-old mind.

She saw the red flash of the ambulance's siren as it turned onto the street. Then she kissed her sister goodbye and picked up Rebecca's baby before running into the house. She spent the next hour by the window, shaking like a leaf, watching the ambulance workers and the police. She tucked Rebecca's dead baby in her sister's cradle and curled up in the corner of the old brown couch that smelled like mold. When she heard a single gunshot ring out—knowing the policeman had to put down the horse—she threw up again.

She didn't sleep at all that night. As soon as dawn broke, she walked down the road to tell her nearest neighbor, Mrs. Hertz, that her baby sister had died in the night, peaceful as can be, in her sleep. Surely God would punish her for all of these lies she was telling. Surely somebody was going to figure out what she had done. But all Mrs. Hertz said was, "God was merciful, Lainey. He knew no child should have to endure Simon Troyer as a father." She grabbed Lainey into her generous-sized bosom for a hug. "I never did understand why your sweet mama ever married that poor excuse for a man, anyhows."

They both knew the answer. A single mother, poor as a church mouse, didn't have a whole lot of choices in 1957.

Mrs. Hertz made one call to the county coroner and the next one to a county social worker. A bead of sweat trickled down Lainey's neck when the coroner arrived. She was petrified he might ask questions about the baby's death, but he just came and took the baby away, like he did two weeks before when her mother passed. She figured the coroner didn't concern himself with poor folks like them. In fact, he acted as disinterested as Simon had the night Lainey's mother lay dying. The day after his wife was buried, Simon told Lainey to take care of the baby and he went off deer hunting, though that couldn't be right because it wasn't hunting season. But maybe he *was* deer hunting. Rules were always optional for Simon.

As the coroner left, the social worker arrived. She took one look at Lainey's living conditions, at the absence of any adult in the home, and whisked her off to a foster home. When Simon didn't appear at the court date to claim Lainey, she became a ward of the state of Pennsylvania. She lived in three different foster homes until she was eighteen. After graduating from high school, she was on her own. She worked for a department store in Harrisburg and saved her money. She had a plan. Her two friends, Robin and Ally, gave her a hard time for being so serious and saving every penny, but Lainey knew what could happen to girls without goals and dreams. Her mother had warned her. She wanted a different life for herself.

All the while, Lainey had never forgotten her baby sister. Giving Colleen up was the hardest, best thing Lainey had ever done. Not a day went by when she didn't wonder a dozen questions about her sister—what did she look like? was she happy?—but she didn't feel plagued with guilt about whether it was the right thing to do. She couldn't think of a better life for a child than to grow up Amish. And now God in his mercy was giving her a chance to see that her sister had a childhood just as she had hoped for her: happy and loved.

Lainey gave up trying to sleep and went to the window to

open it wider. The room she had rented from Mrs. Stroot's sister faced west and was hot and stuffy by evening. She sat on the sill for a while, looking up at a sliver of the new moon. Her feelings felt jumbled. She had come to Stoney Ridge to try to find out information from Bertha about how her sister was doing, but she never planned to reveal her secret. She never wanted to upset her sister's life.

Today, that noble intention turned upside down.

Bertha said she was going to tell Bess and Jonah the truth this summer. It was high time. Bertha said when she saw Lainey in town a few weeks ago, she decided she would do all she could to get Bess out here as soon as she could. Now the time was right, she said. Maybe not today, but soon.

At least Bess would be here all summer. And so would Lainey.

Lainey's thoughts bounced to Jonah. Bertha didn't offer up much information about him—typical of her—but she did say that Bess was his only family. Lainey was sorry to hear that Rebecca hadn't survived the accident. Rebecca had always been kind to Lainey. It gave Lainey comfort to think she might have given her peace in those last moments, laying Colleen in her arms. She remembered Rebecca had been a beauty—small and delicate. It was plain to see how much she and Jonah loved each other. She had thought they were the luckiest two people on earth . . . until the accident.

As she thought about all Bertha had told her today, she found it hard to believe. But life could be like that, she had learned. A single decision, a moment in time, and the ground could shift beneath your feet.

4

When Bess came into the kitchen the next morning, Mammi was pouring batter on the waffle iron while the coffee perked. Mammi had finally relented to Bess's pleading and allowed her to drink coffee, as long as it was half milk. Peering out the window, Bess noticed Billy was already out in the fields among the roses. Unlike other mornings, she wasn't in any hurry to join him. She picked up her fork as Mammi brought her a waffle, then put it down as Mammi sat down and bowed her head. Mammi's prayers were never short.

When Mammi lifted her head, she said matter-of-factly, "You got in awful late."

Bess poured syrup over her waffle. "By nine. You were asleep in the rocker. I didn't know if I should wake you to outen the lights." She had decided against it when she realized that her grandmother had taken out her false teeth. The sight made Bess shudder. Mammi's mouth had looked like a shrunken apple.

"I never sleep."

Bess rolled her eyes.

"Did you have a good time?"

70

Bess nodded, distracted, and chewed slowly.

"Then why are you sitting there with a face as long as a wet week?"

Bess rested her chin on her propped-up hand. "I'm all at sea."

"What's making you so mixed up?"

"Do you know a girl named Betsy Mast?"

Mammi raised an eyebrow at Bess, then her gaze shifted through the window to Billy in the fields, bent over a blooming rose. "Es schlackt net allemol ei as es dunnert." *Lightning doesn't strike every time it thunders.*

"I'm not so sure, Mammi. You know boys." Bess sighed dramatically and took a sip of her coffee-laced milk.

Mammi nodded. "Boys are trouble. But girls is worse." She started filling up the sink with soapy water.

Bess gave up a smile, in spite of her grim mood.

One sure way of surviving heartache was to stay busy, Mammi told her, and shooed her out to join Billy by the roses. Bess picked up a basket on the porch and slowly went out to the field.

Last night, with her chin propped on the windowsill watching the moon rise, she had given her runaway feelings about Billy some serious thought. She'd barely known him a week. Now was the time to reel her heart back in, before she found herself falling off the edge of no return—the way Billy's face looked when he caught sight of Betsy Mast.

So that's the way things were going to be. She thought she had found the man of her dreams . . . but it was only an illusion. A tragic illusion. She sat in the moonlight and shed a tear or two. It didn't take much to set her off, now that she was fifteen. Her feelings were as tender and easily bruised as a ripe summer peach. Even Blackie, her cat, had declared his independence and had taken up barn living. She shed a tear for Blackie too. She missed her father, missed her home and her own bed. She even might miss Sallie and her boys a little. *No, scratch that.* But she did regret ever coming to Stoney Ridge. Even summer school looked more appealing than being stuck here, picking roses near a beautiful boy who hardly noticed her. She sighed, deeply grieved, and climbed back into bed, sure she would never sleep. She turned over once, and it was morning.

As Bess walked out to the roses, she decided that she would avoid Billy as much as possible, picking roses in rows far from him. She bent down to examine a blossom.

"Hey, what are you doing way over there?" Billy called out to her.

She bounced back up.

He picked up his basket and joined her in the row she was working on, making her heart turn in somersaults. "You were right about birds missing from the lake. I went back later last night, to see if I could hear any owls hooting. Nothing. What do you make of that?"

What did she make of that? Looking into his dark eyes, she couldn't make sense of anything. She couldn't think of a single thing to say—she was that tongue-tied around him. He looked particularly fine today too, with his cheeks turning pink from the sun and his shirtsleeves rolled up on his forearms. The wind lifted his hair. He looked so handsome she wanted to reach out and stroke his cheek. Her spirits soared.

Billy Lapp wasn't making it easy for her to fall out of love with him.

Jonah walked out to the shop in his barn, reviewing the facts for the hundredth time. He had tossed and turned last night try-

72

ing to figure it out. What exactly had happened last night to lead Sallie to the conclusion that they now had an Understanding? He had dropped her and her boys off after church, and she had invited him to stay for dinner. There was nothing different about that scenario. He and Bess had often taken Sunday suppers at Sallie's. He remembered saying that the house was awful quiet without Bess. Then, as he said good night, Sallie told him that she was just thrilled they had an Understanding. He was mystified. What had he said?

The morning was so warm that he opened up both doors in his workshop to have air circulate through. As he slid open the barn door, a thought seized him. Sallie was so . . . overly blessed . . . with the gift of conversation that he often found himself not really listening to her. Maybe he was asking himself the wrong question. Maybe the question wasn't what he had said. Maybe it was: what had he not said in reply?

When Lainey heard the bakery door jingle, she looked up, surprised to see Bess. Her blond hair was covered by a bandanna knotted at the nape of her neck, just below her hair bun. She wore a lavender dress under her white apron and she was barefooted.

"My grandmother has a craving for your cherry tarts and sent me down to get some," Bess said, peering into the bakery counter. She looked up, disappointed. "But they're all gone!"

The store was empty and Mrs. Stroot had gone home, so Lainey grabbed the chance to encourage Bess to stay. "I was just going to whip some up. What would you think about staying to help?"

Bess looked delighted. "I'd love to! Mammi is canning zucchini, and the kitchen is so hot that it's steaming the calendar right off the wall. One thing I've learned, if I don't make myself

73

scarce, Mammi will find me some chores." She followed Lainey to the back of the bakery.

Lainey pointed Bess to the sink to wash her hands while she got out the flour and sugar and lard. She felt her heart pounding hard and tried to calm herself. It still seemed like a miracle to her, to think that her sister was right there beside her.

Mammi was waiting out on the porch, arms akimbo, when Bess drove up the drive to Rose Hill Farm. Bess felt a little nervous because she'd been much longer than she said she would.

"Where have you been?" Mammi asked when Bess pulled the buggy horse to a stop by the barn.

"Lainey taught me how to make cherry tarts!" Bess handed Mammi a big pink box before she got out of the buggy, which, she thought, was a smart move. "The bakery was empty and she was just about to make a fresh batch. So she asked if I could help and I thought you wouldn't mind, seeing as how you love them so much."

Mammi opened the box and looked over the tarts. "Well, as long as you were helping her and doing something useful." She took a bite out of a tart and closed her eyes, as if she were tasting heaven.

"Lainey didn't even let me pay for them. She said I earned my keep and she hoped I'd come back again. She said late in the day the bakery is usually empty and she could use my help." Bess hopped down from the buggy and started to unbuckle the tracings on the horse. "Would you mind if I go see Lainey at the bakery now and then? Dad would sure love it if I could bake something new. I told her you wouldn't mind. You don't, do you, Mammi?"

She backed the buggy up from behind the horse and leaned it upright against the barn.

There was no answer, so Bess chanced a look at her grandmother. Mammi's mouth was too filled with another cherry tart to talk.

Three o'clock in the afternoon had become Lainey's favorite time of the day. For the past two weeks, like clockwork, Bess came through the door for another baking lesson. Normally, Mrs. Stroot closed the bakery at three, but when Bess started coming by at that time, Lainey asked if she would mind if the store stayed open a little longer. "I'm here anyway, getting ready for the next day," she told Mrs. Stroot, "and each afternoon we end up selling a few more baked goods. Better first-good than day-old prices."

Mrs. Stroot couldn't argue with logic that turned a profit, but she did say she needed to go home and start dinner for Mr. Stroot. Lainey promised her that she would lock up. So each afternoon, Bess drove Bertha's buggy to the bakery, parked the horse under the shade tree, and spent two hours with Lainey, baking and talking. More talking than baking.

Oh, the things she was discovering about Bess! She learned about Jonah and how he was going to marry his neighbor, Sallie Stutzman, who had twin boys no one could tell apart. And she learned about the boy at school who liked Bess overly much. "Levi Miller is nothing but a bother and a nuisance, Lainey. So . . . childish," Bess said, sounding so very adult. "But we're the only two Amish ninth graders at our public school, so he thinks we're destined for each other." And with that, Bess made a sour face.

There were also things about Bess that Lainey picked up without being told. Earlier in the week, Bess was in the middle of mixing cookie dough when she froze, eyes wide, as she stared out the window. Eventually, she turned back to the cookie dough, but sadness covered her like a blanket. Carefully, Lainey craned her neck to see what had caught Bess's eye out the window. It was that young fellow who worked for Bertha, Billy Lapp, carrying packages for a very attractive Amish girl.

"You're every bit as pretty as she is, Bess," Lainey said. She wasn't just saying that. Bess was going to be a beauty. She was unusual looking, with lovely cheekbones and skin like peaches and cream. And those eyes! They were extraordinary. When she wore a dress of a particular shade of blue, those eyes looked like the waters of a tropical island.

"No. I'm not," Bess said, sounding miserable. "It's hard on an ordinary moth when a beautiful butterfly comes around."

Lainey couldn't help but laugh. "Give yourself a little time. You just turned fifteen!"

Sadly, Bess said, "I don't have time. The summer is flying by."

Lainey's stomach gripped tight. She didn't want to think about that.

Bess looked up at her, a question on her face. "How did you know how old I am?"

And Lainey had no answer for her.

Over two weeks had passed since the Understanding, as Jonah came to think of it, had been formalized with Sallie. By Sallie. He still felt a little stunned, yet the idea of marrying again wasn't altogether unpleasant. It was starting to grow on him, the way Sallie sort of grew on a fellow. She was cheerful, that Sallie. And her boys certainly did need a father's influence. Sallie thought their antics were adorable, but most people ran the other way when they caught sight of those twins. Just the other day, they stripped Jonah's tree of apples and tossed them at passing cars. Mose caught them in the act and quietly took them home to Sallie. If Jonah had caught them, he would have wanted to tan their hides. Yes, those boys needed a father. And living alone this summer gave him a pretty good idea of what the future would hold for him once Bess was grown and gone. He hated it.

Over a month had passed since Lainey had arrived in Stoney Ridge. This July afternoon Bess came into The Sweet Tooth looking pale and worried, with arms crossed tightly in front of her as if she were shivering despite summer's muggy warmth. Lainey tried to teach her how to roll a pie crust, but she could see Bess couldn't concentrate. Bess kept rolling and rolling until the crust was so thin, it was nearly see-through.

Lainey quickly rolled it into a ball and put it in the refrigerator to chill. "You can't let pastry get warm. The shortening needs to be in layers when it bakes, not mixed in."

Bess looked as if the thought of ruining the pastry made her want to cry.

"Is something troubling you, Bess?" At first, Lainey was sure it had something to do with Billy Lapp. But then she had a horrible premonition that maybe Bertha had finally told her the truth.

"No. Yes." Bess's eyes met Lainey's, wide and sea blue. "I'm dying."

"What do you mean?"

"I'm bleeding to death."

Lainey looked her up and down. She didn't see any signs of hemorrhaging. "Where?"

Bess pointed to her stomach. "Here."

"Your stomach?"

Bess shook her head. She pointed lower.

"Oh," Lainey said. Then her eyes went wide as it dawned on her. "Oh!" She put her hands on Bess's shoulders. "Oh Bess, you're not dying. Hasn't anyone ever told you about getting the monthly visit from Flo?"

Bess looked at her, confused. "From who?"

Of course she hadn't been told! She had no mother. Her father certainly wouldn't discuss such a personal thing. Lainey went to the door and locked it, turning the closed sign over. She sat down and patted the chair next to her. "Let's have a talk."

Later that afternoon, as soon as Bess returned to Rose Hill Farm, Mammi showed her a black bonnet she had made for her.

"It's bigger than a coal scuttle!" Bess said miserably. "Mammi, are you trying to turn me into Lancaster Amish?" Her Ohio bonnet was much smaller.

"Nothing of the sort," Mammi said, tying the ribbons under Bess's chin.

Bess could hardly see from side to side. "I feel like a horse wearing blinders."

Mammi didn't pay any attention. "We got us another errand in town."

"Oh Mammi," Bess said, too worried to stir. She didn't think this day could get any worse, but it just had.

Sure enough, Mammi was on a mission to search out that poor sheriff's car. Mammi spotted the empty car out in front of the five-and-dime store and pulled the buggy over.

"Why? Why are you doing this?" Bess asked.

"I got my reasons."

"Then why don't you do the driving?"

"Can't," Mammi said. "I'd be put under the ban." She gave a sideways glance to Bess. "You're safe."

Bess sighed and got into the driver's side. Refusing Mammi anything never worked. She started up the car and drove down the road, a little faster this time—after all, she might as well enjoy this—until Mammi pointed to an empty parking spot and Bess pulled over.

Just like last time, the sheriff came running up the street, huffing and puffing. "Dadblast it, Miz Riehl! You did it again!"

"Did what?" Mammi asked, the very picture of surprise. She pushed open the passenger door and eased out of the car. Bess hopped out and stood beside her.

The sheriff's face turned purple-red. "Now, Miz Riehl, don't be like that."

Out of nowhere, Billy Lapp stepped in front of Mammi and Bess and made a patting gesture with both hands. "You'll have to excuse Bertha Riehl, Sheriff Kauffman. She's feeling her age these days." He made a clocklike motion around his ears with his hands. "I'll make sure these ladies get right on home so they don't cause any more trouble for you."

The sheriff turned to Billy with one hand on his gun holster. "You do that. And make sure that yellow-haired gal stops tempting her granny to a life of crime."

Mammi glared at Billy as he steered them by their elbows to the buggy. Billy tried to help her into the buggy, but she batted away his hand. "Feeling my age, am I?"

He rolled his eyes. "I was only trying to keep you out of jail. What were you thinking?" Mammi wouldn't answer, so he turned to Bess. "And just what do you think you're doing? Why would you ever drive off in a sheriff's car?" He reached out a hand to help her climb up in the buggy.

Still mindful of seeing Billy drive Betsy Mast in his courting buggy the other day, Bess shook his hand off her arm. "We have our reasons," she said huffily as she climbed into the buggy. As soon as they had left the main street, she turned to her grandmother. "Just what *are* our reasons?"

"Why, no reason at all," was all Mammi said, jutting out her big chin.

Later that week, Bess was in the barn, spreading rose petals. She took off her bandanna and wiped her forehead and neck. It was already hot and only nine in the morning. She opened the barn doors to get a crosswind and leaned against the doorjamb for a moment. She scanned the farm as she tied her bandanna in a knot at the nape of her neck. She saw Billy in the fields, Mammi in the kitchen. Hot breezes sighed in the cornfield across the road. A row of crows on the fence line told each other off. A woodpecker was hard at work somewhere high in a treetop. The morning was going on around them.

Suddenly she heard Billy holler like he'd seen a ghost. "Aphids! Bertha! We got aphids!"

The kitchen door blew open and Bertha stood there, arms akimbo. "Aphids?!" She marched out to the rose fields like a general to the front lines. She bent over the rose that Billy was working on, then looked around her. "Why, they're everywhere!"

From the look on her face, Mammi had just declared war on the aphids. She pointed at Billy. "Scoot uptown and bring me back Coca-Cola. Bring back as much as you can carry." She turned on Bess, who was walking over to see the aphid invasion up close. "Run in the kitchen and get five dollars from my special hiding place. You go with Billy to help him carry the soda pop."

By the time Bess figured out that Mammi's special hiding place for her money was an empty Folger's coffee tin—the same place her father kept his money—Billy had the horse harnessed to its traces and was waiting for her. She hurried to join him, delighted at the turn of events that gave her time alone with him. Usually, Mammi was within shouting distance and added her two cents to their conversation. Bess tried to think of something interesting to say, something witty and wise. Just last night, she had been working out a few imaginary conversations with Billy, just in case an opportunity like this—driving together in a buggy—presented itself. But now her mind was empty. She couldn't think of a single thing to say. They were getting close to the store when she blurted out, "Why Coca-Cola?"

"Kills aphids," Billy said without even glancing at her. And then he fell silent.

"What do you suppose it's doing to your belly?" Bess said quietly.

Billy turned to her, a surprised look on his face, before bursting out with a laugh. "Good point." He flashed a dazzling smile at her. His smile seemed as if he had never smiled for anyone else in the world.

Bess felt pleased. She had made Billy Lapp laugh.

Satisfied that the aphids were done in, Mammi spent the rest of the afternoon on another project. Instead of drying the rose petals from today's pickings, she said she was using them to make rose water. She filled a pot with clean rose petals. Then she poured boiling water over them and covered the pot with a lid. She turned off the heat and let the petals stand until they cooled.

Before bedtime, Bess helped Mammi strain the petals from the water. They ended up with the most beautifully colored liquid a person would ever see. The liquid would be kept in the cooler and used whenever they would bake something that called for rose water, and Mammi would sell it in small mason jars. "And we'll charge double at Dottie Stroot's," she told Bess.

Some nights, like tonight, it was so hot that Bess couldn't sleep. She threw off her sheets and went downstairs, finding her way by touch because it was so dark. She opened the back door and stepped into the yard. Boomer followed her out and disappeared into the shadows.

She stood still for a moment. Ohio summers were even hotter, lacking the fresh breeze that seemed to always come through Stoney Ridge. There was just a sliver of a moon and the night was not totally black. She could make out vague shapes: the henhouse, the barn, the greenhouse, the cherry trees.

Blackie slid out of nowhere and wove himself between her legs. Bess picked him up. "You're getting fat! You must be feasting on barn mice."

Blackie jumped down and oozed away, insulted.

She looked up at the velvety night sky, filled with star diamonds. It was a peaceful time. She still went back and forth about being there, but tonight she was glad to be here in Stoney Ridge with her grandmother.

She thought of the things she had already learned to do this summer: how to pick roses and get rid of aphids, how to dry rose petals to make tea and jam, how to make rose water. And how to make a fair profit. How to bake a cherry pie. Mammi told her that was just the beginning of things she needed to learn.

How much more learning can I take? she wondered as she rubbed her head.

Later that week, Mammi made one more valiant effort to steal the sheriff's car. Bess tried to talk her out of it all the way into Stoney Ridge, but Mammi went right on merrily ahead with her plan.

"But why, Mammi? You're going to give that sheriff a heart attack! Why would you want to kill the poor man?"

Mammi set her jaw in that stubborn way and wouldn't answer.

This time, as Bess coaxed the sheriff's car slowly onto the road, Mammi flipped a switch and the siren went on. In the rearview mirror, Bess saw the sheriff run out of the bank and into the road. She pulled the car over and hung her head. Her grandmother was certifiably crazy and she was the accomplice.

The sheriff opened the passenger door for Mammi and helped her out. "Miz Riehl, you are turning into a one-woman crime wave."

Mammi's eyes were circles of astonishment. Stoically, she stiffened her arms and offered her wrists to the sheriff for handcuffing. "Do what you must, Johnny."

Now a crowd started to gather. The sheriff paled. "Aw, Miz Riehl, don't make me do this."

"You are sworn to uphold the law." Mammi clucked her tongue. "Think of all them voters, watching their tax dollars at work. You can't be playing favorites."

"Dadblast it, Miz Riehl! If I didn't know better, I would say you are trying to get yourself thrown in the clink." His face was shading purple.

"Nothing of the sort! But I do get one phone call."

The sheriff narrowed his eyes and thought hard for a moment. "Get in the patrol car, Miz Riehl. You too, missy." He meant Bess.

Mammi slid into the back of the patrol car and patted on the seat beside her for Bess. Bess wanted to die, right there on the spot. But Mammi looked as content as a cat sitting in cream.

The sheriff drove them to his office and took them inside. He pointed to two chairs by his desk. "Can I get you two anything to drink?"

"Nothing for me," Mammi said politely, lowering herself into a chair, "but my Bess here would like a soda pop."

Bess didn't want a soda pop, the way her stomach was turning itself inside out. The sheriff went to the back of his office and brought back a warm Tab. He eased himself down into his chair and leaned back, lacing his fingers behind his head. "Now, Miz Riehl. Let's cut the cackle and come straight to the point. Who do you want to call?"

"Oh, I don't want to call anyone," Mammi said. She pointed at him. "But you can call someone."

The sheriff picked up the receiver. "What's the number?"

Mammi turned to Bess. "What's the phone number to Jonah's barn?"

Bess's jaw dropped open. "Oh no, Mammi, no! You can't tell Dad about us getting arrested! He'll be on the next bus to Stoney Ridge!"

Mammi pushed a few loose gray wisps of hair back into her prayer cap. "Do tell."

5

$\mathcal{A}$s Jonah hung up the phone on the wall of the workshop in his barn, he had to sit down. He couldn't believe what he had just heard from the sheriff. His mother and his daughter were in jail for stealing a police car. In jail! If he hadn't recognized the sheriff's voice, he would have even thought it might be a prank call. Bess had been in Stoney Ridge for only a few weeks. What in blazes had been going on back there?

He had to get there. He had to go, get Bess, and bring her home. As soon as possible. The thought of his precious daughter locked up in a city jail, surrounded by drug addicts and cat burglars and pickpockets and murderers, sickened him. He shuddered. Then he had a comforting thought. No one would bother her as long as his mother was nearby.

He went in search of Mose to tell him that he would be in charge of the furniture business for the next few days.

When Mammi and Bess returned to Rose Hill Farm that afternoon, freed from the sheriff after promising that they would stop taking his car, they found a bucket of water sitting on the porch, two big catfish, mad as hornets, swimming inside. "They are sure ugly fish," Mammi said, "but they make good eatings." She picked up the bucket and took it in the house, but turned toward Bess at the door. "My ladies need feeding. And take the big pail for eggs. Lift *every* hen."

Bess always gathered every one she found, but maybe some days she didn't look as hard as she might. She picked up the pail by the kitchen door and turned to Mammi. "Aren't you wondering where those fish came from?"

"Billy left 'em," Mammi said. "He's done it before."

Bess took off her big black bonnet and hung it on the porch railing. She walked across the yard to the henhouse, cataloging her woes. Her father, understandably, had been astounded to hear that she was at the police station and said he was on his way to Stoney Ridge. He would probably be here by morning, if not late tonight, to take her home. Just when she was starting to feel encouraged about her developing friendship with Billy Lapp.

On the buggy ride back to Rose Hill Farm, Bess had fought back tears. She asked her grandmother, why didn't she just say she wanted to send her home? Why go to all that trouble to aggravate the poor sheriff?

Mammi gave her a look of pure astonishment. "I *don't* want you going home." She turned her gaze to the back of the horse. "I want my boy to *come* home."

"But why?"

"It's high time." Then her jaw clamped shut in Mammi's own stubborn way and she didn't give up another word all the way home.

What troubled Bess the most was that she understood Mammi's logic. In fact, even more worrisome, she thought it was pretty smart. Her father wouldn't have come back to Stoney Ridge under any other circumstance than an emergency. And finding out his daughter was thrown in jail for stealing a sheriff's car would definitely constitute an emergency.

She got a scoop of cracked corn from the feed bin and tossed it around the ground as the chickens tried to peck at her bare toes. Life just wasn't fair, wasn't fair at all. Under the late afternoon sky, all life seemed wrung out.

From the kitchen window came the smell of catfish sizzling in the frying pan. Suddenly, Billy came flying out of the barn, pounding for the house, face first, bellowing like a calf, "No! No! Don't eat it!"

With eyes as big as quarters, Bess watched him jump the steps into the kitchen. She threw the corn on the ground and ran up to the house. Inside, Billy grabbed the frying pan from a startled Mammi and tossed it into the sink. Then he yelped in pain, "Eyeow!" and hopped on one leg. He had burnt his hands from picking up the pan without a rag.

With unusual presence of mind, Bess thrust his hands in the bucket of water the catfish had been in. "*What* is the matter with you?"

He yanked his hands up and she pushed them back in the water. "Those fish. Something's wrong with them. I shouldn't have left 'em on the porch, but that black cat of Bess's was eyeing them in the barn."

"What makes you think something is wrong with them?" Bess asked. She was putting ice from the icebox into a rag and tying it up to make an ice pack.

"Didn't you see them?" he asked.

"They were just as ugly as any other catfish," Mammi offered.

"They didn't have whiskers," he said, taking the ice pack that

Bess offered to him. He leaned against the counter, holding the ice pack between his hands. "And one was missing its eyes. A few weeks ago Bess noticed that birds weren't singing at the lake. So I've been back a few times. She's right. There's no birds up there anymore. And this time, I found these fish up on the shore, practically dead. Something's wrong with that lake."

"Blue Lake Pond?" Mammi put a hand against her chest. "That place is teeming with wildlife. My Samuel used to say he only needed to hold out a pail on the shore and fish would jump in."

"Not anymore," Billy said mournfully.

"What were you planning to do with the catfish?" Bess asked.

"I don't know," he said. "I hadn't gotten that far."

"Something like that happened in Berlin. A company dumped chemicals in a lake. Birds ate the fish and they ended up with strange-looking babies."

Billy's dark eyebrows shot up. "Someone is *polluting* the lake."

"Maybe so," Bess said. "But you need proof." She held up some B&W salve to put on his hands.

He held out his palms. "I don't know what shocks me more." He looked at Bess as she put a dab of salve on his hands. "Someone ruining my lake—" he gave her a sly grin—"or hearing you speak a full entire paragraph that makes sense."

Mammi snorted. "Come around here for breakfast sometime. She babbles like a brook. A person can hardly drink a cup of coffee in peace."

Bess wrapped a rag around Billy's hand and tied it so tight he yelped like a snake bit him and yanked it away from her.

"So how am I going to get some evidence that someone is polluting my lake?" he asked.

Bess put the salve back in the kitchen drawer. "You have to go out there and look for tracks. Maybe even stay out there awhile and watch, at different times of the day. Even at night."

"Trapping!" Mammi said happily, clapping her big red hands together. "Haven't gone trapping in years. Used to be my favorite thing in the world. We'll go tonight."

Later that evening, Jonah Riehl was on the bus heading to Pennsylvania. He gave Mose a note to give to Sallie, telling her he had a sudden errand to attend to. He didn't explain the circumstances. He felt too ashamed of what had happened. He leaned against the window on the bus and tried to sleep, but his thoughts kept him awake. He had been back in Stoney Ridge only once in the last fifteen years—for his father's funeral—since he left it that year after Rebecca died.

It was the trial that made him decide to leave Stoney Ridge for good.

The truck driver who crashed into the buggy, killing Rebecca, had been driving under the influence of alcohol that night. Jonah had to testify against him. It tore Jonah up—he was grieving so deeply for his Rebecca, yet he couldn't ignore the anguish in the truck driver's eyes. He saw the driver's wife at the trial every single day, looking as if she was barely holding herself together in one piece. Who was he to ever judge another man? If he couldn't forgive that man for what he had done, how could he ever expect God to forgive him? In a letter presented by Jonah's bishop, he had asked the judge for mercy. "He has suffered, and suffered heavily. It was a tragedy, not a crime. Sending the defendant to prison would serve no good purpose, and I plead leniency for him."

The state was less generous. The truck driver was sentenced

to six years in prison for reckless driving and involuntary man-slaughter.

Jonah also asked the judge to dismiss a petition for a wrongful death settlement because he was receiving all the financial help he needed from the church. The judge looked at him as if he thought Jonah might have endured more than broken bones in the accident—maybe he had been brain damaged.

The insurance company representing the truck that had struck their buggy and killed Rebecca had offered Jonah a settlement of $150,000. Jonah returned the check to the insurance company with a statement: "I'm not seeking revenge. Our Bible says revenge is not for us."

Someone in the insurance company, astounded by Jonah's letter and returned check, leaked it to the press. Newspaper writers and photographers swarmed to Rose Hill Farm like bees to a flower. Jonah couldn't even go out of his house without someone trying to take his picture and ask for comments. He thought it would blow over, but the story was picked up and reported across the nation. He received hundreds of letters expressing sympathy. And then ordinary folks started arriving at Rose Hill Farm, knocking on their door and wanting to see Bess. That was when he couldn't take it any longer. Every day brought reminders of what he had lost. It was just too painful to stay in Stoney Ridge. Even more so because he knew better. His people were known for yielding and accepting God's will. Yet, deep inside, he was angry with God for what had happened. It made it worse still for him to be among his people and feel like an outsider.

His father understood why he had to move, but his mother didn't. She felt that family belonged together, through thick or thin. Maybe that was why he agreed to let Bess go this summer. It was time to smooth things out with his mother.

His eyes jerked open. How could he possibly smooth things out when his mother got his daughter tossed into jail?

When a round and creamy moon rose above the barn later that evening, Billy came back to Rose Hill Farm to pick up Mammi and Bess in his open courting buggy. It was so small that it tilted to one side when Mammi climbed up on it. Bess was squished between Mammi and Billy and tried not to notice how good Billy smelled—like pine soap. He led the horse up to the turnoff to the lake and drove the buggy to the edge of the trees. Then he hopped out. "I thought we would walk the perimeter and see if we find anything out of the ordinary."

Bess climbed out behind him.

"I'd better stay alert for us all and keep a lookout on things at this end of the lake," Mammi said, stretching out in the buggy seat. She yawned. "I've got eyes like an eagle and ears like an Indian scout." She dropped right off.

Billy and Bess had hardly gone a few hundred yards when they heard the rhythm of Mammi's snores echoing off the still lake water.

"She's as loud as an air compressor," Billy said.

"This is just the prelude snore," Bess said. "Wait till you hear what it sounds like when she's sleeping deep. She rattles the windows. And if you think that's loud, you should stand clear of her sneezes. If I sneezed like Mammi did, I would fly apart."

A laugh burst out of Billy and he stopped to turn around and look at Bess, amazed. "It's nice to hear you finally talking, Bess. Kinda made me nervous at first when I thought we were going to be stuck picking rose petals together all summer."

Bess's knees suddenly felt as quivery as Mammi's green Jell-O salad. Her heart was pounding so loudly she was sure it drowned out her grandmother's snores. She hurried to keep up with Billy's long strides. There weren't many perfect moments in life, she thought happily, but this was surely one of them. Here she was with Billy Lapp, on a moonlit summer night, at a beautiful lake.

"Whatever happened with that lake in Berlin?" Billy said, turning his head slightly to call back to her.

Oh. Apparently she wasn't exactly on the top of his mind like he was on hers. "Well, someone found out it was the chemical company that was dumping their waste in the lake. So then the state of Ohio got involved and the chemical company was fined a bunch of money and had to clean up the lake. Took a few years to come back, but now it's just like it was before."

"How did the state of Ohio get involved?" Billy asked.

"I guess someone notified the police."

Billy stopped abruptly. "Oh," he said flatly. He looked crestfallen.

"What's the matter?"

"Even if we found something tonight, I'm not sure what I would do with the information. You know I can't go running to the police."

Bess snorted. "Tell that to Mammi."

Billy took a few steps and whirled around. "This is no joking matter, Bess. What's the point of trying to find out who's polluting the lake if we can't turn them in?"

"Well, how are you going to protect the lake if you don't find out what's causing a problem?" She walked a few steps to catch up with him. "Maybe you're getting ahead of yourself, assuming it's a person doing wrong. Could be something else entirely."

"Like what?"

"Well, like algae growing. In science class, I learned about some kinds of algae that grow so thick they wipe out any oxygen in a pond, so all the plants and fish die. That might explain what happened to the birds. No fish, no birds." Bess liked science much better than math.

Billy took off his hat and ran a hand through his hair. Then he put his hat back on. "I guess what you're saying is not to get ahead of myself." He started walking again, scanning the shore for some sign of human activity. Too soon, they had walked the rim of the lake and were back at the buggy. Mammi's head was rolled back and she was sawing logs. Billy helped Bess up into the buggy, which startled Mammi out of her deep slumber.

"Sorry to wake you," Bess said.

"I was just resting my eyes," Mammi said. "Find anything suspicious-looking?"

"Nothing," Billy said, untying the horse's reins from the tree. "Not a thing."

"What about that?" Mammi pointed behind Billy. There, on the ground, was a pile of sawdust in between two wheel ruts, as if it had spilled from the back of a vehicle.

Billy bent down and rubbed the sawdust between his fingers. "It's fresh. I can smell the sap." He picked up some more and looked up at the trees. "It's not from these pines. It's from a different wood. Someone brought it here."

"Could sawdust ruin a lake?" Bess asked.

"If there's enough of it," he said.

"I'm feeling a little peckish." Mammi rubbed her big red hands together. "And when I get hungry, I get cranky."

And heaven knows, Bess thought, they couldn't have *that*.

93

Jonah got off of the bus in Stoney Ridge at five in the morning. He walked down Main Street straight to the sheriff's office, but the doors were locked and it was pitch black inside. The town was silent. It drove him crazy knowing that Bess was just yards away from him, locked up in a dirty jail cell. Frustrated, he turned and bumped right into a young English woman as she came around the corner.

"I'm sorry," Jonah apologized and picked up the purse she had dropped. "What are you doing out at this hour of the morning?" he asked. The birds weren't even singing yet.

She looked at him cautiously, then seemed to relax as he handed her the purse. "I work at the bakery. This is when the workday starts. What about you?"

He pointed up the street toward the bus stop. "I just got off the bus. Waiting for the sheriff to arrive."

"You might have a long wait. His hours can be very . . . casual."

Her gaze took in his straw hat and his jawline beard. Her face was lit softly by the streetlight and she smiled. To his surprise, so did he.

"You look pretty harmless. Why don't you wait for the sheriff in the bakery?" She crossed the street and unlocked the door to The Sweet Tooth, then turned on the lights.

He followed her inside but stood by the door. She put on her apron and turned on the lights in the kitchen. He hadn't really noticed what she looked like out in the dark street. He didn't usually pay much attention to English women, but there was something appealing about this one. That face . . . it seemed vaguely familiar. Where had he seen her? He studied the woman more closely as she bustled around in the kitchen. There was a cautious quality in her eyes that made him suspect she'd seen more of life than she wanted to. He felt as if he'd met her before, but of course that was impossible. She was quite a lovely woman, he realized, with fragile, finely carved features and a long, slender neck. And she had been kind to him, even after he nearly knocked her down in the street.

She poked her head out from the kitchen. "If you don't mind waiting a minute, I'll start the coffee."

"I don't mind," he said. He was famished. He hadn't eaten dinner last night; he was too busy trying to pack and get to the bus station in time. He sat down in a chair at a small table and stretched out his legs.

She set down a mug of coffee and a cinnamon roll on Jonah's table. "Cream and sugar?" she asked, glancing at him. Then she got a startled look on her face and froze.

He felt a spike of concern, wondering what had caused her to suddenly look so alarmed. Had he done something wrong? She dropped her eyes to the floor and spun around, returning to the kitchen to get started on the day's baking.

Jonah decided he should leave, that he must have made her uncomfortable, but she started to ply him with questions. Where had he come from? What was it like living there? She was mixing dough and rolling it out and the oven was starting to send out some delicious smells. Before he knew it, she was asking about his family and he found himself answering. He began to talk: slowly at first, like a rusted pump, then things started spilling out of him in a rush.

"Rebecca and I met when we were both only sixteen. She lived in a neighboring district. I courted her for four years, driving my buggy two hours each way to see her on Saturday nights. Sometimes, I would barely arrive home in time to help my father milk the cows on Sunday morning." He gazed into his coffee mug as the bakery lady refilled it. She poured herself a cup and slipped into a chair across from him, listening carefully.

As Jonah lifted the coffee mug to his lips, his mind floated to a different time. "As soon as her father gave us his blessing, we married. Rebecca came to live at Rose Hill Farm and a year after that, our Bess arrived." He glanced up at the bakery lady, wondering if she was listening to him only out of politeness, but the look on her face suggested otherwise, as if she was anxious for him to continue. "Most men wanted a son, but I was glad the Lord gave us a daughter. I knew Bess would be good company for Rebecca." He stopped then and looked out the window at the empty street. "You see, I thought there would be plenty of time for sons. But there wasn't."

"Life can be that way. Things have a way of not turning out the way we expect." She said it so softly, he wondered if it was more his thought than her voice he'd heard.

Jonah caught her gaze and gently smiled. "No, you're right about that."

Then, in a voice that hurt him with its gentleness, she asked, "How did she die?"

His smile faded and he took his time answering. He'd never spoken aloud of Rebecca's accident, not with his parents or Bess, nor Mose. Not even with Sallie. Yet on this morning, the morning he returned to Stoney Ridge, he found himself wanting to talk about Rebecca. "It was a warm April night, just a week or so after Bess had been born. Rebecca wanted to go visit her folks—they were moving to Indiana—and truth be told, my mother was making Rebecca go a little stir crazy. She was always afraid of my mother, was Rebecca." He gave up a slight smile. "My mother can be a little . . . overbearing."

The bakery lady nodded sympathetically, as if she understood perfectly.

"The baby was in Rebecca's arms, sound asleep, and Rebecca had nodded off. The baby's blanket had slipped to the floor. I reached down to pick it up. I took my eyes off the road for just a moment . . ." His voice drizzled off and he closed his eyes tight. "It was the last thing I remember." He covered his face with his hand, but just for a moment. He came to himself with a start and glanced cautiously at the bakery lady. She didn't say a word, but the look in her eyes, it nearly took his breath away. It wasn't pity, nor was it sorrow. It was . . . empathy. As if she understood what a horrific moment that was for him, and how that moment had changed his life.

He hadn't meant to reveal so much to an English stranger. It shocked him, the things that spilled out of him in the predawn of that day. Maybe he was just overly tired and overly worried about Bess and his mother, but talking to that bakery lady felt like a tonic. His heart felt lighter than it had in years.

But this lady had work to do and he had stayed long enough. He stood to leave. "I don't even know your name," he said at the door. "I'm Jonah Riehl."

"I know," she said, giving him a level look. "I know who you are." She put out her hand to shake his.

He took her hand in his. It surprised him, how soft and small it was.

She took a deep breath. "My name is Lainey O'Toole."

Jonah's dark eyebrows lifted in surprise. "Lainey? Lainey O'Toole. I remember you. You were just a slip of a girl. Simon's stepdaughter."

She nodded.

"You disappeared. After your mother died."

She nodded again.

"What happened to you?"

"I became a long-term houseguest of the state of Pennsylvania."

97

He must have looked confused because she hastened to add, "Foster care system. Until I was eighteen."

He leaned against the doorjamb. "What then?" Jonah asked. He was sincerely interested.

"I worked at a department store in customer service. That's a fancy way of saying I listened to people complain. I didn't want to do that forever and a day, so I saved my money to go to culinary school."

"I remember you and my mother baking together in the kitchen at Rose Hill Farm." Those eyes of hers, they were mesmerizing. Full of wonder and wisdom for a woman barely twenty-five, if he counted back correctly. "Are you back home now, for good?"

She didn't answer right away. "I'm trying to do good while I'm here." She gave him an enigmatic smile then. She had flour on her cheek, and without thinking, he almost brushed it away. It shocked him that he would even consider touching a woman like that. There were ten years between them, and a world of differences in every way that mattered.

Still, something about Lainey O'Toole stirred him. He remembered her as a small, worried-looking girl. Simon was a bad-tempered man, lazy and cynical. Even though he lived down the street and passed the house almost daily, Jonah kept a wide path from Simon, and his parents shunned him completely. Jonah saw Lainey's mother only a few times, tossing food out for chickens that lived under the front porch. He remembered her as a faded-looking woman who had probably been pretty in her youth. Lainey used to slip up to the fence that lined the house, quiet as a cat, and just watch him and his father work in the fields or around the barn. It wasn't long before his mother coaxed Lainey into the kitchen, teaching her how to bake. Just taking an interest in her, because no one else seemed to.

98

And here Lainey O'Toole was, a grown woman, standing in front of him.

"Jonah . . . ," Lainey started. Just as she opened her mouth to say something, the sheriff drove by in his patrol car. She snapped her mouth shut.

And now his thoughts shifted to Bess. "I'd better go. Thank you, Lainey O'Toole." He held her eyes as he put his straw hat back on his head, then tipped his head to her and hurried down to the sheriff's office.

Jonah Riehl had a crooked gait. The good leg did most of the work while the weaker one shuffled to keep up, twisting stiffly from the hip. Lainey knew, from Bertha, that was a lasting result of the accident. Her heart swelled with compassion for the man as she watched him walk down the street, leaning on his cane.

She had nearly told Jonah about Bess. That first Sunday afternoon, when Bertha told her she knew Bess wasn't Jonah's daughter, she had made Lainey promise not to tell him or to tell Bess, either. "I'm the one who needs to do the telling," Bertha insisted. "And I will. When the time is right."

Lainey had agreed, reluctantly. Now she regretted that promise. She hadn't expected to be spending so much time with Bess, nor did she ever dream she would meet Jonah face-to-face.

It took her awhile to recognize him this morning, yet once she did, she saw him as he was fifteen years ago, with laughing eyes and a quick wit. When she was just a girl, he used to tease her like a big brother. Never mean-spirited, though. She remembered how kind he was . . . so very kind. He was still kind. And he still had that wavy dark hair, snapping brown eyes, and good-looking face, slightly disfigured by a broken nose. She remembered the day it was broken. He was pitching in a softball game and got hit in the face by a ball. She'd watched from afar and thought she'd never seen a nose bleed so much.

As she saw Jonah head into the sheriff's office, she leaned against the doorjamb and crossed her arms. This summer was turning into something she had never expected. Everything—all of her carefully designed plans—was turning upside down. Would things right themselves again? The oven buzzer went off and she went to check on the bread. Or maybe, she thought as she pulled the loaves from the oven, maybe things had been upside down and were turning right side up.

She set the loaves on cooling racks and pulled off her oven mitts. Either way, she had trusted God with all of this years ago, when she was only ten. And she wasn't going to stop trusting him now. She would see it through.

While Bess was making her bed, she heard a car turn onto the driveway of Rose Hill Farm. She looked out the window and felt her stomach twist into a knot. It was the sheriff. With her father.

She ran downstairs to tell Mammi but found her already on the front porch, ready to greet her son. Like she had been expecting him all along. Bess went outside and stood behind Mammi as the sheriff's car came to a stop and her father opened the door. He climbed out, pulled his suitcase from the backseat, and turned to the sheriff to shake his hand.

"My work here is done," the sheriff said, leaning out the car window. "Stay out of trouble, Miz Riehl." He pointed to Bess. "You too." He made a motion with his hand, two fingers splayed, pointing from his eyes, as if to say "I'm watching you."

After he drove off, Jonah took a few strides to the kitchen porch.

"Jonah," Mammi said calmly.

"So, Mom," Jonah said, just as calmly. "Care to tell me what's been going on?"

Then an awkward silence fell, until Billy appeared out of nowhere. "If they're not going to tell you, I will. Bess had a notion to take the sheriff's car out for a few spins," he said. "Three times, from what I hear."

Bess popped out from behind Mammi and glared at Billy. What had she *ever* seen in him?

"Billy," Mammi said firmly. "Time to move the bees out to the fields. Take Bess with you." She turned to Bess. "Get your bonnet. You'll need it."

Bess went into the kitchen and grabbed her big black bonnet from the wall peg. As she passed by her father, he held his arm out wide to her. "Don't I even get a hello?"

She leaned into him and felt a wave of relief that he was here. She hadn't realized how much she missed him. He wasn't nearly as upset about the police car borrowing as she had expected him to be. But then, her father wasn't quick tempered. She had never seen him angry, not once. Still, she would know if he was upset with her. This morning he looked relaxed, even a little pleased to be here in Stoney Ridge. She hadn't expected *that*.

"Maybe when you're done with moving your grandmother's bees," Jonah said with one dark brow raised, "we can talk about your algebra grade."

She dropped her head. She hadn't expected *that* either.

In the barn, before getting anywhere close to the beehives, Billy rolled down his sleeves, then tucked his pants into his boots. He

101

took out a roll of mosquito netting and covered his hat and face with it. "Better cover up good, Bess," he said, but she didn't appreciate his advice. Billy lifted the mosquito netting to help her wrap it, but she turned away from him. "Bess, don't be childish. You have to protect yourself." He turned her by the shoulders to face him. As he wrapped the netting around her bonnet, she kept her eyes on the ground. "What are you so peeved about, anyway? I was only telling the truth."

She locked eyes with him. "Well, you were wrong. It was Mammi who wanted me to borrow that sheriff's car. I tried talking her out of it . . . but you know my grandmother."

Billy tucked the netting into the back of her apron. "No kidding? That's too bad." He sounded genuinely disappointed. "A couple of fellows were asking me all about you. They think you must act all quiet and shy, but underneath . . . they say . . . sie is voll Schpank." *She is daring.*

Oh no. That meant that everyone in town knew about Mammi's car thievery. "Tell them I'm neither." She pushed his hand away from her waist and rolled her eyes. They both looked ridiculous, covered up with so much mosquito netting, and she couldn't help but laugh at the sight, which got Billy grinning.

"Well, I'll pass that information along." He put the netting on the shelf and picked up a matchbox and the smoker, then placed it on the wheelbarrow. "So what's this about algebra?"

"I see no reason to study math," she said firmly. "No reason in the world."

"I love math," Billy said.

Bess looked at him. "What is there to love?"

"Math is . . . entirely predictable," he said. "There's always a right answer."

"Only for those who make sense of it in the first place."

"You're not looking at it in the right way. Math is based on all the patterns around us. They are constant and repetitious and dependable, like . . ." He looked out the barn window. "Like rows in the fields, ripples in a stream, veins on a leaf, snowflakes. Man-made or natural, those patterns are there. Math is always the same."

She had never thought of math like that. She didn't like to think about math at all.

Billy picked up the wheelbarrow handles and pushed it out the barn door. He waited until Bess joined him, then slid it shut behind her. They walked down the path to the rose fields. "Isn't there anything about learning you love?" he asked.

"Words, I guess. How you can tell by the root the way words get started in the first place. And then how they change over time."

"See? Not so different. You're looking for patterns too."

She pondered that for a while and decided he was probably right, but she still felt suspicious about math.

"Since you're over being mad, I need some advice."

Her heart skipped a beat. Billy came to her for advice? Her madness melted away. "What kind of advice?"

"I'll tell you more when we're done. I need to concentrate." Billy pushed the wheelbarrow down to the beehives in the back of one rose field. As they approached the hives, the buzz grew louder. He lit the smoker and waved it all around the stack of hives. She noticed that he sang softly to the bees as he worked. It touched her, that gentle singing. It was one of the hymns from church, sung in a slow, mournful way. He told her his singing calmed the bees; that they were smart creatures and appreciated a good tenor voice when they heard it. She rolled her eyes at that but couldn't hold back a smile.

Carefully, Billy lifted a hive onto the wheelbarrow as Bess held it steady. A few stray bees buzzed around them, curious. They rotated the hives among the fields where the roses were in bloom. It made for more honey, Bertha had taught him. The bees didn't have to work so hard on the gathering and could concentrate their energies on the honey making. He took one more hive and gently placed it on the wheelbarrow. When he was finished, he emptied out the smoker and they headed to the barn. About halfway there, Billy stopped to make sure the bees weren't swarming, indignant that their homes had been moved. Satisfied, he told Bess she could take off the netting now.

He helped her unwind it from around her bonnet, carefully rolling it up again to reuse. "Yesterday afternoon, I went to the lake and saw the truck dumping the sawdust. Backed right up to the shoreline and lifted the truck bed up and dumped. Deep enough so that it all sank."

She pulled the big gloves from her hands. "Did you say anything to the driver?"

He shook his head. "No. I stayed out of sight."

"What are you going to do with that information?"

"That's what I don't know. That's the part I need your advice about."

Her heart skipped another beat. Maybe Billy was finally starting to notice her. She admired how much he cared about the lake. He was genuinely troubled about it.

"If I tell my father about it, he'll only say that we need to let English problems be English problems, and Amish problems be Amish problems."

"Is that what you think?" she asked.

"I can't just do nothing and let the lake die. God gave us this earth to care for properly. But my father is right about one thing

104

too. It's not my place to get the law involved. It's not our way to demand justice. We leave those matters in God's hands."

Bess shrugged. "It's just letting consequences have a place. There's nothing wrong with that."

"Still," he said, hesitating, and she knew. These kinds of situations were complicated. How could they care for God's earth and not want the lake to be protected? And yet by protecting the lake, they would need to get involved with the law. Billy lifted the wheelbarrow handles and started walking carefully to the rose fields. Bess followed behind, thinking hard.

She stopped as a new idea bubbled up. "Maybe there's something in between."

He turned his chin toward her. "I'm listening."

She took a few steps to catch up to him. "Every afternoon, I've been going to the bakery to visit with Lainey. There's a newspaperman—Eddie Beaker—who comes in after three so he can buy Danish for half off. He's always asking Lainey if she's heard any big news stories. Even not-so-big stories. Any story at all, he said. Just yesterday I heard him complaining to her that he doesn't like summer. Said it's too hot and it always makes for slow news months."

Billy stopped and spun around to face her. "You think maybe he could break the story?"

She nodded. "Mammi says Eddie Beaker is 'a wolf in cheap clothing.'"

Billy smiled, then stroked his chin. "Bess Riehl, du bischt voll Schpank." He tapped his forehead. "Und du bischt en schmaerdes Maedel." *You are daring. And you're a smart girl.*

Jonah leaned against the doorjamb at Rose Hill Farm and looked around the kitchen. It hadn't changed, which comforted him somehow. The wrinkled linoleum floor, the pale green walls and ceiling. Even the bird clock on the wall was the one he had grown up with. He used to think that clock was irritating. Now, it seemed endearing. "I see that the early rain has been good for the roses."

"Now we need sunshine to keep them dry and blooming," his mother completed his thought.

He hung his cane on the wall peg and put his straw hat on top, then sat in a chair. It was the same chair he had always sat in. He knew it would always be his chair. His place in the family. "Bess seems happy. She's as brown as a berry. Looks like she's gaining some weight from your good cooking."

Bertha nodded in agreement. "She came here looking as brittle as a bird. Now she's as fat as a spring robin."

Hardly that, Jonah thought, as Bertha poured two cups of coffee. But Bess's appearance had changed. In just a few weeks, she seemed older, more mature. "The sheriff gave me his side of the story. Mind filling me in on yours?"

Bertha eased into her chair. "I had to do something that would get you back here."

"Why didn't you just ask?"

"I did," she said flatly. "Been asking for years."

So she had. Jonah leaned back. "What is so all-fired important that you need me to be back in Stoney Ridge? Right now?"

His mother took her time answering. She sipped her coffee, added sugar and milk, stirred, then sipped it again. "Simon's dying."

Jonah snorted. "Impossible. Dying would take too much work. He'll outlive us all."

"He's dying all right."

"Where is he? The cottage looked empty."

"He lost that years ago when the bank took it. It's been up for sale for a long time. He's at the Veterans Hospital over in Lebanon."

Jonah sighed. "What's he dying of?"

"Some kind of cancer. Hopscotch disease."

"Hodgkin's?"

"That's what I said." Bertha stood and went to the window, crossing her arms against her chest. "Them doctors are looking for family members. They want bone marrow for him." She turned back to Jonah. "They think it might cure him."

"Don't tell me you're getting tested to give your brother—a man who has done nothing for anybody his whole livelong life—don't tell me you're planning to give him your bone marrow?"

"I tried. I'd give it to him if I could. But I'm not a match." She sat down in the chair. "But you might be." She looked into her coffee cup and swirled it around. "And so might our Bess."

"Bess?" Jonah looked up in surprise. "She's a distant relation to him." He easily dismissed that notion. "What about your sisters? Why don't they get tested?"

"Two did. Three refused because he's still shunned. The two that did—Martha and Annie—they aren't a match." Before Jonah could even ask, she answered. "And their husbands won't let their children or grandchildren test for it."

"Because he's been shunned."

Bertha nodded. "You and Bess . . . you're his last chance."

Jonah exhaled. "What makes you think Simon would accept my bone marrow, even if I were a match? You always said he was as cranky as a handle on a churn."

"You leave Simon to me," she said in a final way.

On the following Sunday, before church, Jonah was buckling the tracings on the buggy horse. Bess and his mother were upstairs getting ready to leave. His mind was a million miles away from churchgoing. He was thinking about what his mother had told him yesterday, about wanting him to take a blood test to try to cure Simon from his cancer. His mother rarely spoke of her brother— Simon had been excommunicated from the church years ago. He wasn't included in family gatherings, his name wasn't spoken, and he was ignored when he was seen, which was often.

Jonah could never figure out why Simon stayed in Stoney Ridge. He moved there right after he was discharged from the army due to an injury. Simon had been drafted in World War II and served as a conscientious objector, stationed as a maintenance worker in a base camp in Arkansas. He was accidentally shot in the foot. He claimed he was cleaning a gun, but the story was vague and changed each time he told it. Samuel, Jonah's father, said it probably went more like this: Simon was doing something he shouldn't have been, like hunting when he was supposed to be on duty, then blamed the Army for the accident. Using his disability pension, Simon bought a run-down home near his sister's farm and ran it down even further. It was as if he enjoyed being a thorn in everyone's side. But . . . that would be Simon. His father said Simon was born with a chip on his shoulder.

Jonah slipped the last buckle together on the bridle and looked up over the horse's mane to see Lainey O'Toole walking toward him.

"Bess invited me," she said, as she took in his confused look. "To church."

"Our church?" he asked, wondering why Bess would have put Lainey in such an unfair position. She might have meant well, but Lainey shouldn't feel obligated to come. "Our church . . . the service lasts for three hours." He knew enough about the English to know they zoomed in and out of church in scarcely an hour's time. Why, the first hymn was just wrapping up after an hour in an Amish church.

Lainey shrugged. "I'm used to that. The church I've been going to the last few years has long services, plus Sunday school."

"The preachers speak in Deitsch."

"I remember. I used to go with your mother." She smiled. "As I recall, those preachers can get a good deal across with just their tone of voice."

A laugh burst out of Jonah. She surprised him, this young woman.

"I can still understand a little bit of Deitsch. Growing up in Stoney Ridge . . . living with Simon those few years, I picked up a bit."

Jonah looked past her to the rose fields, then turned back to her. "Du bisch so schee." *You are so lovely.* Did he *really* just say that? Oh please no. He suddenly felt like Levi Miller, self-conscious and bashful and blurting out ridiculous, awkward compliments.

She gave him a blank look. "I guess I don't remember as much as I thought."

Oh, thank you, Lord! "I said, 'Well then, hop up.'" He offered her his hand and helped her into the buggy. He happened to notice that she smelled as sweet as a lemon blossom.

This was how church was meant to be—pure and simple, Lainey thought as she followed behind Bertha and Bess. This must have been what church was like for the first disciples—no fancy church building with a steeple that grazed the sky. Just a home, shared, to worship in. And God was there.

Today, church was merely a well-swept barn. But God was here. She could feel his presence.

It was such a hot and humid July morning that the host—the Zooks of Beacon Hollow—decided to hold the meeting in the barn, where it would be cooler. The sliding doors were left wide open to let the breeze waft through.

Lainey sat in the back row bench on the women's side, in between Bess and Bertha. Bess whispered to her that they had to sit in the back row because no one wanted to sit behind Bertha—she was too big. She also warned Lainey to watch her head. "Barn swallows might swoop in and steal your hair for their nest if they're in the mood. I've seen it happen. Just two weeks ago, to Eli Smucker's chin whiskers—"

Bertha leaned over and laid a calming hand on Bess, who snapped her lips shut and tucked her chin to her chest.

Lainey had to bite her lip to stop from grinning. She could barely contain the happiness she felt. It nearly spilled out of her. There was no place in the world she would rather be than where she was right that minute. It was a miracle of miracles. On one side of her was Bertha, a woman who had always been good to her, and on the other side was Bess, her very own sister. She could hardly hold back her feelings of praising God.

And to add to her happiness, she was still feeling a little dazed that Jonah had told her she was lovely. She was so startled by it that she pretended she didn't understand him. But she did. It was a phrase Simon said to her mother in those rare moments when he was at his best. Hearing it from Jonah made her stomach feel funny. She glanced at him across the large room. His dark head was bowed, preparing for worship, she knew. Unlike her mind, which seemed to be darting around the room like one of those barn swallows. Where had these new thoughts about Jonah come

110

from? He had always been just Jonah to her, Bertha's son. She remembered that she had thought he was a good-looking young man. She had never been crazy about those scraggly Amish beards. Jonah's was a full, soft brown beard that he had worn since he was twenty. She thought back to being disappointed when he started to grow that beard after he married Rebecca and covered up that fine square chin. His face had so many other interesting features, though, such as high cheekbones and gentle brown eyes that looked at her with warm concern.

Then, as if Jonah had read her mind, he looked up and caught her eye, and she felt a nervous quiver in her belly. She reached down to smooth out her dress as a small, elderly man stood up. A perfect, pure note, as dazzling as a sunrise, floated from his open mouth. The men joined in, then the women, all singing the same slow tune, the same quavery note, almost a chanting. Two hundred voices rising to the barn rafters. They sang for the longest time. Then they stopped, as if God himself was the choir director and signaled to everyone the end of the hymn.

As Lainey inhaled the familiar barn smells of hay and animals, and heard that long, sad hymn, she felt a tidal wave of long-buried emotion. Songs and smells could bring a person back to a moment in time more than anything else. It was amazing how much could be conjured with just a few notes or a solitary whiff. Her thoughts drifted to the church service she had attended with Bertha just a few weeks before her mother had died. The wind that morning had the barest thread of warmth to it. It smelled of the thawing earth, of spring. Lainey suddenly realized that was the last true moment of childhood. The last moment she had been thoroughly happy. A sadness welled up inside her. She shut her eyes and pressed her fingers to her lips. She didn't want to cry, not here. Not now.

And then came the preaching. She was fine through the first sermon, given by an elderly minister. That sermon was told in a preacher's voice, hollow and joyless. It was the second sermon, given by Caleb Zook. She vaguely remembered him as a friend of Jonah's. Caleb was the bishop now, married to the small, copper-haired woman sitting in front of Lainey, who had a baby in her arms and a toddler by her side. Lainey was amazed at how quiet her children were, how quiet all of the children were. When it was Caleb Zook's turn to stand and preach, his eyes grazed the room and rested on his wife's face. Some kind of silent communication passed between them, because he shifted his eyes and noticed Lainey sitting in the back row. He delivered his sermon in English. For some reason, such kindness touched her deeply and made her eyes well with tears. An odd pang of longing pierced her heart. She felt overcome with a desire to belong to this—to these people—forever.

The woman with the child on her hip kept her back turned, slowly ladling the apple butter into small bowls. Bess wanted her to hurry, so she could take out the platter with bread and apple butter and serve the farthest table, where Billy happened to be sitting with his friends after the church service ended. Billy had smiled at her during the sermon. Twice. She thought that when he smiled, he really meant it.

She glanced nervously over at Billy. Sometimes, for no reason, looking at him made her chest ache. It was the tall, strong, splendid sight of him, she supposed.

Bess cleared her throat, hoping the woman would notice she was there, waiting. But this woman could not be hurried. Bess chanced another look in Billy's direction and her heart sunk. Sure enough, Betsy Mast had gotten there first. She was leaning over

Billy's shoulder, filling his glass with sweet tea. The dreamy look on Billy's face as he looked up at Betsy made Bess think about dumping the bowl of apple butter right on his head.

The woman spun around and handed Bess a platter of freshly sliced bread. Bess went to find where her father was sitting instead, to serve him. She looked all over and couldn't find him, so she set the bowl and platter at the nearest table. Then she spotted Jonah, still over by the barn, leaning one arm against the door, engrossed in a conversation with Lainey O'Toole. The way Jonah was looking at Lainey—standing a full foot taller than she did, his head bent down as if he didn't want to miss a word she was saying—something about the sight caught Bess in the heart. She stopped and stared. She'd never seen her father pay such rapt attention to a woman.

Her grandmother came up behind her and silently watched. Then she took in a deep breath and let it out with, "Hoo-boy. Didn't see that coming."

6

On Sunday evening, Jonah told Bertha he had decided to get the test to see if his bone marrow could be a match for Simon. "I'll have the test and wait for the results. But I'm not bringing any of this up to Bess," he told her. "There's no reason to. If I'm not a match, that will be the end of it. I won't let Bess get tested. She's barely related to Simon. The chance of being a match is remote."

Bertha gave a brief nod of her head. "One thing at a time."

He wasn't quite sure what she meant by that, but he needed to turn in for the night. He stood to leave but turned around to face her. "Mom, why are you going to such lengths for someone like Simon?"

"He's the only brother I got," was all she said.

That comment struck him as forever odd. It was similar to what Lainey said at church this morning when he told her that his mother lured him here to be a bone marrow transplant for Simon. She said that Bertha had told her all about Simon's illness, but she hadn't had the courage to see him yet. "I'd like to go with you to see him," Lainey told him. "It's my day off, if you don't mind going tomorrow."

"Are you sure?" he asked her. He knew Simon had treated her badly. Everybody knew. It amazed him that she would even bother with Simon.

"He's the only father I've known," was how she answered him.

So early Monday morning, Jonah met Lainey in front of the bakery and they walked to the bus station to catch the first bus from Stoney Ridge to Lebanon. He felt a little uncomfortable at first, spending an entire day traveling with an English woman, but she soon put him at ease. She started by asking him questions about Bess. It was as if she couldn't get enough of hearing stories about their life in Ohio. He found himself telling her all kinds of stories . . . Bess's first day of school when she came home and told him she quit, that one day was enough. Levi Miller, who overly liked her and left wilted flowers for her in the mailbox until the mailman complained. Her cat, Blackie, who seemed to have abandoned her at Rose Hill Farm and taken up the life of a barn cat. They both started laughing then and couldn't stop. He hadn't laughed that often in a long time, and it felt so good.

Just being with Lainey felt good. He hadn't enjoyed another woman's company so much since . . . well, since he first met Rebecca, he realized with a start. He had taken one look at Rebecca, in her pale green dress that set off her hazel eyes, and he knew she was the one for him. He never wavered, not once. He just knew.

And here he was, with feelings stirring for Lainey. Yet this made no sense. No sense at all. It was downright wrong. Lainey was English. Besides, he felt with a sting of guilt, there was the Understanding he had with Sallie. Oh, this was wrong, wrong, wrong.

And yet . . . he couldn't take his eyes off of Lainey. He found himself memorizing every feature, every expression, of her lovely face. He marveled at her beauty, her glorious black hair that curled around her head like a wreath.

The hour-and-a-half bus ride to Lebanon flew by, and soon they were standing at a nurse's station in the hospital, filling out reams of paperwork. Then they had a long wait until a phlebotomist would be free to draw Jonah's blood for the donor test, so the nurse pointed them to the waiting room.

Lainey looked at Jonah. "Maybe I'll go see Simon while you're waiting to get your blood drawn."

"Not without me," Jonah said firmly. It worried him, having her meet up with Simon after all these years. He remembered Simon to be unpredictable. Granted, his love for the drink had much to do with those moods. But even at his best, Simon was not a pleasant person.

There was something in Lainey's expression right then—a sadness? A longing? He couldn't quite tell. Then she gave him one of her inscrutable smiles and sat down in the plastic chair. He sat down next to her.

"Jonah, why would you be willing to share your bone marrow with Simon?"

He set his cane on the empty chair next to him. "I guess I'm doing it for my mother. Since he was shunned all those years, there hasn't been much we could do for him. But this . . . well, maybe this would give Simon the push he needs to return to the church." He crossed his arms against his chest. "That's what she's hoping, anyway, to encourage him to make things right with God before it's too late."

"Did you ever know that Bertha used to bring us meals on a regular basis?" Lainey asked. "And she would slip my mother money to pay bills."

"What?" Jonah was stunned. "My parents . . . ?"

"No. Not your father. Only your mother." Lainey tilted her head. "Your mother . . . she's something else."

Jonah couldn't believe it. No Amish from their church went near Simon. To do so would risk their own good standing. They were quiet for a long time after that, until he finally asked, "So are you in Stoney Ridge this summer to see Simon?"

Her head was bowed as she quietly said, "He's part of the reason. I need to tell him something." She lifted her head and looked him in the eye, as if there was something she wanted to say. He'd had that feeling before when he was with her . . . as if there was something she was holding back. But then, how could he really know that? He was just getting to know her.

If Simon was part of the reason she was back in Stoney Ridge, what was the other part? He was just about to ask when a large graying woman in a nurse's uniform pointed at him from the door to the lab. "Jonah Riehl?"

He nodded.

"In here. Now." Her lips compressed into a flat line. "Hope you got big-sized veins cuz I've had too many folks in here today with itty bitty veins. Had to poke 'em a hundred times."

His dark eyebrows shot up in alarm. "I'll be back soon," he told Lainey. "Real soon, I hope."

Fifteen minutes later, he came out, unrolling his sleeve. He looked around the waiting room for Lainey, but she was gone.

As soon as Jonah left with the nurse, Lainey went to find Simon. She finally located him on a ward for terminally ill patients. He was at the far end of the ward, and she felt herself trembling as she approached him. When she was about ten feet

117

away, she stopped and watched him for a while. He was sleeping and looked so peaceful. Simon had been handsome before alcohol had thickened his face. He had good features, high cheekbones, and deep-set eyes. Once, he had been a big man. Now, he seemed shriveled, like a grape left out in the sun. His face, once smooth and glossy, was like old shoe leather.

She used to be terrified of him. He could be sweet and charming, but then something minor could trigger an explosive rage.

She remembered one time when she served him a piece of cake she had made and waited by his side, hoping to see if he liked it. He had eaten it in its entirety. Then, instead of complimenting her, he yanked the blue ribbon she won at the county fair for her cherry tart off of the refrigerator and tore it into pieces. "You were getting too fond of that ribbon. Don't you think I've noticed?"

She didn't answer him, which had enraged him.

"Pride goeth before a fall. You should be ashamed!"

She glanced at her mother for help, but her mother looked away. "You're right," Lainey said meekly. "I was too fond of winning that ribbon."

Afterward, her mother had tried to explain to her that it was getting injured in the war that had made Simon so quick to anger. Lainey wasn't so sure. She thought he was born mad, though he was the only Amish-born person she'd ever known who had a temper on him. They were gentle people, she knew that to be true. Gentle like Jonah.

Simon opened his eyes and stared at her. Then recognition dawned in his eyes. Those eyes—icy blue—combined with his mane of thick white hair had always reminded Lainey of a Siberian Husky. "Elaine?"

Elaine, her mother. Lainey supposed she did resemble her mother, at least in coloring. Certainly more than Bess did. Bess took after Simon, that was plain to see. "No, Simon. I'm not Elaine. She died over fifteen years ago. I'm Lainey, her daughter."

Simon peered at her, trying to comprehend what she was saying. He was very ill, she could tell that. "I got married once," he said. "Long time ago, she left me. That's when my life took a turn."

"She didn't leave you, Simon. She died having your baby."

He closed his eyes and was quiet for a moment. After a while, he opened one eye. "I don't suppose you have something to drink?" he asked her, licking his lips.

"There's some water by your bedside." She went to it and poured a glass, then held it out to him.

"I was hoping for something a little stronger," he said, brushing her hand away that held the water glass. "Course, I don't drink much as a habit. Don't have the taste for it."

She knew that was a lie. Simon drank like a fish.

He put his head back down on the pillow and gazed at her. "So, you're Lainey. All growed up."

She nodded.

"I don't have money, if that's what you're after."

"I don't want your money, Simon."

"You must want something. Showing up after all these years, without a word. You're after something. Everybody wants something."

"I don't want anything from you. I wanted to tell you that . . . I forgive you. That's all." She exhaled. "I just want you to know that I forgive you."

He snorted. "For what?"

She dropped her head and didn't see him grab her arm until he had it tight in his grip.

"For what?" he snarled, like an angry dog. "I put a roof over your head and food in your mouth. You weren't even my kid. You should be thanking me."

His grip was weaker than she would have expected. She peeled his fingers off of her arm as calmly as if she was peeling a banana, and stepped back. "You can't hurt me anymore." She took in a deep breath. "No matter what you think, Simon, you do need to be forgiven. And no matter what, I do forgive you."

He seemed not to care in the least. He pointed to the door. "Don't let the door hit you where the dog bit you," was all he said.

His sarcasm slapped her with surprise. She lifted her chin and marched toward the door. Her shoes made a clicking sound down the ward. As soon as she went through the door, she leaned against the wall, trying to compose herself. Hadn't she thought this all through before she even asked Jonah if she could join him today? Hadn't she reminded herself, over and over, not to expect anything back from Simon? And yet, here she was, deeply disappointed. She found herself shivering, as if she was very cold. She heard someone call her name, so softly she thought she might have imagined it. But there was Jonah, walking down the hall toward her. When he saw the look on her face, he held out his arms to her. She burst into tears and sank into him.

Dear Jonah,

Your note said you would be gone only a few days. It has now been nearly a week and I haven't heard a word from you. Should I be planting celery? Can't have an Amish wedding without celery!

Affectionately,

Sallie

"Today's the day, Bess," Billy said when she came into the greenhouse to bring him a glass of lemonade. "We're going to the bakery today to talk to Eddie Beaker."

Bess's eyes went wide. "We? What do you mean, we?"

He took a sip of his lemonade and wiped his mouth with the back of his hand. "You've met him. I don't have any idea who he is."

"I haven't *met* him. Lainey pointed him out, that's all. And you can figure out who he is. He wears a plaid blazer and his hair is slicked back with Crisco and he chews on a cold cigar." She shook her head. "You go. He gives me the creeps."

Billy blew air out through his lips like an exasperated horse.

"What would we say, anyway?"

"Bess, think," he said patiently, as if she were a schoolchild stumped on an easy problem. "We need to be talking about the lake just loud enough so that he overhears us. He needs to think it's his story to break."

She bit her lip. He made it sound simple, but she knew it wouldn't be. It was just like Mammi and the sheriff's car. Same thing.

"Come on, Bess," he said, as she hesitated. "We've got to try and save our lake! You're the one who found out it was polluted in the first place!"

The way he was looking at her, so passionate and fired up, made her fall in love with him all over again. And he had said "our lake," like it belonged to just the two of them. "Fine," she said. "I'll tell Mammi that we're going to buy some cherry tarts from Lainey. She'll be thrilled."

But there were no cherry tarts at The Sweet Tooth today. It was

Lainey's day off, Bess and Billy discovered unhappily when they arrived at the bakery five minutes before three. Mrs. Stroot was trying to lock up for the day and seemed anxious for them to leave. Billy stood in front of the counter, stalling for time, pretending that he couldn't make up his mind about what to buy. Bess kept looking down the street to see a man in a big plaid jacket head this way. Finally, just as Mrs. Stroot was about to shoo them out, in came Eddie Beaker. It was just like Bess had told Billy, he was chewing a cold cigar.

"You go first," Billy told Eddie as he walked up to the glass counter. "I'm still thinking it over."

Mrs. Stroot rolled her eyes.

Eddie pointed to the Danish. "How much?"

"Ten percent discount," Mrs. Stroot bargained.

"Make it half off and I'll take them all," he growled.

As Mrs. Stroot sighed deeply and started to pack the Danish in a box, Billy unrolled his spiel. "I was planning to go fishing, but there's just no fish at Blue Lake Pond." He motioned with Bess to pick up his lead.

"Still none?" Bess asked, too loudly.

"Just the dead ones on the shore," he said.

"Such a pity," Bess said. "And all of those birds gone too." She wished Lainey were here. She would have been able to engage Eddie Beaker into the conversation. He seemed far more interested in the Danish than in the missing wildlife.

Billy sidled closer to Eddie Beaker. "It's the strangest thing. Ever since that paper mill went in, there's been less and less wildlife up there. Now, there's virtually none. Can't figure it out." He looked at Eddie Beaker to see if he was taking the bait. What more of a morsel could he toss to a reporter hungry for news?

Eddie Beaker pulled out his wallet to pay Mrs. Stroot. He

handed her a few dollars, took the change, put it in his pocket, and left the bakery.

Billy exchanged a defeated look with Bess. "Let's go home."

Mrs. Stroot groaned.

Bess woke to the sound of bacon sputtering and popping in the pan. She lay in bed and smiled. Mammi said she would be making pancakes with maple syrup today.

Bess was delighted that her father wasn't talking about returning to Ohio anytime soon. She had assumed they would be heading back as soon as possible, but no. Jonah had told her that he was waiting on blood test results to see if he could help out Mammi's brother with his cancer. And happily, there was no mention of Bess as a donor.

She was glad she didn't have to worry about returning to Ohio. She had enough worries on her plate without adding more.

Her main worry was Billy Lapp. He'd taken up the outrageous notion that Bess could give him advice about how to get Betsy to stop flirting with other boys and just concentrate on him. "I know she's sweet on me," he told her just that afternoon while they were bagging up dried rose petals from the drying frames.

Bess listened sympathetically with her face and about a third of her mind. The rest of her thoughts were on memorizing Billy's face. "How do you know that?" She bent down to scratch a mosquito bite on her ankle until it bled. "Well?" she asked defiantly.

"She tells me so."

Bess straightened up and rolled her eyes to the highest heaven at that comment. "If she's telling that to you, Billy, she's telling that to all the boys."

He scrunched up his handsome face. "Nah. You don't know Betsy like I do."

How could Billy be so smart in rose grafting and mathematics and so dumb when it came to understanding women? The way the male sex thought had her stumped.

Bess had tried to have a conversation with Betsy Mast after church the other day, just out of curiosity. She couldn't deny that Betsy was exceptionally pretty—even more so, up close—but she had a breathy, baby voice and answered questions with questions. Bess asked her if her parents were farmers, and she responded by saying, "Aren't all Amish farmers?" Well, no, Bess told her. Some build furniture, like her father. One fellow manufactures windows. Others even work in factories. Betsy looked at her as if she was describing life on another planet. Bess wasn't sure if Betsy's lantern in her attic wasn't lit or if she was just trying to pretend she was interested when she wasn't.

Billy nudged Bess to bring her back to his problem at hand. "What do you think I should do? Should I tell her I want her to stop seeing other fellows?"

They were working side by side. She enjoyed being this close to him. He smelled of earth and sweat and roses. "I don't know, Billy."

He lifted a frame and leaned it against the wall. "Sure you do. You're a girl, aren't you?"

Charming. At least he had noticed that.

"You can't *make* someone like you." She knew that to be true. "There was a boy in Ohio who drove me cuckoo, he liked me so much. Kept trying to walk with me to school and hold my hand and talked about getting married someday. He hung around me like a summer cold. He even had our children's names picked out. All ten of them!" She shuddered. "If he had just left me alone, maybe I would have taken notice of him." Probably not, though. Everything about Levi Miller was annoying to her.

Billy lifted the last empty frame and set it against the wall. He swiveled around on his heels, his head cocked. "Okay, I'll try it! I knew you'd have an idea of what to do. You're a peach." He smiled, exposing two rows of very white, straight teeth. Possibly one of his best features, Bess assessed. Either that or the cleft in his chin.

Bess turned away. *Don't tell me I'm a peach*, she thought. *Tell me I'm . . . what? Beautiful? Hardly. The love of your life? That would be Betsy Mast. A loyal friend? Oh, that sounds like a pet dog.* So what did she want? Why was she so determined to keep on loving him, knowing that he loved another?

She had no answer.

In the middle of her musings, Billy surprised her with a loud and brotherly buss on her forehead. He grabbed his hat and waved goodbye as he left the barn for the day. She went to the open barn door and watched him walk down the drive, hat slightly tilted back on his head, whistling a tune as if he didn't have a care in the world. Blackie—fatter than ever from hunting all those barn mice and birds and other things Bess didn't want to think about—came out of his hiding place and wound himself around her legs. She bent down to pick him up, the traitor.

She wasn't sure what she had said that gave Billy a better plan to woo Betsy, but she knew she wasn't going to wash that kiss off of her forehead for a very long time.

Billy hurried through his chores that afternoon to get home, shower, and change, so he could hightail it over to the volleyball game at the Yoders'. He was grateful to Bess for giving him such good advice. Bess was turning out to be a valuable resource. He hadn't really had a friend who was a girl before. Bess was easy for him to talk to, maybe because she was a good listener. When Bess told him the story about the fellow who overly liked her, it hit him like a two-by-four. That was just the way he'd been acting toward Betsy.

It made so much sense. Betsy was more than a year older than he was. The last time he had tried to talk to her about courting, she tilted her head and asked him how old he was.

"Eighteen," he said. "Nearly nineteen."

Betsy gave him a patronizing look. "You can't even call yourself a man yet."

"Years aren't everything," Billy said. "I'm taller and stronger than most grown men."

Betsy had smiled and let him kiss her on the cheek, but he knew she never took him seriously. Of course not. He'd been acting immature, fawning and obsequious. Girls didn't like that, Bess had told him. That came as a surprise, but most things about girls came as a surprise to him.

Starting tonight, he was going to ignore Betsy. Not talk to her. Not even look at her.

When Billy arrived at the Yoders', he found his friends huddled together in a sad circle. "Who died?" he asked his best friend, Andy Yoder, who claimed to also be head over heels in love with Betsy. But Billy wasn't at all concerned. Andy was always in love with somebody.

"Haven't you heard? Betsy Mast ran off. We think she's with an English fellow who works at the Hay & Grain. Guess they've been planning it for months now." Andy looked as if his world had just imploded. "She's just been using all of us as decoys, so her folks wouldn't catch on."

That night, Bess was sleeping deeply until a noise woke her. She opened her eyes and tried to listen carefully to the night sounds. She wasn't entirely used to Rose Hill Farm yet, the way the walls creaked or the sounds of the night birds, different from Ohio birds. At first she thought the sound must have been Mammi's snoring, but then she heard something else. Something thumped the roof by her window. She hoped it was a roof rat. Or maybe Blackie, finally coming out of that barn for a visit. Where was Boomer when she needed him? Probably snoring right along in rhythm with Mammi.

She tiptoed out of bed and looked out the window. Sometimes at night the leaves rustled branches at the window, but she didn't see leaves or branches. A shape was down there and it scared her half to death. She was just about to scream when she heard the shape calling up to her.

It was Billy, below her window, waving to her. He cupped his hands around his mouth and whispered loudly, "Get dressed and come down! I need to talk to you!"

Bess's heart sang. She never dressed faster in her life. She stuck herself twice as she pinned her dress together. She bunched up her hair into a sloppy bun and jammed her prayer cap over it, then quietly tiptoed down the stairs and slipped out the side door.

Billy was pacing the yard, arms crossed against his chest. When he saw her, he stopped and motioned to her to come. "Let's go to the pond."

He had left his horse and courting buggy on the road so that he wouldn't waken Mammi and Jonah, he said, so they hurried down the drive and climbed in. Bess looked back once, but the large farmhouse looked silent. Billy slapped the horse's reins and kept his eyes straight ahead. He didn't say a word, but Bess didn't care. Here she was on a perfect, moonlit summer night, being secretly courted by Billy Lapp. This was the most wonderful, splendid moment of her life. She wanted to remember every detail of the evening so she could relive it during dreary moments—math class came to mind—when she returned, inevitably, to Ohio. The night was dark, so she chanced a glance at Billy, admiring the determined way his jaw was sticking out, the stern set of his mouth, his two dark eyebrows furrowing together.

All of a sudden, Bess's dreamy hopes evaporated, like steam rising from a tea cup. She felt something was wrong, but then she was always feeling that and it never was. "Billy, is something bothering you?"

He took in a deep breath. "She's gone, Bess. She ran off with an English fellow who worked at the Hay & Grain." He wiped his eyes with the back of his sleeve.

"Who?"

"For crying out loud, Bess! Who do you think? Betsy!" He jerked the horse's reins to sharply turn right onto the path that led to Blue Lake Pond. He pulled back on the reins and stopped the horse at the end of the level space, then hopped down and tied the reins to a tree. He sauntered down to the water's edge, looking bereft.

Bess stayed in the buggy, watching him, half furious, half delighted. A part of her was disappointed that Billy used her as a listening post for his troubles. The part that felt delighted Betsy was gone made her feel shamed. What kind of person took delight in another person's downfall? She knew that wasn't right and she breathed a quick apology to the Lord for her sinful thoughts. But from the start she knew what kind of girl Betsy was, that she never did care about Billy or see how special he was. Betsy

Mast wasn't good enough for Billy Lapp. Then she caught herself. That, too, was a sinful thought, and she had to apologize again to the Lord.

Goodness. Love was a tricky business.

She could see that Billy was suffering, and she tried not to be too glad for it. She sighed and hopped down from the buggy to join him.

"This is the worst summer on record," he said mournfully. "My lake is ruined. My love life is ruined." The words gushed out of him, heartfelt. He pressed a fist to his breast. "I love her so, it's like a constant pain, right here in my chest." He glanced at Bess. "You probably don't understand that kind of love."

Oh, I understand it all right, Bess thought. Love that burns so hot and fast it makes you act crazier than popping corn on a skillet.

He was sitting at the water's edge with his elbows leaning on his knees. "It's your fault, you know."

Her jaw dropped open.

"It is. If you had only given me the idea of ignoring her before today, maybe she would have taken me more seriously." Billy looked up at the moon. "I should have told her how much I loved her. How I was planning on marrying her. I shouldn't have waited."

Bess rolled her eyes. One minute he's ignoring Betsy. The next minute he's professing undying love.

"It's just that . . . I've never felt like that about anyone before. And I'm sure she was in love with me. I'm just sure of it."

Bess plopped down on the shore next to him. "Lainey said she's seen Betsy zooming around town in that English fellow's sports car all summer."

Billy froze. "That's not true."

"Lainey wouldn't lie about that," she said softly. "And you must know she was spending time in other boys' courting buggies." She looked away. "Even I knew that, and I've only been here a little over a month."

"That is a lie!" Billy shouted.

"No, it is not. You know it's the truth. I've seen Betsy in Andy's buggy and Jake's buggy and—"

Billy scrambled to a stand. "Aw, you don't know what you're talking about! She told me to my face that she was pining only for me!"

Bess rose to her feet and brushed off her dress. "Billy . . . you must have had some inkling—"

"Why am I even trying to talk to you about this? You're nothing but a child! What would you know about love?" He spun around and marched to the buggy.

Bess opened her mouth, snapped it shut. How *dare* he call her a child! She stomped up to the buggy. "Betsy Mast was never sweet on you! You got caught up like all the others with her . . . her curves and big lips and wavy hair. There was nothing in the attic." She tapped on her forehead. "Kissing don't last. Brains beats kissing every time."

Billy stared at her, as if he was trying to absorb what she had said. Finally, she threw up her hands in the air, turned, and marched up to the road to walk back to Rose Hill Farm.

She was halfway down the dark road and thought she heard a rustling noise in the berry bushes along the road. She stopped, slowly turned, looked back. The movement behind her also stopped. Each time she paused, it happened. Was Billy really going to let her walk all of the way home by herself? She was determined not to look behind her to see if he was coming, but now she was sure she heard a loud scruffling noise. Why, it was as loud as a bear, she started to think, though she had never actually come face-to-face with a bear. Bears liked berry bushes, she knew that for a fact. Yes, it definitely sounded like something was following her. A spooky owl hooted, wind cracked in the trees, and something else made a slithery noise that she hoped wasn't a snake, because she was afraid of snakes.

Just when she was about to run for her life, she heard the gentle clip-clop of Billy's horse pull up the road.

When he was beside her, he called out in his soft, manly voice, "Bess, hop in."

She continued walking quickly up the road, stubborn but pleased he had come for her.

Billy slowed the horse to a stop and jumped out, putting his hand on her shoulder to turn her to face him. "Bess. Don't be like that. I'm sorry I called you a child. I'm just . . . upset."

He looked so heartbroken and sad that her madness dissolved. He guided her back to the buggy and helped her up. They rode home silently, and he let her off at the edge of the drive so she could sneak back in the house.

Morning came too early. Bess couldn't stop yawning throughout Jonah's prayer before breakfast. Mammi handed her a cup of coffee without any milk in it. When Bess looked into the cup, puzzled, Mammi said in her matter-of-fact way, "Awful hard to sleep with a full moon blasting through the window. Goings-on outside look as bright as daylight."

Bess froze. Her eyes darted between Jonah, who was spooning strawberries onto his hot waffle, and her grandmother, quietly sipping her coffee with a look on her face of pure innocence. There was no end to what Mammi knew.

7

The weather all week was sunny and mild with no sign of rain. Late one afternoon, Lainey found Caleb Zook out in his cornfield, walking among the rustling whispers of the stalks. He was a tall man, yet the green stalks nearly reached his chin. He waved when he saw her and came through the path to meet her by the fence.

"We met at church on Sunday," she said, putting out her hand to shake his. "I'm Lainey O'Toole."

"I remember." He smiled. "I remember you as a girl too. Bertha brought you to church now and then."

His warmth surprised her. She would have thought a bishop would act stern and serious and cold with an Englisher. But Caleb Zook wasn't cold. Not cold at all. "I was hoping to have a talk with you sometime."

"Now is as good as any," he said kindly, though she knew she had interrupted him. "Shall we walk?" He hopped over the fence and joined her along the road. "What's on your mind?"

"There's something I've been thinking about. I've given it a lot of prayer, and thought, and more prayer. And more thought."

She had too. It was something she couldn't get out of her mind. The more she tried, the more she felt God pointing her in this direction. And it was a frightening direction. She wouldn't be in charge of her life, not anymore.

He cocked his head, listening intently.

"I want to become Amish."

Caleb took off his hat and spun it around in his hands. "You want to become Amish?" he asked her. "Amish go English, but English don't go Amish. At least, not very often. I can only think of a few converts." He looked up at the sky. "Oh, lots of folks come and say they want a simpler life, but they don't last more than a few months. It's just too hard on them. The language, living without modern conveniences. They just didn't understand what they'd be giving up."

"Their independence," she said quietly.

"Yes. Exactly that." He looked at her, impressed. "Folks don't realize that being Amish is much more than simple living. It's giving up self for the good of the community. It's giving up individual rights because you're part of a whole. It's called Gelassenheit. There's not really a way to say what it means in English."

She nodded. "I know enough about the Amish to know what you're getting at. But that's the very reason I want to become Amish." Her gaze shifted past him to the corn in the fields, swaying in the wind. "For just that very reason—to be part of a whole. To belong." She crossed her arms against her chest. "I don't know if you can understand this, but I've never really belonged to anyone or anything. Until I was ten, I watched all of your families, always wishing I were part of one."

Caleb listened, spinning his hat. "Have you thought of joining an English church? Wouldn't that give you what you're looking for?"

She dropped her chin to her chest. "I've always belonged to God. He's been the one thing I've been able to count on. I've always gone to church, even on my own, even when I was living with different foster families." She lifted her head. "But there's still a part of me that wants something more. I thought finding a career would be the answer, so I saved up my money for culinary school. That's where I was heading when I ended up in Stoney Ridge this summer. But now that I'm here, I know it's something else that I want." She swept her arm out in an arc and gathered her fist to her chest. "I want this." She owed so much to the Amish. It was through them, years ago, when her sorry childhood was at its bleakest point, that she met the Lord. It was one of those mornings when Bertha let her tag along to church. Lainey couldn't understand much of the service, but there came a moment when she knew God loved her. It was during a hymn, a long, mournful Amish hymn, and it was as real as if God spoke to her, telling her that he knew her and loved her and not to worry. He would be watching out for her. She couldn't explain how or why, but she knew it was true, and that assurance had never left her.

Caleb looked at her with great sincerity. "Being Plain . . . it's not easy, Lainey, even for those of us born to it."

"I know more about being Amish than you might think," she said. "Do you remember Simon, Bertha's brother?"

He dropped his eyes. "Of course."

"Simon had it all wrong, about being Amish." Caleb was about to interrupt, but she put a hand up to stop him. She knew what he was going to say. "Oh, I know he was excommunicated. But he was raised Amish and thought he understood what it meant. He emphasized all the wrong things. He would rail against pride and then scold my mother for decorating a birthday cake for me with

134

icing. He would say God was watching everything we did, like an angry parent, then he would go out drinking until the wee hours."

She could see Caleb wasn't sure what she was trying to say. She tried to make it more clear, but this was hard. She was telling him things she had never told anyone else. "Even back then, I knew he was missing the heart of it all. He didn't understand God the way I knew him, not at all."

Caleb raked a hand through his hair. "I have to ask. Does this have anything to do with Jonah Riehl?"

She looked at him, stunned.

"I noticed the two of you talking together after church on Sunday."

Her eyes went wide with disbelief. Why would talking together make the bishop think she wanted to join the church? "No! For heaven's sake, no! Nothing could be further from the truth. Jonah will be leaving for Ohio any day now. Bess said he's planning to marry someone there. I'm staying right here, in Stoney Ridge."

Caleb spun his straw hat around in his hands, around and around. She could see he was thinking hard. "Spend one week without using electricity."

Lainey's eyes went wide. "What will I tell Mrs. Stroot at The Sweet Tooth?"

He smiled. "No. Not at the bakery. But at home. You might find yourself heavy-hearted in your soul for machine-washed clothes and flipping on a light switch and other things in life that you have taken for granted."

Lainey was sure she wouldn't be so heavy-hearted. She had grown up poor, accustomed to going without luxuries. "Before I came to Stoney Ridge, I worked at a department store, listening to people's complaints about the products they bought." She shook her head. "All day long, I listened to complaints. It struck me one day that people were hoping these products—these things—would bring them happiness and satisfaction. But they never did." She looked up at him. "Because they can't."

Caleb listened carefully to her. "One week without electricity. Then we'll talk again." He put his hat back on his head and laid his hand on the fence post. Before turning to go back to work, he added, "For now, Lainey, I'd like you to keep this to yourself. Just something between you and the Lord God to work out. I'll be praying too."

She did write weekly to her two friends, Robin and Ally, but she would never dare tell them about this new plan. They would think she was certifiably crazy. "Bess knows."

Caleb tilted his head and smiled approvingly. "Then we'll keep this between the three of us." He jumped back over the fence.

Lainey watched the top of his straw hat until he disappeared among the cornstalks before she started back down the road. The funny thing was, going Amish was Bess's idea in the first place, a week or so before Lainey went to church with her. Bess and Lainey were baking muffins one afternoon at the bakery and talking about what they imagined a perfect life to be. Lainey described growing up Amish, and Bess looked at her, surprised. "Well, why don't you become Amish, then?" Lainey laughed, but Bess persisted. "I mean it. Why not?"

Lainey hadn't taken her seriously, but she hadn't stopped thinking about it ever since. And then when she went to church last week, she felt an even stronger pull. So then she started to pray about it, long and hard, asking God to tell her all the reasons why she *shouldn't* become Amish. But all she sensed from God was the same question Bess had posed, "Why not?"

She ran through all the logical things: she didn't know their customs or language, she didn't dress Plain, she would have to give up modern conveniences. Many things that she took for granted would be forbidden, like listening to the radio or watching television for entertainment. Then there were the deeper aspects to being Amish: humility and obedience to authority and denying self. Those weren't exactly popular concepts in the world she lived in.

It didn't make any sense, yet she couldn't deny what was stirring in her heart: a deep-down longing to join the Amish church and community. She wanted a place amongst them.

For the rest of the week, Bess avoided Billy as best she could, but he was so sulky, he didn't even notice.

"That boy looks like he's been poked in a private place," Mammi noted, watching him walk to the barn one morning. She finished drying the last dish at the kitchen sink and hung the dish towel to dry. "Anything to do with Betsy Mast running off?"

How did Mammi know everything that went on in this town? "It's not fair! It's just not fair," Bess cried, dropping her head on her arms at the kitchen table. "How could he be so sweet on a girl who would leave her church and family?"

Mammi shot her a warning glance. They should be worried that Betsy's soul was in peril, not throw stones at her. Bess knew that, but it was hard not to feel despair over the situation.

"The only fair I know hands out ribbons for canned pickles and prize tomatoes," Mammi said calmly. She eased her big self down onto a kitchen chair. "Things happen for a reason. Best to leave it in the Lord's hands."

"Do you think Billy will pine after her *forever*?" Bess glanced out the window as he came out of the barn and went over to the greenhouse.

"Forever is a big word for a fifteen-year-old. No sense tearing through life like you plan on living out the whole thing before you hit twenty." She leaned back. Bess was sure she heard the chair groan. "But he's no fool, that Billy Lapp."

Bess had no desire to listen to Billy's woes about Betsy Mast, but the situation at Blue Lake Pond was another matter entirely. Last night, lying in bed, she gave the matter serious thought and had a brainstorm. In the morning, she took out a sheet of white paper and started to write. She described the vanishing wildlife, the sawdust on the shoreline, the truck seen coming in and out dropping a load of paper pulp. She even included the license plate of the truck. She signed the letter, A Friend of the Lake. She addressed the letter to the *Stoney Ridge Times*, attention: Letter to the Editor, put a stamp on it, and tucked it in the mailbox so the postman would pick it up. She hoped the good Lord would understand that she wasn't just doing this to help Billy Lapp. She really did care about that lake.

Then she waited. And waited. But there was no sign of any activity at Blue Lake Pond other than the truck dropping paper pulp into it on a regular basis.

After lunch one day, Bess and Mammi washed the dishes and swept the room, and now Mammi was mending a torn dress hem while Bess was cutting scrap material into quilt pieces. They sat close to the window for better light—it was raining again. Jonah was in the greenhouse fixing a broken window.

"Mammi, I've been thinking," Bess said.

"Mebbe you should have tried that in math class," Mammi said.

Bess paid no attention. She was getting used to her grandmother. "I just don't know what else we can do about Blue Lake Pond. Billy and I have tried to get the attention of the right people, and they just don't seem to care."

Mammi's brow was furrowed and she rubbed her forehead, thinking hard. Then a look came over her. You had to study hard to see any expression at all on Mammi's face, but it was a look Bess was coming to know. She could tell Mammi was having one of her sudden thoughts. Mammi slammed her palms down on the table, stood, grabbed her bonnet off of the hook, and opened the door. "You coming?"

Bess followed behind her to help get the buggy ready. It wasn't long before Mammi went flying into town and pulled the horse to a stop at the sheriff's office.

Bess's heart nearly stopped. "Oh no. Oh no no no. I am not telling that sheriff about this. I don't want to get the law involved and then have to testify and . . . oh no." Bess crossed her arms against her chest. "I am staying right here."

"Suit yourself," Mammi said agreeably. "Here he comes now."

From across the street came Sheriff Johnny Kauffman. "Well, well, well. It's Miz Riehl and her granddaughter. Out on another crime spree?"

Mammi ignored his question. "Johnny, it's time you came out to dinner at Rose Hill Farm. I was thinking catfish. Battered and fried."

The sheriff's eyebrows shot up. He was practically licking his chops. "Your cooking is legendary, Miz Riehl."

"Saturday lunch then. We'll be looking for you." She climbed back in the buggy. "You wouldn't mind bringing the catfish, would you? You being such a dedicated fisherman and all. From Blue Lake Pond? No better catfish than Blue Lake Pond."

The sheriff looked pleased. "I haven't been out that way all summer." He clapped his hands together. "What time you want me at your farm?"

Mammi whispered to Bess in Deitsch, "What time does that paper truck make the drop?"

"Two on Saturdays," Bess whispered back.

"Twelve noon," Mammi said decidedly. "I want those catfish still jumping."

"I'll be there, Miz Riehl." He looked pleased. "You can count on it."

As they drove off, Bess tried to object, but Mammi waved her off. "You leave him to me."

Bess spent the drive home trying to think up Mammi-proof, ironclad excuses to absent herself from Saturday's lunch. *Nothing.* Nothing came to mind.

On Saturday morning, Mammi picked out two plump chickens to roast. By eleven, they were plucked, dressed, and in the oven. At twelve thirty, the sheriff turned into the drive at Rose Hill Farm and parked, all riled up.

"There wasn't a fish to bite," he told Mammi. "Something's *wrong* with that lake."

"Do tell," Mammi said, looking surprised. "Why, just last week, Billy Lapp said there's no birds out there anymore." She shook her head. "It's a misery, all right."

"She means mystery," Bess whispered to the sheriff.

"No, she's right," the sheriff said, looking quite bothered. "It

140

is a misery. I sure was looking forward to Bertha Riehl's catfish, battered and fried."

"We'll have to make do with chicken," Mammi said. "Bess, go call your dad from the barn. Tell him dinner is ready."

The sheriff ate heartily, but as he left, Bess and Mammi noticed he turned left instead of going right into town. Mammi said she had a hunch he was heading back out to Blue Lake Pond.

Early Wednesday morning, Billy came running up to Rose Hill Farm, hollering for Bess at the top of his lungs. Bess and Jonah and Bertha were having breakfast. He burst into the kitchen.

"Look at this, Bess!" He held a newspaper up in his hands. The headline read "Schwartz Paper Company Fined for Poisoning Blue Lake Pond."

"Somehow, it worked!" Billy was overjoyed. "That Eddie Beaker took the bait!"

Jonah asked what bait he was talking about and Billy tried to explain. Bess opened her mouth to interrupt and point out that the story wasn't written by Eddie Beaker at all but by another reporter. But before she could cut a word in edgewise, Mammi shot her a silencing glance.

Jonah read the article aloud: "'The Schwartz Paper Company has been fined for discharging millions of gallons of untreated paper pulp into surface water at Blue Lake Pond. Sheriff John Kauffman of Stoney Ridge blew the whistle on one of the worst pollution offenders in Lancaster County. While fishing one day, he noticed that the lake seemed to be absent of fish. The sheriff began an investigation and discovered that the Schwartz Paper Company had been dumping gallons of untreated pulp straight from their mill into Blue Lake Pond.'" His voice picked up the pace as he read through the more factual parts of the story: "'Tremendous amounts of material discharged into the lake used up the oxygen in the water. Fish and aquatic life died from lack of oxygen. Mill wastewater also carries large amounts of suspended solids, such as wood fiber, that could smother underwater habitat for scores of fish and invertebrates such as insects and mussels . . .'" His voice trailed off. He scanned to the end of the article. "The company has admitted negligence and will pay the costs to return the lake to its original pristine condition." Jonah put the paper on the table and looked up. "The sheriff's been given a special commendation from the governor."

After Billy had left the kitchen, Jonah stroked his beard. "Curious, isn't it? Sheriff was here on Saturday. Story broke on Monday." He cast a sideways glance at his mother.

Mammi paid no attention. She stifled a rare smile and appeared pretty satisfied with the way things had turned out. "Well. That's that." She nodded, as if a great mystery had been solved.

Jonah had to leave a contact number for the hospital to call about the results of the blood test, and Lainey had offered the bakery's phone number since Bertha didn't have a phone. Plus, she said, someone was at The Sweet Tooth most every day. So Jonah had quickly slipped into the habit of dropping by the bakery very early in the morning—just to see if the hospital had called—when the town was still sleeping and Lainey was already at work. He would sit at the table by the window while she baked, and they would talk. Too soon, they would hear the noises of Stoney Ridge waking up, of the squeaky bicycle wheels that belonged to the paperboy as he rode down the street and the thump of the newspaper as it hit the shop doors. Of a car engine sputtering to life.

Of a dog barking excitedly and another answering back. And then Jonah would get to his feet and prepare to go. He had to make himself leave. It seemed to him that the sweet smells that came out of that bakery—well, they could make a man forget everything in the world and follow its fragrance wherever it led.

As he shaved his cheeks, getting ready to head out the door this morning, his eyes fell on Sallie's letter, received just yesterday. It made his stomach hurt a little.

Dear Jonah,

It has been more than two weeks since you left for Pennsylvania. Mose Weaver is working full-time taking care of your furniture business. I'm worried about the poor man, he works so hard. You left an abundance of undone work for him. I need to bring him lunch each day just to keep up his strength so that your business doesn't suffer.

Fondly,

Sallie

P.S. I went ahead and planted celery. It is starting to come up. Plenty for the food, plenty for the table decorations.

He thought he would try to call the shop today and speak to Mose, just to make sure he wasn't overwhelmed by the workload. He was going to need to stay in Stoney Ridge awhile longer. For his mother's sake. For Bess's sake.

Oh, who was he kidding? It was for his sake. He couldn't get Lainey O'Toole out of his mind. It thrilled him to death. It worried him to death.

8

Early one morning, Mammi stood at the foot of the stairs to give Bess a wake-up call. She banged a spoon against a metal pan. "And bring down your sheets," she hollered up the stairs.

"I'm doing the laundry today," Bess hollered back down the stairs. Lainey had the morning off and was coming over. For once, Bess knew something that her grandmother didn't know. Lainey had told her she spoke to the bishop about going Amish, and Bess was so thrilled by the notion that she quickly offered to help. Today, she was going to give her a lesson on how to work a wringer machine. They had talked yesterday and picked out today for a laundry lesson because Jonah would be gone all day at an auction with Caleb Zook. And Mammi had plans to go to a neighbor's for a quilting frolic. Lainey wanted to keep quiet about her interest in going Amish. Bess wasn't sure why it was so important to keep it mum—she thought it was *wonderful* news—but she respected Lainey's wish.

"Good! I'll go back to bed and sleep till noon!" Mammi called out.

"Thought you didn't sleep at all!" Bess yelled back with a smile in her voice.

"Mebbe I'll just have to give it a try one of these days. See what Ohio folks find so appealing about it."

Bess laughed out loud. She looked out the window and saw her grandmother cross the yard to go to the henhouse, as she did every morning. A feeling of love for Mammi swept over her. How could she have ever been so frightened of her? She thought of those first few days when she arrived at Rose Hill Farm. She had been deathly worried her grandmother would be relentless about her getting a blood test for bone marrow to help Simon, but she never mentioned it after that first time. Not even when her father arrived in Stoney Ridge. She knew her grandmother continued to visit Simon at the hospital once a week, but she never discussed him with Bess. She didn't even ask Bess to go with her. In fact, Bess had nearly forgotten about Simon.

When her grandmother disappeared into the henhouse, Bess turned her attention back to her project. She had just finished writing out another list of Deitsch vocabulary words for Lainey to memorize. She looked the list up and down. Earth. *Erd*. Mountain. *Berig*. Ocean. *See*. It struck Bess that this might have been what Adam and Eve felt like, having to learn the names of everything. The first job God gave Adam: inventing language. *Not* math. She'd have to remember to point that out to Billy Lapp.

She folded up the list and stuffed it in her pocket. She glanced out the window again and saw Lainey coming up the street with a pink bakery box in her arms. Mammi saw her too. Good. Maybe Mammi would be too busy thinking about what was in that box to wonder why Lainey was here.

Not likely. Her grandmother didn't miss a thing.

Lainey had spent a week now going without any electricity in her little rental room. She had to admit, it was harder than she thought it would be. Bess was a big help, showing her that it didn't have to mean living *without* power—she just had to do things differently. Bess loaned her a gas lamp with a fierce-looking fabric wick and showed her how to fill it with kerosene. They bought a little propane camper stove to use for heating food.

"It's a small version of what we use," Bess told her. "If you can start getting comfortable with kerosene and propane, you'll find that most everything else comes easily."

Lainey had tried to make chicken corn rivel soup for dinner last night using the propane stove. The soup wasn't so bad, but the rivels were inedible. Instead of turning out like dumplings, they tasted like lumps of school paste.

One thing that took getting used to was sitting in a room so dimly lit. She kept the gas lamp close to her so she could read, and it cast its glow in a circle around her while the rest of the room remained dark. It seemed so different from the English way of lighting up the entire room and then some, especially on a rainy day.

Bess gave her fifty words to learn each day, then quizzed her on them and corrected her pronunciation. She said the easiest way to learn a language was to be just like a toddler again, matching words for objects, so your ear became attuned. Bess was a hard taskmaster, Lainey thought with a smile. Lainey had taken German in high school, so she had a head start, but Deitsch was a dialect of German. Similar but different. Everything was slightly skewed, like how you felt when you looked in a wavy mirror.

This morning, she followed Bess down to the basement. Two

large galvanized tubs were waiting, side by side, filled with hot water that Bess had brought down from the kitchen. On one of the tubs was fastened a wringer.

Bess tossed in some shavings of Mammi's soap and swirled it around until it lathered. "Mammi's soap lathers up real good. Vile smelling, but it does lather up."

Bess took a sheet and placed it in the tub. Lainey's eyes went wide when she saw Bess pick up a plunger to swirl the water.

"I've only used that to unclog a toilet," Lainey said.

Bess snorted. "Not around here. Mammi still uses a privy." She rolled her eyes. "I've tried talking her into letting Dad put in indoor plumbing till I'm blue in the face. Now it's Dad's turn to persuade her." After a few minutes of plunging, Bess fed the sheet through the wringer, then put it in the second tub to rinse it. Again, she plunged and plunged, then fed the sheet into the wringer.

Lainey helped with the next sheets. By the end of wringing them, she was panting hard. "This takes some muscle, doesn't it?"

Bess laughed at that. "This is just bedding for three people. Imagine what it's like for most Amish families."

Now Lainey understood why she saw clotheslines up at Amish farmhouses every day of the week except Sunday. It must take an Amish housewife hours every day to keep a family in clean clothes.

Bess looked up at her over the wringer. "How do you do your laundry?"

"At the Laundromat. You have to sit there for a few hours so no one steals your clothes."

Bess's head snapped up. Lainey could see that the thought shocked her. Stories about the English fascinated Bess. To her, they seemed so complex, so filled with odd contradictions. Lainey knew what Bess was thinking: how could it be better to use electricity when it meant you had to worry about your clothes getting stolen?

By the time they got the big basket of sheets outside and hung on the line, the sheets were half dry and Bess and Lainey were wet through. Lainey's black hair hung in damp tendrils. Bess's blond hair was flying every which way out from under her prayer cap.

Lainey slipped a clothespin on the last sheet. The wind pushed against the damp sheet, making it fluff and lull in the air like a sail on a ship. The scent of roses lingered around them. For some odd reason, the morning's work was deeply satisfying. Far more satisfying than she ever felt at a desk, listening to people complain about their purchases. Their stuff. She wondered what Robin and Ally would say to that. They loved their stuff.

The Amish used time in a different way, Lainey thought, walking back to town after the laundry lesson with Bess. As she had watched Bess work, she noticed that her movements were unhurried. She never seemed to be rushing through a task so she could get on to something else, something better. To Bess, it was all good, all worth her time. Lainey thought of how she and her English friends would jam their schedules full so they could fit in more. And yet they were always running out of time! The Amish had the same amount of hours in a day, lived busy, productive lives, but somehow they seemed to have an abundance of time for all that really mattered. Lately, she felt as if she were on a fence, in between Amish and English worlds. Watching, evaluating. With every passing day, Lainey felt herself drawing closer to the Amish way.

Jonah had come up with an idea to build Mammi a roadside stand so folks wouldn't always be wandering up to the farmhouse. Bess knew Mammi didn't like to have English strangers wandering around Rose Hill Farm, mostly because they interrupted her work and they talked too long. Mammi was so pleased with Jonah's suggestion that she decided to expand her line of rose products to sell at the stand. Besides rosebushes, she sold rose petal jam, rose petal tea, potpourri, rose water, and now, she decided, she would add rose-scented soap.

Mammi had always made her own lye soap. It smelled like woodsmoke and could take the top layer of skin right off of a person. Bess thought it was a fine idea to try rose-scented soap.

Jonah told her that if she wanted to sell the soap, she should probably stop using animal fat and switch to vegetable shortening or coconut oil. Mammi looked shocked, and it wasn't often that she could be shocked.

"Where did you learn so much about soap making?" Mammi asked Jonah.

He told her he might have learned a thing or two in his life, and Bess thought he was starting to sound an awful lot like his mother.

When Mammi started to collect ingredients around the barn workshop for her rose soap project, Bess had a hunch she was going to have the raw end of this new business prospect.

To be sure, the very next morning Mammi set Bess to the chore of cleaning out the old soap kettle. That ancient kettle hadn't been thoroughly scraped out since it was new. Bess had to roll the cast iron kettle in the grass and climb halfway in with a wire brush to loosen the clinging, foul-smelling lye soap. Even Boomer wouldn't come near her. Blackie came to investigate, then scampered away before slowing to a stiff walk, his white-tipped tail arrogantly upstanding.

Near the barn, in the shade of a big tree, Billy was helping Jonah build the roadside stand. He walked past her once or twice and shook his head. It was hot and sticky work, and by the end Bess reeked of old lye soap.

When the kettle was finally scraped clean to her grandmother's satisfaction, Mammi brought out the ingredients for the rose soap. She cooked the soap outside, over an open fire, despite weather that had turned beastly hot and humid. The air felt so heavy it was hard to breathe, but Mammi soldiered on, which meant Bess had to also. Mammi experimented until she was satisfied with the right blends. Using rose water instead of plain water at the end of mixing the glycerin and oils together gave it a heavenly scent. Mammi wanted to get it perfect before they poured the soap into molds and let it cure in the barn for a few weeks. At last, she had the perfect combination.

"I need a victim," Mammi said, eyeing Bess's prayer cap. "Let's wash your hair."

Bess smelled of such sour smoke that she was happy to get her hair washed, but she hoped to high heaven Mammi's soap wouldn't leave her bald in the process. Mammi brought out a new wash pan and filled it with fresh water from the pump. Jonah and Billy had finished the stand and were building a foundation for it down by the end of the drive, so the two women had plenty of privacy. Bess pulled out her pins to let down her hair. Her hair fell to her waist. She bent over a big washtub and Mammi lathered her head.

"That burning your scalp at all?" she asked Bess.

"So far, so good," Bess said. Actually, it felt good, so good, with gentle suds and a sweet smell.

Mammi rinsed out her hair with clean water, again and again, until it squeaked. Then she took the tub and leaned it upright against the house before she went back inside. Bess wrung out her hair and let the air dry it. She sat very still, with her back to a tree, staring into the sky as she combed her hair out. The clouds were scudding overhead. There was quiet, and soft summer air, and time to think. She closed her eyes, just for a moment, and drifted to sleep.

Moments later, or maybe an hour, she opened her eyes and there was Billy. He was smiling at her with his thrilling white smile. She hoped her white blond hair looked like shining waves of water, blowing gently in the breeze.

Her eyes closed again, and when she opened them, he was gone.

Early the next morning, Lainey waited for Jonah to come into the bakery. She kept peering out the window, looking for him. She smiled when she saw him turn the corner. She looked forward to their visits and was surprised at how comfortable it felt to be with him. She had a cup of coffee ready for him and let him sit down before she gave him the message from the hospital.

She sat down across from him. "They said you're not a match. You have three HLAs that match, but Simon needs six HLAs." She scrunched up her face. "I'm not really sure what that means."

Jonah stirred his coffee solemnly. "It means that even though we have the same blood type, there are different antigens in the blood."

She thought he would be relieved by the news, but instead, he seemed distressed. They amazed her, these Amish. They genuinely cared about people who were difficult to care for. The timer for the oven went off and she picked up her mitts to take the Morning Glory muffins out. She was ashamed to realize that she wasn't sure she would give Simon her bone marrow, at least not as readily as Bertha and Jonah had offered theirs. Had she really forgiven him, then? Or was it a conditional forgiveness? Only good as long as he didn't ask anything of her. Was that truly forgiveness?

Jonah was watching her face as she took the muffins out of the pan. He stood and came to her. "What's troubling you?"

She finished setting the hot muffins on a cooling rack. "I told Simon I forgave him for being such a pitiful father. But the truth is, I'd only given him a small piece of forgiveness. The part that benefited me. I released my anger toward him for how he treated me and my mother. But I don't want the best for him." She took off the mitts and placed them on the counter. "I'm not even sure if I care if he lives or dies." She looked away. "That must shock you."

He leaned his back against the counter, his arms crossing his chest. "It doesn't shock me. I remember Simon's drinking and his get-rich-quick schemes. And his temper." He locked eyes with her then, and before she knew it, he brushed a curl of her hair away from her eyes.

His touch was so gentle, feathersoft, it nearly undid her. She was finding herself attracted to Jonah despite her best efforts to ignore—even stamp out—those feelings. Falling for Jonah didn't make any sense. But still, there was . . . just . . . something about him. She felt so safe with him, as if she could be entirely herself. She had never felt this way about a man before. But she couldn't forget about the Sallie woman back in Ohio. Jonah had never mentioned her to Lainey, and Bess didn't mention her either, other than that one time. But Lainey hadn't forgotten.

She tucked her hair behind her ear. "I'm amazed you don't feel relieved that you're not a match."

"I'm not relieved." He crossed his arms again. "I wish I had been a match. Since I'm not, my mother will be after me to get Bess tested. She's brought it up nearly every day. I keep telling her there's no way it would work. Bess is Simon's grandniece. But you know my mother. She gets like a dog with a bone over things."

Lainey felt a cold shock run through her. She turned away from Jonah so quickly that she dropped the empty muffin pan and it clattered as it hit the ground, echoing throughout the bakery.

Billy had offered to show Bess how to graft roses, so when the weather cooled off one day in late July, with gray skies threatening rain, he told her today was the day. Good grafting weather. He showed her how to pick out the strongest rootstock, healthy and undamaged. Then they went out to the rose fields to cut some slips.

"Your grandmother said she has an order for ten plants of white sweetheart roses," Billy said. He pointed out the best plant. Then he pulled out his knife and made slanted cuts from branches, quickly wrapping them in a wet dishrag. "Don't want the cut pieces to dry out."

Raindrops started to splatter their faces as they hurried back into the greenhouse. Inside, the air was warm and musty. Billy made an assembly line with rootstocks and slips. First, he dipped the slips into a powdery substance to help the root take, then carefully matched each slip to a rootstock branch before wrapping it with gauze. "Roots may not be glamorous, and they aren't even seen, but they're the source of a rose's strength," he told her, as if he were a teacher and she a student.

"Like people," Bess murmured.

"How's that?" he asked absently.

153

"It was in one of the sermons last week. 'If our roots go deep in the knowledge of God and our lives are hidden in Christ, we'll be strong. More likely to survive the storms of adversity.'" She surprised even herself by remembering what the minister had said. It was Lainey's influence. The more time she spent with Lainey, the more interested she became in spiritual things. Lainey quizzed Bess and Jonah after each church service. She understood more and more Deitsch now and was eager to piece together what she was learning. Her enthusiasm was contagious. "I'm thinking of joining the church," Bess said aloud to Billy. She had been considering it, but it gave her a shiver to say it aloud. It seemed more real.

Billy glanced at her. "I already did. Last year." He put away the powder. "If you know it's right for you, no point in putting it off, is the way I see it." He brushed one palm against the other. "But you are awful young. Not sure the bishop would allow it."

She rolled her eyes at that slight. She was, after all, nearly sixteen. She doubted Billy was much older when he became a member. He had joined at a younger age than most boys did, but that didn't surprise her. Billy wasn't like most boys. In many ways, he seemed already grown-up, solid and unwavering. Except when it came to girls. In that area, Bess thought, his judgment was quite poor. Abominable.

Billy liked to talk while he worked, and Bess loved listening to him. Today, he told her that he wanted to buy his own farm as soon as he turned twenty-one. "No mortgage, either. I've been saving every penny. I want to own my land free and clear. You see, land is a trust, Bess," he said, starting to sound like a preacher. "I think it's something you hold onto for a lifetime. Something a man passes on to his sons. And his sons pass on to their sons. Land should be cared for and improved in every generation—just the way your grandparents have done here at Rose Hill Farm—and that way, we're passing on a legacy."

Bess studied Billy as he worked. She felt keenly aware of every detail. She liked being this close to him. The rain was coming down hard now, soughing on the roof above them. She pretended for a moment that she and Billy were married, working side by side on their farm. Talking together, laughing together, making plans together. She wished this moment wouldn't come to an end, wished she could stretch the morning and make it last forever. Why was it that three hours in school felt like a week, but three hours with Billy Lapp felt like mere minutes?

The morning melted away too soon. The rain ceased and a bright sun flooded the space with light as Bess fell more in love with Billy than ever. Unfortunately, he showed no sign of feeling anything more for her than a kind of platonic friendship. But he hadn't mentioned Betsy Mast all morning. That thought made Bess happy.

And then it was noon and Mammi was calling to Bess to stop for lunch, which meant Billy would head home. She sighed. Time spent with Billy was always over too soon.

Dear Robin and Ally,

Work at the bakery is going well here in Stoney Ridge. So well that I've even given some thought to postponing culinary school. But don't worry; I haven't decided anything for sure.

Love,

Lainey

At lunch one day, Bess mentioned to Mammi and her father that Lainey would be dropping by later in the afternoon. Afterward, as Bess was washing dishes at the kitchen sink, she happened to glance out the window and notice her father by the pump. His head was under the pump. Then he skinned off his shirt and was washing his entire upper region. He was soaping seriously and Bess grinned. Her dad had never said so, but she had a sneaking suspicion that he and Lainey were growing sweet on each other. They shared smiles with their eyes and stole glances at each other when they thought no one was looking. But Bess saw and it suited her just fine. She had a hope for her father and Lainey, but she knew it was best to keep that thought quiet. She knew when to leave things be.

When Lainey arrived at Rose Hill Farm, Mammi was over at the Yoders', helping to clean the house for church that weekend. Another neighbor had come to ask for Jonah's help to catch a runaway horse. The house was empty but for Bess and Lainey. This afternoon was working out better than Bess had even hoped.

She told Lainey she was going to teach her how to sew using a treadle sewing machine.

Lainey looked dubious. "I can't even sew a button on my blouse."

"Good news," Bess said. "No buttons." She laid out a few yards of dusty plum–colored fabric and spread a thin tissue pattern over it. As soon as she had smoothed it all out over the fabric, she pinned one edge and pointed to Lainey to start on the other side.

"What are we making?"

Bess smiled mysteriously. "A dress."

After cutting out the pieces, Bess threaded the machine and started to push the pedal with her foot, causing the needle to go up and down at a steady speed. She sewed one seam and then turned it over to Lainey. "You do the other side. Just sew a straight line."

It took awhile for Lainey to get the rhythm, to pump her foot steadily so the machine would work. "You made it seem so easy, Bess. It's harder than it looks!" But then it came together. She held up the shapeless dress. "Done!"

"Not hardly," Bess said. She took two sleeves and pinned them to the main section. "Watch carefully. Curves are trickier." She whipped off one sleeve and let Lainey take her place.

After Lainey finished, Bess held it up and frowned. "Pull out the stitches and we'll do it again."

So Lainey did. Two more times until Bess was satisfied. They worked the rest of the afternoon and took the dress downstairs to press out the wrinkles.

Bess showed Lainey how to light the pilot light for the Coleman iron. They drank sweet tea while they worked in the kitchen. Lainey ironed the dress and held it up for Bess's approval. "There you go! A new dress for you."

Bess shook her head. "Not for me. It's for you."

Lainey looked stunned, so Bess added, "I don't know if or when you feel the time will be right to start wearing our garb, but I thought it would be good for you to have a dress. For when you're ready."

Lainey looked at the dress. "Should I try it on?"

Bess nodded, pleased. "There are pins on my bureau top."

Lainey felt strange, taking off her blouse and skirt and putting on this Amish dress for the first time. She wasn't even sure what kind of underwear they wore. She forgot to ask Bess. Did women even wear brassieres? Well, she would be wearing one today, that's for sure. One step at a time.

She slipped the dress on and tried to figure out how the pins should be placed so they wouldn't work themselves loose. She had heard a taxi driver who came into the bakery complain about all the loose pins he found in his cab's backseat after driving Amish women on errands. She folded the front pieces across each other and tried not to jab herself as she pinned them shut. Bess and Bertha never seemed to complain about the pins, but she knew they would take getting used to. Laid out on the bed were a prayer cap and a white apron. Lainey smiled. Bess had this all planned out ahead of time. She hesitated for a moment, but then decided to try them. She slipped the prayer cap on her head. It perched uneasily on her curls. She was growing out her hair, but she knew the covering probably looked silly. She tried to tuck her hair back under the cap. She had watched Bess do it one day and was shocked to see how long her hair was. Below her waist! She told Lainey it had never been cut.

Lainey put pins through the cap to hold it in place, the way she'd seen Bess do it. Then she pinned the apron into place and turned around slowly, trying to decide if she felt any different. She had pins holding her together from head to waist. There wasn't a mirror, so she wasn't as self-conscious. She had been wearing less and less makeup the last few weeks and hadn't even missed it. Well, the first day or two she had felt practically naked, but then she relaxed. She even started to like feeling less made-up, more natural. Maybe that's another secret the Amish have, she realized. If you aren't looking in mirrors all the time, you aren't thinking about how you look all the time. Your mind is freed up for other things.

She went downstairs to show Bess. Moving quietly as she

always did, she found Bess washing dishes by the kitchen sink and said, "Well, what do you think?"

Bess whirled around, startled, dripping soapy suds on the floor. "Oh Lainey! Seller Frack bekummt dich!" *That dress becomes you!* Then her eyes darted nervously to the other side of the room.

Lainey looked to see what had distracted Bess. Jonah was standing by the door, staring at her. "Ya. Ich geb ihr allfat recht." *Yes, I agree with her.* His smile got lost somewhere in that quiet moment.

Now, Lainey felt different.

Dear Jonah,

It has been over four weeks since you left. Mose has been working as hard as a pack of mules for you, but he did take time out to stake the tomato plants in the garden for me. And take us for a picnic down by Miller's Pond. And he built a treehouse for the boys with leftover wood from the furniture-making business. He said you wouldn't object. Would you?

Yours truly,

Sallie

P.S. The celery patch is nearly six inches tall!

It took Jonah a few days to get up his nerve to tell his mother about the blood test not being a match for Simon. He had dreaded this conversation. He waited until Bess had gone to the barn, and then he quietly told her. He sat sprawled in his chair, one arm hooked over the back.

"I know," Bertha said. "They sent a letter with the results." Out of her apron pocket she pulled a letter from the hospital.

Jonah closed his eyes. "How long have you known?"

Bertha looked up at the ceiling. "Let's see. A week."

Jonah rubbed his forehead. "I know what you're thinking. And I'm not going to agree to it."

"Bess is old enough to make the decision for herself."

"She's still a child."

"Fifteen years old is no child. Why, when I was a girl—"

"I know, I know," Jonah interrupted. He'd grown up hearing plenty of hardship stories that started with that sentence. "There's a remote chance, anyway, that Bess would be a match. Why take the risk?"

Bertha slapped her palms on the table and glared at him. "Why not?"

Right then, Jonah realized that the simplest, easiest thing to do would be to have Bess take a blood test. That way, the results would show his mother what he already knew—that Bess could not possibly be a match. "Okay." He surrendered his hands in the air. "If she agrees to it, Bess can have the test."

He thought his mother would be ecstatic or, at the very least, satisfied. He was giving her what she wanted. Instead, her gaze shifted to the window. From the look on her face, it seemed as if she just had a sense of something dreadful coming to pass.

That night, Jonah asked Bess to sit out on the porch with him to watch the sunset. She knew he had something on his mind. It was a clear night. They watched the sun dip below the horizon and the sky turn a bruised blue. Then he told her about his mother wanting her to get the blood test. Bess sat on the porch steps, hugging her legs, with her chin leaning on top of her knees as she listened to him.

"I want you to pray about this tonight. I don't want you feeling any pressure to have the test."

Bess turned her head toward him. "You were willing to give Simon your marrow, weren't you?"

Jonah nodded. His heart ached in a sweet way when he saw the earnest look on her face. "I was willing, but that doesn't mean you have to. The blood test is pretty simple, just a prick in your arm. The marrow test is a much more complicated procedure. You'd have to have general anesthesia and stay in the hospital, and it will be a little painful. The chance of you being a match is highly unlikely. I can almost rule it out. It's just that your grandmother . . . well, you know how she can be once she gets an idea in her head."

Bess lifted her eyebrows. "Sie is so schtarrkeppich as an Esel." *She is as stubborn as a mule.*

This time Jonah had no trouble smiling. "It seems very important to Mammi that we at least rule it out."

Bess shrugged. "I guess I can understand that. Simon is her brother."

"But that doesn't mean you have to do this, Bess. If you'd rather not, I would never make you do it, no matter what Mammi has to say about that."

"But you were willing. To give Simon your bone marrow."

"I was willing."

"And Mammi was willing?"

Jonah nodded again. He knew his daughter's tender heart. "Bess, I don't know if he . . . deserves such mercy." He told her the entire story, all that he knew, about Lainey and her mother and how Simon treated them. He was surprised to realize that

Lainey had never mentioned Simon to Bess. He knew the two had grown close this summer. He could see Bess was shocked when she learned Simon was Lainey's stepfather. She grew quiet for a long time. Jonah wondered why Lainey had never told her, but then he decided that she was probably protecting Bess. Knowing what he knew of Lainey, he thought she was trying not to influence Bess one way or the other.

They sat quietly for a long time, watching the stars fill the sky. Finally, Bess lifted her head and gave him a soulful look. "Simon may not deserve our mercy, but Lainey is always telling me God has a different perspective on mercy."

Those words cut into him as real as a sharp knife. That old disquiet filled him again, gripping his chest like an actual pain. He had discovered something about himself this summer— something that shamed him deeply. He had believed in God all of his life, but did he truly believe God was sovereign over all? Did he believe that God's ways were truly merciful?

Fifteen years ago, he would have said yes. But after the accident that killed Rebecca, a part of him had stopped counting on God the way he had before. As if God couldn't entirely be trusted.

And so Jonah had run. He had run from God, the same way he had run from his memories. It was too difficult to remain in Stoney Ridge, driving by the accident site nearly every day where Rebecca had died, constantly reminded of what he had lost.

Lainey had just as many reasons to leave Stoney Ridge as he did, yet here she was. Back, facing the very things that haunted her. She was even willing to face Simon in the hospital. When she had come out of Simon's ward into the hallway, the look on her face nearly sliced his heart in two. It was filled with sorrow, but not for herself.

It was filled with sorrow for Simon's lost soul.

Billy hadn't been planning to go to the gathering tonight. It was Bertha Riehl who pinned him to the wall to go and take Bess along too. That woman had a way of getting what she wanted. She didn't ask directly, she just stared at you until your knees buckled and you caved in.

He wasn't in much of a party mood, and hadn't been, and probably never would be again, since Betsy Mast's departure. He still couldn't believe she had up and gone. He had had so many plans for their future together. As soon as he turned twenty-one, he was going to buy some land to farm. He knew just the kind of house he wanted to build for himself and Betsy: it would have a southern exposure, and a barn on a right angle, and a pond to fish and swim in. A pond that would be safe from polluters.

In his vision, his father and brothers would see what he had done—bought a parcel of fine land, married the most sought-after girl in the district, started a thriving business—and they would treat him with respect, not just as the baby of the family. Der Kaschde. *The runt of the litter*, his brothers called him.

But that dream was gone now. What irked him most was that he thought he knew Betsy. He thought she would want the same things. It still stunned him that she was gone. She had left her family, her church. She had left him for another man.

Bess had told him once that he had made up the idea of Betsy in his head. Maybe he didn't really know her at all, she pointed out.

He glanced over at his cousin Maggie, talking a mile a minute, and Bess on the other side of her. Bess was in a cranky mood today. The day had started out fine. She had been helping him get some plants ready to sell to a customer this morning, and he told

163

her his latest theories on Betsy's departure. She grew quieter and quieter, like she was getting a headache, and didn't say goodbye to him when her grandmother called her in for lunch. Girls could be like that, he was learning. Moody and unpredictable.

As soon as they reached the yard where the gathering was held, Billy jumped down, tied up the horse, and sauntered off to join his friends at a game of volleyball. He didn't even notice where Maggie and Bess had gone until Andy Yoder pulled him aside.

"Who's that?" Andy pointed across the yard to a tight knot of girls.

"Who?"

"The blond."

"The skinny one? That's Bess. Bertha Riehl's granddaughter."

Andy snorted a laugh. "Maybe you need eyeglasses. She ain't so skinny now. Seems like she's got a different shape up above." He handed the volleyball to Billy and walked across the yard to meet Bess.

Billy watched Andy make his way to sit next to Bess. It occurred to him that Bess was going to be quite a nice-looking girl. It was a thought he'd never had.

After volleyball and dinner, then hymn singing, Billy was ready to go home. When he found Maggie, he told her to go get Bess and he would meet them at his buggy.

"She already left," Maggie told him. "With Andy Yoder."

Bess woke up in the morning with a firm resolution: last night was the final time she would cry herself to sleep over Billy. She could feel how swollen her eyes were and wondered if she could sneak out to the garden to snatch a cucumber without Mammi spotting her. She had heard girls talk about putting cucumbers on their eyes as a cure. She tiptoed down into the kitchen and was glad to find it empty. She was just about to open the side door when she spotted Mammi, picking beans and filling up her apron, talking to Billy in the garden. Bess couldn't go out there now.

Maybe pickles would work. She grabbed a jar from the pantry and hurried back upstairs. She opened the pickle jar and lay down on the bed, placing a sliced pickle over each eye. Within seconds, her eyes were stinging from the vinegar. She jumped up and reached for a pitcher of water. What a terrible idea! Her eyes were bloodshot now and even more swollen-looking than before. A sharp scent of dill and vinegar hung in the air.

An hour later, she was in the barn spreading rose petals when Billy came in with a freshly filled basket. "Where do you want them?"

She kept her head low and pointed to an empty tray.

He carefully spread the petals out, single layer, on the screen. "So Andy Yoder took you home last night?"

She shrugged. That was her business and no one else's.

"You could have at least told me. I wasted time looking for you."

Bess looked up, pleased. "You did?"

"Sure." Billy shook out the basket and set it on a shelf with the other baskets. "Last thing I want is to have your grandmother sore at me for not bringing you home."

Charming. "Well, she's not sore at you." She gave him a sideways glance. "She thinks Andy Yoder is a fine fellow."

"Bertha Riehl said that?" he asked, amazed. "Andy isn't very selective about girls. He'll take any female who smiles his way."

She brushed past him to go to the farmhouse.

165

He sniffed the air as she walked by him. "Strange. I keep getting a whiff of pickles."

Jonah was about to turn off the kerosene lamp in the kitchen and head to bed when a knock on the door surprised him. He opened the door to find Lainey standing there in the moonlight.

"Jonah, I would have come sooner, but I was working late tonight in the bakery for a big order tomorrow. A call came for you today. From the hospital." She bit her lip. "Bess is a perfect match for Simon. Six for six."

Jonah was stunned. "How could that be? How could that possibly be true?"

Lainey looked past him with a hard stare.

Jonah turned to see what she was looking at. His mother was on the bottom stair. It looked as if she had come down, overheard them, and was starting to tiptoe back up.

"Tell him, Bertha," Lainey said in a firm voice.

Bertha stopped in her tracks.

"Tell me what?" Jonah asked, looking from his mother to Lainey and back again.

Lainey and Bertha locked gazes. "If you don't tell him, I will."

"Oh, I'll tell him. I said I would and I will." Bertha scowled at Lainey but sat down at the kitchen table.

The tendon of his mother's jaw was working, so Jonah knew to prepare himself for a revelation.

Bertha looked at him carefully, paused a long while to gather her thoughts, then slapped her palms on the table and turned to Lainey. "Fine. You tell him."

Lainey gave Bertha a look as if she couldn't believe what a coward she was. She dropped her head and let out a deep breath. She pulled out a chair across from Jonah. "This is a story that goes back to that night fifteen years ago when you and Rebecca and . . . your baby . . . were in that horrible accident."

Jonah stiffened.

But Lainey didn't waver. She told him the entire story, she didn't leave anything out. When she was done, she looked directly at him. "I switched those babies, Jonah. Your baby for my little sister."

Jonah was stunned silent. The kitchen was so quiet that the sound of a fly buzzing against the window echoed through the room. He stared at Lainey as if she had been speaking in a foreign language. The full realization of what she said slowly started to dawn on him. *No. It couldn't be. It couldn't possibly be true.* He had trouble speaking—the words tangled up in his throat, and he had to stop and unravel them before he could say what he needed to say.

In a hoarse voice, he spoke at last. "You were only ten. You must not be remembering clearly. You must have it mixed up."

"I remember it right, Jonah," Lainey said softly. "I'll never forget that night."

"But . . . how? How could you . . . how would you even know if a baby was dead?" He leaned forward in his chair. "Maybe she wasn't. Maybe—"

Lainey shook her head. "She died instantly. I know I was young, but I knew she was gone." Her eyes welled with tears.

In a tight voice he said, "But I was told my daughter was completely unhurt. I was told it was a miracle."

"I put my baby sister in Rebecca's arms—to bring her comfort—and waited until I heard the sirens. I just stayed right by

167

the two of you, telling you over and over again not to quit. Not to give up. But by the time the ambulance arrived, I had made a decision."

Silence fell over the table. Jonah's mind struggled to grasp what Lainey was saying. He grabbed hold of the table, feeling like the victim of a hurricane, his life strewn to pieces. Everything seemed to be floating.

Bess wasn't really his daughter. It shocked him to the core.

Then he had an even greater shock. His eyes met his mother's and he realized that she wasn't at all surprised. She *knew* this. She knew this!

As if Bertha could read his thoughts, she crossed her arms defensively against her chest. "Yes, I knew about this, Jonah. I knew. The night of the accident, I went to the hospital and found out Rebecca had passed and you were in bad shape. They said the baby had come through the accident unharmed. A miracle, they called it. They kept her overnight for observation. Then the next day, she was given to me to take home. But she wasn't our Bess. By that time, I had already heard about Lainey's sister's passing and put two and two together. I went to the county morgue, to be sure. I planned on telling you, but it got harder and harder, and then . . ." Her voice drizzled off.

He lifted his eyes to look at his mother. "And now you've finally come clean because of Simon."

Slowly, Bertha nodded. "When Lainey showed up out of the clear blue sky, I knew the time had come."

"How could you do that? How could you lie to me for fifteen years?"

"Some things are just worth a little bit of trouble."

Jonah exploded. He rose to his feet and leaned his palms against the table. "Don't you dare make this sound like something trivial!"

Bertha didn't back down. She looked straight at him. "You needed that baby, Jonah." She pointed a strong finger on the table. "And she needed you."

Once again, silence covered the room. In a voice so calm he hardly recognized it, he said, "Tomorrow, Bess and I will return to Ohio. This topic is closed. Forever." He stared at Lainey, hard, for a long moment, then reached for his cane and went up the stairs.

At breakfast, Bess could tell that something had happened between her father and grandmother, but she had no idea what had made her father decide to leave Stoney Ridge so suddenly. It saddened her when he told her at breakfast. She tried to object, but she could read the stubborn look on his face. There was no changing his mind. And Mammi, as usual, wasn't talking.

Bess went up to her room to pack up her belongings. As she folded her dresses and aprons into her small suitcase, she could hardly believe how attached she had grown to Mammi, to Lainey, to Rose Hill Farm. To Billy. It had been only two months, yet she felt as if she belonged here. As if this was her home.

She heard her father call to her to come downstairs. She looked around the room one last time to brand the image on her memory: the pale green walls rimmed with pegs for clothing. The scratched-up wooden floors. The small wooden bed with Mammi's hand-made starburst pattern quilt on top, the nightstand with a glass oil lamp, the windowsill where she sat some nights, watching the moon rise and cast shadows over the rose fields. She sighed and trudged down the steps.

Billy was out front, waiting for them by the buggy. Jonah had asked him to drive them to the bus station to catch the noon bus. She walked up to him and he took the suitcase from her.

169

"What's going on with your dad?" he whispered. "What's the big rush to leave town?"

Bess shrugged. "Just needs to get back to his business, I guess," she said nonchalantly. Bess felt a small sense of dignity rise up in her. After all, Billy had disappointed her tremendously. Maybe it was good that she was leaving. Maybe he would pine for her. Maybe he'd even write long letters to her.

"I'll go scrounge up that black cat of yours," he said, heading over to the barn.

Blackie! She'd nearly forgotten him.

Mammi and Jonah came out to the buggy.

"What's keeping Billy?" Jonah asked, looking anxiously at the barn.

Not a moment later, Billy let out a large whoop. He came outside, cradling two small kittens in his arms, with an angry Blackie trailing behind. "Hey, Bess! So much for your scientific skills! I thought you said your cat was a boy!" he cried out, laughing.

Bess ran over to see the kittens. Blackie curled around her legs. She looked back at her father. "I can't take them! They're hardly a day or two old!"

"They'll stay," Mammi said decisively. "Their mother stays too. She's a decent mouser after all."

Bess gave each kitten a kiss and let Billy take them back to the barn where he found them. She reached down to stroke Blackie, but he . . . she . . . glared at her and hurried after her kittens.

Bess watched them go and turned to say goodbye to Mammi. When their eyes met, Bess felt tears choke in her throat. She ran to her grandmother and threw her arms around her big shoulders. She felt Mammi's arms reach up to pat her on her back. When Bess finally let go, Mammi took off her spectacles, breathed on them, and rubbed them with her apron. Needed polishing, she said.

Jonah offered his mother a stiff handshake. Mammi held onto his hand extra long, Bess noticed, as if she didn't want to let go.

But Jonah was undeterred. He went to the buggy just as a pony and cart pulled up the drive. It was Andy Yoder, carrying a bouquet of wildflowers in his arms.

When he reached the yard, he reined the pony over to the buggy and jumped off the cart. "What's going on?"

"They're heading back to Ohio," Mammi said, glaring at Jonah.

Andy looked horrified. "But why?" When no one answered, he looked to Bess, but she only shrugged. Then he turned to Jonah. "Well, could I at least speak to Bess? Privately?"

Jonah rubbed his forehead as if he had a headache coming on, but he climbed into the buggy. Mammi stayed put.

Andy gave a sideways glance at Mammi before thrusting the wildflowers at Bess. "What would you say if I wrote to you? Would you write back?"

Billy came out of the barn and stopped abruptly when he saw Andy handing the wildflowers to Bess. "We'd better get going if you want to make that noon bus, Jonah," he said in a loud voice. He climbed into the buggy.

"He's right, Bess," Jonah called out.

Andy looked stricken. Bess got into the buggy and sat in the backseat.

"Write to me, Bess!" Andy yelled as Billy slapped the reins to get the horse moving.

Bess leaned a hand out the window to wave to Mammi and Andy and the rose fields and the house and Blackie.

When Billy turned left onto the road, Bess said to her father, "I want to say goodbye to Lainey."

"No time," Jonah answered, eyes on the road. He spoke sharply but without conviction.

"We're going right past the bakery and it won't take but a minute," she said firmly.

Jonah didn't respond, so Billy pulled the horse to the hitching post. Lainey came out as if she had been expecting them. Bess ran into her outstretched arms.

"I don't know why he's doing this, Lainey!" Bess whispered. "Something's happened to make him upset."

Lainey didn't answer at first. Then she pulled back and held Bess's arms. "Being here . . . it's hard for your father. It brings up a lot of sad memories. Things he'd rather forget about. Give him time. He'll come around." She hugged Bess again and released her.

Jonah came toward them. "Bess, hop in the buggy. I'll be there in a moment."

Bess went to the buggy to wait with Billy. She kept her eyes on her father. Lainey was saying something to him, but he didn't say anything back. He looked away while she spoke, as if he didn't really want to hear it.

"He'll be in love with a new girl by week's end," Billy said crisply.

Bess's gaze was fixed on her father and Lainey. "I don't think so. I've never seen him like this."

"What do you mean? He's like this all the time."

She turned to Billy. "Who?"

"Andy Yoder. He's girl crazy."

Bess rolled her eyes.

"I'm only looking out for your welfare."

Bess turned back to her father and Lainey. He was saying something to her now, something that made Lainey look hurt.

He returned to the buggy and gave a nod to Billy to get going. Bess waved to Lainey, who blew a kiss at her and waved back, slow and sad.

Jonah and Bess's quick departure left Billy with a vague unease, as if he had left the barn door open or forgot to water the new rose graftings. Something just didn't feel right. What was Jonah's big hurry about, anyway? Billy clucked to old Frieda to get her moving faster. This horse moved plenty fast for Bertha but acted like a tired old nag for everybody else.

His thoughts drifted to the way Jonah and Lainey looked—so serious—when they were talking to each other outside the bakery. If he didn't know better, he would say they looked like their hearts were breaking. But that couldn't be right. A straight-up fellow like Jonah Riehl would never get involved with an English girl. Bertha Riehl would have him drawn and quartered.

But what did he know about love? He thought Betsy was straight up, and he sure was wrong about that. *Oh Betsy, Betsy, I thought I knew you*, Billy lamented as the horse plodded along.

He felt himself slipping back into what Bess called his Betsy funk. He tried to snap out of it by thinking again about Jonah and Bess and Lainey. Bess had been trying to figure out what Jonah and Lainey were saying to each other while he was trying to warn Bess not to count on Andy's devotion for longer than a minute. Bess was awfully innocent about boys, though she didn't seem to appreciate his warning. She had told him to hush.

"They're saying something important," she scolded him, watching Jonah and Lainey. She squinted her eyes, trying to lip-read. "She's asking him if it would have been better to be raised by *that* man. He's telling her that he thinks living with the truth

173

would have been better. No . . . best." She shrugged and blew out a breath. "*What* is going on with those two?"

As Billy turned the horse right into Rose Hill Farm, he felt an odd feeling stir in the pit of his stomach. It surprised him, that feeling. Bess wouldn't be there anymore.

Gone would be their daily challenge: he would give her a math problem to figure out, only to have her give him a vocabulary word that he had to puzzle over. She didn't think she was very smart, but he thought differently. She knew about things he'd never heard of: Latin names of birds that visited the rose fields. She would hold her head in dismay as he butchered the pronunciation. She said he did to Latin what her grandmother did to English. Bess was interested in everything: how to graft a rose, how to gather honeycombs without making the bees mad, even how to track animals. He never knew anyone with such curiosity. He thought about how her eyes always widened when she thought deeply. He would wait and lean in her direction, as a sunflower would follow the sun, for whatever illumination was sure to follow.

He felt a strange ache in his heart, a different kind of ache than Betsy Mast's devastating betrayal. He was going to miss Bess.

9

$\mathcal{B}$ess had never seen her father like this before.

Jonah was carrying a burden, heavyhearted. He hardly said more than a few words during the long bus ride to Ohio. When they returned to the house late that night, Sallie rushed right over and Bess's heart sank to her knees. Bess fled upstairs to open up the windows, she told Sallie, and let the house cool off. It was so hot and stuffy inside that candles had melted in their holders. She didn't intend to eavesdrop, but Sallie and Jonah were outside on the porch, right below her window.

"My oh my, but you gave me a start!" Sallie was saying. "I was beginning to think you weren't coming back at all! Not at all!" She spoke so quickly that her words blurred together.

Jonah said something so quietly that Bess couldn't make out what he said.

"If you were much later, I was afraid we'd have to wait until December to get married. But November will still work. Not a minute too soon, mind you. We're already way behind schedule. Not to worry, not to worry! It will all get done!" She started listing out all that she had already done—made a list of people

175

to invite, made a list of foods to prepare, decide which house to live in . . . but that could be discussion for another day, she told Jonah. Then Sallie gave up a rare pause. "You do still want to get married, don't you, Jonah?"

There was silence down below. *Oh please, Dad. Please, please say no!*

"Yes," Jonah finally answered, loud and clear. "Of course."

Bess's heart sank. She tiptoed to another room to open the windows and get a cross breeze. She knew when to leave things be.

Maybe, Lainey thought, maybe it was just as well that Jonah had left before anything more serious developed between them. She had a lot of thinking to do about her future, and being around Jonah made her mind a little scrambled. She didn't like feeling scrambled. She liked having plans laid out, even and straight. Not that plans couldn't be changed. They could.

In fact, she was changing her plans this very day.

Earlier today, Lainey had met with the realtor, Ira Gingrich, wanting to have an informal conversation about the purchase of Simon's former house. She had thought long and hard about this. She prayed about it every time she walked past the cottage. She felt as if there was something about that cottage she couldn't ignore—as if it was a metaphor for how she felt about her life. God was in the business of restoring things. People too. The old could be made new.

Ira Gingrich was a plump, easygoing man with pink skin and white hair, who sat with his hands resting on his belly. The house had been on the market for three years, without a bite, he said sadly. When Lainey made a ridiculously low offer on it as a joke, he squinted at her in confusion. Then a sudden smile creased his face.

"Sold!" he shouted and jumped to his feet, thrusting his hand out to grab Lainey's and pump it up and down.

Stunned speechless, she was suddenly the owner of a dilapidated, run-down, neglected house sorely in need of some love and attention.

That night, in her little room, she went over her finances and felt rather pleased. The money she had saved up for culinary school would suffice as a down payment. She thought she would talk to Billy about doing some renovations for her. She had a lot of confidence in Billy's abilities. She had noticed how carefully he worked at Rose Hill Farm. If he didn't know how to do something, he would find out. She figured out that her bakery hours would cover her mortgage payments . . . just barely. Even still, she didn't regret this turn of events. Not at all. For the first time in her life, she had a home of her own. And she hoped and prayed that Jonah would come to his senses and at least let her be a sister to Bess. She had squelched the hope that was stirring within her heart for Jonah.

It was probably a good thing that he left when he did, she told herself. Over and over and over. After all, she thought, it made things simpler.

Ira Gingrich sped up escrow so Lainey would close on the house by Friday. Bertha observed that nobody had ever seen Ira Gingrich move this fast, not even at quitting time at the bank. She said he was moving that escrow through like a greased sow before Lainey could think twice and change her mind. Lainey started a list of things she would need: a bed, sheets, a table, chairs. She wondered if Bertha might have a few extra pieces of furniture to loan in that big attic at Rose Hill Farm.

By the time Friday dawned, Lainey woke up more excited than she had ever felt about anything in all her life. She wished she could be sharing the day with Bess and Jonah. Instead of missing them less, she found she was missing them more. Especially Jonah. Every morning when she went to the bakery, she expected him to be there, waiting for her. And often at night, as she had closed up shop, he would happen to stop by to walk her home. She hadn't even realized how often Jonah filled her thoughts. It worried her. She had only known him a month's time. Was Caleb Zook right? Was she planning to get baptized for Jonah's sake?

No. She had an unwavering certainty that it was more than that. She had been longing for something all of her life . . . and when her VW Beetle died on Main Street in Stoney Ridge, it wasn't long before she knew she had found what she had been looking for. She wasn't one to think that only the Amish were Christians . . . she'd been around too many types of people to know that God cared about the interior condition of a person's heart, not their exterior labels. But for her, she knew she worshiped God best here. What she liked best was that being Amish, to her, meant that every part of her life was a testimony to God.

She had given away her clothes and makeup and was wearing the garb now. Even at the bakery. Mrs. Stroot took one look at her, shook her head, and blamed Bertha Riehl. It took Lainey a few days to feel comfortable, to get used to startled stares. After a while, she decided that the reason the Amish wore Plain clothes was to identify them as belonging to God. So each time she was reminded she was dressing differently from others, it drew her attention to God. She liked that.

As she was dressing this morning for work, it dawned on her

that she had an answer to the bishop's nettlesome question: if Jonah Riehl was the reason she was going Amish, that reason was gone. Most likely, he was planning his autumn wedding to that Sallie woman in Ohio whom Bess had mentioned once or twice.

And still, Lainey was determined to become Amish.

Bertha Riehl burst into the bakery midafternoon on Friday as Lainey was pulling chocolate chip cookies out of the oven. "Been to see Simon. He's only got a few weeks left. They said we should take him on home. Let him die in peace."

Lainey set the trays on the counter to cool. She took off the mitts. "You're awfully kind to do that, Bertha." She slid a spatula under each cookie to loosen it.

Bertha eyed the cookies. "Do what?"

Lainey put a warm cookie on a plate and handed it to Bertha. "For taking in your brother. For seeing him out."

Bertha took a bite of the cookie. With a full mouth, she said, "I'm doing nothing of the kind."

Lainey looked up, surprised. "Where will he go?"

Bertha kept her head down over her plate with the cookie.

The terrible truth dawned on Lainey. "Oh Bertha, you can't be thinking I would take him in!"

Bertha snapped her head up. "Why not? You got a house now."

"But . . . but . . . why can't *you* have him?"

There was never a more surprised look on a person's face. "Simon was shunned."

"That was so long ago! The bishop would certainly understand. Simon is dying!"

Bertha nodded. "Mebbe so. But my Samuel wouldn't hear of it. If he were still living, it would give him a cardinal arrest."

That remark didn't surprise Lainey. It was always Bertha who had come visiting, bringing casseroles and tucking money under the sugar bowl. Never Samuel. People often made the mistake of blurring the Amish together, assuming that because they dressed alike and looked alike, their thoughts ran alike. But that assumption was wrong. Bertha and Samuel Riehl were as different as two people could be. She remembered every detail of Samuel: the clear-rimmed glasses and broad smile, the grandfatherly bald head like a warm, bright lightbulb. He seemed so trustworthy and kind, and he was, as long as it fit inside the Amish box.

Lainey came to herself with a start. While Jonah had his father's warmth, he also had his father's strict observance to rules. How had she not seen this before? Now she understood why Jonah left Stoney Ridge so abruptly after learning Simon was the real father of Bess. He was his father's son.

A combined sigh of impatience and exasperation from Bertha jolted Lainey back to her present dilemma. "Bertha, that house is a disaster. It's not safe! There's no way anyone could live in it . . . for weeks! Maybe months! I don't even take possession of it until the end of today."

"We'll help."

Lainey didn't know what to say. Her stomach twisted up in a firm knot. "I have to think about this, Bertha. You can't just bully me into it."

Bertha lifted her eyebrows as if she couldn't imagine what Lainey was talking about. "Just don't take too long. He's getting ejected from the hospital next Friday," she said at the door.

"What if Simon doesn't agree? Have you thought of that?"

"You leave Simon to me," she said. "He may be a tough caricature, but he's still my baby brother."

Lainey covered her face with her hands. When Bertha Riehl got her mind set on something, you'd just as well prepare to see it through.

Ira Gingrich handed Lainey the keys as soon as he received her cashier's check. She left his office holding those keys so tightly that they made a red indentation in her palm. Ever since Bertha had paid her that visit to the bakery and told her she should take in Simon, she had been filled with doubts about buying this cottage. She had an inner debate with herself. *If our possessions belong to the Lord, why is it so hard to share them with others in need?* And Simon certainly needed *someone*.

But then she would go back to wondering why *she* needed to be the one to help him. She began to question if becoming Amish was such a wise thing, after all. If they believed so strongly in community, why would she be left on her own to take care of Simon? Maybe she had glamorized being Amish. Maybe it wasn't any different than so many other Christian churches. Big intentions, little action. A mile wide and an inch deep.

She walked to the cottage and stood outside of it. A small bead of sweat trickled down her back. What had she gotten herself into? And was it too late to get out of it?

She heard a noise, like a very loud woodpecker, coming from inside the house. Slowly, she went up to the porch. The noise was definitely coming from inside. It sounded like a team of woodpeckers. She was just about to push the door when it flew open. There stood Billy with a hammer in his hand and nails in his mouth.

He took the nails out of his mouth and grinned. "Saw you standing out front with a dazed look on your face."

Behind him came Bertha, with a broom in her hands. Past the two of them were a few other men whom Lainey had seen at church. Through the front room, Lainey could see some women scrubbing the kitchen.

"What's going on?" Lainey asked.

"Billy's fixing loose cupboards in the kitchen. Them two men are working on the chimbley. I'm cleaning with them ladies." She spread her big arm out. "It's called a working bee. More are coming tomorrow." She took in Lainey's stunned look. "It's what we do."

Lainey clapped her hands to her cheeks. "I don't know what to say."

"I told you we'd help," Bertha said, starting to sweep the cobwebs out of the ceiling corners.

"But . . . I didn't really expect it. It's just so touching. So . . ."

Billy shrugged. "Amish," he said. As if that explained everything.

Lainey nodded as tears started to well in her eyes.

"It certainly gives a person something to compensate about," Bertha added. She gave up a rare smile.

"It does, Bertha," Lainey said, talking through her tears. "It definitely gives a person something to compensate about." That clinched it for her. Any lingering doubts she had just vanished. She wasn't alone. She would tell Caleb Zook this very weekend that she wanted to be baptized as soon as possible.

Bess watched the clouds float across a sky so bright a blue it shimmered, and her thoughts turned to home. But it wasn't

182

Berlin, Ohio, that she was thinking of. She was thinking of Rose Hill Farm. She felt as unsettled as a yanked-up weed.

This summer, she had grown to love her grandmother. She began to notice how hard Mammi worked and how old she was getting. She wanted to be there with her, helping her grow roses and make jam and tea and rose water and soap. It troubled her to think of Mammi alone on that big farm.

She was worried about her father too. She had thought if she left him be, he would work himself through this sulky mood. But two weeks had passed and he was still moving through each day in slow motion, as if weighed down by something. By contrast, Sallie was moving like a runaway train with their wedding plans.

Tonight, as they finished up another silent dinner, she spoke up. "I got a letter from Lainey today."

Her father didn't respond, didn't even look at her. Bess decided to give him most of the details anyway.

"She said Simon is nearly dead. The hospital, according to Mammi, is ejecting him by week's end." Bess hoped her father would react, reminded of his mother's way of mangling English words.

The ghost of a smile flickered across Jonah's face, but he didn't make a comment. He moved his fork around on his pie plate.

"I'm not sure I should be telling you this, but I'm not sure I shouldn't, either. Lainey is getting baptized this fall. She's becoming Amish."

Jonah stilled, but he kept his eyes downcast. "She is, is she?"

Bess nodded. "All summer long I've been teaching her how to do things without electricity. And I was teaching her Deitsch."

Jonah took that information in silently. He avoided Bess's eyes.

She bit her lip. "Dad, won't you please tell me why we left Stoney Ridge so suddenly?"

Jonah's face set in warning lines. Bess could see the shutters coming down.

He eased back in his chair. "Things are . . . complicated, Bess."

"Maybe if you told me about it, I could help you uncomplicate things."

Jonah gave her a slight smile. "Things happened long ago that you wouldn't understand."

She felt offended. Nothing irked Bess more than when someone inferred she was a child. Usually, that someone was Billy Lapp. "Try me."

"Oh Bess . . . some things are best put away." He dropped his chin to his chest as if he was fighting something inside himself. He was quiet for a long while and Bess let him be. She knew not to push him. He was like Mammi that way. He let his fork drop on his plate. "Your blood test came back as a perfect match for Simon."

She *knew* it! She just knew this had something to do with that blood test. Her father was so protective of her. She looked into his kind, dark eyes and reached out for his hand. She took a deep breath. "Then we need to go back to Stoney Ridge. As soon as possible. I want to give my bone marrow to Simon."

Jonah looked at her, horrified. His voice nearly broke on the words. "Why? Why would you do that? It's a painful procedure. And for a man who . . . a man like him." He raked a hand through his hair, as if he was struggling with how to grapple with this. "Maybe it's just consequences for the life he's led. I'm not at all sure we should interfere. Maybe it's Simon's time to pass. Maybe it's . . . God's will."

Bess's gaze shifted out the window. "I asked Lainey what she remembered about Simon. She said he slept till noon, then took a nap. He could lie as smooth as new cream. And that was on his good days. When he got to drinking spirits, she said he was like another person. So mean he could make angels weep. Once he made her kneel on uncooked rice until she had cuts in her knees." She turned back to Jonah. "I asked Mammi what made him so mean and she said he was just born that way."

She got up out of her seat and went to put the dishes in the sink. "Lainey bought Simon's old house with her cooking school money. She's taking him in. To die." She filled up the sink with hot water and added dish soap. She swirled the water with her hand to make it sudsy. "I guess if Lainey can do that, after how he treated her, if she can forgive him . . . well, if my bone marrow could give him a chance to live and maybe to love God through it . . . then I should at least offer it to him." She wiped her hands on a rag and turned to her father. "I *need* to do this, Dad."

Jonah rubbed his face with his hands for the longest time. Finally, he stood, walked over to her, and put his arms around her. Bess burrowed her face into his shoulder.

"We'll leave in the morning," he finally said in a husky voice.

Jonah looked out the window as the bus drove over the bridge into West Virginia. Bess had drifted off to sleep and was starting to lean her head against his shoulder. He felt such tenderness toward her. She was hardly the same girl he sent off in a bus to visit his mother. He had always thought of Bess as excitable as a hen walking on hot coals, never able to keep still, always jumping up with some further excitement. Yet gentle too. He had worried that others might take advantage of Bess's gentle ways. A part of him felt his mother had taken advantage of her, deciding she was a last-ditch cure for Simon. He felt a hardness toward his mother that plagued him.

But it was starting to dawn on Jonah that he didn't need to worry about Bess the way he used to. Next to him was a calm, assured young woman who knew her mind. She had grown up, slower than she wanted, faster than he realized.

Bess jolted awake and looked at him as if she hadn't been asleep at all but had been thinking. "Don't you wonder how two people from one family—like Mammi and Simon—could begin their lives at the same point and somehow take turns that would lead them to such very different lives? I mean, are we born who we are, or does life make us that way?"

That is an eternal question, Jonah thought, as he watched Bess drift back to sleep. *Take you and Lainey. You started in the same point, took a turn, and then seem to be ending up leading very similar lives.*

They arrived at Stoney Ridge not long after dawn. Bess wanted to see Lainey first thing, hoping she'd already be at the bakery. Jonah said to go ahead without him. He had an errand of his own. He walked Bess to Main Street, saw the lights on in The Sweet Tooth, and then told her he would meet her later at Rose Hill Farm.

She didn't ask him any questions, but she did put a reassuring hand on his shoulder. "Everything is going to turn out fine, Dad."

When did they switch roles? he wondered as he walked the road that led to Caleb Zook's farmhouse, Beacon Hollow. When did Bess become the parent and he become the child?

Jonah found Caleb in the dairy barn, just as he had expected. The cows had been milked and Caleb was stacking the emptied-out milk cans into the sink to be washed. Jonah stood for a while, watching him work. Caleb had been Jonah's closest childhood friend. They did everything together—hunt and fish, swim, skip school. They stood together as witnesses for each others' weddings. And Caleb was by his side to help him when Rebecca died. When Jonah moved to Ohio, they lost touch. *No*, he corrected himself. *I lost touch. With everything and everyone from Stoney Ridge.*

Caleb rinsed out the last bucket and hung it upside down on a wall hook to dry. That was when he noticed Jonah. "Well, well. Skin me for a polecat." Caleb looked pleased. He picked up a rag and dried his hands as he walked over to Jonah. "Heard you had returned to Ohio."

"I did," Jonah said. "Now I'm back." He shook Caleb's hand. "Would you have time for a talk?"

"For you, Jonah, I have all the time in the world." Caleb led Jonah down to two lawn chairs that sat under the willow tree, along the creek that ran parallel to the road.

Jonah watched the water make its way around rocks. Caleb didn't press him, and Jonah expected that. Caleb always had a way of knowing how to work with others. When Jonah heard Caleb had become a minister, then a bishop, he knew the Lord had chosen well for the district.

A mother sheep bleated for her lambs, and the two hurried to find her. The sun was just starting to rise as Jonah took a deep breath. "Caleb, I learned something that has turned my world upside down."

Caleb leaned back in his chair. "Well, my friend, let's see if we can make things right side up again."

Jonah spilled out the entire story, leaving nothing out. Caleb didn't say a word. He just sat there, letting Jonah work through his tangled thoughts and feelings.

"This summer," Jonah said, "it's like I've woken up after a long sleep." There'd been joy this summer, in seeing his mother and Bess grow so close, and in meeting Lainey, he told Caleb. But there was pain too, as he was reminded of Rebecca and the life they should have had together. And now, there was fear. He hadn't been able to tell Bess the whole truth, about Simon being her father. What if he did tell her and she told Simon? If Simon did get well, would he take Bess away from him?

"Lainey was only ten years old and she was trying to give her sister a better life. She was keeping a promise to her mother. I understand that." Jonah looked up at the sky. "But my mother! She knew, yet she didn't tell me the truth." He wiped his eyes with his palms. "How do I forgive her for that, Caleb? How do I forgive my mother for coaxing Bess here this summer to be a bone marrow donor for Simon?"

Caleb took his straw hat off of his head and spun it around in his hands. Finally, he looked over, past Jonah, to the large vegetable garden on the side of the house. "I've been trying something new this summer. I've got a compost pile working just for kitchen scraps."

Jonah looked sideways at him, alarmed. Did Caleb not hear him? What did a compost pile have to do with all that had just spilled out of him?

Caleb leaned forward in his chair. "Composting is a miracle, really. It starts out with carrot scrapings and coffee grinds and banana peels. And then you give it time and the sun warms it and God turns all of that rubbish into something wonderful and useful. Something we can use and spread in the garden."

Jonah tilted his head. "You're trying to make an analogy of composting to the lie I've been living with for fifteen years?"

"I guess I am." Caleb smiled and set his hat on his knee. "The funny thing about composting is that it ends up benefiting us. Nothing is beyond God's ability to repair. Even kitchen scraps. He is all-powerful."

Jonah glared at him. "So you're saying that I just forgive and forget?" He thrust his fist against his chest. He felt so angry. He felt so cheated. "Something as big as the fact that this child I've been raising isn't really mine?"

"Isn't she?" Caleb asked, holding Jonah's fixed gaze. "Could Bess really be any more your daughter?"

Jonah dropped his eyes to the ground. Caleb was right. Bess *was* his daughter. He had to fight back a lump in his throat.

"Nothing can ever change that, Jonah."

Jonah looked down at the creek. "You probably want me to tell Bess the whole story."

"I'm not the one to tell you what to say or what not to say. You'll have to pray long and hard about that matter. I do understand that it's heavy information for a child to bear."

"She's not a child any longer. She's grown up years this summer."

Caleb smiled. "There are seasons in our life that are like that."

The sun was up now, filtering through the trees, creating shadows over the creek.

"As far as forgiving your mother," Caleb said, "Peter asked Jesus, how many times should he forgive another? Peter wanted a statistical count. And Jesus responded with a story. 'Not seven times, but, I tell you, seventy-seven times.' Jesus was teaching him that we don't live by careful bookkeeping. Through God's mercy, bookkeeping has given way to extravagant generosity." He paused for a moment. "So this is your story, my friend."

They spoke no words for a long while, and yet the silence didn't seem uncompanionable.

Then Caleb placed a hand on Jonah's shoulder and added, "There's someone else you need to think about forgiving."

Jonah looked at him with a question.

"Yourself," he said softly. "For the buggy accident."

Jonah winced. He started to protest, to give the pat answers that he always gave—God was in control. God knew best. God has a purpose in all things. But he couldn't say the words. He stopped and leaned forward, resting his elbows on his knees, holding his head in his hands. "I should have prevented it. I should have been paying closer attention to the road." His voice grew hoarse. "It's hard enough to accept that I could have prevented Rebecca's death ... now I've learned that my daughter died in that accident too. I was responsible for them." He covered his face with his hands and his shoulders started to shake. Something broke loose inside of him and he began to weep. He couldn't even remember the last time he cried. He didn't even cry when he learned that Rebecca had passed. He just felt numb. But now, this morning, he felt fresh, raw, searing pain, as if the accident had just happened. He was spilling out grief he had stored for fifteen years, his chest heaving and racking with sobs.

Caleb sat quietly until Jonah's tears were spent. Finally, he spoke. "You didn't cause that accident, Jonah. It's hard to understand why God allowed it, but we trust in God's sovereignty. Your wife and baby's lives were complete. And now we trust they are in the presence of our Almighty Lord." The faint clang of a dinner bell floated down to the creek. He rose to his feet. "Breakfast is ready. Jorie's probably wondering where I've disappeared to. I know she'd be pleased to have you join us."

"Thanks, Caleb. Another time."

Jonah started to rise, but Caleb put his hand on his shoulder. "Why don't you stay here awhile and talk this all out with the Lord? I find it's my favorite place to hammer things out with him."

As Jonah eased back down, he asked Caleb, "So you think Bess should give Simon her bone marrow? A man such as him?" He looked away. "You remember, Caleb, how he treated Lainey and her mother. How the sparkle drained from them." And what life would have been like for his Bess, too, had she been raised by Simon. Lainey had pointed that out to him, but he hadn't listened to her.

Caleb rubbed his forehead. "Are we going to be part of condemning a man? Or are we going to be a part of releasing him from condemnation?" He sat back down again. "Jonah, we want to share in this world, of forgiving and being forgiven. Even such a man as Simon."

It wasn't easy, though. Even for Caleb. Jonah could see this was a temptation for both of them, to let consequences fall as they would. To let Simon pass away without a hand of kindness offered to him. Except for the hand of Bertha. Suddenly, Jonah felt a slight softening toward his mother. He realized how hard this must be for her, what a difficult spot she was in. Despite everything, Simon was her brother.

Caleb added, "You probably know this, but Lainey O'Toole is planning to be baptized."

"Bess told me," Jonah said.

"When she first came to me a while back, I told her to go without electricity for a week. That usually changes folks' minds right off. They miss their radio and hair dryer and television too much. But she didn't bat an eye. She's been learning our language and choring without modern convenience. Even still, I had to make sure she wasn't doing this on a whim."

191

He nodded.

"I asked her why, and she told me she truly believes that she can serve and love God best by being Plain." Caleb lifted his eyebrows. "Sure wish some of our members felt that way. Quite a few of them claim to be meditating during church." He raised his eyebrows. "An activity that looks suspiciously similar to dozing." He rose to his feet. "God always has a plan, doesn't he?"

Jonah looked up at Caleb and did his best to offer up a slight smile. He wished he had Caleb's unwavering faith. Ever since Rebecca—and his baby—had died, he had been able to summon only a pale shadow of the faith he once had. For how could a loving God let a twenty-year-old young mother and her newborn baby die in a careless accident? If God was sovereign, then his sovereignty seemed frightening. It was a question Jonah had never been able to work through to a comfortable solution.

Caleb watched him carefully, as if reading his thoughts. "God may allow tragedy, Jonah, just like he allowed his Son to have a tragic death." He leaned closer to Jonah. "But God is a redeemer. Never, ever forget that truth."

Once a week, on her day off from the bakery, Lainey traveled to Lebanon to visit Simon. She brought him baked goods and a magazine or a puzzle. He was not looking well. He had become even more pale and thin, with dark circles under his eyes. Today, she found him on the patio, getting some sun. Simon, who had always looked so sure of himself, seemed hollow and fragile.

He opened one eye when he heard her. "What's in the box?" he asked in a gruff voice.

"Doughnuts. Jelly filled. Your favorite, if I remember right."

192

"I never liked doughnuts." He held out his hand, palm up, for a doughnut.

She opened the box and handed him one. He ate it carefully, as if he had sores in his mouth, and jelly dripped down his chin. She wiped it off with a tissue and he let her. It amazed her to see Simon helpless. "So the nurse said they're going to release you."

He narrowed his eyes. "They just want the bed. Government can't bother themselves with a dying vet. Even one with a purple heart."

Lainey tried not to roll her eyes. She had heard that purple heart line many times before. "It was Bertha who talked them into releasing you. She thought you'd be better off in a home."

"I'm staying right here. I got my rights."

She knew the truth was that he had no place to go. He was a pathetic, lonely old man who was dying. She looked at him with eyes that were not hard or cold. She saw him objectively. "I'd like you to come home with me."

Simon didn't move a muscle. He didn't even blink.

"I bought the old cottage and neighbors helped fix it up. We're going to rent a hospital bed for you and keep it downstairs in the living room, so you feel like you're part of things."

He eyed her suspiciously. "If you're looking for money, I told you I ain't got none."

She smiled. "I don't want your money, Simon, even if you had any."

"Then why would you be bothering with a sick old man?"

That was a question she had asked herself and prayed over ever since Bertha suggested—no, informed her—she should take in Simon. She finally decided the answer was because she was able to make something right in at least one tiny corner of the vast house of wrongs. It was another thing she was learning from the

Amish. "Everybody needs somebody in this world to help them through. I guess you're stuck with me." *And I'm stuck with you,* she thought but kindly didn't say.

Simon tucked his chin to his chest. She thought his hands were trembling a little. Maybe not. Then he lifted his head. "I like my coffee strong, and served right at six a.m."

A laugh burst out of Lainey. "Oh, I see you're already giving orders." She stood. "I'll go talk to the nurses about getting you released."

He put his hand on her forearm to stop her. He looked up at her, and for the first time she could remember, he didn't look full of mockery. He looked scared. "Lainey, why?"

She patted his hand, the way she would a child. "Your debt is canceled, Simon. That's why."

Jonah hadn't seen Lainey yet. Nor had Bess. When he returned to Rose Hill Farm after talking to Caleb, Bess was already there. Apparently, it was Lainey's day off from the bakery and Bess couldn't find her anywhere.

By late afternoon, Jonah drove the buggy down to Lainey's cottage to see if she had returned yet. There was no answer at the door. It amazed him to see that cottage transformed. It had been well worthwhile to fix it up. It was starting to look the way it was probably intended to look, years ago, when it was first built by the original owners. It was a lovely little house, with good bones and a solid foundation. He could still smell the fresh paint. New windowpanes replaced the broken ones.

He sat on the porch steps to wait for her. He had been worried to hear that she was going to live in this house—the one where her mother had died in childbirth. He put a hand to his forehead. She died delivering his Bess! Right here. Another discovery that hadn't occurred to him. How could Lainey live in a house that sheltered so many unhappy memories? He couldn't have done it.

His back was stiff from sitting for so long, so he got up to stretch. He hoped she would return soon. Soon it would be more dark than day. He walked down the pathway and around to the back of the house. He peered inside the window and recognized some furniture and an old rug from Rose Hill Farm's attic. He should have known his mother had a hand in this. He walked all around the perimeter of the house, stopping by a small, newly planted rose garden. He smiled. More evidence of Bertha Riehl. He walked around to the front and then he saw Lainey. She stood by the road, watching him, wearing a Plain dress—lavender that brought out her eyes. Her hands were clasped before her to keep them steady.

"Lainey," Jonah said softly as he approached her.

"You came back," Lainey said. "There's so much I need to explain—"

"Would you take me to see my child's grave?"

She nodded. "We can go right now."

They didn't speak in the buggy as Jonah drove them to the town cemetery. Lainey led him straight to the back where her mother was buried. A small grave marker was next to it. He could see that the two graves had been recently weeded. They looked cared for. By Lainey, no doubt.

"I'll give you some privacy," she said quietly, and went to wait in the buggy.

Jonah knelt in front of his daughter's grave. And for the second time that day, he wept.

As Jonah drove away from her cottage, Lainey stood by the road and watched until his buggy had dipped over the rise and was out of sight. They had stayed at the cemetery and talked for hours. It was as if they were filling each other in on the last fifteen years of their lives. They talked until the shadows got longer and still had more to say to each other. It wasn't until long after the dusk turned to darkness and the stars came out in the clear sky that Jonah said he should be getting back to Rose Hill Farm. But he didn't look at all as if he wanted to leave.

10

The next morning was a church Sunday. Bess dressed quickly and offered to go down the road to pick up Lainey and come back for her father and grandmother, but Jonah said he wouldn't mind going. He said old Frieda needed a little warming up, but Bess wasn't so sure. Her dad came back late last night, whistling. Even Mammi noticed how happy he seemed. You had to know Mammi pretty well to decipher a difference in expression, but Bess thought she hadn't stopped looking pleased ever since she and Jonah had arrived.

Bess wished her father would hurry old Frieda along. She hadn't seen Billy at Rose Hill Farm yesterday. She knew he would be at church this morning, and so she took extra care with her hair. She even pulled a few strands loose behind her cap and tried to curl them into tight ringlets. She didn't think anyone would see since they sat in the back bench, but she hoped maybe Billy might notice. Betsy Mast often had corkscrew curls slipping under her cap and down her neck. But then, Betsy had thick, curly hair, and Bess's hair was thin and straight.

She spotted Billy by the barn the minute they arrived at the

197

Smuckers'. He was surrounded by a group of friends; they were laughing over some joke. Mammi took her time getting out of the buggy from the backseat, which gave Bess a chance to furtively glance at the boys while pretending to help her down. She saw Andy Yoder spot her with a delighted look on his face. Billy hadn't noticed her yet. He had turned around to talk to someone else. As soon as Bess climbed out of the buggy, Andy was at her elbow.

"Bess! You're back! Hallelujah! You look . . . wonderful." Andy's admiration was unqualified. "I was just this minute trying to talk Billy into making a trip to Ohio to see you! But he made it sound like we were going to the far side of the moon."

Bess stifled a smile. Andy was the kind of person that sometimes told you unexpected things.

"Don't listen to a word this fellow tells you," Billy said, approaching them from behind.

Bess whirled around to face Billy. "Which words?" Her heart was pounding like an Indian war drum. She was sure Billy could hear it.

Billy looked at her as if he was seeing her for the first time. For a few seconds, he was literally unable to find words. "The second part," he said simply.

Then it was as if the mist had cleared and they went back to their old ways.

"Missed picking rose petals, did you?" he asked.

She grinned and held out her palms. "Especially the thorns. When the last cut healed, I told Dad we needed to return. My hands looked too good."

Billy and Andy peered at her hands as if they were made of fine china.

Jonah handed the reins of the horse to one of the Smucker sons and interrupted them. "Well, boys—"

198

Bess cringed at the undue emphasis her father placed on the word "boys." Couldn't he see that Billy was a man?

"—it's time we went in to the service." Jonah put a hand protectively on Bess's shoulder to steer her to the house for meeting.

Around three o'clock, they left the Smuckers' to return to Rose Hill Farm. Bess invited Lainey to join them for supper, and Jonah couldn't hold back a smile. As he turned the buggy into the drive, he felt a jolt. Bess let out a gasp.

There, on the front porch, patiently waiting, was planted Sallie Stutzman, her twin sons, and Mose Weaver.

Jonah swallowed hard. In his haste, he had completely forgotten to tell Sallie and Mose that he and Bess were leaving.

Over breakfast on Monday, Bess asked her grandmother if she would take her to see Simon in Lebanon as soon as it was convenient. Mammi said it was convenient right now and grabbed her bonnet to head out the door. Sallie and her boys and Mose were staying at Rose Hill Farm, and Sallie's "cheerfulness," Mammi said, was making her dizzy.

They didn't talk much on the bus ride. Something was building inside of Bess, something she had discovered last night as she watched everyone at dinner. She was so sure she was right that she felt as if she might explode. Finally, she blurted out, "Oh Mammi! Whatever are we going to do?!"

Mammi had been looking out the window. She turned to Bess as if she had forgotten she was there. "About what?"

About *what?* Wasn't it obvious? "Dad loves Lainey and Sallie loves Dad and Mose loves Sallie and Lainey loves Dad! If we don't do something quick, the wedding is going to happen because Dad is too honorable to tell Sallie no. That's what!" Sallie hadn't stopped talking about the wedding last night. That dinner was one of the most painful moments of Bess's life. Her father looked stricken, Mose kept looking at Sallie with this terrible longing—Bess knew Mose well enough to know that his mild look held *terrible* longing—and Lainey! Poor Lainey! She hardly said a word. When Jonah offered to drive her home, she refused him, flat out.

Mammi turned back to the window and exhaled. "We let nature take its course. *That's* what." She patted Bess's leg. "That's what we do. Never forget that."

Bess turned that thought over and over in her mind, not at all convinced it was the best plan. Didn't Mammi care? Didn't she want her dad to be happy?

Just before they reached Lebanon, Mammi asked, "Does that little round gal ever stop talking?"

"No," Bess said glumly. "She never does."

"Them two boys ever stop wiggling?"

Bess shook her head. "Not even in church."

"Does that tall fellow ever say a word?"

Bess scratched her prayer cap. "None that I recall."

"Hoo-boy," Mammi said. "Nature has her work cut out for her."

After they arrived at the hospital, Mammi went in search of a bathroom and Bess knew *that* could be a long wait, so she decided to go ahead to Simon's ward. She tiptoed up to his bed. She could see he had grown much weaker than the other time she had visited. Sweat gleamed on his face, like he was feverish.

"If you're another vampire, go away," Simon muttered without opening an eye. "I don't have any more blood to give."

"But I'm not . . . I'm not a vampire," Bess said. "It's me. It's Bess. Bertha's granddaughter. Jonah's daughter."

"Well, well. It's the holy howler." He groaned. "If Bertha sent you here to get me to confess my sins before I kick the bucket . . . tell her no thanks."

"She didn't," Bess said quietly.

Simon didn't respond.

"Would it be such a bad thing, though, to confess your sins?"

Now he looked at her. "It wouldn't be if I didn't enjoy sinning so much."

Bess had never heard of anyone who enjoyed sinning. She gave him a look of great sadness. "I'll pray for you, for your soul."

"Have at it," Simon said mockingly. "I'm afraid all those childhood lessons in holiness slid off me like hot butter off the griddle." He pointed to the door. "Now go look for where the carpenter made a hole."

She supposed that was his rather impolite way of telling her he wanted her to leave him alone. For a brief moment, she thought about not going through with the bone marrow operation. Simon would never appreciate the gift.

And yet, she wasn't doing it for him. She was doing it for God. And for Mammi. She bit her lip. "I came here today to tell you some good news. It turns out we're a match, you and I. I can give you my bone marrow."

Simon lay very silent, but he was listening, she could tell that.

201

"So instead of going home with Lainey to d—," Bess gulped back the word, "um, you're going to be getting some medicine to help your body get ready for the transplant. In another week or so, I'll have the procedure. Harvesting the marrow, they call it. Then they'll give it to you and, hopefully, it will cure you right up."

He still didn't look at her. He didn't say a word.

"I guess it won't be that fast," Bess said, rambling now. "Sounds like it will take a while to graft. They called it grafting, which is interesting, because that's what we do with the roses at Rose Hill Farm. We graft them onto better rootstock. Then they're stronger and healthier. I guess that's just what it will be like for you. You'll get stronger and healthier. That's the plan, anyway." She ran out of things to say. "I just wanted to tell you the news myself."

Simon lifted his chin. "I'll have to think on it."

"Well, think a little faster," Mammi said. She had come into the ward and eased into a chair beside Bess.

Simon frowned at his sister. She frowned back at him.

"Well, Bess," he said, "don't expect me to thank you."

Bess lifted her chin a notch. "I don't. I don't expect a thing."

"Good. As long as we're clear on that." But he did look at her, right in the eyes.

Bess held his gaze. "We're clear on that."

"Simon, anybody ever tell you it's hard to put a foot in a shut mouth?" Mammi said, standing to leave.

Everything was happening so fast that Jonah didn't know what to do. Sallie had settled into Rose Hill Farm like she wasn't going to budge. The dining room table was covered with wedding invitations that she was busy addressing. Mose, too, seemed to be in no hurry to leave, and even though the fate of their business troubled

Jonah, he was thankful for Mose's presence. Mose acted like a self-appointed shepherd to those boys, and it was a good thing. They *were* little monsters, just as Bess had said. How had he never noticed? The first day, they ran their scooters into his mother's most cherished rugosa and broke the bush at the stem.

His mother went so still it scared him, like the quiet right before an Ohio tornado hit. When she finally spoke, it was in a chilling voice. "Bess, go get Billy Lapp. Tell him we got us an emergency."

The second day, those boys knocked over a shelf of freshly canned rose petal jam in the barn when they were horsing around. The third day, they forgot to latch Frieda's stall and she wandered into the vegetable garden, trampling a row of tomato plants.

And he would never forget the look on Lainey's face when she was introduced to Sallie on Sunday. He had never mentioned Sallie to Lainey . . . it never occurred to him to mention her. But Sallie started right off with wedding talk, and Lainey responded with forced cheer, like daffodils in January. When he offered to give her a ride home—hoping for a chance to explain—she gave him a firm "No."

It made him feel sick to his stomach.

Dear Robin and Ally,

I haven't written in a while because so many changes have been happening so quickly and I didn't know where to begin. First of all, I bought a cottage with my savings. A fixer-upper would be a generous description. It's the home I lived in as a child. And I am going to be taking in my stepfather, Simon Troyer. He's been quite ill. I've told you about Bess. We've grown as close as . . . well, she's like a sister to me.

And to answer your question about men: no. There are no men of interest in Stoney Ridge. None whatsoever.

Love, Lainey

For the actual bone marrow transplant, Simon had been moved from the Veterans Hospital down to the hospital in Lancaster, where a specialist worked who was skilled at performing the relatively new procedure. Bess would be given a general anesthesia, and the marrow would be removed from her hip bone. She would stay one night, just for observation, and be allowed to go home the next morning.

The night before the operation was scheduled for Bess was one of those hot late-August nights that never cooled off. She had trouble sleeping, so she got up and went outside to get some fresh air. She sat on the porch steps and gazed at the stars. Somehow, the night sky gave her a sense of the majesty of God. She seemed so small and he seemed so big. In the distance, a horse whinnied and another answered.

"Bess?"

She looked out toward the yard and saw the silhouette of a person. "Billy! What are you doing here?"

Billy hesitated. "I forgot my books." He looked toward the barn. "In the barn. I forgot my books." He kept his books in Bertha's barn because his brothers teased him for being a bookworm.

"And you couldn't wait until morning to read?"

"No. I was right in the middle of a good part. What are you doing out here?"

"Couldn't sleep."

He walked up to her. "It's a brave thing you're doing. Giving Simon your bone marrow."

"I'm not at all brave," she answered truthfully.

"Are you scared? About tomorrow?"

She squeezed her elbows. "Maybe a little."

"Think it will hurt?"

"I'm not too worried about the pain. They said it's not much more than a bad fall on ice. I've suffered through plenty of those. It's more . . ."

He sat beside her on the porch steps. "What?"

"Well, I've never had general anesthesia before. Where do you go, when you're put to sleep like that? I won't even dream, the nurse said. I mean, where does your soul go?"

Billy didn't answer for a long time. "Caleb Zook said once that our great hope is when we're absent from the body, we're present with the Lord." He looked over at her.

She thought about that for a while in the quiet of the night. That answer satisfied her. It gave her peace. "Thank you, Billy."

"Bess?" Billy asked, husky-voiced.

She turned her face to him to see what he wanted. He held her face in both his hands and kissed her very softly on the lips. Then he drew away. She could hardly breathe, so stunned by the kiss.

He tucked a loose strand of hair under her cap, and then gently grazed her cheek with the back of his hand. "Good night." He stood and took a few steps down the walkway before turning slightly. "I'll see you in the morning. I'm going to the hospital."

His tone was so sweet that it made her heart flutter. She was just about to tell him that he forgot his books again, but then she realized that he hadn't come over for the books at all. Billy had come over this night because he was worried about her. It gave her the shivers, even on a hot night like this.

❦

It was the longest day Jonah had ever known. As soon as Bess arrived at the admitting office, the hospital machinery moved into action. She was whisked away in a wheelchair with barely time enough to wave goodbye to everyone who had come with her that morning: Bertha, Billy, Sallie and her boys, Mose. And Lainey, who was keeping a considerable distance from Jonah.

Jonah waited with Bess in the pre-op room. Machines hummed softly and white-soled shoes whispered up and down the halls. A nurse came into the room. "We just got word that the doctor is getting prepped." After she left, Jonah and Bess sat in silence. Suddenly, this was real.

Jonah leaned down to smooth her hair from her face. "You," he pronounced, "will wake up and still be the same girl who cannot be bothered to study for a math test and vanishes when there are chores to do and goes to sleep reading with the light on." But all he heard himself say was the first part of the sentence: "You will wake up and be the same girl . . ." That's all he was praying for.

The anesthesiologist came in and put the mask over Bess's mouth and nose. He told Jonah to count aloud to Bess, but instead, Jonah recited the Lord's Prayer in Deitsch. It was Caleb Zook's suggestion. He recommended having Bess hear the words "Thy will be done" before she fell asleep. When her eyes drifted shut, the nurse ushered him out to the waiting room.

Lainey looked so worried that Jonah wanted to take her in his arms and tell her everything would be all right. But of course he couldn't.

And there was part of him that wasn't sure everything would be all right. A terrible fear came over Jonah, a feeling he struggled to disown. He knew he must yield absolutely to God's will and trust in his ultimate mercy. "Not my will but Thine be done," he had told Bess before she slipped into unconsciousness. He had spent a lifetime reciting that prayer and wanted to believe it. But the fear of God's will was there, nonetheless. He still struggled against yielding to God's will, and he prayed desperately that God would bring Bess back to him, whole and well.

He looked over at his mother, sitting in a plastic chair with her head tucked down and her hands clasped together in her lap. He wondered if she felt worried too. She was more a woman of action than of words and worry. Her eyes were closed, either praying or meditating or . . . she let out a loud snore. A laugh burst out of him, Lainey too. He looked at her then; his brown eyes met hers, and they shared a smile. Sallie had been telling Mose something and caught the look that passed between Lainey and Jonah.

She stopped talking. Sallie Stutzman stopped talking. Her eyes darted back and forth between the two of them.

Jonah felt like he was a boy caught with his hand in the cookie jar. Guilt washed over him and he made sure he didn't look in Lainey's direction again.

It seemed like an eternity, but it was really less than an hour before the doctor came to the waiting room, searching out Jonah. The doctor seemed a little startled to find a large group of Amish jump to their feet, eyes fixed on him.

"She's fine," the doctor reassured everyone. "Bess is awake now. We're just going to observe her for a while, make sure no complications develop, and then we'll put her in a regular room for the night."

"Can I see her?" Billy asked.

Jonah turned to Billy with an eyebrow raised.

"Uh, I mean, can her father see her?" Billy stumbled.

"In a little while," the doctor explained.

"What about Simon?" Bertha asked. "When will he be getting

Bess's marrow?" Simon had been in isolation for over a week and hadn't been allowed any visitors because of risk of infection.

Jonah felt shamed. He hadn't even given a passing thought to Simon. *Forgive me, Lord*, he prayed quickly.

"It's actually easier for him to receive the marrow than it was for Bess to give it," the doctor said. "A needle is inserted into the cavity of the rear hip bone where a large quantity of bone marrow is located."

The doctor became quite animated with such a rapt audience. "We harvested about one to two quarts of marrow and blood. Bone marrow is actually a spongey material, found inside the bones. While this may sound like a lot, it really represents only about 2 percent of a person's bone marrow, which the body replaces in four weeks."

Billy looked as white as a sheet. Bertha told him to go sit down and put his head between his knees so he wouldn't faint.

"Men don't faint," he said in a weak and pale voice, but he let her help him to a chair. "They might pass out, but they don't faint."

"Whatever handle you want to call it by, you look like you're just about to do it," Bertha told him.

"Everything's getting ready for Simon now, and I'm going to head in and take care of that." The doctor clapped his hands together. "Hopefully, the donation will 'take' and make its way into the central shaft of larger bones to restore stem cell function."

Billy groaned, then stood abruptly and hurried down the hall, in need of a men's room.

Bertha watched him weave down the hall and shook her head. "That poor boy's going off his feed again."

Early the next morning, Billy went over to Rose Hill Farm to finish chores as fast as he could. Billy had told Bertha he would take her to the hospital to meet everyone for Bess's release this afternoon. For the last two days, he had felt an odd anxiety and he hadn't been sleeping well, as if something wasn't quite right and he didn't know what.

He was walking up the tree-lined drive when he heard Boomer barking up a fury in the rose fields. He glanced at the house and was surprised there was no buttery glow from a lantern light in the kitchen. Usually, he could see Bertha at the stove and smell something delicious frying. Even though he had just eaten a full breakfast at home, his stomach would begin to rumble in happy anticipation. Not today, though. The farmhouse looked dark and cold.

He jogged over to see what Boomer's ruckus was about, then slowed as he approached him. A chill ran down his spine when he saw the frantic, wild-eyed look in the dog's eyes.

Then he discovered what Boomer was troubled about. Bertha Riehl was lying on her side, as if she had laid down to take a nap among her roses. Billy rushed to her and rolled her on her back. Her eyes were closed, her lips were blue, her face was white, and he could see she wasn't breathing. She'd been gone for a while. She had been out spraying Coca-Cola on her roses when she passed. She looked utterly at peace. He held her hand for a while, tears streaming down his face, unsure of what to do next. Boomer rested his big woolly head on Billy's shoulder.

Billy took a few deep breaths, trying to steady himself, and went up to the farmhouse. He was looking for Jonah, before he remembered Jonah was spending the night at the hospital with Bess. It looked like their company—Sallie and her boys and that Mose—were gone too. Probably at the hospital, Billy figured. Billy rubbed his face with his hands. His father would know what to do. He hated leaving Bertha like this, but he couldn't move her on his own. Boomer was standing guard by her. He bolted down the drive and ran home to fetch his father.

Billy knew word would trickle quickly through the community about the passing of Bertha Riehl. He had to act fast to get to the hospital in Lancaster as quickly as he could. His father tried to insist they get Caleb Zook to tell Jonah and Bess the news about Bertha. "That's what bishops are for," he told Billy. "They know best how to say these things."

Billy was tempted, but he knew, deep down, he needed to be the one to go. Part of being a man was not avoiding hard things. He changed clothes and his father drove him into town to catch the bus to Lancaster.

"Maybe I should go with you," he told Billy.

"No, I need to do this myself." Billy wasn't sure how he was going to break the news to Jonah about Bertha's passing. But he had to get to them before they returned to Rose Hill Farm and found a group of women gathered, preparing the house for the viewing.

Just before he hopped on the bus, his father stopped him by placing a hand on his shoulder. Billy turned to him, and his father didn't say anything, but there was something in his eyes—a look that said he was pleased with him. He couldn't remember ever seeing that look from his father before.

Not an hour later, Billy arrived at the hospital and found Jonah and Lainey and everyone else sitting in the waiting room.

"Billy!" Lainey said when she spotted him. Then she grew solemn, sensing from the look on his face that something had happened. "What's wrong?"

Billy sat near them, struggling to speak. Lainey took hold of

210

his hand to give him strength. "It's Bertha," Billy started, then tears filled his eyes. "She's gone." He had to stop and wipe his eyes with the back of his sleeve. "I found her in the roses." He covered his face then, unable to continue.

Jonah heard the words come out of Billy's mouth, but he couldn't understand them. It was as if everything had stopped. The sound of the nurses' shoes as they hurried up the hallways, the clocks ticking, the elevator opening and shutting. He looked at Billy and felt pity for him. Poor Billy. He was suffering. And then he looked at Lainey, with tears running down her cheeks. Sallie started to tell Mose a list of things they needed to do for the funeral. It was like Jonah's mind had shut down and he wasn't able to process the meaning behind the sentence, "She's gone."

His mother had passed? She was dead?

Like a fog lifting, the full meaning behind those words started to sink in to him. Then the pain rushed at him, as real as an ocean wave, and he felt the tears come. Billy crouched down beside him and Jonah put his hand on Billy's head. They sat there for a long while, until a nurse came and timidly interrupted to let them know Bess was ready to go now.

Jonah nodded and wiped his face with his handkerchief. "I need to tell her."

"I'll go with you," Lainey offered.

"*I* should go," Sallie said as she rose to her feet.

"No," Lainey said, giving Sallie a firm look. "No. I'll go."

Sallie looked confused, then hurt, but Mose put a gentle hand on her arm. Jonah didn't have the presence of mind to do anything more.

Before walking into Bess's room, Jonah took a deep breath and prayed for God's strength. Bess had grown so close to his mother this summer. More and more, she was acting like her too. She even cooked like his mother. He opened the door a crack and saw her waiting by the window, dressed and ready to go.

"How are you feeling?" Lainey asked her.

"Not too bad," Bess said. "A little sore. They won't let me see Simon, but they did tell me it went well for him."

Jonah nodded. "So I heard."

Bess picked up her bonnet and cape. "Let's go home."

Jonah pulled up a chair for Lainey to sit in. "Bess, something has happened."

Bess looked curiously at her father. Then she gasped. "It's Simon. He's dead, isn't he? All this effort, and he's dead."

"No. Simon is fine." In a twist of irony, Simon *was* fine and his mother was dead. Jonah pulled the curtain around her bed to give them privacy from the other patients. Then he leaned a hip against the bed frame, crossed his arms against his chest, and lifted his face to Bess. Gently, he told her that her grandmother had passed this morning while she was out tending the roses. He waited, expecting her to break down.

Bess turned to face the window. She hugged her elbows as if she was holding herself together.

Lainey walked up to Bess and put her hands on her shoulders. Softly she said, "It was your grandmother's time. She'd done everything she needed to do. She brought Simon back to his family. She brought you and your dad back to Stoney Ridge." Lainey turned Bess around to look at her. Bess was dry-eyed. "God's timing is always perfect. You see that, don't you? Her life was complete." She spoke with conviction.

Jonah remained silent as Lainey said those words. He was amazed by her, nearly in awe. But it distressed him to see Bess so quiet. It wasn't like her. Two years ago, when their pet dog had been hit by a car, she had cried for two days straight. "Are you all right, Bess?"

Bess nodded but didn't say a word.

"When you're ready," Jonah said, "Billy is waiting for us in the hallway."

"I'm ready now," was all Bess said in a voice unfamiliar to him.

It was afternoon by the time they returned to Rose Hill Farm. The hardest moment of all came as the taxi drove up the drive-way. Knowing Mammi wasn't there—and wouldn't be there ever again—made Bess feel an unbearable pain in her chest, as real as if she had been stabbed.

Everyone in the taxi was aware of Mammi's absence. She saw the tight set of her father's jaw. Billy kept his chin tucked to his chest, Lainey just went ahead and let the tears flow. Sallie was quiet, which was a great blessing. Even her boys seemed to know they needed to be calm and still, but it helped to have Mose sit between them in the back of the station wagon.

Rose Hill Farm wasn't empty. The news had spread quickly throughout Stoney Ridge. Friends and neighbors were in and around the farmhouse, cleaning it from top to bottom in prepa-ration for the viewing and the funeral. The women fussed over Bess, but all she wanted was to go upstairs and lie down on her bed. She was stiff and exhausted after an uncomfortable night. Her hip felt sore and so did her heart—aching for her grandmother. It was the bitterest kind of heartache she had ever felt—an ache that burned and gnawed. She hoped that tears would come in solitude and help wash away the pain. It seemed a terrible thing that she couldn't shed a tear for Mammi. She had loved her grandmother more than she had even realized. She knelt by her window and looked out over the rose fields, wondering where it was that her grandmother had lay down and died. But still no tears came, only the same horrible ache of grief.

When she finally went downstairs, she learned that the undertaker had returned her grandmother's body. The women had dressed Mammi in burial clothes and laid her out in the front room. One had stopped all of the clocks in the house at the early morning hour they assumed Bertha had died. They would be restarted after the burial.

Bess walked slowly into the front room. Mammi didn't look like Mammi, she thought as she stood next to her grandmother's still body, lying on the dining room table. Jonah came up behind her and put his hands on her shoulders.

"She's really gone," Bess whispered. "You can tell. Whatever it was that made her Mammi is gone."

"Gone from us, but gone to God," Jonah told her.

At first, Boomer seemed to be in everyone's way, all the time. Bess knew he was looking for Mammi, and it nearly broke her heart. She knew what he was thinking: almost everyone else in Stoney Ridge seemed to be in and out of Rose Hill Farm, doing errands of kindness, but there was no sign of his mistress.

Later that day, Boomer went missing. Bess called for him and put food and water out on the porch, hoping he would return. He seemed to have disappeared.

It was a muggy, rainy day when Bertha Riehl was buried, three days after she passed. Jonah and Bess stood by Bertha's graveside and viewed her for the last time in the large, plain pine coffin.

Jonah stood looking down at his mother. Her face was relaxed and serene, but Bess was right—whatever it was that made her Bertha—her soul? her pneuma?—it was gone. *Our bodies are just a shell, a house, for our eternal souls.*

How differently he would have done things if he'd known his mother was slated for death this summer. How much time he had wasted. He felt moved with a deep grief for the years lost between them. And yet, on its heels came a quiet joy. Coming back to Stoney Ridge last week had been no accident. He and his mother, in the end, they made their peace. Just in time.

He saw Billy lean close to Bess and whisper, "Are you okay?"

Bess nodded without looking up. She was calmer than Jonah would have thought possible, considering. His mother would be proud of her.

The lid of the coffin was nailed shut and lowered into the ground; the young men—Billy was one of them—picked up their shovels to heave dirt. When the first loud clump of dirt hit the coffin, Bess broke down with a loud sob. Jonah took a step toward her, but Billy had already handed his shovel to another boy and was at Bess's side. He patted her on the back to comfort her, handed her his handkerchief, then as her weeping grew worse, he steered her by the shoulders to lead her to his buggy.

On the drive back to Rose Hill Farm, Billy couldn't find any good words to ease Bess's sorrow. Several times he almost had the right thing. But always he stopped. He couldn't bear it any longer. He turned the buggy down a side road and pulled the horse to a full stop. "Go ahead, Bess," he said as he put his arms around her. "Cry it all out. I'm here. No one's here to see. Have a good cry."

And so she clung to him and wept and wept until he thought that her body would never stop shaking with the sobs and the grief. He didn't think a body could have so many tears to cry, but maybe girls were made with more tear ducts. It was good, though, to have her finally show some emotion. It worried him to see her tearless. It just didn't seem like Bess.

"It's not that I'm crying for Mammi, Billy," she said between sobs. "I know she's in a better place. And she's with Daadi now. I'm crying for me. What will I do without her?"

Finally, the wave of sorrow subsided and Bess's sobs turned to sniffles. When he thought she seemed all wrung out, with not another tear left to shed, he wiped her face with his sleeve and took her home.

As soon as the house had emptied out that evening, Jonah went outside to get some fresh air. He checked that Frieda had water and alfalfa hay, then lingered in the barn for a while. He swept the floor of rose petals and knocked down a few spiderwebs. He just didn't want to go inside. Sallie would be waiting for him and he couldn't face her. He couldn't deny that she had been a wonderful help these last few days. She seemed to know how to get things done in a matter-of-fact, efficient way.

But all he could think about was how much he wanted to be with Lainey. To talk to her about his mother. About Bess. About Simon. About everything. She had participated in every part of the viewing and the funeral, was accepted by the community as nearly one of them—he noticed that folks weren't switching to

English anymore when she came in a room. And he would be forever grateful for the support she had provided to his Bess.

But Lainey continued to avoid him. He couldn't blame her at all, but he didn't think he could abide much more of it.

Jonah hung up the broom and slid the door open to find Sallie walking toward the barn in the dusk. "Shall we walk awhile?" she asked him.

They headed down the drive to the road without saying a word to each other. The strange thing, he realized, was not that he wasn't talking. It was that Sallie wasn't talking. In fact, now that he thought about it, she hadn't said much at all lately. She was as silent as a Sunday afternoon. Then, with a start, he realized why.

She knew.

"Sallie," he started.

She held up a hand to stop him from continuing. "Tomorrow, Mose and I and the boys, we're heading back to Ohio. School starts soon for my boys and I don't want any trouble with that terrible truant officer. And Mose is awfully worried about the business."

Jonah knew that wasn't true. Mose didn't worry about a thing. Sallie was only being kind.

"Sallie," he started again.

She held up another hand. "I'm sorry, Jonah. I just don't think things are going to work out for us. I need a man who . . ."

Who wants to be married to you? Who wants to be a father to your boys? Or maybe, Jonah thought, cheeks burning, *who isn't in love with someone else?*

". . . who isn't quite as complicated."

Jonah stopped short. A laugh burst out of him, the first laugh in a very long time. It surprised him, that laugh. He felt as if a tremendous burden had lifted. "You're right, Sallie. You deserve someone who isn't as complicated as me." He *was* complicated. He spent fifteen years grieving, then finally fell in love with someone new—a woman who wasn't even Amish. Not yet, anyway.

Sallie smiled at him then, a genuine smile. All was well. As they headed back to Rose Hill Farm, she started to tell him about something cute one of her boys had said today. And she didn't stop talking all the way up the drive. Jonah found that he didn't mind a bit.

11

At Billy and Maggie's urging, Bess went to the youth gathering on Saturday evening, a few days after Mammi had been buried. She wasn't in much of a mood for socializing—though her spirits had risen temporarily after Sallie left for Ohio and she learned that the wedding was off for good. Her father had seemed anxious to have her go out tonight. He said it would do her good to get out of the house. She couldn't deny that she always enjoyed watching Billy play volleyball. He was such a good athlete. He had been so kind and attentive to her this last week. It made the upheaval of the last week more bearable. She still struggled with the reality of Mammi's passing, and she missed her dearly. She kept repeating to herself Lainey's reminder: her grandmother's life was complete. This was God's time to call Mammi home.

Bess sat on a rock in the shade by herself, content to be left alone, half paying attention to the game until it came to an abrupt halt. Billy held the ball in his hands, as if frozen. His eyes were glued on a buggy that had just pulled into the yard. Bess's gaze shifted from Billy to the buggy. A clump of girls had arrived and spilled out of the buggy, one by one. The last girl climbed out, scanned the yard, then flashed a dazzling smile when her eyes rested on Billy. It was an awful, heart-stopping moment for Bess as she recognized Betsy Mast, looking fresh and lovely in a pink dress.

Billy dropped the ball and made his way over to Betsy. His back was to Bess and she couldn't imagine what he was saying to her, but she could see Betsy's face clearly. Betsy's eyes sparkled as she laughed and joked with him. Bess's heart sank.

Everyone at the youth gathering learned about Betsy's return in record time, though what they heard bore little relation to the facts. Maggie said that the English boy had refused to marry Betsy and dumped her back at her parents' farm. Andy heard that Betsy tired of the English life and wanted to return to her Amish roots. Someone else said that Betsy heard Billy Lapp had made clear his feelings for Bess at her grandmother's funeral— and hightailed it back to stake her claim on him.

Bess spent the rest of the evening doing her very best to appear at ease, but she kept one eye on Billy and Betsy. At first, she noticed that Betsy was her usual flirtatious self, tilting her head, looking up at Billy from the corner of her eyes, playfully striking him in mock punishment for something he said. As the sun went down, they stood off by themselves. Betsy became serious, speaking to him insistently while he seemed to protest innocence. They both looked at Bess, and she guessed they were talking about her.

Was that good? she wondered. *Probably not.*

Betsy could see that Billy's mind was on other things. They were in his buggy after the youth gathering, parked by the shoreline of Blue Lake Pond. Andy had offered to take Maggie and Bess home, and he was grateful for it. Billy needed time to talk to Betsy alone. His mind was darting in a hundred different directions, like a moth to a flame. Betsy shifted a little closer to him on the buggy seat as she tried to explain again why she had left suddenly and why she had returned.

"What about that English fellow?" he asked her. He'd asked her twice before, but she kept changing the subject, turning it around to accuse him of flirting with Bess.

"You're not going to listen to rumors, are you?" She sidled a little closer to him. "He just gave me a ride to see a friend." She put a hand on his forearm. "I needed to see the other side, Billy. Just to see, before bending at the knee. You understand, don't you?"

She batted her long eyelashes at him, and he knew he couldn't stay mad for long. She really was a beautiful girl. He saw her familiar features as if for the first time, and he was enchanted again by her sparkling green eyes, her dainty nose, and the determined set of her jaw. Her mouth, he realized, did not quite fit the rest of her face: those lips were too full. It was a mouth made for kissing, and the thought that he might never kiss it again filled him with despair.

Maybe he could understand why she left, after all. Everybody had doubts. Wasn't it better to work that all through before getting baptized? That was what the ministers had told him before he was baptized. Better to not take the vow than to take it and break it. "So are you planning, then, to join the church this fall?"

Betsy was looking up at Billy with her red lips in a big *O* of surprise. "Why do you ask, Billy?" Then she leaned up against him and put her lips on his and he felt his mind start to spin. Kissing Betsy always had that effect on him.

Later, after he dropped her at home and was driving the buggy back to his farm, he realized that she had answered his question with a question and given him no answer at all.

As soon as Bess had left with Billy and Maggie to go to the youth gathering, Jonah hurried to Lainey's cottage. Yesterday, he had said goodbye to Sallie and her boys and Mose, and he wanted to be the one to tell Lainey the news of their departure, before Bess had a chance to tell her at church tomorrow. He found her in the backyard of her cottage, trying to turn sod over with a shovel.

"What are you doing?" he asked.

She looked up, surprised to see him, and wiped her forehead with her sleeve. "Making a space for a vegetable garden." Then she turned her attention back to the sod.

It was hard work, what she was doing. But that wouldn't stop Lainey, he realized as he watched her huff and puff. If she made up her mind to do something, she would see it through.

"Maybe I could help," he offered.

She gave him a sideways glance. "No, thank you." Her tone was crisp.

He came closer and put a hand on the shovel's handle. "The place you've chosen gets too much afternoon shade. A vegetable garden needs at least six hours of sunlight a day." He scanned the yard. "Over there, away from the cottage, would be better."

She blew air out of her mouth, exasperated. "You're right."

She released her grip on the shovel and sat down on the porch steps. He set the shovel against the house and sat down next to her.

"I'll dig the sod for you. This week. Right now, even."

"I can get Billy to do it. You've got your . . . houseguests . . . to tend to."

He glanced at her. "Lainey, she . . . they . . . they're gone. Sallie and Mose and her boys . . . they went back to Ohio." He dropped his cane, leaned back against his elbows, and stretched out his legs, crossing one ankle over the other. "Autumn is coming, and Sallie's boys need to start school and Mose needs to tend the business. I need to stay here and see to my mother's estate." He lifted his head. "Sallie and I . . . we had a talk the other night. There isn't any Understanding between us . . . not anymore."

Lainey stared at her balled fists in her lap.

"It's for the best," Jonah continued, his voice steady and strong. "We have different . . . ideas of marriage. We want different . . ." We want different people, he wanted to say, but he didn't finish the sentence. He glanced at her between sentences, wondering what she was thinking. Unlike Bess, whose every thought revealed itself on her face, Lainey was hard to read. She was cautious and careful about her feelings. He watched her intently, waiting for a response.

Lainey lifted her head and looked at the area Jonah had pointed out as a good spot for a vegetable garden. "Maybe . . . maybe that might be a better spot for the garden."

"It's important to start with the right spot," Jonah added with a smile, not at all sure they were talking about a garden plot. He rose to his feet and reached for the shovel. "The right spot makes all the difference."

He took off his jacket and threw it on the ground, then marked out the space for the garden before he began to dig. Lainey found a spade and worked alongside him, breaking up clumps of grass.

Jonah felt happy and whole for the first time in what felt like forever. The deep calm had been missing before, but not now. Not anymore.

Yesterday afternoon, Lainey had been stunned when Jonah told her that Cheerful Sallie had returned to Ohio. As he spoke, she kept thinking this was a moment when people pinch themselves in case they're dreaming. She kept her hands in a tight ball and pinched the inside of her palms, just to make sure. And it hurt! she found, relieved.

He had dug up a patch of earth for her to make a garden and agreed to stay for dinner in lieu of payment, and soon everything slipped back to normal between them. He stayed after dinner and helped her with dishes, leaving only when he thought Bess might be due in from the gathering. She could tell he didn't want to leave, and knowing that made her heart sing.

And today, Jonah said he wanted to go with her to the hospital to learn about all of the postoperative treatment that Simon's convalescence would require. She was pretty sure Jonah must think she was crazy to take him in, but he didn't say so. Instead, he helped her think through the details she would need for Simon, such as ordering a hospital bed. And then he listened endlessly as she described her plan to start a pie-baking business. She wouldn't be able to work at the bakery anymore because she needed to be available for Simon. Mrs. Stroot crumbled when she had told her this morning that she was quitting the bakery. She crumbled even more when Lainey told her she planned to bake pies from her home.

"You'll run me clean out of business!" Mrs. Stroot had wailed.

"I'd never do that to you, Mrs. Stroot! Never! How could I possibly hurt a person who has been so good to me? I thought I'd only make pies on days when the bakery is closed. I just need enough money to cover the mortgage."

Mrs. Stroot shook her head and wiped her tears. She gave Lainey a satisfied smile. "I have a better idea. I'll buy your pies and sell them here. Fifty-fifty."

They shook on the arrangement, and Lainey had her first customer.

Lainey could hardly wait to tell Jonah about the conversation with Mrs. Stroot. He had barely lighted from the buggy when she rushed to meet him with her news. "She wants me to bake pies for her every week! She said I could vary the fillings by what's in season. And we even talked about down the road. That's what she called it. 'If this works out, Lainey, down the road, we can think about adding your signature cinnamon rolls.'" She looked at him with her black eyebrows raised in delight above her wide blue eyes.

The brackets around Jonah's mouth deepened ever so slightly, and his eyes tightened at the corners. Quietly he said, "Well then, perhaps we should see about getting you an oven."

Her face fell. She hadn't thought about such practicalities. It was so like her, to jump into a lake before she learned to swim. Her enthusiasm for her plans always did carry her away. Of course she would need an oven! And a refrigerator. And a stove top. Her kitchen was sparse, only a table and two chairs, provided by Bertha. "I'll have to go to Lancaster for that."

Jonah tilted his head. "Are you thinking you'll use electricity? The cottage isn't set up." Then his gaze shifted beyond her.

She knew what was behind that question. She had planned to be baptized this fall, but that had to be postponed because of Simon. If she were baptized, she would have to shun Simon. She would wait.

Jonah had never asked her about joining the church. She was getting to know him well enough to know that he was watching and waiting, letting time provide the answer. "No. Not electricity. Bess has been teaching me how to cook on a propane stove top. And how to use a woodstove too."

Jonah looked back at her. "You could get those things, used, at an auction."

She nodded. "Then I'll go to an auction."

Jonah stifled a patronizing smile. "Make out a list and I'll get what you need."

"I can take care of these things." *I can take care of myself*, was what she meant.

Jonah gave a short laugh. "Might be a little hard to purchase items at an Amish auction, Lainey. You don't speak Deitsch."

Now her spine stiffened. "I'm learning." But she was a long, long way from being fluent.

He walked up to her. "I'm offering to help. Would it be so hard to accept it?" He searched her eyes.

Yes, she thought, suddenly shy. *More than you could imagine.* She'd always had a hard time accepting help from others. Depending on others. Trusting others.

But she was trying to get past that obstacle. It was part of what she was learning this summer. How could she become Amish if she didn't learn how to rely on her community? It would be like missing the forest for the trees.

She wiped her hand on her apron and held it out to him to shake. "Then I accept your help."

Jonah looked at her extended hand, then took her hand in his. They remained that way for only the briefest moment, touching palm to palm; she was the one to pull away.

She gave him a shy smile. "Thank you."

226

Dear Robin and Ally,

Isn't the start of autumn wonderful? The air is getting crisp in the morning and evening, and apples are falling off the trees! Don't you just love autumn?

So . . . perhaps there is a man of interest in Lancaster County after all.

Love,

Lainey

P.S. By the way, did I happen to mention that I'm becoming Amish?

Jonah took the time to find out what the state requirements would be to get permits and a license for a commercial kitchen. Then he drove a wagon to an auction and purchased a used propane refrigerator and stovetop oven, delivered them to Lainey's cottage one hazy and humid September afternoon, and hooked them up for her. The sky had begun to cloud over and the kitchen grew dim, so Lainey held a lamp over his head while he worked. She studied his face in the shifting light of the flame. Once, he caught her eye and smiled. She considered how attractive he was—the type of man who was clearly comfortable in his own skin and had grown up unaffected by his good looks.

When he finished, he stood and turned on the gas to the stove. When she saw the pilot light fire up, she clapped her hands together and said, "How can I ever thank you?"

Jonah looked down at her. He was quite a bit taller than she was. "I should be thanking you, Lainey."

She wanted to ask why but could see he had something on his mind. He seemed to be carefully arranging his thoughts, so she remained quiet.

"There's something I've been meaning to tell you. The night of that accident, when you stayed by the buggy until the ambulance arrived. You kept saying not to give up . . ." He swallowed hard. "I remember. I remember hearing your voice and I held on to those words. They helped me stay alive." His eyes became glassy with tears and he wiped them away with a laugh. "I can't stop tearing up this summer. It's like I'm shedding a lifetime of bottled tears."

They locked eyes for a long moment, then she leaned toward him. She stroked his face softly. He caught her hand and held it to his lips. He kissed it with his head bent over it so that she couldn't see his eyes.

A month had passed since Simon's bone marrow transplant. Jonah and Lainey were seated in hard plastic chairs in an office as a nurse explained what to expect after Simon was discharged. His blood counts were returning to safe levels, the nurse said.

"Does that mean the bone marrow transplant worked?" Jonah asked.

"The transplanted marrow seems to be engrafting," the nurse said. "We're cautiously optimistic. But I have to warn you that recovery can be like a roller-coaster ride. The patient may be irritable and unpleasant with the caregiver. Helplessness is also a common feeling among bone marrow transplant patients, which can breed further feelings of anger or resentment."

"Even more than usual?" Lainey asked.

"One day a patient may feel much better, only to awake the next day feeling as sick as ever." She gave Lainey a bright smile. "So if his daily blood samples continue to show that he's producing normal red blood cells, he can go home by the end of this week."

"So soon?" Lainey asked in a dull, polite way.

"By the end of this week," the nurse repeated cheerfully.

Jonah had a funny feeling the staff was eager to have Simon leave.

"In the first several weeks," the nurse continued, "he'll be weak and tired and will want to sleep and rest frequently. He'll need to return to the hospital for frequent follow-up visits for medication, blood transfusions, and monitoring."

"And then?" Jonah asked. "How long until he can take care of himself?"

"Recovery from a bone marrow transplant is lengthy and can take up to six months to resume normal activities, including returning to full-time work."

Jonah and Lainey exchanged a look of shock. Six months!

"During the first three months after the transplant, he'll be vulnerable to complications due to the fact that his white blood cell counts will be very low and incapable of providing normal protection against everyday viruses and bacteria. So he'll have to avoid crowded public places such as movie theatres and grocery stores to avoid contact with potential infection." The nurse clapped the file shut. "And he really shouldn't have any friends visiting for a while."

Jonah's eyebrows shot up. "Well, *that* shouldn't be a problem. Simon has no friends."

That made the nurse burst out with a laugh. "Will wonders never cease?"

The first morning after Simon was released from the hospital and moved into Lainey's house, he rang a bell at five in the morning to wake her to help him find the bathroom. At six, he rang it again for coffee. At seven, he complained that the eggs she had scrambled for him were cold.

Bess came by in the early afternoon to see if Lainey needed any help. Stoney Ridge was experiencing an Indian summer, and it was too hot to pick rose blooms. Jonah wanted to keep the rose petal harvest going, though he still hadn't decided what to do about Rose Hill Farm or their home in Ohio, either. The roses were in their second bloom, and they had to work quickly in this heat to get those roses picked and dried. Lainey smiled to see the Band-Aids covering Bess's hands.

Lainey made Simon lunch, went back to the kitchen to clean up, only to have Simon ring the bell again. "I don't like crust on my sandwiches," he complained to her. "I don't like crunchy peanut butter, only smooth. I asked for a Coke, not milk. Do you think I'm a six-year-old?"

Lainey took his plate back to the kitchen and cut the crust off of his sandwich, then took it back to him with a Coke.

Bess sat in the front room and watched this ongoing interaction. The third time Simon rang the bell to complain, Bess stood abruptly and held a hand in the air to stop Lainey from taking his plate back to the kitchen. "So, you don't like your lunch?" Bess's voice was dangerously calm.

"Dang right I don't like that lunch. Didn't like breakfast, neither." Simon turned to Lainey. "And I didn't like the coffee. I told you I want it strong."

Bess picked up the bell, walked to the door, opened it, threw the bell outside, and closed the door.

Simon did not make any further comments through the rest of lunch. He didn't thank Lainey for it, but he didn't complain about it, either.

For the next few hours, Bess helped Lainey roll out pie crusts in the kitchen, and they talked quietly to each other as they worked, while Simon rested. Finally, sounding hurt that he was being left out of the conversation, Simon called to them to ask what kind of pies they were baking. Bess had just taken a pie out of the oven and stood at the door, holding it in her hands with hot mitts. "Apple and pumpkin."

Lainey pulled out a rack for Bess to set the pies on and asked Simon what his favorite pie was.

He scowled at her. "I only like two kinds of pie: hot and cold."

Bess and Lainey laughed at that, genuinely laughed, and Simon's mournful, hound-dog face brightened a bit.

Not much later, Lainey and Bess were cleaning up the mess they'd made in the kitchen when an ear-busting woof came from the front of the cottage. Bess dropped the wet dishrag and hurried to open the front door.

"Don't open that door!" Simon hollered from his bed. "We're getting bombed!"

"That's no bomb! That's Boomer!" Bess said, clapping her hands in delight. She threw open the door and in charged Boomer, looking a little thinner and smelling pretty bad. He jumped up on Bess, then Lainey, then put his dirty front paws on Simon's bed.

"Get that mutt out of here," Simon yelled. "He smells like he was on the wrong end of a fight with a polecat!"

"This is Mammi's dog, Simon," Bess said. "His name is Boomer. He's been out mourning for Mammi. But now he's back. We'll give him a bath and he'll be as good as new."

"Fat chance of that," Simon muttered.

"If you wouldn't mind keeping Simon company for a few minutes," Lainey told Bess after they gave Boomer a bath, "I've got some laundry hanging that I need to take down." She picked up an empty laundry basket and went to the backyard. Having a house of one's own took getting used to, Lainey had quickly realized. There was always some little thing to be done. It wasn't a big house, but there were plenty of chores.

She took her time taking the dry clothes off the line. Hanging laundry was something she found she enjoyed doing. Pinning clothes up and letting the sun permeate them with its warmth was so much better than sitting in a dark Laundromat guarding a machine. Bess had told her once that working is a form of prayer. At first, Lainey had trouble understanding that. But now, she could see it. She thought it meant the kind of work that came from caring for others.

When Lainey came back inside, she found Bess helping Simon drink from a glass of water. It was touching to see Bess, this child who had grown up with another life and another father, reaching out to this man. When Bess tossed that bell out the front door, it was like Lainey was watching some other girl entirely. Bess was so confident and clear about how to handle Simon. She handled him better than Lainey ever did. In fact, it just occurred to Lainey, she handled him the way Bertha used to. Bertha never stood for any of Simon's bluster.

Lainey tiptoed to the bedroom to fold the clothes. When she came back out, she found Simon had drifted off, and Bess was curled up in a corner of the couch, sound asleep. Boomer was on the foot of Simon's bed, snoring.

Later that week, Bess stood on the porch at Rose Hill Farm and waved goodbye to Andy Yoder after he had dropped off a bushel of ripe apples from his family's orchard. Before turning

232

onto the road, Andy looked back and yanked off his straw hat. He stood on the wagon seat, holding the horse's reins in one hand, waving his hat in a big arc with the other.

The thing about Andy Yoder, Bess was finding, was that you just couldn't put him off. He was cheerful and funny and full of life, and totally convinced that she loved him. Which of course she didn't. It wasn't that she was immune to Andy's charms; it felt nice to be admired. He told her today that he thought she looked like an angel: smooth skin with large, bright eyes and a mouth shaped like a bow. He stared at her mouth when he said it, and it made her stomach do a flip-flop. Andy was like that: chock-full of sweet words and lingering gazes and always willing to share every thought.

But as fun as Andy was, Bess knew her heart belonged to Billy. Each day, they worked in the rose fields or in the greenhouse and talked about all kinds of things. Conversation was so easy between them, even their good-natured arguments. Sometimes, when he was in a professorial mood, she couldn't understand half of what he said. Her thoughts often wandered to imagining that this would be their life: the two of them living side by side, day by day, for always.

Esther Swartzentruber told her at church that Billy was spending a lot of time with Betsy Mast, but Bess knew it couldn't be so. Not after that week when she had the surgery and he had kissed her, ever so gently, and had been worried for her. Not after he had comforted her when her grandmother died. Even Mammi had said Billy Lapp was no fool. Surely, Esther was just spreading rumors.

Bess reached down and hoisted the basket of apples onto her hip. Mammi also used to say that a rumor was "something with truth on the trail," and a flicker of fear ran through her.

233

Billy Lapp wiped his brow. He had worked a few hours at Rose Hill Farm, teaching Jonah about Bertha's rose business, then spent another hour replacing shingles on Lainey O'Toole's roof. He still needed to get home and help his brothers with the oat shocks. Threshing day was tomorrow, and they needed to knock the shocks down to ready the rows for pitching. Billy had done some research to calculate the best time to harvest the oats. He'd recommended this week to schedule their farm for the community's threshing rotation, and for the first time ever, his father had listened to him. The weather cooperated, and this oat harvest looked to be one of the best they'd had in years. Just this morning, his father was discussing tomorrow's pitching and had given him a nod of approval in front of everyone. That was no small thing.

Billy hopped down from the roof and packed up his tools. Then he told Lainey he was heading home, and she handed him a slab of blueberry peach pie she had just pulled from the oven. It was a recipe of her mother's, she said, and she was trying to improve it.

Billy looked up at the sky and was relieved to see the clouds didn't look as threatening as they had an hour ago. If they worked fast, they might be able to get the north field finished before it got too dark. And wouldn't his dad be pleased with that?

He took a bite of Lainey's blueberry peach pie, then another. It was delicious, that pie. It struck him that Bertha had done the same thing with her roses: took something old and made it new. Maybe that's what life was all about—taking the lot you were given and making it better, he thought, finishing off the rest of that pie slab in two bites as he hurried down the road.

The nurse had been right about the roller coaster of emotions Simon would experience, yet that was nothing new to anyone who had dealings with him. At times, Lainey could see that he was making an effort to be pleasant. Or at least, not unpleasant. And then, hours later, it was as if he used up all of the niceness he had, which wasn't in great supply to begin with. He would slip back to constant complaining, mostly about her cooking. Lainey could brush off most of Simon's insults but not those about her cooking. That area was off-limits. She told him that he was welcome to cook for himself.

He gave her a hard look. "You're in no position to be giving me lectures."

There was a moment's silence.

Lainey thought of what Bess would say. She pulled up a highback chair and sat next to him. "The truth of it is that I am in a position to be giving you a lecture. The way I see it, you have two choices. You can stay here, but only if you stop complaining about every little thing. Or . . ."

He narrowed his eyes.

"Or you are free to leave." Lainey was firm.

She had him there. He had no place to go.

He glared angrily at her. "Women are the devil." He said it at least three times a day.

And yet it was Jonah who had the most difficulty tolerating Simon. He dropped by the cottage often, to help Lainey with house repairs or to take her on an errand to town. But he was cool to Simon and had little patience for him. If Simon dared make a vague complaint against Lainey, Jonah would put up a hand to cut him off. In turn, Simon acted cautious around Jonah, as if he knew not to cross him.

As Simon's health improved, he liked to talk. While Lainey

worked in the kitchen, he would tell her stories about all of the near riches he'd had in his business dealings. Since she was in the other room and working on her pies, she was able to only half listen. But Jonah didn't want to hear the stories, even if he was working on a house repair in another room and Simon was in the front room. He never said a word, but he would quietly get up and go outside.

One afternoon, Lainey followed Jonah outside to the vegetable garden. He had given her some spinach seedlings to get in the ground, but she hadn't had a chance yet. He picked up a hoe and raked a neat furrow. She put a hand on his shoulder and he stopped digging.

"I just can't listen to him, Lainey. This chasing after rainbows and borrowing money from people—never paying anyone back. Simon's spent a lifetime living on the near brink of disaster. It just sickens me to think this would have been the life my Bess would have had."

"But she didn't," Lainey said quietly. "She grew up with you. The life she's had with you is the only life she's ever known."

He finished marking the row. "I can't seem to find a way to tell Bess. I can't see what good would be served if she were to know Simon was her father."

"Is that what you're concerned about? Whether it would be good for Bess to know?"

"I don't want her to be hurt. Or confused."

Lainey sat down on the back step and patted the step in silent invitation for Jonah to sit beside her. He lay the hoe on the ground and sat down. "I'm not sure it's up to us to decide whether truth is good for us or not. Truth is just . . . truth. I guess it's how we respond to it that makes it good or bad."

Jonah looked away. "Lainey, why are you doing this?" He took off his black hat and raked a hand through his hair. "I have an easier time forgiving the truck driver—a stranger—who caused the accident that killed Rebecca and our baby, than I do Simon, for abandoning you and Bess like he did."

Lainey didn't answer for a while. "That truck driver was remorseful. Forgiveness comes a little easier when a person asks to be forgiven."

"Maybe. But that doesn't explain you. You're not even Amish, yet you're able to give Simon something I—who lived my whole life in the Amish church—can't." He turned to her. "Why?"

Lainey lifted her head to the sky. "For a long time, I felt abandoned. And so lonely. I still do, at times. I think it will always be my Achilles heel. But a few years ago, I went to a church service and the pastor happened to be preaching on the difference between divine forgiveness and human forgiveness. I knew I couldn't forgive others without God's help. He said that we fail in the work of grace and love when there is too much of us and not enough of God. That thought stayed with me. Too much of me and not enough of God. Once I understood that and asked for God's help, I was able to forgive Simon and stop condemning him." They sat together there for a long time before Lainey added, "I learned how to love from watching your mother. I know she could scare a body half to death, but a person knew she could fail and still be loved. I think even Simon knew that about your mother. I think that's why he never left Stoney Ridge. She might have been the only person who really loved him."

Jonah tucked his chin. "Rebecca was always frightened by my mother."

Jonah was bringing up Rebecca's name more and more and it made Lainey glad. She wanted him to feel comfortable talking about her. She didn't want him to feel as if he had to forget her.

He glanced at her. "You never were frightened by my mother, were you? Even as a young girl."

"I always knew there was a tender heart inside that gruff exterior."

Lainey smiled at him, and Jonah smiled back at her.

She reached out and jostled his knee. "Listen. Simon's still telling the story."

Sure enough, they could hear Simon's voice through the window, carrying on as if they were still in the kitchen. Jonah gave a short laugh. "Are you seeing much improvement in him? Other than his talking voice is back in working order?"

"Little by little. He's not needing as much sleep. He took a walk to the end of the road yesterday."

Jonah tucked a curl behind her ear and stood to leave. "Good. Maybe there is an end in sight."

And then what? Lainey wondered, watching Jonah head out to the street toward Rose Hill Farm.

Caleb Zook made a point of stopping by to see Simon every Sunday afternoon. Lainey was amazed. Caleb had no responsibility for Simon since he had been shunned. But Jonah said Caleb was like that. He said Caleb had always managed to be sincere about his faith without becoming legalistic. It wasn't that rules were optional to Caleb. She noticed that he didn't entirely ignore Simon's shunning: he didn't sit at their table for a meal with Simon. Once she offered a plate of cookies to the two of them while they were talking in the living room, but Caleb politely turned her down. Jonah told her later that Caleb shouldn't be offered food from the same plate that had been handed to Simon. And Caleb didn't touch Simon, not even a handshake. But he still showed genuine concern and interest in him. He seemed to believe that there was something to redeem in Simon.

All men of God should be like Caleb Zook, Lainey thought more than once.

"Do you really believe Simon can change?" Lainey asked him one Sunday as she walked with him out to his buggy after he had paid a call on Simon. "Or are you just saying that because you're the bishop and that's what you're supposed to think?"

Caleb laughed at her candor. "Simon always was chock-full of brag and fight." He put on his hat. "But, yes, I think he can change if he wants to. God wants all men to come to him."

Lainey wanted to ask him more but waited to see if he was in a hurry to leave. When he didn't get in the buggy right away, she blurted out, "What made Simon the way he is?" It was a question Lainey had often wondered and wished she had asked Bertha. She did ask Jonah once, but he had no idea. As long as he could remember, Simon was just thought of as the black sheep.

Caleb leaned against the buggy, one long leg crossed over the other, his arms crossed against his chest, that black hat still shadowing his face. "I'm not sure there's an easy answer to that question. I don't think there's one event. But I do recall my mother saying that Simon's mother died bringing him into the world, and his father was a hard man to please." He stopped as a thought seemed to come to him. "A little like Billy's father. Always wondered if that might be why Bertha took such an interest in Billy." He stared down the road for a moment, then turned back to Lainey. "Simon was the last child and only boy in a string of females, and life seemed to be a little more difficult for him— learning in school, getting along with others, learning a trade. He grew up being told he couldn't do anything right. Maybe there came a point when he believed it. It became a way of life for him. A habit. Maybe it was easier to just go ahead and disappoint people in advance. Maybe that's how he has felt about God." He unknotted the buggy reins from the fence. "He's softening, though. Little by little. Bertha would say, 'En Baam fallt net uff der eracht Hack.' *One stroke fells not an oak.*"

Lainey frowned. "Bertha also said, 'You can't make good hay from poor grass.'"

Caleb grinned. "Now, now. How could a man be at death's doorstep and not have some change in his heart?"

Lainey was unconvinced. To her, Simon didn't seem capable of change.

Caleb caught the look on her face. "Let me put it another way. Before Simon's body could accept Bess's bone marrow, the doctors had to kill off his own marrow. Only then would his body be able to accept the new marrow, Bess's sacrifice. There's a spiritual part of this. The way I see it, he's a new man. It's just taking awhile to break those old habits, to kill off that old marrow. That old way of life."

That was a new thought to her.

"But," Caleb warned, "it might take time." He shrugged. "No matter. God has plenty of time. It's one thing he's never short of."

Lainey rolled her eyes. "God might have time, but I'm running out of it. Patience too. It's like trying to take care of a bear with a toothache."

Caleb laughed. "Lainey, now that Simon is getting more energy, maybe you should think about putting him to work for you." He climbed into the buggy. "Work does a soul good. Even a tough old codger like Simon."

As she watched his buggy drive down the road, she wondered if what Caleb said could possibly be true. Could Bess's sacrifice to Simon be changing him, inside out?

She heard Simon's voice yelling for her to hurry his dinner. *Fat chance.*

12

*J*onah and Lainey were heading back to the cottage from buying supplies in town. They were on the top of the rise when Rose Hill Farm came into view. This was Lainey's favorite vantage point. She could barely make out the rooftop of her cottage down below, hidden by trees, but it gave her comfort to realize how close their homes were. Suddenly a car honked loudly and careened around the buggy, upsetting the horse so that Jonah pulled quickly over to the side of the road and stopped.

"Dutt's weh?" he asked Lainey. *Does anything hurt?*

"A little scared but not hurt," she said.

He raised his eyebrows. "You understood?"

She lifted her chin. "I understand a lot more than you might think."

He grinned at her. "I'm sure you do." He looked back at the horse. "I haven't known Frieda to rear before."

Lainey looked up the road at the small speck of a black car, now far up the road. "It wasn't Frieda's fault. It was that car's."

Jonah got out of the buggy to calm the horse down. When

they arrived at the cottage, they found that little black car parked out front.

"Oh no," Lainey said, worried. She hopped out of the buggy and hurried inside while Jonah hitched the horse to the fence.

There in the living room were her English friends, Robin and Ally. Simon, looking delighted to be in the company of two young women, was entertaining them with stories.

It was Robin who recognized Lainey first. Robin was not quite beautiful, and certainly not pretty, but men had always been attracted to her. She had a straight nose and a strong jaw, and her green eyes were large and clear. She was not smiling when she saw her friend; in fact, she wore a slight frown. She was studying Lainey, her gaze moving slowly over her prayer cap, her blue Plain dress and white apron, then back up to her starched white cap again. "You look so . . ."

"Plain?" Lainey offered.

"Then it's true," Robin said. "What you wrote to us. We thought you were joking. They've got you in their clutches. It's a cult, just like he said."

"*Who* said such a thing?" Lainey asked.

"Him," Ally answered, pointing to Simon. Ally was round and pleasant looking. There was something friendly and understanding about her face.

Lainey glared at Simon. "Don't listen to him. He's always saying crazy things. Being Amish is not a cult."

"It's a cult of the worst sort!" Simon said. "Seems all sweet and rosy as long as a fellow toes the Amish line. But just put a toe over the line a very little bit and folks will come down on you like a wolf on the fold." He folded his arms across his chest. "If that's not a cult, I don't know what is."

243

Ally was staring out the front window at Jonah, who was looking over the black car. "Who's he?"

"That's her boyfriend!" Simon called out. "He's been bringing twigs and leaves and starting to build a love nest, just like a couple of doves in springtime." He made a sweeping gesture with his hand. "She's getting baptized just so she can throw me out on the streets. Shunning me just like the rest of 'em."

Lainey lifted her palms and looked at Simon. "Why do you say these things?" She had told him once that she would postpone her baptism until he recovered and could live on his own, just to avoid any complications of his shunning. How had he twisted that around?

Robin walked up to the window and stood next to Ally to peer at Jonah. Lainey looked over their shoulders. Seeing him at a distance the way a stranger might see him, she felt a surge of tenderness for him. He was such a fine-looking man.

"Oh sheesh," Robin said. "She's gone off the deep end for sure. It's worse than we thought."

Jonah had a pretty good idea to whom the black car belonged. Lainey had told him about her two English friends she used to live with, that they were good-hearted but ran a little wild. He saw the two of them watching him from the window. He took his time getting the horse some water, stalling, trying to settle his unease. Would Lainey be tempted by her friends to return to the world?

Maybe this was good, he tried telling himself as he emptied the water bucket. Now was the time for Lainey to find out if an Amish life was what she truly wanted. To be sure she was hearing God's guidance correctly. And before his feelings for her were at the point of no return, he had to admit, hoping he hadn't already passed it. Cautiously, he approached the cottage porch.

Lainey met him outside. "My friends are here." She had an uncomfortable look on her face. "They think I've gone crazy."

Jonah looked down at her earnest face and tried to hold back a grin. "Have you?"

Her face relaxed into a smile. "No more than usual."

When she smiled like that, with her full-lipped mouth, it always made Jonah think of kissing her. He was seized by an urge to take her in his arms, but instead he reined in those stray thoughts and said, "Then let them see that. They're here because they care about you. Let them see you're still you."

Lainey nodded and turned to go into the house. She stopped and whirled back around. "I just . . . apologize in advance for anything they say that might be considered . . . offensive."

Jonah gave her a reassuring smile and followed behind her into the house.

Lainey gestured toward Jonah. "Robin, Ally, this is my friend Jonah Riehl."

There was an awkward silence as the two women looked him up and down. Then the taller of the two, the woman whose mouth was pursed tightly—Robin—took a few strides forward to shake his hand. The gesture struck him as insincere; he could see a mocking intelligence in her eyes. He turned to the other woman to shake her hand. Ally had a small, round face on top of a small, round body. The image of a sparrow following behind a raptor flickered through his mind.

"I noticed one of your car tires is nearly flat," Jonah said.

"We've been running on three tires since we hit Lancaster," Robin said, as if it didn't seem to matter.

"If you have a spare, I could change it out for you," he offered.

Robin exchanged a curious glance with Ally. "I thought you Amish folks didn't want anything to do with cars."

Now it was Jonah's turn to exchange a glance with Lainey. "Knowing about something and using it are two different matters." He took off his coat and tossed it on a chair, then rolled up his sleeves and went out to the car.

After Jonah went outside, Ally turned to Lainey. "That sweet old man was just about to rustle something up for us in the kitchen. We're starving!"

Sweet old man? Simon? Lainey heard a curse fly out of the kitchen and hurried in to find Simon in the middle of frying up a loaf of scrapple. He was rubbing butter on his hand. A curl of black smoke was rising up from the frying pan. Lainey grabbed a dishcloth and pulled the heavy cast iron pan off of the burner.

"Scrapple?" she asked Simon as she put his hand under cool water. "Why would you offer scrapple to my friends at this time of day?" She cracked the window open to fan out the smoke.

"They wanted something Penn Dutch," he said, carefully examining his hand.

"Fine," Lainey said, pulling forks out of a drawer. "If that's what they wanted, then that's what they'll get." She had just bought a loaf of scrapple in town because Simon had pestered her to get some for breakfast.

It irked her to see Simon bend over backward, acting as charming as could be toward her two friends. To her, he always sounded quarrelsome, even if he wasn't. Why, he had never even cooked before! She pulled plates from the cupboard and napkins and took them to the table. By the time she got everyone something to drink, Jonah had returned from changing the tire. He took one look at the burnt scrapple and said he should be leaving.

"Please, Jonah. Don't go. Sit down and visit." She wanted him to get to know her friends and for them to get to know him. Plus, Simon was on better behavior when Jonah was around. She pointed to the place she had set for him at the table.

Too late, Lainey remembered that Jonah couldn't sit at the same table with Simon. He hesitated, an uncomfortable look passed over his face, until she jumped up and offered him a glass of iced tea. Then, instead of sitting down, she nonchalantly leaned against the kitchen counter and he followed her lead. She had seen Caleb do the same thing once. Still respecting the rules of the church, but without making a scene or being rude to others.

Jonah took a sip of iced tea. "So, what is it you two do in Harrisburg?"

"We're cosmetologists," Ally said.

"They study the stars," Simon said to Jonah, thumping the bottom of the ketchup bottle over his plate.

Robin snorted and Lainey exchanged an amused glance with Jonah. "That would be cosmology," Lainey whispered to Simon.

"Same thing," Simon said.

"Not hardly," Robin said. "We work at a beauty salon."

"Ha!" Simon said. "It is the same thing. You're turning coal into diamonds!" He grinned at his own joke.

For some reason, it irritated Lainey even more that Simon could laugh off Robin's correction. If she had corrected him, he would have barked at her.

Ally poked carefully at the scrapple with her fork. "What's in this?"

"Offal," Simon said, sawing a piece of scrapple with his fork. Ally looked up. "Awful?"

"Yup," Simon said. "Hog offal. Heads, heart, liver, and other scraps. All mixed together with cornmeal and flour." He took a bite and chewed it. "Guess that's why they call it scrapple."

Robin made a face. "It sounds awful!"

"Yup," Simon said. "That's what I've been telling you. Offal."

Lainey gave a sideways glance with a smile to Jonah, and Jonah smiled back at her. An intimacy passed between them that shut everybody else out. It only lasted a moment, but no one at the table missed it.

After Jonah left, Lainey showed Robin and Ally upstairs to the spare bedroom. She felt as if she should brace herself, now that they were alone.

"Why, this room is as bare looking as the downstairs!" Robin said, walking into it. There were two twin beds covered with handmade quilts, and a simple nightstand between them. No curtains on the windows, no rugs on the floor, no pictures or posters on the wall. It was a Plain room.

Lainey looked around the room as Robin and Ally did, then her gaze came back to her friends. As they stared at each other, the air seemed to acquire a prickly tension but the silence dragged out.

Finally Robin let out an exaggerated sigh. "You can't actually be thinking of wanting to marry that simple farmer, can you?" she asked, flopping on the twin bed. "Why, he even smells like a farm!"

Lainey liked the way Jonah smelled—of hard-work sweat. It blended with the other scents of summer, of sweet clover and mown hay. He had spent the morning helping a neighbor thresh in his fields.

"Simon told us that Jonah's house doesn't have toilets," Ally said, eyes as big as saucers. "Or running water."

Lainey winced. "Rose Hill Farm belonged to his mother and she died recently. He's installing indoor plumbing right now." It was the very first project Jonah started work on after his mother had passed, and Bess couldn't have been happier.

Ally sat down on the other bed. "Has he told you he loves you?"

"Not in so many words," Lainey said, handing them towels. "The Amish don't use terms of endearment the way we—you—do. They show how they feel about someone by example." Like the time Jonah cut a cord of wood for her and stacked it neatly into a pile by her front door. She thought of him preparing the vegetable garden for her, then helping her to plant. Or accompanying her on medical appointments for Simon. Even changing her friends' tire today, without being given a word of thanks. Were those things not evidence of love? She knew her thoughts showed on her face, and her cheeks grew warm. "Jonah Riehl will make someone a fine husband," she added. She wasn't sure why she felt as if she needed to defend him.

"Oh, will he really?" Robin asked in mock amazement. "I'll grant you this . . . if he shaved off that beard and took a shower and got a haircut and wore a T-shirt and blue jeans, he could be a looker. But what about that cane? And his limp? How old is this guy, anyway?"

"Not old at all," Lainey said in a crisp tone. She thought Jonah was quite marvelous just the way he was: wise and kind and wonderful.

Robin stood and pointed a finger at Lainey. "And you? You

always told us you weren't the marrying kind. Not Lainey O'Toole!"

Robin's words rankled Lainey. It was true, she had said many times marriage wasn't for her. Hadn't she thought this whole thing through a hundred thousand times before? But that was before she met Jonah and grew to care for him. It was a frightening thing—to realize that you wanted to love and be loved more than you could have ever imagined.

"Do you actually think he's going to marry you?" Ally asked. "Wouldn't he be driven off for marrying someone out of his commune?"

Lainey stiffened. "No one ever said anything about getting married." That was the truth. Jonah had never hinted at marriage in any way, shape, or form. He seemed to carefully avoid any discussion of their future. She didn't know if he was planning to return to Ohio or stay here in Stoney Ridge. All she knew for sure was that Sallie Stutzman had married his business partner, Mose, and he didn't seem bothered by the news. Lainey often wondered if Jonah even thought about marrying her at all; she thought about it all the time. "And the Amish do not live in communes. Nor is it a cult."

"But what about culinary school?" Ally asked. "You scrimped and saved for years! It was your dream!"

Lainey shrugged. "I've learned more about cooking in the last few months here than I ever could in a formal school. Here, food means more than nourishing a body. Sharing a meal nourishes a community. It's like women are feeding a big family."

"That's another thing Simon told us about," Ally said. "Amish women are oppressed. They're always serving the men and the men are controlling and mean-spirited. The women can't speak their mind and they have to do whatever their husband tells them to and they have no self-esteem and they have at least a dozen babies—"

"And you ... Miss Independent!" Robin interrupted. "How many times have you given us a lecture about respecting ourselves and not falling in love with every guy that looks our way? About how we should have goals and plans? And how a man would only derail our dreams?"

Ally nodded in silent agreement.

Robin lifted her hands in the air. "But along comes a guy in a beard and a buggy—who walks with a cane and has a teen-aged daughter, no less—and Lainey falls for him, hook, line, and sinker." She looked back at Ally as if to say "what is the world coming to?" then turned to face Lainey. "Well, honey, if you're not derailed, I don't know what is."

Lainey sat down on the bed. "Listen, you two. I'm *going* to become Amish. Not *because* of Jonah. This has nothing to do with Jonah."

Robin and Ally exchanged a doubtful glance.

"I'm becoming Amish because that's what I think God wants me to do." Once she said it aloud, she realized that was exactly what it was. She truly believed God was leading her in this direction.

Robin put her hands on her temples, as if she had a headache. "I'd like to think your bonnet is on too tight, but you always did go a little overboard with the God stuff. I never imagined you'd go this far."

Stung, Lainey felt no need to reply. Without a word, she rose to leave and went downstairs to start dinner. Still upset, she decided to go sit on the porch steps for a few minutes of solitude and watch the sunset. Why did it seem that when a person really started listening to God, others assumed that person had gone off the deep end? Maybe because God does lead us into unusual places. She looked up at the streaks of red that blazed out from the dying sun. What was it Jonah said? Red sky at night is a farmer's delight. Red sky at morning, a farmer takes warning.

The wind unfurled strands of her loosely pinned hair and pressed her dress to her legs. She smoothed out the apron over the blue dress Bess had made for her. Maybe she shouldn't be so hard on Robin and Ally for their concern. If someone had told her six months ago that she'd be dressing in simple garb and living a Plain life, falling in love with a Plain man, making a life in Stoney Ridge, she would have laughed out loud.

But she was here and so very glad to be . . . where life was simple, where people cared for each others' needs, where faith in God and life blended together as one. This was where she belonged.

She noticed the first star appear on the horizon. Looking up at the bruised blue of the evening sky for a few minutes—at the vast and empty sky—always cut human problems down to size. A short laugh burst out of her as she rose to her feet. *Maybe it is a little crazy.* But it was a crazy that suited her.

All through dinner and into the evening, Robin and Ally tried to convince Lainey to return to Harrisburg with them, but she wouldn't budge. She tried to explain her feelings, but they couldn't see her point of view.

"Can't you just be happy for me?" Lainey asked them at last. "I'm still me. I might be wearing a Plain dress and living without modern conveniences—"

"I'll say," Robin interrupted with a sneer.

"—but I'm really, truly happy." Lainey could tell that they still didn't believe her, and it hurt her. The three of them had been friends since high school; Robin and Ally were the closest thing to a family that she'd ever had. The way they looked at her—especially Robin, but Ally always followed Robin's lead—was almost as if she had to choose one or the other, the Amish life or her old friends. Why did it have to be that way?

She would have thought it to be the other way around, that Jonah might frown on her English friends. She knew there were some Amish who avoided the English as much as possible, as if they might be corroded by worldly rust. Jonah didn't seem to share that belief. As he left her cottage yesterday afternoon, he had quietly suggested to her that she might bring them to Rose Hill Farm tomorrow afternoon. He said he wanted them to meet Bess.

On Sunday morning, Lainey tiptoed into their room at seven to ask if they would join her for church. She thought that maybe, if they could see the gathering for themselves, if they could see the kindness and the sincerity of the people, then they would understand why she felt so drawn to this community. If they could only see what a wonderful father Jonah was to Bess, then maybe they could see why she cared for him. And if they could meet Bess, they would understand why Lainey wanted to be close to her. She wanted Robin and Ally to come to her church because it was becoming so much a part of her, the backbone of her life.

Robin opened one eye and said emphatically, "No. Way."

Bess couldn't wait to meet Lainey's English friends. Her father had told her what he knew about them, but it wasn't much. Lainey had mentioned their names to Bess once or twice, but then she would change the subject, as if she just wasn't sure how to combine her past with her present. Bess was curious about them. She knew they were important to Lainey, and she was eager to know everything she could about her. Lainey fascinated Bess.

After a light lunch that followed church, Bess, Jonah, and Lainey returned to the cottage. As Jonah hitched the horse's reins to the fence post, they heard Simon singing. It sounded slurry and strange and off-key. And loud. Very, very loud. Jonah motioned for the two to stay put while he went inside. He opened the door carefully, then pushed it wide.

He looked back at Lainey with a look of sheer disgust. "Er is gsoffe." *He is drunk.* Jonah's patience for Simon hung by a thread.

Lainey and Bess went to the door. A near empty bottle of an amber-colored liquid was on the floor and Simon was sprawled on the couch, singing at the top of his lungs. The smell of alcohol oozed from him, sour as old sweat. His eyes shone too brightly.

Lainey stomped over to him and picked up the bottle. "Where did you get this?"

Simon's chest heaved as he drew in a ragged breath. "Don't even think about sharing," he said, slurring his sibilants.

"Your English friends is my guess," Jonah said. He took the bottle from Lainey and poured it out on the grass.

"Did Robin and Ally give that to you?" Lainey asked.

"They . . . might have . . . left it behind," Simon said. "They went into town to get a new tire, then came back and waited for you, but you took too long. They had to get to Philly by nightfall for a rock concert. Said to say goodbye." He waved his hand carelessly in the air.

Silence covered the room. Bess saw the disappointed look on Lainey's face. Jonah saw it too. How could her friends leave like that?

But then Lainey stiffened her spine. "Did you ask them to buy you that booze?" she asked.

"All of you, quit looking down your noses at me!" Simon snapped. "People been looking down their pointy little judgmental noses at me for as long as I can remember. Nobody believes in me! Nobody has ever been in my corner!"

Eventually his voice grew slower, his hand movements less exaggerated. His arms fell to his sides, and soon his head began to hang as if it were a great weight. Then he stopped altogether. His face was white, but he was not going to ask for mercy, or understanding, or a second chance.

Bess felt a surge of pity for him. She took in his thin, greasy hair and his long, white narrow face. There was some sincerity in the way he spoke. If this was his version of his life, then this was his life.

"Very well, then," Lainey said. Something in her tone made them all look at her. "You should leave now, Simon. If that's how you feel, if that's what you think—after all Bertha went through to bring Jonah and Bess here, and after all Bess went through to donate her bone marrow, and after all I've been doing just to get your sorry hide healthy—if that's how you feel, you should leave this afternoon."

It was more decisive even than Bess would have been. She looked at Lainey in admiration. So did Jonah. There was no hate, no revenge in her tone. Just a simple statement of the position. It startled Simon just as much.

Something clicked then. Simon knew she meant it. He looked at them, one by one, as if he had never seen any of them before. Defeated, he retreated.

255

Simon turned a corner after Robin and Ally's visit. He grew noticeably stronger and healthier. He stayed in the spare bedroom now and cheered when the truck drove away with the rented hospital bed. He still napped quite a bit, but his face gained color and he was filling out some.

But Lainey's determination to become Amish felt tangled up after her friends' visit. It was the seeds of doubt about Jonah they had planted that ate at her. They were shocked that he had never said he loved her nor hinted at a life together. Ever since, it had bothered her too.

She knew it was silly to think that words alone would reveal if a man loved a woman. How many times had she mopped up her friends' messes after they had their hearts broken by a man who had professed love? Too many times to count. Words were cheap, she knew that.

But there was a part of her that longed to know how Jonah truly felt about her. Did he care about her the way she cared for him? She knew he had a lot to do to sort out Rose Hill Farm, but she wondered if he was planning to return to Ohio soon. What about his business there?

Would he ever tell her he loved her?

Did he need to?

She felt as if she was staring at a fork in a road. One way of thinking was the English way: that words expressed how a person felt.

The other road was the Amish way: that action took the place of words.

It was her friends' visit that showed her how truly English she was. Becoming Amish was so much more than learning their language and their ways. It was changing how she perceived things, even small things. Things like terms of endearment.

If she felt this way about hearing the words "I love you," how many more things were there that she didn't even understand yet? Like being submissive to a husband. What if a husband made wrong decisions? And Robin was right about one thing: Amish women always served the men first. She'd seen Amish women out in the fields, working side by side with their husbands, but she'd never seen an Amish man in the kitchen. Why did Amish men seem to have a complete pass on domestic duties? And what about her little pie business? She loved to bake. How could she keep her business if she had a dozen babies?

She kept these internal musings to herself, but whenever she was alone, the doubts slipped back, as persistent as a buzzing fly that needed shooing away.

Maybe this path wasn't right for her, after all. Maybe becoming Amish was really impossible for an English person. Maybe it wasn't too late for her to leave and return to her original plan—to attend culinary school.

And have a life of independence. Unencumbered.

Alone.

After Sallie had left for Ohio, Jonah told Bess that they needed to stay for a while to clean out Rose Hill Farm and straighten out Mammi's affairs. Bess was thrilled. She loved Stoney Ridge. She adored Lainey. She was hopelessly in love with Billy. And, to add icing to the cake, it meant she could avoid repeating algebra. But it also meant they had a big job to tackle. Mammi never threw anything away. Each day, Bess and Jonah tried to clean something out—a closet, a desk, a bureau. Bess felt as if she was having an opportunity to peek in on her grandparents' lives. Especially Mammi's. She cherished anything that helped explain her grandmother to her. Mammi seemed the sort who'd never really been young, yet here Bess was, finding letters and notes Mammi had written and received years and years ago.

She missed Mammi more than she could have ever imagined. She hated waking up to the shock of remembering that she was gone. Tears would come to her eyes at unexpected moments during the day, then they would disappear just as quickly. But always, like a shadow, there remained a sharp tug of loss.

Her deepest regret was that she was just starting to understand her grandmother and her unexpected ways . . . and then she was gone. Bess had never lost anyone close to her in such a sudden death. This must have been what her father felt after her mother died in that accident. Like a fresh wound that was slow to heal.

But God's ways were always best. She knew that to be true.

One evening, Jonah had already gone to bed but Bess was wide awake. She decided to brew herself a pot of chamomile tea. Once the kettle boiled, she went out into the garden, mug in hand. There would be a hard frost tonight, the first one of autumn. She drew the cold air into her lungs, and when she breathed out again, her breath hung in the air for a moment in a thin white cloud, quickly gone. The air had a touch of wood smoke in it from somebody's fire. She shivered and turned to go back inside.

Bess decided to finish cleaning one last desk drawer before going to bed. She found an unmarked large envelope and opened it. In it were yellowed newspaper clippings. That struck Bess as strange, because her grandmother didn't read anything but the Amish newspaper, *The Budget*, and these were clippings from the *Stoney Ridge Times*. She picked up the lantern and went to the kitchen table. She laid the clippings out on the table. As she realized what she was reading, she started to tremble. The articles were about the buggy accident that killed her mother. There was even a grainy but gruesome black-and-white picture. She saw the mangled buggy and the horse lying still in the background. She held it up to the light. She could hardly make it out in the background, but an ambulance had its back doors wide open. She touched the picture gently. Was that her mother on the stretcher?

There were other clippings too. Ongoing ones of the trial her father had to testify in against the driver who rammed into the buggy. It touched her deeply to see the quotes her father had made. He was just a young man, only twenty-one years old, newly widowed, with a child to raise. Yet he was quoted with such clarity and rightness. And then there were other clippings—ones that described how stunned the nation was to learn of a man who turned down an insurance settlement. There were pictures of her dad in the article. She could tell he was trying to keep his head down, away from the cameras. No wonder her father had felt the need to leave Stoney Ridge. He was such a private man.

She gathered up the clippings to slip back in the envelope. One small clipping dropped on the floor. She stooped to pick it up and held it by the light. It was a death notice, only one paragraph long, of a newborn baby that had died of sudden infant death syndrome. *Parents: Elaine O'Toole Troyer (deceased) and Simon Troyer. Surviving sibling: Lainey O'Toole.*

She read it again and again, confused. Lainey had never mentioned having a sister. She wondered why Mammi would have kept that clipping. Was it because it was Simon's only child? But why in this envelope? Then she noticed the date. Lainey's baby sister had died the same day as the buggy accident. She slipped the clipping back into the envelope. Tomorrow, she would ask Lainey about it.

13

ainey heard the rumble of thunder in the distance and hurried outside to take the laundry down before the rain began. The air had grown thick and heavy this afternoon, signs of a storm coming. Lightning cracked again, this time much closer. So close her ears hurt. She knew this rainstorm would hit with a fury. She looked up to see Bess hopping over the fence to join her. Under Bess's arm was a large manila envelope.

"What are you doing here in this weather?" Lainey asked her, folding a stiff towel. When Bess didn't answer, she tossed the towel in the laundry basket and turned to face her.

Bess had an odd look on her face. "I was cleaning out Mammi's desk and I found this." She handed Lainey the manila envelope. "Open it."

Lainey sat down on the back steps to the kitchen and opened the envelope. She drew in a quick breath when she read the headlines on the yellowed newspaper clippings. She flipped through the clippings and stopped when she saw the obituary about Colleen. She glanced up in alarm.

Bess pointed to that clipping. "Why would my grandmother have kept that? Why . . . in that very envelope?"

Lainey's heart felt fierce with panic. It was time for Bess to know the truth, she was sure of it. Bertha Riehl had felt the same way. Jonah should have told her long ago. It was time.

But it should be Jonah telling her this truth.

She patted the seat beside her, but Bess shook her head. Lainey bowed her head and was silent for a moment, offered up a silent prayer for God to give her the right words, then she lifted her chin and met Bess with a level gaze. "There's a story I need to tell you. It's about you and me. About Jonah and Rebecca." She told Bess everything, every detail. She kept looking up to see how Bess was taking the news. Bess stood with her arms crossed tightly against her chest, an inscrutable expression of calm on her face. Lainey rose to her feet and reached a hand out to touch her. "Bess, can you tell me what's running through your mind?"

Bess kept her gaze on the fluttering sheets, as if concentrating on how the gusts of the wind lifted them.

"Bess?" Then Lainey heard Simon shouting for her from inside the house. She tried to ignore it, but the calls grew louder and louder. She sighed. "Let me just check on Simon and I'll be right back."

She went inside to discover Simon ranting about a window left open. The wind was giving him a chill, he complained. She slammed the window shut, rolled her eyes at Simon, and went back outside to finish her conversation with Bess.

But when she went back outside, Bess was gone.

Lainey hurried to Rose Hill Farm to tell Jonah that she had told Bess the truth: that Simon was actually Bess's father. She found him feeding hay to Frieda in the barn.

Jonah was stunned. For a long time he said nothing, seem-

261

ing unable to take it in. The rain was coming down harder now and pounded the metal roof like a drum. Then, as the truth of it dawned on him, he looked bewildered. "You told her about Simon?" he asked her.

"She asked me, Jonah. She had a bundle of newspaper clippings that your mother had saved. In it was one about the death of Simon's baby. She asked me specifically if I had any idea why Bertha had saved that clipping."

His face had gone all white and taut. "But why? Why would you tell her?"

Lainey waited a heartbeat before she said, "I wasn't going to lie to her."

"You could have waited."

"For how long, Jonah? When were you ever going to tell her? You've been avoiding this conversation for months!"

"Maybe she didn't *need* to know. Maybe some things are best left alone."

He looked so anguished. She wanted to put her arm around his wide shoulders, to try to console him with her touch. But he seemed suddenly brittle, as if he might break if she were to touch him. She was desperate to give him some kind of comfort, but she didn't know how. What could she say to him in these circumstances? Every phrase that came to mind seemed inadequate.

He turned to face her. "Where did she go? She must be upset."

"I don't know where she went, but she wasn't upset," Lainey said, her voice surprisingly soft. "She really wasn't."

He glared at her. "How could she *not* be upset?"

She folded her arms against her chest. "You underestimate her, Jonah."

"Oh? You think you know Bess so well after just a few months?" Now he was clearly livid. "Then where *is* she?"

That, Lainey couldn't answer.

"In this pouring rain, why isn't she home? Where is my daughter?" He grabbed a bridle and went to Frieda's stall, quickly slipping the bit into the horse's mouth and buckling the buckles. He led her by the reins out of the stall and toward the door. Just as he was about to leave the barn, he turned to Lainey and looked at her with anger in his eyes.

"If something happens to her, Lainey . . . if anything . . ." He shook his head as if to stop himself from saying more, then left.

The rain hit with a fury. It was cold and sharp and falling sideways in the fierce wind. Jonah barely noticed it. When he heard what Lainey had done, he felt such panic grip his chest that for a moment he couldn't breathe. He was furious with Lainey. She had no right!

"Bess is *my* child!" he said aloud. The words tore out of him, from some deep place, some old, long-buried hurt. He had to find Bess and explain. But where could she possibly be? He felt as if the world had become very fragile. Very dangerous.

As he rode the horse past the Lapp farm, it occurred to him that Billy might have an idea where Bess might be. The two had spent hours together this summer and it had given Jonah cause for concern. Bess was too young to be thinking seriously about boys. Then, suddenly, a well of hope bubbled up. Maybe Bess went to Billy to find comfort.

He turned the horse around and galloped toward the Lapp farmhouse.

❧❦

As soon as Billy saw the frantic look on Jonah's face and heard that Bess had gone missing—that she was upset about something—he had a pretty good idea of where she would have gone.

"Give me an hour," he told Jonah. "If I'm not back in an hour—no, give me an hour and a half—then you can go looking. But there's no sense in both of us getting soaked to the skin. I think I know where she is." He grabbed a slicker and went to the barn.

Jonah followed behind him. "Then tell me and I'll go find her."

"It's too hard to find. Trust me, Jonah." Billy saddled up his pony. "You go home in case she returns there." He rode away before Jonah could object.

About a month ago, he and Bess had found an abandoned crow's nest at Blue Lake Pond, high on a ledge but protected from the rain by the branches of a sheltering tree. He knew she was there, as sure as if he could see her. When he got to the lake, he tied the pony's reins to a tree trunk. The wind was lashing through the trees, and the pony shifted its weight from foot to foot, uneasy, but the fury of the rain had eased up. Billy hiked up to the ledge, slipping a few times. There on the ledge, shivering and drenched, was Bess, hugging her knees to her chest. When he called her name, she looked up, startled, and put her fingers to her lips. She pointed to the nest. There was a black crow, staring down at both of them.

"I've been watching her land in that tree. She thinks she owns it, that it's her tree. She takes off and lands again, watching me watching her. That's what crows do. She's living her crow life," she said softly, eyes fixed on the bird.

264

Billy sat down next to her. "Your dad is steaming like a kettle. Said something has upset you."

"I'm not upset."

With a measured glance, he realized she was speaking the truth. She didn't seem at all upset. Wet, cold, and shivering, but she was calm. She had a look on her face that seemed peaceful. Andy always said she looked like an angel, and right now, he was right.

She turned her face to the sky, like a flower, and smiled softly. "Billy, isn't it a wonder? That the crow is here? God made nature so things can get fixed again." She turned to him. "Blue Lake Pond will have birds and fish again."

He'd been so relieved that Bess was where he thought she'd be, he hadn't even given the appearance of the crow a second thought. "Why, you're right." He scanned the lake and heard a woodpecker somewhere, hard at work, hammering a tree. He smiled.

"God does it with people too. Makes it so that they can find their way back to him." She rested her chin on her knees. "You know what I love about looking up at the sky? It helps me to remember that I am so incredibly small and God is so immense." She lifted her face to the sky. "Behind those clouds is an ocean of stars, limitless in its infinity, so large, so large, that any of our problems, even the greatest of them, is a small thing."

Billy wasn't really sure what she was talking about, but the day was dying and they were wet and cold. He knew Jonah was out of his mind with worry. He stood and gave her his hand. "Maybe you can save your philosophizing for home, by a warm fire, in dry clothes."

Jonah had given Billy an hour, like he agreed, but now that hour was up and he was going to find his Bess. He was putting on a rainproof cloak and his black hat when he saw a pony heading up the drive with two figures on its back. He ran out the door and down the porch steps. He could see them now, Billy in front with Bess holding on to him from behind. A powerful wave of relief flooded over him, like the relief that follows the first rainstorm after a long summer drought—swift, complete, overwhelming.

The first thing Jonah did was to wrap Bess in a large towel and make her sit down by the fire.

"I'm sorry to worry you, Dad," she told him, and she saw tears prickle his eyes.

He brought her a cup of hot tea and kept fussing over her as she tried to explain how she felt. She could see he was worried sick. Billy had warned her as he left to return home.

Bess knew she should have been shocked by what Lainey told her today, or at least terribly upset. But instead, she was filled with a strange sense of destiny, as if God had spared her for a reason. She told Jonah she felt blessed, having him for a father, and that only made his eyes water up again.

"It's like the roses, Dad. I'm a branch that's been grafted onto this good tree. Your tree. An Amish tree. And the great root of God sustains us." That thought had come to her while she was sitting on the ledge, and she had rolled it over and over in her mind. She liked how it sounded.

Her father bowed his head. She wished she could make him understand that it was all right. That everything was going to be all right in the end, just like Mammi had said it would be.

She went to him and knelt down by his chair, putting a hand

over his. "Please don't blame Lainey, Dad. She was only telling me the truth." There was something else that occurred to her on that ledge, something wondrous. A wide smile broke over her face. "Dad, do you realize that Lainey is my half sister?"

Lainey knocked tentatively on the door to Rose Hill Farm, unsure of what kind of reception she would get from Jonah. A few hours ago, he had seemed so angry with her, and—from his point of view—she couldn't really blame him. Nor did she agree with him. But she had to know that Bess was home safely.

"Lainey," Jonah said as he opened the door. He put a hand to his forehead. "I was going to come down tonight. Bess is here. She's fine. She's safe."

Lainey exhaled with relief. "Good. I mean, I'm glad she's home." She turned to leave.

"You . . . were right. She wasn't upset. Not upset at all."

She turned and looked at him. "But you didn't believe me."

He looked uncomfortable, but he didn't dispute her. "She's upstairs, changing into dry clothes. Would you come in and wait for her?" His eyes were pleading.

"No. But tell her I stopped by." She saw a hurt look cross his face, and straightaway she wished she had not sounded so curt. All that mattered right now was that Bess was home.

She started to leave, but Jonah touched her arm lightly to stop her. His voice dropped to a whisper. "She said that she felt as if God had a purpose in all of that. By protecting her."

Lainey gave him a direct look. "She's absolutely right."

Jonah took a step closer to her. "Lainey. I'm sorry for doubting your judgment. Your judgment is far better than mine about these matters."

"We can talk about it tomorrow."

"I didn't want to lose Bess."

"You love your daughter." Her voice was flat—without salience. "It's normal to want to hold on tight to those we love."

"Maybe there's such a thing as holding on too tightly." He looked away. "Tonight I wondered if God might be testing me, the way he tested Abraham with Isaac." He folded his arms against his chest. "As if he wants me to figure out if I trust him completely or not."

Lainey softened a little. "It's the worst place to be, half trusting, half not."

He rubbed his forehead. "That's where I've been for the last fifteen years. Stuck right in that very place. The worst place to be. I haven't really been living, I've just been tiptoeing around, trying to avert disaster."

"It doesn't work," Lainey said, quiet but firm. "You just end up missing the life you have." Through the window, she saw Bess come down the kitchen stairs and look around the room for her father. "Go. Talk to her."

Jonah reached out his hands to her. "Come in with me. Let's talk to her together."

Lainey hesitated. Doubts about Jonah had been buzzing around her all afternoon. She shook her head. "No. I'd better get back."

Jonah watched her carefully. Her words and posturing were bold, but only skin deep. As if she was on a precipice. "Lainey, please?" His question, and the gentleness in his voice, disarmed her. He kept his hands extended, waiting for her to take a step toward him. Just waiting.

A silence came between them then. A silence she could feel, for it was thick with words that had never been spoken.

Jonah's face opened for an instant: trust and hope.

She felt a sense of perspective wash over her. This was *Jonah*.

Her Jonah. Jonah wasn't the kind of man Robin and Ally thought him to be—mean-spirited and controlling. Why, in fact, she suddenly realized they were describing a man like Simon! Jonah wasn't like Simon, not at all. Just the opposite. He asked her opinion about things and really wanted to know her thoughts. He helped her set up her pie business. Why had she allowed Robin and Ally to influence what she knew to be true? How could she have let that happen? Her friends said Amish women had no self-esteem. If only they had met Bertha Riehl! Bertha had a stronger self-esteem than anyone she'd ever known. And Bertha was Amish to the core.

Lainey's heart lifted. She knew Jonah's heart—knew it in some fundamental, important way. Yet she'd held herself back from him, not trusting this love that had come so unexpectedly, from such an unexpected source. She looked at him long and hard, tears in her eyes, then reached out and tangled her fingers with his. He tugged on her hands and drew her close. She felt his arms go round her, and they clung to each other as if it were the most natural thing in the world.

On Tuesday evening, Mrs. Stroot dropped by Lainey's cottage with an order for one hundred little six-inch pumpkin pies and seventy nine-inch pecan pies for the Stoney Ridge Veteran's Day Parade, to be delivered on Friday afternoon. Lainey was thrilled and quickly agreed when Mrs. Stroot told her about the order. She needed the money; setting up a home business had cost more than she expected, and her savings account was dwindling rapidly.

The gray light of an autumn dawn was beginning to appear at the window as Lainey sat at the kitchen table the next morning and decided she must have temporarily lost her mind. How could she possibly bake that many pies in such a short amount of time? She was still getting accustomed to a propane stove. Not every pie turned out like the one before. Even with Bess's help, she was facing a daunting task. She sat at the kitchen table, notepad in her hand, and tried to make a list of all of the ingredients she would need. Then she put the pencil down and stared at a point on the ceiling.

"I can't do it," she said to herself. "It's my own fault. I got greedy. I thought I could do it, but I can't."

"Yes, you can," Simon said.

Lainey hadn't even noticed that he had come into the kitchen for coffee and had been watching her. "My pies are too inconsistent. I would need to make double the quantity, just to make sure I have ones to sell."

Simon lifted one shoulder in a careless shrug. "I'd sooner have a slice of your worst pie than anyone else's best."

Lainey's head snapped up. She couldn't believe her ears. Was Simon actually paying her a compliment? She couldn't quite tell.

He looked away, embarrassed. "Keep writing that list. I'll head into town and get the supplies. You better get moving."

Tears came into her eyes. "Simon . . . I don't know what to say . . ."

"Don't say anything or I'll take back my offer," he groused, but he looked pleased.

There followed two of the busiest days Lainey had ever known in her life, and certainly so for Simon. The two of them, plus Bess and even Jonah, rolled out endless mounds of pastry dough, cracked open pecan shells for the nuts until their fingers were stained and blistered, stirred fillings, and sampled the results. The kitchen, in a white fog of flour, had a heavenly scent of vanilla

270

and cloves and pumpkin and blackstrap molasses. The pies were laid out on baking racks, like little works of art. Lainey displayed a streak of perfectionism; only the best would be delivered to Mrs. Stroot. She had to keep sending Simon up to the store for ten-pound bags of sugar and another big can or two of Crisco. He went without complaint, which amazed her. He drove Jonah's horse and buggy as if he'd done it every day of his life. Boomer rode along as shotgun, just the way he had accompanied Bertha. Simon liked to gripe about Boomer, but he whistled for the big dog to come along whenever he was going anywhere.

By Friday morning, Lainey had the pies ready for delivery in pink boxes that Mrs. Stroot had provided. Jonah and Simon, with Boomer shadowing him, took the pies over to the lunch grounds for the parade. Then they came back for the pies that didn't make the cut and delivered those to grateful neighbors.

"She's been working me like a whole pack of bird dogs," Simon groused to Caleb on Sunday afternoon. "She's aiming to put me back in the hospital and kill me for certain." Boomer lay sprawled right by Simon's side.

Lainey was used to him now and paid no attention to his tone of voice. "Don't you lie to the bishop, Simon," Lainey called out from the kitchen. She wiped her hands on her apron and leaned against the doorjamb. "But I will say you've been a big help. I couldn't have done that big order for Mrs. Stroot this week without you."

Simon turned to Caleb. "That's the gospel truth. I saved the day." He stroked Boomer's big head.

Then Simon smiled—for the first time, thought Lainey—and it was not a smile that lasted long. But still, Simon had smiled.

Billy tossed some pebbles up at Bess's window late one evening. He cupped his hands around his mouth and whispered loudly, "Can you come down?"

Bess's heart left the ground and sailed into the night sky. She dressed quickly and hurried downstairs. Maggie had said she was pretty sure he was courting Betsy again, but Bess didn't believe it. Would he be coming to see her now, if he were still interested in Betsy?

She opened the kitchen door as quietly as she could and met him at the bottom of the stairs. She stopped on the last step so she was eye level to him. She couldn't pretend; she was thrilled to see him. But her delight seemed to distress him. A flicker of fear came and went through her, but she dismissed it.

"Oh Bess," he said, taking her hand and holding it to his face.

Bess's intuition rang an alarm. Something was badly wrong, she felt sure, though she did not know what. She looked into his eyes. His face was working with emotion. He was struggling for words. She could almost hear him trying out different words in his head.

"I need to tell you something. I want you to hear it from me first." He swallowed hard. "It's about me. About me and Betsy. We're going to get married. Soon. Betsy doesn't want to wait."

So it was true. Bess said nothing, unable to take it in. She blinked away tears and looked down to hide her confusing emotions. Then one strong feeling broke through: disappointment that felt like a knife wound.

Billy grasped her arms and pulled her close to him. "You know, don't you? That you've meant something special to me?"

He kissed her mouth. It was a new kind of kiss, different from the one he had given her the night before her surgery. It was as if he was determined to remember the moment. She realized, with dismay, that he was thinking this would be their last kiss.

She clung to him, wanting it to go on forever, but all too soon he drew away and turned to go down the drive. Bess stared at him as he walked away, chin to chest, hands jammed in his pockets, beautiful in the moonlight. So this is what it felt like to have your heart break.

When Billy was out of sight, Bess went back to the house, up to her room, closed the door behind her, and lay down on the bed. Her body started to shake with sobs. Once she started to cry, it was hard to stop. She cried because she had lost Billy for good. She cried because life seemed so unfair sometimes. She cried because she missed Mammi. She wanted her grandmother.

Billy walked home from Rose Hill Farm that night feeling lower than any man on earth. He hated hurting Bess like that. Her face looked so trusting, so eager to please, when she first came outside to him tonight. Unfortunately, she looked particularly pretty. Her soft white skin seemed to glow, and the light blue dress she was wearing made her eyes the color of a tropical sea.

Then, after he told her about planning to marry Betsy, her face looked as pained as if he had wounded her. It tugged at his heart, and tears came to his eyes. He had to look away so that she would not see. He wished she would have yelled at him or thrown something at him. The disappointed look on her face cut him to the quick. He had dreaded telling her about him and Betsy. What he truly feared, he realized, was hurting Bess. He could bear her anger; it was her pain he could not face.

She must have heard some gossip about him and Betsy. She

must have noticed how he had been unable to meet her eye the last few weeks. But she seemed shocked by his news. It shamed him, how she always believed the best in him.

Could he be in love with two different girls at the same time? And such different girls. Bess was so full of curiosity, eyes as big as saucers, and her face would light up with excitement over new things. He found himself thinking of her at the oddest moments, when he saw a soaring Cooper's hawk or found a hummingbird's nest with that delicate fir bark lining its cup. He'd never forget how thrilled she was when he brought her the newspaper clipping that the United States Supreme Court agreed to hear the case of *Wisconsin vs. Yoder*. With her face lit up with happiness, she kissed the clipping and declared she was never going to have to step into a school again as long as she lived. He thought it was ironic that she was so glad to be done with school. She was the smartest girl he knew.

But then there was Betsy. He'd been crazy about Betsy for as long as he could remember. Finally, she seemed to be equally as smitten with him. They kissed every chance they got: behind the barn at gatherings, when they met on the road, in the buggy, and—best of all—when he was at her house and her parents went off to bed and they found themselves alone. He thought about kissing her before he dropped off to sleep, and it filled his mind as soon as he woke up. He lived for those moments.

So why did he often feel a painful jumble of anxiety?

He rubbed his hands over his face, exasperated. What was wrong with him? What kind of man was he?

He would have liked to have slowed things down with Betsy, but she seemed insistent to get baptized and married soon. Six months ago, he would've jumped at the chance to hear Betsy Mast say she would marry him. Now, it made his stomach twist up in a tight knot. In fact, it suddenly occurred to him that he hadn't actually *asked* Betsy to marry him. They were necking down by the pond and she started talking about how nice it would be to not have to stop but to wake up in each others' arms every morning. He must have murmured that he agreed because next thing he knew, they had a meeting set up with the bishop. He knew he had to talk to Bess before they spoke to Caleb Zook.

Billy loosened his collar. Lately it felt like it was cutting off his air supply.

Jonah could see that Bess was hurting. She was quiet and pale and her eyes were swollen like she'd been crying. These were the moments when he longed for a wife. Bess needed a mother. He hoped she would talk to Lainey about whatever was bothering her, but Lainey was taking Simon to the hospital today for a checkup. Usually, that meant a long day.

When Billy came by early today to say that he needed to quit working at Rose Hill Farm, Jonah put two and two together and had a pretty good idea about what was troubling Bess. Last week, Lainey had tipped him off that she had seen Billy with a girl in his courting buggy a couple of times lately.

He found Bess in the barn, Boomer by her side, gathering up the dry petals and stuffing them into bags. They sounded like crackly tissue paper as she stuffed. His heart went out to her. Her head was down and her shoulders slumped. He saw a dried tear on her cheek.

"Bess, I need to tell you something."

She kept working, kept her head down.

"There's something I've discovered that you and I have in common." It was never easy for him to say things out of his heart, but there was something he needed to say. "When we love someone, we love them with our whole heart."

She put the bag down and bent down to pat Boomer.

It's funny, he thought, that it's always easier to talk about important matters with our eyes turned away. He let his cane slip to the floor, leaned his hip against the table that held the rose petals, and folded his arms against his chest. "I've learned something this summer. I've learned that I have a tendency to make a person I love too important. They start filling the spot that only God should hold in my life. I did it with Rebecca, and when she passed, I felt that great void for far too long. I've done it with you, and when I found out that Simon was your father, I felt that void again." He chanced a look at her. "The Lord has to keep teaching me the same lesson. To hold on a little more lightly to others and to trust him in a deeper way."

He crossed one boot over the other. "Lainey is a good example for us. She's always depended on God in just the right way." He was a better person for knowing her. Lainey had an ability to make him revise his stiff attitudes—like his attitude about Simon. Or about telling Bess the truth. It was an uncomfortable process, but she was so often right. And he had nearly lost her, that night. He had held himself so close and tight, so afraid to love again after Rebecca died. "When we left to go back to Ohio, Lainey was sorry and she missed us, but she wasn't devastated. She left us in God's care." He looked up at Bess. "And the Lord brought us back here, didn't he?" But he knew that things rarely turned out nice and neatly in this life.

Bess stood and picked up a handful of rose petals, letting them slip through her fingers back onto the table. "I don't think the Lord is going to bring Billy and me back together. He's marrying Betsy Mast."

So *that's* what had happened. Jonah put his large hand over Bess's. He wished he had better words, softer ones. "Then we can trust in God's plan for Billy and Betsy. And trust God has another plan for you. A good plan." ·

With that, Bess dove into his arms. They stood there for a while, with Jonah's chin resting on her head, until Boomer stood abruptly, hackles raised, and let out a huge bark. He tore outside and kept barking as he ran down the drive.

"Someone must be coming," Jonah said. "I'll go see who Boomer is scaring half to death." Before he turned to go, he stroked her cheek with the back of his hand. "Things have a way of turning out in the end."

She gave him a slight smile. "That's what Mammi used to say."

The taxi had dropped Lainey and Simon back at her cottage from the hospital. Lainey was so happy she felt as if she were floating. She made Simon a cup of his favorite tea and told him she would be back soon, that she had an errand. She hurried up the hill to Rose Hill Farm, practically bursting with happiness. She stopped to pet Boomer at the bottom of the hill and when she looked up, there was Jonah. She walked up to him, a smile wreathing her face.

"Simon's well, Jonah. He was given the all clear by the doctors! He still has to be tested every six months, but he can go back to living a normal life . . . whatever normal means for Simon Troyer."

Jonah put his arms around her waist and swung her in the air, laughing. "We can finally make plans!"

"What kind of plans?" she asked him boldly when he set her down. She needed to know.

He took in a deep breath. "Plans to marry, you and me," he said in a voice as dry as toast. "That is, if you're willing to have me."

When she didn't answer, his face grew worried. He suddenly looked so earnest and vulnerable and sincere that any doubts if he loved her evaporated, like steam from a cup of hot tea. In its place swept a feeling of assurance, of safety, of tenderness, and an overwhelming love. The love she felt for him was so strong it burned her every breath.

The next moment she was in his arms and they were kissing. She thought she must be dreaming, but she felt the grip of his strong arms around her, felt the passion and warmth of his kiss. She didn't need to hear him say the words "I love you." She knew.

From the side door of the barn, Bess watched her father with Lainey. She couldn't hear what was being said, but she could tell they were happy. And in love, that was plain to see. Her grandmother had spotted that from the first time they laid eyes on each other.

Boomer came charging back up the hill to join Bess and collapsed by her feet, panting heavily. When Bess saw her father bend down to kiss Lainey, she turned and closed the barn door. She knew when to leave things be. She smiled, though, as she went back to work. Wouldn't Mammi have been pleased by this turn of events?

Caleb Zook said no to Billy and Betsy's engagement. He explained gently that he felt they needed more time, especially after

Betsy's very recent time spent running around. This time next year, if they still felt the same way, then he would be pleased to marry them. After Betsy went through instructions for baptism, of course.

Billy was visibly relieved. He even felt as if his shirt collar wasn't tightening up on him, like he'd been feeling for a few weeks now. He tried to encourage Betsy on the buggy ride home, but she was stunned silent.

When they got to her parents' home, she stayed in the buggy, her eyes on the back end of the horse, and calmly said, "We should elope."

There wasn't much Billy would refuse Betsy, but that was one thing he was firm about. "Oh no. We don't go against the bishop. I don't aim to start a marriage off on the wrong foot." He glanced at her. "To tell you the truth, I agree with Caleb. I always hoped to marry you, Betsy, but I imagined it in a few more years, after I turned twenty-one." He gently stroked her cheek. "We've got our whole lives ahead of us."

She kept her chin tucked to her chest. "My whole life starts now." She turned to him then and gave him a deep, searching look. "You're a very nice boy, Billy. But you're still just a boy." Then she hopped out of the buggy without a word and walked to her house.

He had the strangest feeling that she was saying one thing but trying to tell him something else entirely.

The next week, Betsy Mast left again. Maggie hurried over to Rose Hill Farm to tell Bess the news. She found Bess in the backyard, taking down laundry from the clothesline just as the gray sky began to darken to twilight.

"Betsy's gone to stay with an aunt in Maryland."

"Oh," Bess said.

"An *aunt*," Maggie stressed, whispering in a low, conspiratorial voice.

"So you said."

"She's having a baby, Bess." Maggie's eyes were bright with the scandalous details.

Bess gasped. "You shouldn't be spreading tales, Maggie."

"I'm doing no such thing! I overheard her father talking to my dad. And my dad is the bishop, you know!"

Bess was so surprised that for a second she froze. "Billy's baby." *My Billy.*

Maggie buried her face in her hands. "No, Bess. *Not* Billy's. *Think!* That English boy at the Hay and Grain! He just used her and dumped her. He had no intention to marry her. That's why she came back. She was trying to trick our Billy into marrying her!"

But Bess knew better. "Billy might not have known all the details, but he was still willing, Maggie." She felt a little sorry for Billy. She even felt a surge of pity for Betsy. Life hadn't turned out the way Betsy had expected.

Maggie put her hands on her hips. "Are you trying to tell me that you're over Billy?"

"I guess I am." And oddly, Bess meant it.

She remembered how she had ached all over at the very thought of him. That soul-deep ache—it was less painful now.

14

*J*onah walked up and down the sidewalk in Harrisburg, trying to get the nerve to walk into the Shear Delight Hair Salon. He had never been inside such a place—had never even noticed them before—and he felt a little terrified. He could see women of all ages seated in chairs with large plastic capes around them. Some were sitting under enormous metal globes. He walked past one more time, steeling himself, took a deep breath, and went inside.

The receptionist took one look at this tall, lanky Plain man with a black hat on and her mouth fell open. As she recovered herself she blurted out, "Here for a trim?"

"No!" Jonah answered, flustered. "No . . . I'm here to see, um, Robin and Ally." He pointed to them toward the back of the long room.

"They're with clients right now. Have a seat and I'll tell them you're here."

Jonah sat down next to an elderly woman with blue-ish colored hair. The woman kept staring at Jonah. He was accustomed to stares by the English, but he felt his cheeks grow warm. Or maybe it was the sour stink of the place. He had never smelled such toxic fumes before; they made his eyes start to water. He thought the smell of a hog farm was the worst smell on earth, but this hair salon was inching it out. He picked up a magazine, opened it, and quickly dropped it back on the table when he saw the contents in it. He crossed his legs, then uncrossed them, then rubbed his hands together, then tried to look out the window. The blue-haired woman continued to stare at him.

Finally, he heard Robin's voice ring out loudly from the back of the store. "No way! An orthodox rabbi is here? For us?"

He turned his head toward Robin's station and rose to his feet as he saw her make her way toward him. He reached out a hand to shake hers, but her hands were covered with black mud.

She lifted her hands in the air. "Sorry. I'm doing a dye job on Mrs. Feinbaum."

He could tell she didn't recognize him, but Ally did. She had walked up behind Robin and peered over her shoulder.

"Jonah!" She elbowed Robin. "This is Lainey's boyfriend." She turned anxiously to Jonah. "Is Lainey all right?"

"She's fine," Jonah said. "I was hoping I could speak to you both. Just for a moment."

Ally and Robin exchanged a look. A woman in a chair with black mud covering her head was calling for Robin in a worried voice. "I gotta finish up Mrs. Feinbaum, then I can take a break," Robin said.

Jonah nodded and went back to sit down.

The blue-haired woman continued to stare. "You a Quaker?" she asked in a reedy voice.

"No," Jonah said. "Amish."

The woman frowned. "You don't pay taxes."

"Yes, I do," Jonah said patiently.

"You don't fight in the military."

"That's true. But we do serve. As conscientious objectors."

"Still. Not the same."

Jonah hoped the conversation could end with that.

"I don't understand how you can live in this country and reap all the benefits and not do your part."

Jonah sighed. The fumes in the salon were giving him a headache. He hoped this errand would turn out well. He was starting to think it was a terrible idea.

Just as the blue-haired woman opened her mouth to provide Jonah with another opinion, Ally and Robin approached. He leapt to his feet.

"I've only got ten minutes before I need to rinse Mrs. Feinbaum," Robin said.

Jonah glanced at the blue-haired woman, who was still glaring at him. "Could we go outside?"

Out on the sidewalk, Jonah explained that he and Lainey were planning to be married soon.

Robin frowned. "I figured as much."

"I came to invite you both to the wedding," Jonah said.

"Where's Lainey?" Ally asked. "Why didn't she come?"

"She doesn't know I'm here," Jonah said. "When you left . . . without saying goodbye, I think she felt a little hurt."

"Couldn't be helped," Robin said brusquely. "Your church service took too long. We had to go."

"Robin," Ally said in a coaxing tone. She was weakening, Jonah could see by her expression. She looked at him. "That's awful sweet of you, to come all this way."

"You are Lainey's family," he said. "Just because Lainey is choosing"—he emphasized that word—"to become Amish, it doesn't mean you won't continue to be an important part of her life. She . . . we . . . want you to be there. At the wedding. And in her life. In our life."

"Aw," Ally said. Her face got all soft and tender. "You really love her, don't you?"

Robin rolled her eyes. "I gotta get back to Mrs. Feinbaum." She bit her lip. "We'll think about it." She put her hand on the door handle to the hair salon. "I think she's gonna wake up one day and regret this whole ridiculous phase she's going through. And then what?"

Ally waited until Robin went inside. "Don't mind her, Jonah. She's bitter because she just found out her boyfriend has been cheating on her. As soon as she gets over that, she'll be happier that Lainey has found true love."

"Then, you'll come to the wedding?" he asked.

"Oh . . . I don't know about that. I guess it depends how long it will take Robin to get over things." She scrunched up her face. "I've found it's always best to wait until Robin's not riled up. Then I'll try talking to her." She turned to go inside. "No promises. But . . . I'll try."

She pulled the door open wide so the blue-haired lady could leave. Jonah saw the lady aim for his direction and he decided now would be an excellent time to return to the bus station and wait for the bus to Stoney Ridge.

Jonah and Lainey decided to let Simon stay in the cottage after they married, with the understanding that he had to take good care of it and he had to start going to church.

Simon looked grieved and shook his fist. "Here it comes. I knew it! I *knew* it! It's blackmail!"

"We're not telling you to go to the Amish church," Jonah

explained, "unless, of course, that's where God's leading you. But you have to go to some church. You have to worship God."

"That's out-and-out blackmail!"

But they held firm and he reluctantly agreed to the conditions.

As Lainey dressed for church one Sunday morning in mid-December, she realized that she no longer felt strange in Plain clothing. In fact, she would feel strange if she weren't wearing it. When she was in town last week, she noticed the types of clothing that young girls wore, even in winter: miniskirts, low-cut tops. Six months ago she wouldn't have thought twice about how much skin showed. Now she felt embarrassed for them.

When Jonah and Bess came by to pick her up, she asked Simon—as she always did—if he would like to join them for church. He was seated at the kitchen table, drinking coffee.

He gave her the same answer he had given her for three or four months, "Now, why would I want to do that?"

If she had time to spare, she would try, always without success, to give him reasons why he should come. But today, this special day, she had no time to waste.

She hurried out to the buggy and smiled when she saw Bess and Jonah. She squeezed Bess's hand. She was so glad they were sharing this day. Today, they were going to be baptized.

"I only wish Mammi were here," Bess said quietly.

"Knowing my mother," Jonah said, "she had a hunch this is how things would work out." He smiled at both of them. "Probably planned it all along."

For the last few weeks, Lainey and Bess had been attending a class of instruction, studying the Confession of Faith, with the ministers. Yesterday, they had one more opportunity to meet with the ministers and "turn back" if they so desired. The ministers, including the bishop, had emphasized that to them again and again: it was better not to make a vow than to make a vow and later break it. But Lainey and Bess had no doubts.

It was a solemn morning. Lainey and Bess wore new clothing they had made specially: black dresses, black prayer caps, long white organdy aprons, white organdy capes, black stockings, and stiff black oxfords. They filed in and took their seats in the center section near the minister's bench. They sat silently through the service, heads bowed, in anticipation. When the time came, the deacon left the service and returned with a small pail of water and a tin cup. Caleb turned to Lainey and Bess. He reminded the applicants that the vow they were about to make would be made not to the ministers or to the church but to God. He asked them to kneel if it was still their desire to become members of the body of Christ.

So Bess and Lainey knelt.

Caleb asked them a few simple questions, which they answered. Then, the deacon's wife untied the ribbons from Lainey's cap and removed the cap from her head. Caleb Zook laid his hands upon her head, "Upon your faith, which you have confessed before God and these many witnesses, you are baptized in the name of the Father, the Son, and the Holy Spirit, Amen." The deacon poured water into Caleb's hands, cupped above Lainey, who was still kneeling, and it trickled down over her hair and face.

Then it was Bess's turn.

When the rite of baptism was completed, Caleb took the hand first of Bess, then Lainey, and said, "In the name of the Lord and the Church, we extend to you the hand of fellowship, rise up."

As they stood, the deacon's wife greeted them with a holy

kiss and retied their prayer caps, one by one. Lainey searched for Jonah's face as she waited for Bess's prayer cap to be retied. Their eyes met and locked, and she was completely undone when she saw the tears streaming down his face.

Jonah's heart felt pierced. He had prayed for this moment for fifteen years. To watch Bess, his daughter, bend at the knee, and then to have Lainey, his soon-to-be bride, do the same, felt like a perfect and holy moment. As if the heavens parted and he had a brief glimpse into the great and wondrous plans of God, weaving all things together for good. He would never, ever forget this day.

It was a powerful moment for a parent to watch his child join the church. He couldn't help thinking of the little girl Bess used to be. He wished she could have stayed a little girl, but she was growing up. Growing into a lovely, wise young woman.

He could hardly wait for Caleb to conclude the service and announce his and Lainey's wedding plans. They were going to be married on a Thursday, the week before Christmas, at Rose Hill Farm. He felt a growing impatience, eager for Caleb to wrap up.

Caleb wasn't usually long-winded, but today he seemed to be drawing out his sermon, a long admonishment to the congregation to be helpful to new members. Then he began to give instructions to Lainey and Bess to be faithful to the church and to the ministry. Jonah felt a little relieved when he concluded the sermon with Romans 6. Caleb kept making furtive glances toward the door. Jonah didn't think anyone else noticed, but he was puzzled by it. It seemed as if Caleb was going to preach forever today. Then the other ministers offered their statements of approval of Caleb's message, but Caleb had run over so long that they were mercifully brief. Finally, Caleb rose to his feet and asked everyone to kneel for prayer. Just as he finished the prayer, Jonah thought he heard the door squeak open, cautiously. He opened his eyes and saw Caleb motion to someone with his hand.

All eyes turned to the door. It was Simon. Bess let out a gasp, and Lainey and Jonah exchanged a baffled look as Simon made his way down the aisle to the bishop, head held high. Boomer trailed along behind him. Caleb extended his hand to Simon, as if he had been expecting him. Slowly, Simon knelt, facing the church, facing his family. Boomer settled down beside him as if he had found the perfect spot for a winter's nap. Caleb read a short message from the Bible, about how the faithful shepherd didn't rest until he found that one lost sheep.

And then it grew quiet.

In a quavering voice, Simon said, "I am that lost sheep. I have sinned against the Lord God. I confess to the sin of pride. I confess to the sin of drunkenness. Oh, and laziness too. I've got a nasty temper on me. I wasn't much of a husband to my Elaine." He glanced over at Lainey. "I might not be much of a father, neither." He looked up at the ceiling rafters. "And there might be a few other sins I'd like to keep private between just me and the Lord." He wiped tears off his face with the back of his sleeve. "But I want a fresh start. I'm ready to repent."

Caleb placed his hands on top of Simon's head. "After a sinner was brought to the Lord Jesus Christ to repent, he told the sinner, 'Go and sin no more.'" Caleb helped Simon rise to his feet. "This is our brother, Simon, home for good." He reminded the church members that Simon was now a member in good standing. "Geduh is geduh." *What is done and past cannot be called again.*

288

His sins would not be spoken of. The Lord God had wiped them clean, he said. They were gone.

Caleb then announced the upcoming wedding of Jonah Riehl and Lainey O'Toole. As folks turned toward Jonah, he thought he probably looked like a fool, grinning from ear to ear. But he didn't care. This was quite a day.

"Let us sing our closing hymn," Caleb said, with one hand clasped on Simon's shoulder. With the other hand, he motioned to the Vorsinger.

As if the cue from Caleb was meant for him to set the key, Boomer let out a bark and, in a rare moment, the church rocked with happy laughter.

A week before Jonah and Lainey's wedding, on a gray mid-winter day, Caleb Zook dropped by Rose Hill Farm, looking for Bess. He found her in the greenhouse where she was checking to see that young rose graftings were protected from the cold.

He walked around the greenhouse, examining the plants. Bess was surprised to see him and wondered briefly if she had done something wrong. In Ohio, the bishop didn't tend to call very often unless there was some unpleasant business to deal with. She could tell Caleb Zook had something on his mind and it was making her nervous. He slowly made his way to where Bess was working. She was wrapping plants in burlap and tying them with twine.

"So, Bess, have you thought about whether you're going to let Simon know that he's your real father?"

Bess froze. She hadn't expected *that*. She looked at him. "You told me that could be my decision."

"I still stand by that."

She went back to wrapping the roses. "Jonah is my real father."

Caleb took off his hat. "Yes, but—"

"I guess that's my answer," Bess interrupted. She surprised herself. Normally, she would never speak so forthrightly to an elder, much less interrupt one. But there was something about Caleb Zook that made her feel as if she could speak her mind to him. "Simon might be my actual father, but Jonah is my *real* father. Day in and day out, year after year. I just don't think Simon needs to know anything different." She gave him a direct look. "I have prayed long and hard about this, and for now, I would like to keep my secret."

Caleb looked at her for a long while, then put his wide-brimmed black felt hat back on his head. "Then that's how we'll leave things." He turned to go but stopped at the door and put his hand on the doorjamb. He looked back at her. "For what it's worth, I think you're right. For now. Maybe for a long, long time. Someday, though, I hope Simon will be told. It would be nice for him to know that his life has counted for something good in this world."

Jonah and Lainey's wedding day was sunny but bitter cold. Several friends came from Ohio for the event, including Mose and Sallie—now newlyweds—and Sallie's rambunctious twins, plus Levi Miller, the boy who liked Bess overly much. His head and body were finally growing to fit his ears, Bess had noticed, relieved, when she laid eyes on him yesterday. And his hair didn't stick straight up anymore. It usually looked like somebody had just held him under the water pump.

The furniture at Rose Hill Farm had been moved from the

first floor to the second and the entire house had been cleaned. Tables were provided so that the meal would be served inside, but the barn would be where the wedding service would be held. The church wagon brought the wooden benches to fill the now bare floor. The church wagon provided dishes, glasses, and silverware, but one neighbor loaned their good dishes—with a pink rose pattern—for all of the tables. Other neighbors pooled their water glasses, pitchers for lemonade and coffee, cups and saucers, and small glass dishes for pickles and condiments.

Jonah and Lainey didn't have any frills, but Bess was allowed to order paper napkins engraved with the name of the bride, groom, and wedding date: JONAH AND LAINEY RIEHL, DECEMBER 16, 1971. The Eck, the special corner table, was the place for the bride, groom, and the witnesses, Bess and Simon. It was draped with a royal blue tablecloth and held a small two-tier wedding cake that Lainey had made and iced herself.

For the last few days, it seemed nearly every female member of the church had been at Rose Hill Farm. These experienced cooks, all red with heat and hurry, were preparing the meals to serve to 250 guests. The menu for the noon meal included roast duck and chicken, mashed potatoes and gravy, dressing, cold ham, coleslaw, corn, homemade bread, two kinds of jelly in cut-glass dishes, and a variety of cakes and cookies. A second meal would be served later. Smaller though, since most folks would have need to return home for choring.

That morning, Bess helped Lainey get ready upstairs. Lainey had made the dark blue dress herself. She tried to pin the white cap on, but she kept dropping pins on the floor.

"Look at me, Bess! My hands are trembling!"

Bess laughed. "It's an important day! You're entitled to be a little nervous."

She scooped up the pins from the floor and picked up a comb to brush Lainey's hair into a bun. It was growing longer now and could at least be gathered into a small knot, but curls were always escaping along the nape of her neck. Bess sighed. Those were just the kinds of curls she had always wished she had. She placed the cap gently over Lainey's head and pinned it into place.

They heard a car pull into the drive. Lainey went over to the window and gave a short gasp. Bess came up behind her. "Why, that's . . . that's Robin's car. Look! There they are! Robin and Ally!" She turned to Bess. "Did you . . . ?"

Bess shook her head and smiled. "Not me. It was Dad's idea. He went all the way to Harrisburg to invite them to come. Said they're like family to you and it wouldn't be a wedding day without them." She laughed. "Can you imagine Dad in a beauty salon?"

Lainey clapped her hands together. "Oh Bess. I never dreamed that God would give me all of this. You. Jonah. Simon. I never thought I'd have a family of my own."

Bess sat on the bed. "I think Mammi knew. But then she claimed to know when anyone in this town so much as sneezed."

Lainey sat next to her. "You're right. I think somehow she did. She always seemed to know things—"

"—even before they happened," Bess finished.

They both laughed and stopped quickly when a knock came on the door.

"Bishop said it's time," someone said from the other side. "We're just waiting on the bride."

Late that evening, after most folks had gone home, the young people piled into a couple of buggies and went down to Blue Lake Pond for a bonfire on the shore. The air was biting cold and the wind stung Bess's ears as she walked across the crunchy frosted shoreline to the huge blazing fire. The boys were still dressed in their Sunday best: black and white, with vests. The girls were trim and neat with crisply pressed white aprons under their dark capes. Before Bess sat down, she glanced behind the bonfire to the lake that unfolded before her, silvered by frost and moonlight.

Andy and Levi made a space for her between them. Exhausted but happy, Bess plopped down on the ground. She was surrounded by so many friends, new and old, all sitting in a great circle. It was peaceful here and she felt content.

The clouds that had been in front of the moon scudded past, and for a few minutes it was almost as bright as daylight. Bess noticed someone come up tentatively behind the circle, waiting, as if he wasn't sure he belonged. It was Billy Lapp. She had seen him once or twice at church but hadn't spoken to him since Betsy had left. He had been at the wedding service today, and she saw him sitting with Andy and other friends for the meals, but Bess was busy helping Lainey and her father.

A few people waved to Billy, but he held back and didn't join in. His eyes sought out Bess's before joining the circle. She smiled at him. Her welcome was real.

Somebody moved over to make space and Billy sat down in the casual way he always sat: legs apart, elbows on his knees. Andy Yoder began to sing and the others joined in. Their breath streamed out in white ribbons.

Bess's gaze returned to the fire. She listened to the voices in the dark, happy to know that Billy was a part of things, spending time with all of their friends around the fire. But she was even happier to realize he no longer gave her such a stomach-dropping feeling. It wasn't so long ago that being in such close proximity to Billy would have a physical effect on her. Her stomach would quiver, her cheeks would grow warm, her heart would pound, and her imagination would run away from her. Thoughts of Billy had filled her mind from the moment she woke until she fell asleep. She even imagined his face in the clouds, or in a fire such as this, or in the shimmering reflection off Blue Lake Pond. That was the way it had been for a very long time, ever since she had first met him.

Tonight, all she saw in the fire were flames and smoke and sparks. She looked up at the sky. Nowhere in the clouds did she see the handsome face of Billy Lapp.

Billy had been watching her. When he caught her eye, he pointed subtly toward the trees—a signal to meet him. Out of curiosity—or was it habit?—she slipped away to join him. They walked along the shoreline until they were out of view of the others.

Billy stopped and turned to her. He swallowed hard. "Bess, would you let me take you home afterward?"

Bess looked at him, her eyes went all around the face that she had loved so much, every line, every crease of the skin so dear to her.

If she agreed to go home with him tonight, it would be so easy. They would be back to where they had been before. In time, Betsy Mast would be forgotten.

But Bess would always wonder. What would happen if Betsy came back again? Or if she had never left? It was too much to ask. Bess didn't want to wonder and doubt and worry anymore.

"No, Billy." Her voice was gentle and polite and sincere. "But thank you anyway."

His face was surprised and sad. More sad than surprised.

He began to say something.

"Bess, I do care for you . . ." Then he stopped.

294

Bess waited quietly. His words drifted on the still night air. "I never meant to . . ." He stopped again.

"It's all right, Billy," Bess said. "Really." It *was* all right. "Mammi used to tell me: 'Gut Ding will Weile haben.'" *Good things take time.* She used to think Mammi meant food—like not rushing the making of a pie crust—but now Bess realized she meant other good things too. Like love. And the mending of a broken heart.

Maybe someday, when the time was right, Bess and Billy would find their way to each other. But maybe not. That time would be far off in the invisible future. And if there was one thing Bess had learned she couldn't see at the age of fifteen, it was ahead.

She thought she saw tears in Billy's eyes and looked away quickly. Then she walked quietly past him to go back to the fire to join her friends.

Discussion Questions

1. Conflict and reconciliation are central themes in *The Search*. Discuss the ways in which the characters come to peace with their past.

2. What kind of a woman was Bertha Riehl? As you were reading, what was your reaction to her? Did your opinion change over time?

3. As Jonah puts Bess on the bus to go to Stoney Ridge, he tells her, "Be careful because—"

   > Bess teased him that each time he said goodbye to her, even as she hopped on the school bus, he would add the caution, "Be careful, because ..." *Because ... I won't be there to protect you. Because ... accidents happen.*

   What is Jonah really afraid of? How does he finally come to terms with that fear?

4. In one scene with her two visiting friends, Lainey defends

her decision not to go to culinary school, as she had planned. "I've learned more about cooking in the last few months here than I ever could in a formal school. Here, food means more than nourishing a body. Sharing a meal nourishes a community." What did she mean by that? In what ways is the Amish relationship to food and meals different from mainstream society's?

5. Simon spent a lifetime trying to be "significant." What finally spoke to his heart? Do you think his change was permanent?

6. What kind of future do you see for Bess and Billy? Do you think they will end up together? Or do you think Bess has outgrown Billy?

7. Do you think Bess will ever tell Simon that he is her biological father? Do you want her to tell him? Why or why not?

8. What did you learn about Amish life in reading this novel?

Acknowledgments

I'd like to express my deep appreciation to my family, near and far. To my sister, Wendy, and daughter, Lindsey, and good friend, Nyna Dolby, who generously shared their insights and also read an early draft of this manuscript. A heartfelt thanks for reading this manuscript with tough and loving eyes, offering candor and guidance. As always, enormous gratitude to my agent, Joyce Hart, for being so wise, warm, and steadfast. I'm very grateful to all the people at Revell, especially my editors, Andrea Doering and Barb Barnes, who make my books so much better.

And above all, abiding gratitude goes to the Lord God, for his wisdom on matters seen and unseen.

Suzanne Woods Fisher is the author of *The Choice*, the bestselling first book in the Lancaster County Secrets series. Her grandfather was raised in the Old Order German Baptist Brethren Church in Franklin County, Pennsylvania. Her interest in living a simple, faith-filled life began with her Dunkard cousins.

Suzanne is also the author of *Amish Peace: Simple Wisdom for a Complicated World*, a finalist for the ECPA Book of the Year award, and *Amish Proverbs: Words of Wisdom from the Simple Life*. She is the host of **"Amish Wisdom,"** a weekly radio program on **toginet.com**. She lives with her family in the San Francisco Bay Area and raises puppies for Guide Dogs for the Blind. To Suzanne's way of thinking, you just can't take life too seriously when a puppy is tearing through your house with someone's underwear in its mouth.

Don't miss the third novel in the Lancaster County Secrets series!

Meet Suzanne online at

Suzanne Woods Fisher

suzannewfisher

www.SuzanneWoodsFisher.com

To Follow Her Heart, Must She Leave the Community She Loves?

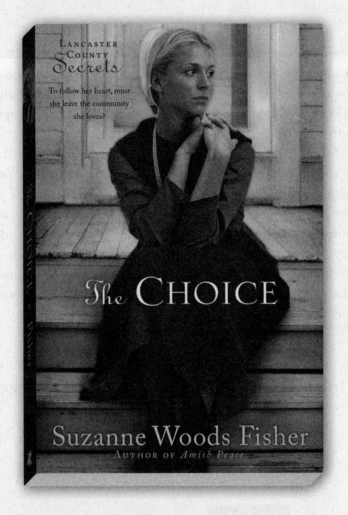

Don't miss the first novel
in the Lancaster County Secrets series!

50